A SHORT HISTORY OF
WORLD WAR II
1939–1945

A SHORT HISTORY OF
WORLD WAR II
1939-1945

Brigadier PETER YOUNG

THOMAS Y. CROWELL COMPANY

NEW YORK   ESTABLISHED 1834

ACKNOWLEDGEMENTS

Gratitude for their very kind permission to include in this volume passages from the undermentioned works is due to the following authors (or their executors, trustees or representatives) and publishers.

E. P. Dutton & Co., Inc., for the quotation from *Russia at War: 1941-1945* by Alexander Werth, copyright © 1964 by Alexander Werth; and for the quotation from *Panzer Leader* by Heinz Guderian, translated by Constantine Fitzgibbon, published 1952. Harper & Row for the quotation from *The Struggle for Europe* by Chester Wilmot. Holt, Rinehart and Winston, Inc., for the quotation from *The Battle for Stalingrad (The Beginning of the Road)* by Marshal Vasili Chuikov, translated by Harold Silver. Houghton Mifflin Company for the quotations from *The Second World War*, Vol. I, and *The War Speeches* by Sir Winston Churchill. David McKay Company, Inc., for the quotation from *Defeat Into Victory* by Field Marshal the Viscount William Slim, 1961. The Macmillan Company for the quotation from *El Alamein* by Michael Carver. The United States Naval Institute, Annapolis, Maryland, for the quotation from *White Ensign (The Navy at War)* by S. W. Roskill, copyright © 1960 by the U.S. Naval Institute. University of Oklahoma Press for the quotation from *Panzer Battles: A Study of the Employment of Armor in the Second World War*, by Major General F. W. von Mellenthin, copyright © 1956 by the publisher.

CONTENTS

CONTENTS

ILLUSTRATIONS

MAPS

ACKNOWLEDGEMENTS

I wish to express my gratitude to some of those who have helped me in the preparation of this book.

To D. W. King, Esq., O.B.E., the Librarian of the Ministry of Defence (Army Department): who is always ready to put his vast knowledge and the resources of his great library at the disposal of the military historian.

To Colonel R. W. S. Norfolk, O.B.E., T.D., D.L., who drew the maps.

To Lt.-Colonel G. A. Shepperd, M.B.E. (retd.), Librarian of the Royal Military Academy Sandhurst, for much help and support, but especially for his assistance with the maps.

To my colleagues Antony Brett-James, John Selby, Christopher Duffy and David Chandler: the first two for reading the typescript and for many valuable suggestions and corrections; to the other two for their help in the selection of the illustrations.

To Lt.-Colonel A. H. Farrar-Hockley, D.S.O., O.B.E., M.C., who first encouraged me to take on this project.

Last, but really foremost, to my Wife – she typed it.

INTRODUCTION

Exactly twenty years ago today the Second World War, 'Hitler's War', ended in Europe. The death roll was 30,000,000, for this was unlimited war and claimed its victims among civilians and soldiers alike.

The twenty years that have passed have done little to prove that the human race has rejected violence as a means of attaining its political ends. Extreme nationalism, so far from losing ground, is more violent than ever, with emergent nations producing régimes patterned, if not on Hitler's Germany, on Mussolini's Italy. For all the good intentions of the United Nations this world is still not a fold of innocent sheep, 'If you won't be a wolf the wolves will eat you' as the Bedouin say. The late Joseph Stalin, a realist if ever there was one, is reported on one occasion to have enquired: 'How many divisions has the Pope?' It is an attitude that still prevails.

Perhaps we are destined to see a third and yet more terrible World War, for it may be that we are incapable of learning from our history. It is certain that the techniques of such a war would differ vastly from those of the 1939–45 period. Even so we may do well to ponder upon the fate of a generation which, appalled by the horrors of the First World War, sought to appease evil men, and found itself plunged, all unprepared, into a yet more deadly struggle.

Yateley.   PETER YOUNG
8 May 1965

LIST OF ABBREVIATIONS

ARP: Air Raid Precautions.

BBC: British Broadcasting Corporation.

BEF: British Expeditionary Force.

CINCPAC: Commander-in-Chief, Pacific.

COMSOPAC: Commander South Pacific.

COSSAC: Chief of Staff to the Supreme Allied Commander (Designate).

E-BOAT: British term for German motor-torpedo-boats.

FFI: French Forces of the Interior.

LCA: Landing Craft, Assault.

LVT: Landing Vehicle, Tracked (Amphtrac).

OKH: Oberkommando der Heeres – High Command of the Army.

OKW: Oberkommando der Wehrmacht – High Command of the Armed Forces.

RA: Royal Artillery.

RAF: Royal Air Force.

SHAEF: Supreme Headquarters, Allied Expeditionary Force.

USAAF: United States Army Air Force.

CHAPTER ONE

THE COMING OF WAR

1919

18 Jan.	Paris Peace Conference.
19 Jun.	German Fleet scuttled in Scapa Flow.
28 Jun.	Treaty of Versailles signed.
19 Sep.	Treaty of St Germain signed: the break-up of the Austrian Empire.
	Establishment of the Weimar Republic in Germany.

1920

	First meeting of the League of Nations. Germany, Russia, Turkey and Austria excluded. The U.S.A. not represented.
10 Aug.	Treaty of Sèvres signed: the break-up of the Ottoman Empire.
	Hitler founds the Nazi Party.

1922

28 Oct.	Mussolini marches on Rome.

1923

11 Jan.	French occupy the Ruhr.
24 Jul.	Treaty of Lausanne.
	Hitler's abortive Munich *putsch*.

1924

21 Jan.	Death of Lenin.
22 Jan.	First Labour Government in Britain.
16 Aug.	London Conference, Dawes Plan accepted.
	Agreement to evacuate the Ruhr.

1925

26 Mar.	Hindenburg elected President of Germany.
1 Dec.	Treaty of Locarno between Germany, England, France, Italy and Belgium.

1926

31 Jan. British evacuate Cologne.
Germany admitted to the League of Nations.
The General Strike in Britain.

1928

The Kellogg Pact disavows the use of force.

1929

Second Labour Government.
The Wall Street crash.
Remarque publishes *All Quiet on the Western Front*.

1930

Allied troops evacuate the demilitarized Rhineland.
The Maginot Line planned.

1931

Coalition Government in Britain under Ramsay Mac-
Donald.
18 Sep. Japan invades Manchuria and leaves the League.

1932

1 Mar. Manchuria becomes the Japanese puppet state of
Manchukuo.
German right to rearm recognized.
The Lausanne conference ends reparations.

1933

30 Jan. Hitler appointed Chancellor of Germany.
27 Feb. The Reichstag fire.
17 Mar. Japan leaves the League of Nations.
14 Oct. Germany leaves the League of Nations.

1934

26 Jan. Germany and Poland sign ten-year non-aggression pact.
30 Jun. Night of the Long Knives. Purge of the Nazi Party.
25 Jul. Murder of the Austrian Chancellor, Dollfuss, by the Nazis.
2 Aug. Death of Hindenburg. Hitler becomes both Chancellor
and President.

1935

13 Jan.	The Saar plebiscite.
16 Mar.	Hitler reintroduces conscription.
2 May	France and the U.S.S.R. sign five-year mutual assistance treaty.
18 Jun.	Anglo-German Naval Pact. Germany permitted to build her navy up to 35 per cent strength of the British fleet.
3 Oct.	Italians invade Abyssinia.
18 Nov.	The League of Nations 'imposes' economic sanctions on Italy.

1936

7 Mar.	Germany repudiates the Treaty of Locarno. Germany remilitarizes the Rhineland.
5 May	The Italians occupy Addis Ababa.
17/18 Jul.	Outbreak of the Spanish Civil War.
25 Oct.	Germany and Italy form the Rome-Berlin Axis.
25 Nov.	Germany and Japan conclude the anti-Comintern Pact. Neutral Belgium withdraws from alliance with France.

1937

7 Jul.	The Japanese invade China.
5 Nov.	The Hossbach meeting. Hitler expounds his programme to his service chiefs.
13 Dec.	Japanese sack Nanking.

1938

4 Feb.	The OKW set up.
14 Feb.	Opening of Singapore naval base.
13 Mar.	The *Anschluss*. Germany annexes Austria.
28 Sep.	British fleet mobilized.
29 Sep.	The Munich Agreement between Hitler, Chamberlain, Mussolini and Daladier.
Oct.	Germany annexes the Sudeten district of Czechoslovakia.

1939

15 Mar.	Hitler proclaims Bohemia and Moravia a German Protectorate.
22 Mar.	Lithuania cedes Memel to Germany.
29 Mar.	Britain decides to double the Territorial Army.

1 Apr.	End of Spanish Civil War.
7 Apr.	Italy seizes Albania.
27 Apr.	Britain introduces conscription.
28 Apr.	Hitler denounces the Anglo-German Naval agreement and the Polish Non-Aggression Treaty.
12 May	Great Britain and Turkey sign a defensive agreement.
22 May	Hitler and Mussolini sign 'the Pact of Steel'.
23 May	France and Turkey sign a defensive agreement.
23 Aug.	Non-aggression pact signed between Germany and Russia.
25 Aug.	Anglo-Polish treaty signed. Japan leaves the Anti-Comintern Pact.
31 Aug.	British fleet mobilized.
1 Sep.	Germany invades Poland. Britain and France mobilize.
2 Sep.	Britain introduces compulsory military service for all men between 18 and 41.
3 Sep.	11 a.m. Great Britain declares war on Germany. 5 p.m. France declares war on Germany.

'The angel of peace was murdered, killed consciously and deliberately in 1939.'   DR WALTER HOFER.

'HITLER'S War' is not a bad title for the Second World War, for he was its architect. But in fact two wars waged quite separately, though more or less simultaneously, made up the struggle. These could be called the German War and the Japanese War.

The German War lasted from 1 September 1939, when Hitler's armies invaded Poland, to 8 May 1945 when they surrendered. This was in effect a continuation of the 1914–18 'Kaiser's War: it was the Germans' second throw to achieve their national aspirations – the hegemony of Europe and perhaps eventually of the world.

The Japanese War ran from 7 December 1941 (the date of their attack on Pearl Harbor) to their surrender on 15 August 1945. Their aim was simply to establish Japanese domination of the Far East.

Although the Germans and Japanese were allies, their two wars hardly impinged on each other at all, except that the Allies, especially the United States, had to decide which to fight first.

In a positive sense the main responsibility for these two wars rests squarely on the Germans and the Japanese, for it was they who took the intiative. They were prepared to use war as a means of attaining the objects of their state policies.

In the First World War (1914–18) the Central Powers – Germany, Austria-Hungary, Turkey and Bulgaria – had fought France, Russia, Great Britain, Italy, the United States and their allies and had been defeated. In consequence the ancient Austrian Empire had been carved up along lines dictated by 'Self-determination'. The Imperial Russian government had been succeeded by the Communist system, the Imperial German government had given way to a Republic. But the only major power to disappear altogether was Austria-Hungary.

We have Napoleon's word for it that in war the 'moral' is to the 'physical' as three is to one. The effective legacy of the First World War was in the sphere of morale. For the Allies, except the United States, it was the ten million dead that laid their cold hands on the

5

generation whose future they had fought to assure. Isolationism in America, pacifism in England and defeatism in France were the reaction of too many of the survivors. An atmosphere was created in which it was difficult for any politician to stand up to the growing power of Hitler and Mussolini. In this negative sense the Allies themselves were responsible for the War. 'Fear and be slain.'

The League of Nations, to which all disputes were to be submitted before any resort to the use of force, had, in theory, the backing of economic and military sanctions; but in fact it was so gravely weakened by the absence from its counsels of the United States, that it was doomed from the outset.

In 1918–19 the Germans, who had no mean opinion of their soldiership, were bewildered to find themselves on the losing side. They felt themselves cheated by the settlement, the *Diktat of* Versailles. War is a political act. Therefore the degree of violence employed must always be governed to some extent by considering the settlement that is to follow. The settlement after the First World War may have solved certain problems; it also produced a fresh crop.

Hitler had no difficulty in stirring up German resentment against the Versailles 'slave treaty'. It had deprived the Fatherland of all her colonies, given back Alsace-Lorraine to France, internationalized the Saar, made Danzig a Free City and left the Allies in occupation of the Rhineland. Reparations too had been heavy – £6,000,000,000 – and failure to pay had led Poincaré, violently anti-German as he was, to order the occupation of the Ruhr in 1923. Even after the Lausanne Conference (1932) put an end to reparations, Hitler found no difficulty in keeping German resentment alive.

'This is not Peace. It is an Armistice for twenty years', had been Marshal Foch's comment on the Treaty of Versailles, and in a way it had been a remarkably accurate forecast. Yet the provisions of Versailles were laid aside long before 1939. Only the bitterness remained, valuable propaganda material for Hitler on his avenging progress. That Hitler was encouraged by the feeble politicians of neighbouring countries, by pacifists everywhere and by the woolly-minded dreamers of the League of Nations Union cannot be denied. But their responsibility was a negative one, whether born of good intentions or merely of ignorance and fear.

The overwhelming majority of the people living in Europe in the 1920s and 1930s, and their leaders, hated the thought of a Second World War. Yet, given the conditions prevailing after the Peace

Treaties, it would have been strange indeed if the legacy of the First World War had not been a second.

'War is the continuation of state policy by other means,' General Karl von Clausewitz, the author of *Vom Kriege*, calmly assures us. However logical his aphorism may have seemed to one who had served in the Napoleonic Wars, many who had been through the First World War thought it wholly unreasonable. The idea that they had fought 'the War to end War' was widely held, at least among the English-speaking contestants. But Hitler was a disciple of Clausewitz.

Few indeed among the victors were willing to consolidate their political position at the risk of the sort of losses they expected in a further war. People everywhere were profoundly impressed by the development of modern weapons, especially bombing aircraft, though these last were as yet far less formidable than they believed. And, whatever one may have thought in 1939, the Germans themselves were not without misgivings as to the possible consequences of their leader's policies, much as they enjoyed their earlier fruits. Without Hitler to lead them the Germans would hardly have set out a second time to conquer Europe. In the words of Professor Trevor-Roper: 'The Second World War was Hitler's personal war in many senses. He intended it, he prepared for it, he chose the moment for launching it; and for three years, in the main, he planned its course.'[1] In that sense the Second World War was certainly Hitler's War. Yet the causes of the struggle were complex and the fighting took place in many theatres widely dispersed over the face of the earth.

In 1914 war had blown up practically unheralded, but the steps that led to the explosion of 1939 were clearly marked. We need trace its origins no further back than the day when Adolf Hitler became Chancellor of Germany. It is true that in the Far East Japan was already pursuing a course of comparable violence, and that in Mussolini the new dictator seemed to have a model and a mentor, but neither Japan nor Italy would have risked a Second World War had Germany remained peaceful.

Adolf Hitler was born at Braunau in 1889, the third child of an Austrian customs official. His father, who was over fifty when the boy was born, had a stubborn though passionate nature. He wanted Hitler also to become an official and sent him to a secondary school. But the boy wanted to be an artist, and left school in 1905 without

[1] Hitler: *War Directives*, p. xiii.

the customary Leaving Certificate. His report described his command of the German language as inadequate. From this period dated his love of Wagner's operas, which he first heard at Linz, and his intense German nationalism.

His father died in 1903 and in 1907 his mother allowed him to enter the Academy of Fine Arts in Vienna. His progress was unsatisfactory. He returned to his home where with great gentleness he nursed his mother through her last illness – cancer of the breast. Her death and the consequent break-up of the home left him badly shaken. Returning to Vienna he eked out a pitiful existence as a casual labourer and a painter, sometimes without a roof, sometimes without an overcoat. In 1910 an acquaintance described him: 'From under a greasy, black derby hat, his hair hung long over his coat collar. His thin and hungry face was covered with a black beard above which his large staring eyes were the one prominent feature.'[1] He was 'lazy and moody . . . he disliked regular work . . . He had none of the common vices. He neither smoked nor drank and . . . was too shy and awkward to have any success with women. His passions were reading newspapers and talking politics.'

'One evening,' Hanisch relates, 'Hitler went to a cinema where Kellermann's *Tunnel* was being shown. In this piece an agitator appears who rouses the working masses by his speeches. Hitler went almost crazy. The impression it made on him was so strong that for days afterwards he spoke of nothing except the power of the spoken word.'[2]

It was from this period also that his anti-Semitism dates. 'The black-haired Jewish youth lies in wait for hours on end,' he wrote, 'satanically glaring at and spying on the unsuspecting girl whom he plans to seduce . . .'[3] It has been suggested that sexual envy was at the root of Hitler's hatred of the Jews. It is certainly not unreasonable to suppose that frustrated sex was the mainspring of his paranoia.

When Hitler was 25 the First World War broke out. Although an Austrian national, he was allowed to enlist as a volunteer in the 16th Bavarian Reserve Infantry Regiment,[4] and served throughout the war as a company runner. He won the Iron Cross, Second Class (November 1914) at the first battle of Ypres, and was at the front

[1] Bullock: *Hitler. A Study in Tyranny*, p. 29.
[2] Bullock: p. 30.
[3] Hitler's *Mein Kampf*, p. 273.
[4] Called the List Regiment after its first commander. Rudolf Hess was in the same unit.

until he was wounded during the battle of the Somme (7 October 1916). He returned to the front in March 1917, as a lance-corporal, and was at Arras, at Third Ypres, and in the Ludendorff offensive in the spring of 1918. Before he was gassed in October 1918, he had won the Iron Cross, First Class, a rare distinction for an N.C.O. Despite his good record as a soldier he was never recommended for a commission. One of his comrades thought him 'a peculiar fellow. He sat in the corner of our mess holding his head between his hands, in deep contemplation. Suddenly he would leap up, and, running about excitedly, say that in spite of our big guns victory would be denied us, for the invisible foes[1] of the German people were a greater danger than the biggest cannon of the enemy.' Such an eccentric, however brave and patriotic, was hardly likely to commend himself to officers of the Kaiser's army.

After the war he plunged into politics, founding the Nazi party and developing his talent for demagogic, almost hypnotic, oratory. The Munich beer hall *putsch* of 1923 put him in Landsberg prison for 13 months and gave him time to set down his political testament in *Mein Kampf*, a work which outlined his unmoral views and unscrupulous methods quite plainly. Unfortunately his turgid prose was too boring to attract the close attention of Western politicians, who remained ignorant of the menace which his rapid rise brought in its train.

Germany was hard hit by the depression: there were 9,000,000 unemployed in the winter of 1931–2; among the middle classes many were bankrupt. Hitler's clearcut solutions to the miseries attributed to Versailles had a fresh appeal. By 1932 the Nazis had 14 million votes and, as leader of the majority party in the Reichstag, Hitler was entitled constitutionally to his appointment as Chancellor (January 1933). The Reichstag fire the following month – which, incidentally, may well have been started by the Communist Van der Lubbe – gave him a splendid opportunity to pose as a crusader against Bolshevism. Now followed a reign of terror not only against Jews, Liberals, Socialists and Communists but also against his own Brownshirt followers, many of whom were liquidated on the Night of the Long Knives (30 June 1934). Hitler's followers had butchered not only Captain Roehm and a number of his Nazi Brownshirts, but General von Schleicher and his wife, and General von Bredow. Yet

[1] He referred, of course, to Jews and Marxists.

there were still responsible French and British statesmen who supposed that we could exist in peace side by side with a dictator who could treat his own nationals in such a way. The Gestapo, censorship, arson, beatings and the concentration camp were the instruments of the new régime. Indoctrination – most efficiently run throughout the Nazi era by Dr Goebbels – fought the battle for mens' minds. Mass rallies captured the minds of the German people, who were caught young and enlisted in the Hitler *Jugend*. School text-books were re-written. But the best propaganda of all was full employment. Little the Germans cared that the Nazis were taking up the slack by the expansion of the armaments industry.

Hitler, like Bismarck before him, had certain long-term national aims. How these were achieved was relatively unimportant to him. The course of his strategy was settled; his tactics were entirely opportunistic. His general objective being clear in his mind, he had the advantage over opponents who did not know where he meant to go. Those who believe that he intended nothing more than a revision of the Treaty of Versailles are very much mistaken, for he had nothing but contempt for the mild revisionism of the Weimar Republic. Hitler, like Philip II, Louis XIV, Napolean I and Kaiser Wilhelm I before him, fought for nothing less than the hegemony of Europe. It was his intention to establish a land empire double the size of the existing Reich, a world power comparable with the United States.

That is not to say that world domination was necessarily his aim. Though the French and British Empires might be dismembered in his triumphant progress, this would be incidental to his Grand Design. It was said of Napoleon I that like the witches of old his power ceased at running water. In a sense this was true of Hitler also for he himself distrusted the water. 'Cyprus would be lovely,' he once said, 'but we can reach the Crimea by road.' He was talking of nothing more grave than the holidays the German people were to have when his war was over, but still it was to the East that his strategic thinking led him. It was the black-soil region of South Russia and East Europe that was marked down as the *Lebensraum* of the German people. The 1914 frontiers figured prominently in his speeches, but not in his thinking, for the frontiers of his Reich would lie far beyond. And what he could not get by peaceful means, he planned to take by war.

Hitler expounded his long-term plans on 5 November 1937, when he made a speech at Hossbach. His audience consisted of the service chiefs, Generals Blomberg and von Fritsch, Admiral Raeder, Göring, and the foreign minister, von Neurath. Hitler stated his main assumptions: that Germany must have more territory and that it was necessary to take it by force. The question was When? He himself had come to the conclusion that 1938 or 1939 would be the time to strike. By the period 1943–5 Germany would be much stronger, but her foes would have completed their rearmament and would be even stronger. He would concentrate on building aircraft and tanks, the weapons for quick victory. The shortcomings of his more conventional arms were to be clouded by the barrage of propaganda that surrounded his warlike preparations.

Hitler was going to be 50 in 1939. He felt that he could not wait much longer. Thus by his usual mixture of instinct and calculation the Dictator faced the risks inherent in his designs. And in 1933 when Hitler had at last come to power the risks were by no means evident, for it was in 1932 and 1933 that the wave of pacifism had been at its peak. It was in 1933 that the Oxford Union passed its motion 'That this House would not fight for its King and Country.' This pronouncement by the young men who were to provide, at least in part, the leaders of the next generation of Britons gave comfort to our enemies everywhere, especially Mussolini. The young gentlemen had little inkling that their maiden political joustings would be taken seriously. The assumption that the intelligentsia of any generation really speak for the great, rugged, sound, inarticulate mass of Britons is in any case to be regarded with suspicion. 'It was easy to laugh off such an episode in England, but in Germany, in Russia, in Italy, in Japan, the idea of a decadent, degenerate Britain took deep root and swayed many calculations. Little did the foolish boys who passed the resolution dream that they were destined quite soon to conquer or fall gloriously in the ensuing war, and prove themselves the finest generation ever bred in Britain. Less excuse can be found for their elders, who had no chance of self-redemption in action.'[1]

The British, like any other people, need leadership. They need someone they can trust to tell them what they are thinking! When rearmament first began, it had no real popular support. But the Spanish Civil War changed all that. At long last men realized that some things can be resisted only by force. Franco's form of Fascism was one of these. Nothing that Hitler had done thus far had had

[1] Churchill: *The Second World War*, Vol I, pp. 66–7.

anything like the psychological impact of this Spanish sideshow. Yet Hitler was already far on his sinister journey.

In 1935 Germany accelerated the pace of conscription and in 1936, against the advice of his own generals, the Dictator got away with his first great international coup when he broke the Locarno agreement, which guaranteed existing frontiers and renounced the use of force. He then proceeded to reoccupy the Rhineland. which the Allies of 1918 had meant to demilitarize for ever. Hitler did not expect that this reoccupation of his own back garden would mean war. And he was right.

There followed the *Anschluss* with the Dictator's own homeland (1938), which stirred up comparatively little resentment, at least in Britain. Again Hitler did not expect war, and again he was right. Meanwhile Mussolini, not to be outdone, was overrunning Abyssinia. The dismemberment of Czechoslovakia followed in 1938-9, with Mussolini, now the pupil rather than the master, trying to keep up by invading Albania. Meanwhile, unhindered by the distracted powers, Japan pursued her conquering course in China.

The long torment of the Spanish Civil War, with Fascist and Communist support making one side as unattractive as the other, dragged out its weary course from 1936 to 1939 – the bloody curtain-raiser to a bloodier tragedy.

Through all this, British and French politicians, with the notable exception of Winston Churchill, retained their trust in the continuance of peace with a doggedness worthy of a more hopeful cause. Thus they served to reflect rather than to lead the opinion of their nations; and this, in a nutshell, was that a government should 'seek peace and ensue it'. In Britain this idea had actually led to disarmament, but none of the other European powers had been so idealistic – or so simple – as to follow her lead.

After 1918 successive British Governments had assumed that there would be no major war for ten years, an assumption that did not die in 1928. Not until 1934 was it decided that a measure of re-armament was desirable, but by 1936, the time of the Rhineland crisis, no great progress had been made. By that time neither Italy nor Germany was attempting to conceal that they were building up huge armies, while it was calculated that Japan was spending 46 per cent of her national income on armaments.

No British government thought for a moment of preparing public opinion to accept similar sacrifices. Economic rather than strategic considerations dictated the nature of the rearmament programme, which was devised purely for *defensive* war. By April 1938 the government had reached the conclusion that in a war with Germany the British should confine their contribution to naval and air forces. A large expeditionary force should not be despatched to the Continent; the role of the Army would be home defence and the defence of British territories overseas. The rearmament programme provided for increases of coastal and air defences, but for a minute field force of five divisions. No provision was made for its reinforcement, and the Territorial Army was only to be supplied with training equipment.

It was obvious that, should a second World War come, France and Great Britain would be allies, but it was not until six months before the declaration of war that Staff talks began. The French made it clear that their first objective would be the defence of French territory. They intended to remain on the defensive, maintaining an economic blockade until they had built up sufficient forces for an offensive against Germany.

The Anglo-French staffs assumed that they would probably be opposed by Italy as well as Germany, and that the enemy, while greatly inferior to us at sea and in long-term economic strength, would be superior on land and in the air. It would be years before allied military strength could be built up. Thus in the days of air forces, tanks and mechanization, the best the planners could hope for was to compel the Germans to indulge once more in the static trench warfare of 1914–18. Such a war would obviously demand a great number of divisions. The French were not unnaturally dismayed to learn that the British proposed to contribute at the outset no more than two regular divisions.

It was not until the end of March 1939 that the British government abandoned its belief that, in a war against Germany, it could avoid sending an army to the Continent. On 29 March the Cabinet decreed the doubling of the Territorial force, following this on 27 April by the introduction of conscription. That summer army reservists were called up for training and the Fleet and the Royal Air Force were partially mobilized. All this was some comfort to the French.

Meanwhile Germany had taken Bohemia and Moravia under her protection (15 March), and seized Memel, the chief port of Lithuania. Hitler had denounced not only his non-aggression pact with Poland but his Naval Agreement with Great Britain, besides signing the so-called 'Pact of Steel' with Mussolini. There was little in all this to surprise the most innocent observer, but the news of Germany's agreement with Russia (the Moscow Pact of 23 August) was totally unexpected. Chamberlain's Government riposted with the Anglo-Polish Defence Alliance (25 August) a bluff which Hitler called with stunning speed.

The Führer did not take this guarantee seriously, for he was convinced that his war with Poland could be localized. The British declaration of war, however, took him by surprise. Dr Paul Schmidt, his interpretor, recorded his reaction. 'Hitler was petrified and utterly disconcerted. After a while he turned to Ribbentrop and asked "What now?" '

Whatever the truth of this report, Count Ciano's diary records the following exchange, which took place at Salzburg on 11 August 1939.

CIANO: 'Well, Ribbentrop, what do you want? The Corridor or Danzig?'

RIBBENTROP: 'Not any more. We want war.'

And so at 11 a.m. on the morning of 3 September Great Britain and Germany went to war for the second time.

CHAPTER TWO

POLAND, 1939

1939

31 Aug.	The Germans invade Poland.
1 Sep.	Great Britain mobilizes.
3 Sep.	Great Britain and France declare war.
8 Sep.	Russia mobilizes.
12 Sep.	Fall of Lemberg.
17 Sep.	The Russians attack Poland.
18 Sep.	The Russians occupy Vilna.
	The Polish Government escapes into Roumania.
27 Sep.	The Commander of Warsaw asks for an armistice.
28 Sep.	Modlin surrenders.
29 Sep.	Moscow: Ribbentrop and Molotov partition Poland.
6 Oct.	End of organized Polish resistance.

'Fall ich in Donaustrand? Sterb ich in Polen?'
HUGO ZIMMERMANN, 1914.

HITLER'S forces conquered Poland in eighteen days. Europe had
seen no such thunderbolt of war since Napoleon struck down
Prussia at Jena. From a professional viewpoint the German soldiers
had excelled even their ancestors of 1866 and 1870. The famous
Schlieffen Plan had failed to win the First World War in 1914 and to
earn its title of the new Cannae. Now General von Brauschitsch
really brought off a double envelopment worthy of the name. It was
a strategy which the Polish dispositions greatly favoured. Marshal
Smigly-Rydz, not unnaturally, wanted to protect Poland's industrial
areas, and to do this he deployed the greater part of his forces along
the 1,700 mile frontier. This meant that he was strong nowhere.

It was not Polish morale that failed. The Poles simply were not
strong enough. General Ironside had been impressed when, just
before the outbreak of war, he had witnessed 'a divisional attack-
exercise under a live barrage, not without casualties'[1] – not the sort
of manoeuvre practised in the British Army of 1939. But patriotism
and *élan* were simply not enough: the Germans poised to strike from
East Prussia and Pomerania, from Silesia and Slovakia, outnumbered
the Poles in everything but horsed cavalry.

The German fleet commanded the Baltic as effectively as the
Luftwaffe was to command the skies. East Prussia, despite the
Polish Corridor, was not really cut off from the Reich.

Against nine armoured divisions the Poles could pit a dozen
cavalry brigades and a handful of light tanks. Even in artillery and
infantry the Germans outnumbered the Poles by at least three to two.
And in any case the defending army was not given time to complete
its mobilization. In addition the Germans, whether in the air or on
the ground, were incomparably better equipped.

Even had Polish morale been higher than German, which was
not the case, sheer force of numbers would have redressed the balance.

[1] Churchill: Vol. I, p. 312.

But it was not physical considerations alone that made the German victory a foregone conclusion. Their whole approach to warfare was fresh. The Poles were fighting by the rules of 1918: the Germans had invented a new set.

This new concept was the *Blitzkrieg*, which could be summed up as Surprise, Speed and *Schrecklichkeit*.[1] Surprise was achieved partly by means of the Fifth Column[2] – there were two million Germans living in Poland – and partly by the simple device of striking without a declaration of war. The novel tactical combination of armour with the support of dive-bombers rather than conventional artillery was another surprise. So was the way in which the Germans were prepared to drive their armour deep through the crust of the Polish defences, by-passing pockets of resistance, and disregarding the fact that their flanks were unprotected.

Schrecklichkeit was a matter of deliberate policy. The bombing of towns and villages got the population on the move. On the roads they obstructed the movements of such reserves as the Poles possessed. Machine-gunning the columns of refugees added to the confusion – a confusion deepened by the activities of the Fifth Column.

At dawn on 1 September the Germans launched their invasion. Two days later the Polish Air Force had ceased to exist, much of it destroyed on the ground. A week later the Germans were in the outskirts of Warsaw, and the defending army was already split up into groups. The Poles had fought bitterly and not altogether without tactical successes. Polish infantry made night attacks on the head-quarters and parks of armoured divisions, compelling the Germans to provide their tanks and armoured cars with powerful searchlights so as to blind their assailants and light up the fields of fire. Yet such successes were rare.

As early as 5 September Guderian's corps had had a surprise visit from Hitler, who had driven along the line of the previous advance. At the sight of a smashed Polish artillery regiment Hitler said: 'Our dive bombers did that?'

'No, our panzers,' Guderian replied.

Hitler was astonished to be told that the Battle of the Polish Corridor had cost Guderian's four divisions no more than 150 killed and 700 wounded. Again the Dictator was amazed. In the First World

---

[1] Frightfulness.

[2] An expression used since the Spanish Civil War, when General Franco claimed to have four columns advancing on Madrid, and a fifth concealed within the city.

War his regiment had had over 2,000 casualties on its first day in action. Guderian explained that even against a tough and courageous enemy tanks were a life-saving weapon.

And resistance was not tough everywhere. Lieutenant Baron von Bogenhardt describes the advance of the 6th Motorized Regiment from Slovakia:

'There was virtually no resistance . . . There was a certain amount of sporadic fighting when we got to the river barriers, but the *Luftwaffe* had already cleared the way for us. Their Stuka dive-bombers were deadly accurate, and as there was no opposition they had it all their own way. The roads and fields were swarming with unhappy peasants who had fled in panic from their villages when the bombing began, and we passed hundreds of Polish troops walking dejectedly towards Slovakia . . . there were so many

19

prisoners that nobody bothered to guard them or even tell them where to go.'[1]

General Kurzea, whose forces at Posen had been by-passed, drew in troops from Thorn and Lodz and boldly counter attacked towards Warsaw with twelve divisions. The Germans reacted violently and by the 19th the battle of the Bzura was over. Still it was a gallant effort.

Meanwhile the battle of the Vistula was being fought out. Lemberg fell on the 12th, and on the 17th the German pincers closed near Brest-Litovsk.

The Russians had crossed the eastern frontier on the 17th, taking Vilna next day. The Polish government was compelled to flee to Roumania. Warsaw held out until the 27th and the fortress of Modlin until the 28th.

Walter Schellenberg of the German Foreign Intelligence Service saw Warsaw just after the capitulation. 'I was shocked at what had become of the beautiful city I had known,' he wrote, 'ruined and burnt-out houses, starving and grieving people. The nights were already unpleasantly chilly and a pall of dust and smoke hung over the city, and everywhere there was the sweetish smell of burned flesh. There was no running water anywhere. In one or two streets isolated resistance ... continued. Elsewhere everything was quiet. Warsaw was a dead city.'[2]

In this way a nation of 33 million people with an army that might, fully mobilized, have numbered 1,700,000 men, was crushed almost before the war had begun. The cost to the Germans was 10,572 killed, 5,029 missing and 30,322 wounded.

On the Western Front the German and Allied armies sat and looked at each other. The Poles had hoped, not unreasonably, that their Allies would show some signs of life, but it was not to be. Having spent a great deal of money on the Maginot Line the French were not attracted by the idea of leaving it behind them.

The victors lost no time in arranging the fifth partition of Poland. On 28 September the Foreign Ministers, Ribbentrop and Molotov, met to revise the Moscow Pact. The Russians annexed 77,000 square miles of Poland, with most of her oil and 13,000,000 inhabitants. The other 73,000 square miles, with 22,000,000 people and most of the

---

[1] Flower and Reeves: *The War* (*1939–45*). p. 11.

[2] Goebbels had the stricken city plastered with posters showing a wounded Polish soldier pointing to the ruins and saying to Neville Chamberlain: 'Anglio! Twoje Dzieto.' 'England! This is your work.'

manufacturing areas, came under the 'protection' of the Reich. By the end of the year the conquerors had executed 18,000 Poles for 'offences' of one sort and another.

But the Poles had not fired their last shots in the war. Disaster did not break their spirit any more than it had done in the days of Dombrowski.[1] At the capitulation of Warsaw a Polish general made a remark to von Manstein which may be translated: 'The wheel always turns full circle.'

[1] General Dombrowski (1755–1818), Polish patriot.

CHAPTER THREE

SIDESHOW IN FINLAND

1939

29 Nov.	Russia severs diplomatic relations with Finland.
30 Nov.	Russia invades Finland.
14 Dec.	The Soviet Union is expelled from the League of Nations.

1940

2/15 Feb.	Timoshenko breaks through the Mannerheim Line.
12 Mar.	Peace signed between Russia and Finland. The Treaty of Moscow.
15 Jun.	Russian troops occupy Lithuania, Latvia and Estonia.

'The Russians have learnt much in this hard war in which the Finns fought with heroism.' MARSHAL TIMOSHENKO.

Germany and Russia had rewarded themselves more or less equally for their very unequal share in the Polish campaign, but the Russian military machine remained untested. It was soon to show its form: a watching world found it singularly unimpressive, especially when compared to that of the Germans in Poland.

On 30 November, Russia, bent on securing territory which she considered vital for her own strategical security, invaded Finland. It seemed obvious that a nation of 180,000,000 would make short work of one of 3,200,000. But in fact Finland held out for three and a half months. A comparison of the initial strength of the two armies does nothing to explain this:

	Russia	*Finland*
Divisions	100	3
Officers and men	*c*.1,000,000	33,000
Tanks	3,200	?
Aircraft	2,500	96 (mostly obsolescent)

The Russians were very far from showing any mastery of the new German technique of the *Blitzkrieg*. They hoped to gain their ends by bombing, in order to break the morale of their victims. They also counted on a rising of the Finnish workers.

The Finns, like the French, had their Line, called after their able Commander-in-Chief, Field-Marshal Mannerheim. This covered the Karelian Isthmus between Lake Ladoga and the Gulf of Finland. The defensive works were far less elaborate and expensive than those of the Maginot Line, but they served their turn.

It was not particularly intelligent of the Russians to attack in November. An elementary knowledge of their own history should have shown them that it was in the cold of November 1812 that Napoleon's Grand Army had dissolved.

The Red Army ploughed forward through a terrain of wooded ravines cloaked in deep snow, its tanks and transport compelled to stick to the miserable forest roads. Finnish ski patrols, the 'White Death' (Bielaja Smert), in their white winter garb, harassed the flanks, shot up convoys, cutting off not merely stragglers but entire formations, which had to be supplied by air. Russian casualties were heavy. Still they had almost complete command of the air. According to Douhet's[1] theories the Finns should not have lasted a fortnight. When the end came it was not the bombing tactics of Douhet or the *Blitzkrieg* tactics of Brauschitsch that brought it about, but the techniques of 1916.

In February, Marshal Timoshenko concentrated 27 divisions against the Mannerheim Line, and the biggest barrage since Verdun preceded the assault. Mannerheim records that in the fighting that

[1] See Chapter 24 for Brigadier-General Douhet's ideas.

26

followed, the Soviet armour, which hitherto had been a disappointment to the Russians, supported their infantry effectively. 'Their twenty-eight and forty-five-ton tanks, armed with two guns and four or five machine-guns, contributed decisively to their penetration of our lines.' The Finns held out with the greatest resolution but were gradually overrun. By the middle of the month the Russians had broken through and surrender was inevitable. Finland was compelled to cede the Karelian Isthmus, as well as the town of Viborg (Viipuri) and a military base on Hangö Peninsula.

Mannerheim's estimate of the losses is of interest. According to him the Russian losses were about 200,000 killed. Thousands of the wounded died of cold while waiting for medical attention. The Finns lost 24,923 killed, missing and died of wounds, and 43,557 wounded. The Finns never at any period had more than 287 planes (162 fighters); they lost only 61. The Russians lost at least 684 planes and perhaps as many as 975, besides about 1,600 tanks.

Allies and Germans alike sympathized with Finland. Both were delighted to see the poor showing of the Russian army, and so the real lessons of the campaign were lost. It seemed that the Russians were no more efficient in 1939 than they had been in 1917.

But Mannerheim was well aware of their good points, which included a 'phenomenal ability to dig themselves in'. The Russian infantryman was brave, tough and frugal, but lacking in initiative. The artillery, an *élite* arm in the old Tsarist army, had suffered from the loss of its old officer corps. Still they had an astonishing mass of modern guns of great rapidity of fire and range and apparently inexhaustible supplies of ammunition.

The Finns, like the Germans in Poland, had underlined the value of mobility, which could offset lack of numbers. The influence of climate and terrain on tank warfare was demonstrated. Douhet's ideas on bombing were shown to be suspect. Mannerheim tells us that about 150,000 explosive and incendiary bombs (7,500 tons) killed 700 civilians and wounded 1,400. Considerable destruction was done. 'Total air war was in our country met by a calm and intelligent population whom danger merely steeled and united more strongly.'

Stalin, whose purges had done so much to impair the efficiency of the Soviet Army, now set Timoshenko to work to overhaul it.

CHAPTER FOUR

THE WAR AT SEA, 1939–40

1939

19/31 Aug. 30 Ocean-going U-boats sail for their war stations.

21/24 Aug. The pocket-battleships *Graf Spee* and *Deutschland* sail for the Atlantic.

26 Aug. The Admiralty assumes control of all merchant shipping.

3 Sep. The liner *Athenia* sunk by U-30.

RAF bombs entrance to Kiel Canal and German warships.

5 Sep. President Roosevelt orders organization of Neutrality Patrol.

14 Oct. The *Royal Oak* sunk by U-47.

Nov. Germans using magnetic mines.

Neutrality Act repealed by United States Government. War material to be supplied on 'cash and carry' basis.

21 Nov. *Scharnhorst* and *Gneisenau* sink the *Rawalpindi*.

13 Dec. The battle of the River Plate.

17 Dec. The *Graf Spee* scuttled.

1940

16 Feb. The *Altmark* boarded by the *Cossack* in Norwegian waters.

12 Mar. British ships to be 'degaussed' against magnetic mines.

> *'The Royal Navy of England hath ever been its greatest
> defence and ornament; it is its ancient and natural strength –
> the floating bulwark of our island.'*
>
> (SIR WILLIAM BLACKSTONE: *Commentaries 1765-1769.*)

ON 3 September Mr Chamberlain appointed Mr Winston Churchill First Lord of the Admiralty as well as a member of the War Cabinet. 'On this the Board were kind enough to signal to the Fleet, "Winston is back".'[1] Half-hearted measures were to characterize the first six months of Allied operations on land and in the air. But there was no phoney war at sea. As if to emphasize this, the ss *Athenia* was sunk without warning by U-30 off the coast of Donegal on the very day that war was declared. There was heavy loss of life.[2] Oddly enough this atrocity was in direct contravention of Hitler's own orders. It has been suggested that the submarine's captain, Lemp, mistook the liner for an armed merchant cruiser. It is more probable that he believed such attacks to be permitted by his government.

Unilateral abrogation of international treaties was habitual with Hitler. Nevertheless it is worth recording that in 1936 his representatives had signed the London Protocol, and had joined the other powers in denouncing submarine warfare against merchant shipping. When on 12 December 1939 the British submarine *Salmon* intercepted the *Bremen* off the Norwegian coast she forbore to sink the 52,000 ton German liner. 'Magnificent, but not war,' one might say, and as late as 1941 unrestricted attacks on German merchantment were only permitted in certain declared areas. Later in the war British and United States warships became less inhibited.

In the early campaigns of the war the Germans enjoyed a marked superiority both in the air and on land. At sea they were outclassed from the first, for British maritime power, though insufficient to meet every possible call, was still a very formidable instrument. The French navy, too, was both powerful and efficient. When war broke

[1] Churchill: Vol. I, p. 320.
[2] Among the 112 lives lost were those of 28 American citizens.

out in 1939 the Allies had, generally speaking, the means to control the seas and oceans of the world for their own purposes and to deny them both to the German enemy and to his potential allies. Even so its personnel rather than its material resources was the Royal Navy's strong suit in those days.

The Royal Navy was manned by long-service volunteers. Most officers began their careers at 13 and the majority of the men started their shore training at 16. At 18 the men signed a 12-year engagement. They could re-engage for a further 10 years and so qualify for a pension. Men in their second term of service provided most of the Petty Officers and Leading Rates. These men, masters of their special crafts, deeply imbued with the traditions of the service and with knowledge of the sea, were the backbone of the Navy.

The numerical strength of the Royal Navy was not very great. It amounted to nearly 10,000 officers and some 109,000 men and 12,400 Royal Marines. The reserves called up on mobilization were about 73,000 officers and men. Some were pensioners; others belonged to the Royal Fleet Reserve, which consisted of men who had not re-engaged after their initial 12 years' service, as well as men from the Merchant Navy. The Royal Naval Volunteer Reserve, 6,000 strong, consisted of enthusiastic amateurs who had trained in their spare time. Including reservists the Royal Navy totalled some 200,000. As the war went on the Navy expanded to four times this size and at its peak in mid-1944 it totalled 863,500, including 73,500 of the Womens' Royal Naval Service (Wrens).

The parsimony of successive governments had seen to it that these splendid men should hazard themselves to a great extent in obsolescent warships. This is especially true of Britain's 15 capital ships, 13 of which had been built before 1918. When war broke out in 1939 four new battleships (the *King George V* class) were building, but they would not be ready for another 18 months. The position as regards cruisers, destroyers and submarines was not nearly so black. Britain and the Dominions had 25 large and 38 small cruisers[1], with 19 more on the stocks. All but 21 had been completed between the wars. Of the 168 destroyers, about two-thirds were relatively modern. There were 69 submarines, mostly of recent construction.

Since the days of Queen Elizabeth I Britain had frequently made effective use of her maritime strength in 'combined operations' – Quebec (1759) and Aboukir Bay (1801) are obvious examples. But

---

[1] Including six old cruisers converted to anti-aircraft escorts.

despite the lessons of history the Royal Navy had virtually no landing craft in 1939, a defect for which 'the Blue Water school' deserves as much blame as financial stringency.

But by 1939 command of the sea was a question of air as well as purely maritime strength. Unfortunately senior officers, as well as politicians, were peculiarly reluctant to observe that flying as well as floating bulwarks were essential. The traditions of Nelson's day could still be a strength, when the techniques of Jellicoe's were already outdated. War found us with a mere six aircraft carriers. Of these 'one was a very small ship, four were conversions from battleship or battle-cruiser hulls, and only one (the *Ark Royal*) was new and had been specifically designed as a carrier. Six new fleet carriers of 23,000 tons, capable of operating 35–55 aircraft, had been laid down since 1937; but, . . . none could be ready to join the fleet for many months'[1] This was an extremely unsatisfactory position at the outset of a war in which carrier-borne aircraft were to play a leading part.

Aviation was another weak point in the Royal Navy's panoply. Here again the conservatism of the Admiralty hierarchy was to blame. In 1918 2,500 naval aircraft had been transferred without demur to the newly-formed Royal Air Force. For twenty years the Admiralty had been responsible for the development of carriers while the Air Ministry had been responsible for the design of their aircraft! Under this Gilbertian arrangement it was hardly likely that the latter would spend its meagre funds on producing torpedo-bombers. It is not unfair to say that in 1939 the Royal Navy was in possession of some of the finest museum pieces in the world – the Swordfish, the Skua, the Roc and the Sea Gladiator.

Coastal Command, the Cinderella of the Royal Air Force, had only achieved independent status in 1936. In 1937 it was agreed that 291 aircraft should be allotted to it for convoy escort and reconnaissance duties over the North Sea. Another 48 were to be stationed at convoy assembly points abroad. But by 1939 less than two-thirds of this modest total were available, and they were slow and obsolescent Ansons. 'Unfortunately Coastal Command crews had received no training at all in anti-submarine warfare; and the belief that to destroy a U-boat from the air was a comparatively easy matter was all too widely held. This and the fact that our anti-submarine

[1] Roskill: *The Navy at War*, p. 25.

bombs were completely useless prevented any results being accomplished for a very long time.'[1] Fortunately the ineffectiveness of these bombs soon became obvious from the results of attacks by friendly aircraft on British submarines!

The bases of the British fleets left much to be desired. Until April 1938 it was thought that Rosyth would be the main base of the Home Fleet in any new war with Germany. Thereafter there had been a failure to push ahead with the defences of Scapa Flow, which had been demilitarized after World War I and was still far from secure.

The Mediterranean Fleet was in similar difficulties. Malta, long its main base, was too vulnerable to possible Italian air attack, and in 1939 it was based, thanks to the Anglo-Egyptian treaty of 1936, on Alexandria. The Mediterranean Fleet, 'at the time the finest naval force in the world' was 'greatly handicapped by the inadequacies of the base organization which had been extemporized somewhat hurriedly in Egypt'.[2]

In 1938 the Chamberlain Government, never remarkable for its strategic foresight, had excelled itself by surrendering – voluntarily and unconditionally – rights to naval bases in Eire. Berehaven and Lough Swilly had proved invaluable in World War I. Belfast and Londonderry in Ulster were not adequately equipped as bases.

The German Navy, though outnumbered by the Home Fleet, consisted entirely of modern vessels, (the Germans being generously deprived of all their older units in 1918).[3] Moreover all their capital ships, whose displacements were supposedly limited by treaty, greatly exceeded their published tonnage. Their U-boat strength was only 56 – slightly less, surprisingly enough, than British submarine strength – and the Admiralty actually regarded the German surface vessels as a threat to merchant shipping. While entertaining no illusions as to German regard for treaties, they did not expect she would again indulge in unrestricted submarine warfare, because of its effect on neutral opinion, especially that of the United States. Even so, effective plans for organized convoys were laid before war broke out. German merchant shipping was 'almost immediately, swept off the face of the oceans'.[4] A vigorous blockade of Germany was enforced and neutral ships were intercepted and searched for contraband cargoes. This interference, though long recognized as the

[1] Roskill: p. 45.
[2] Roskill: p. 24.
[3] Roskill: p. 34.
[4] Roskill: p. 36.

legitimate right of a belligerent, was resented by some neutrals. On 7 November the United States declared the waters round France and Britain a war zone and prohibited American shipping from entering. This move, of course, was greatly to the disadvantage of the Allies, but was mitigated by the repeal of the Neutrality Act. This meant that the Allies could buy war material in America, so long as they could pay for it and were prepared to import it in their own ships. The so-called 'Cash and Carry' order was the first of a number of measures by which President Roosevelt began to give very real support to the Allies.

As in 1914, the Royal Navy succeeded in convoying the British Expeditionary Force to France without the loss of a single man. By June 1940, 500,000 men and 89,000 vehicles had made the crossing in one direction or the other.

By the end of 1939 the First Canadian Division had safely crossed the Atlantic. The *Queen Mary* and, later, the *Queen Elizabeth* were bringing Australians and New Zealanders to Egypt. The greatest secrecy necessarily surrounded these and similar movements. Their success was yet another proof, were any needed, of the value of sea power.

By October a barrage of 3,600 mines had been laid in the Straits of Dover and only one U-boat succeeded in passing through the straits safely, while three were lost. Thereafter the Germans sent out their Atlantic patrols round the north of Scotland. In September and October several U-boats sent to lie in wait off Scapa Flow were sunk by destroyers before they had done any damage. Fortunately they had at this time an inefficient magnetic torpedo pistol. It was probably due to this that *Ark Royal* escaped U-39 on 14 September.

Meanwhile from his War Room the First Lord was prodding his subordinates into a counter-offensive. 'There can be few purely mental experiences more charged with cold excitement than to follow, almost minute to minute, the phases of a great naval action from the silent rooms of the Admiralty.'[1] It was an excitement that proved irresistible and led to interventions that were not invariably fortunate. One such probably led to the loss on 17 September of the fleet carrier *Courageous* (48 aircraft), while employed, with a small screening force, on submarine hunting. This disaster receives the strongest comment from the Official Historian '. . . this was by no means the last occasion on which the old fallacy regarding the

[1] Churchill: *The World Crisis*. Vol. II, p. 132.

alleged superiority of seeking for enemies in the ocean spaces instead of convoying shipping with the greatest possible strength, and so forcing the enemy to reveal his presence within range of immediate counter-attack, reared its hoary head in British circles. Half a century previously Mahan had condemned it; and after World War I both Admiral Beatty and Admiral Sims, USN, went on record with similar opinions based on their recent experiences; yet in 1939 the whole massive weight of historical evidence was again ignored.'[1]

Having the initiative, the Germans were able to send out every U-boat fit for sea before hostilities began. By March 1940 they had sunk 222 ships of 764,766 tons – about 100,000 tons per month. The Germans had lost 18 – about one-third – of their U-boats. Only 11 new boats had been commissioned, for the *Führer* had not as yet given high priority to their construction. That he meant Britain ill, none need doubt, but desire oft outruns performance. Not the least of Hitler's blunders was his failure to comprehend that to destroy a maritime power you require a fleet.

In the first few months of the war Hitler had considerable success with one of his 'secret weapons' – the magnetic mine.[2] These were sown by aircraft, and by the end of October 1939 they had already sunk 50,000 tons of Allied shipping. In November only a single channel into the Thames was open, and 27 ships (120,958 tons) were lost. Then on 23 November one was dropped on land. It was dissected by Lt.-Commander J. G. D. Ouvry. His courage enabled the Admiralty to devise an effective counter-measure, known as de-gaussing. A belt of energized electrical cable was installed with the object of neutralizing the ship's magnetic field by a counter-current so that the magnetic needle in the German mine would not detonate its explosive charge.

On 8 October a German flotilla, including the battle-cruiser *Gneisenau* and the light cruiser *Köln*, made a brief foray into the North Sea. Admiral Sir Charles Forbes swiftly positioned his force to cover the passages to the Atlantic, and the Germans beat a hasty retreat to Kiel. At the end of this operation the battleship *Royal Oak* anchored in Scapa Flow, and there on the night of 14 October, U.47 sent her to the bottom, with the loss of 833 lives. One is compelled to admire the boldness of Lieutenant Prien's exploit. This disaster had the effect of hastening our efforts to complete the defences of Scapa.

[1] Roskill: p. 41.
[2] Oddly enough the British had laid a few magnetic mines in 1918.

On 23 November another German foray led to the sinking of an old converted liner of the Northern Patrol, the *Rawalpindi* (Captain E. C. Kennedy), by the battle-cruisers *Scharnhorst* and *Gneisenau*. In the best traditions of the service the liner fought to the last. The Germans were jubilant, but it was not much of a victory although they escaped they had failed to dislocate Allied Atlantic shipping. Their superior intelligence at this time was due to German cryptographers having broken the British naval cipher.

The *Graf Spee* had already sunk nine British ships[1] (50,089 tons) when three British cruisers under Commodore H. Harwood, who had always believed that she would eventually be attracted by the traffic off the River Plate, concentrated 150 miles east of the estuary. The *Graf Spee* appeared 24 hours later (13 December). The German pocket battleship outgunned the three British ships, but Harwood had long since thought out his tactics, and engaged from two different directions so as to compel Captain Langsdorff to divide his main armament. A running fight followed in which *Graf Spee* crippled the *Exeter* so severely that he had a good opportunity to finish her off. The concentrated fire of the 6-inch guns of the *Ajax* (Captain C. H. L. Woodhouse) and the *Achilles* (Captain W. E. Parry) was sufficient to distract him. Langsdorff, whose ship had suffered considerable damage, now steered for the coast, harried by the two light cruisers. At 7.25 an 11-inch shell put both *Ajax's* after turrets out of action and Langsdorff had his second chance to clinch the deal. Harwood turned east, making smoke, but finding that the German was still in flight, resumed the pursuit towards Montevideo.

Langsdorff was impressed, 'You English are hard' he said afterwards. 'You do not know when you are beaten. The *Exeter* was beaten, but would not know it.' Surely, he thought, the cruisers would not have pressed home their attack if heavier ships were not coming up to their support? He made for Montevideo.

Feeling in Uruguay was strongly pro-Allied and Langsdorff did not get permission to stay in port beyond the legal limit of 72 hours. The British let it be known that *Ark Royal* and *Renown* were at Rio de Janeiro. They were in fact thousands of miles away. Harwood had only been reinforced by the cruiser *Cumberland*. Langsdorff considered that he needed at least two weeks to make his ship seaworthy for he had received some 70 hits, but on 18 December, watched by

---

[1] In justice to Captain Langsdorff it must be recorded that not a single British merchant seaman lost his life in any of these sinkings.

great crowds of spectators, he put to sea. The British cleared for action only to be informed by their single spotting aircraft that the *Graf Spee* had been blown up and scuttled by her own crew. Langsdorff, perhaps unduly pessimistic, had become convinced that to continue the fight would be to run the risk of his ship falling into British hands. On 20 December he committed suicide.

The moral effect of the Battle of the River Plate was out of all proportion to its size. To the British people, so far starved of victories, there was something about the sureness with which Commodore Harwood's weak squadron hounded its mighty adversary to her watery grave that recalled the great days of British naval history. It seemed an earnest of better times. Neutrals too, began to wonder whether the British were really as effete as they had been led to believe.

The humane Captain Langsdorff had transferred the crews of his victims to his supply ship, the tanker *Altmark*. In February Admiral Forbes received warning that she was moving down the Norwegian coast. She was escorted by two Norwegian destroyers, whose senior Norwegian officer alleged that the *Altmark* had been searched at Bergen, was unarmed and was making lawful use of territorial waters. Mr Churchill now intervened and with his strong backing Captain P. L. Vian laid the destroyer *Cossack* alongside the tanker and boarded her as in the days of old. The ship was found to be armed, but, after a feeble resistance, 299 prisoners were rescued. It would be idle to deny that this action was an infringement of Norwegian neutrality, but this evidence of resolution was no bad thing in the eyes of neutrals as well as the British public. The howl that went up from Goebbels' propaganda machine was gratifying!

In December 1939 the submarine *Salmon* made a patrol in which she sank U-36 and torpedoed the light cruisers *Leipzig* and *Nürnberg* which were covering a mine-laying foray to the east coast.

Little success came the way of the Allies in the first six months of the war, but such victories as they did enjoy were won by the Royal Navy.

CHAPTER FIVE

NORWAY, 1940

1940

16 Feb.	The *Altmark* exploit.
9 Apr.	Denmark and Norway invaded. Denmark capitulates. Oslo, Kristiansand, Trondheim, Bergen and Stavanger taken.
10 & 13 Apr.	Sea fights at Narvik.
15 Apr.	A British force lands north of Narvik.
16 Apr.	General Carton de Wiart lands at Namsos.
18 Apr.	General Paget lands at Aandalsnes.
19 Apr.	British troops occupy the Faroes.
2/3 May	The British re-embark from Namsos and Aandalsnes.
10 May	Mr Chamberlain resigns, Mr Churchill becomes Prime Minister.
14 May	Allied troops land near Narvik.
27 May/ 4 Jun.	Dunkirk.
28 May	Allies capture Narvik.
8 Jun.	Allies quit Narvik.
9 Jun.	Norwegian army capitulates.

A 'campaign for which the book does not cater'.
GENERAL CARTON DE WIART.

THE Norwegian campaign is one of the most illuminating in the whole war, showing at every stage how chance and *friction de guerre* influence the decisions of commanders and throw their plans out of gear.

Hitler was not fond of the sea, nor have the Germans any tradition of amphibious warfare. Nevertheless in Norway, albeit at the cost of the greater part of their surface fleet, they brought off a combined operation on the grand scale.

As usual there was no declaration of war. Surprise was achieved by a mixture of treachery and timing. The Fifth Column organized by Major Vidkun Quisling played its part. Trojan Horse tactics were used: German soldiers concealed in innocent-looking coal-ships were in position before the fighting began. Far more important was the teutonic precision of the staff work which achieved simultaneous landings at all the main Norwegian ports. It was only by the narrowest of margins that they failed to end the campaign at a stroke.

Curiously enough it was the Allies who moved first. On 8 April they laid minefields in order to deny the use of Norwegian territorial waters to vessels carrying contraband of war to Germany. British relations with Norway had already been strained by the *Altmark* incident. Now Norwegian suspicions that they were being dragged into the war were deepened. With a population of 3,000,000 and an army of 13,000 they were not anxious to cross swords with the Third Reich.

On 9 April the Germans, despite a non-aggression treaty for which Hitler himself had asked, invaded Denmark. In Copenhagen the Palace Guard opened fire on the invaders, but King Christian X, unwilling to witness the massacre of his army of 14,550, ordered a cease-fire.

Meanwhile the German plan to seize the main Norwegian ports was unfolding itself. The Admiralty had got wind of a German foray

NORWAY

0 50 100 150 200 250
MILES

ATLANTIC

OCEAN

LOFOTEN ISLANDS

Narvik

Bodø

Iron Ore Mines

Mo

Mosjoen

SWEDEN

Namsos

Trondheim

Andalsnes

Vaagso

GULF

OF

BOTHNIA

Hamar

Bergen

Oslo

Horten Oscarsborg

Stavanger

Stockholm

Lillesand

Kristiansand

Allied Landings
German held towns
National Borders

as early as the 7th, though a report from a neutral minister in Copenhagen of a German expedition to Narvik and Jutland was unfortunately deemed 'a further move in the war of nerves'. Sir Charles Forbes sailed from Scapa Flow at 8.15 p.m. on the 7th. The Home Fleet seems to have had three capital ships, six cruisers and 21 destroyers at sea – no aircraft carriers be it noted. 'On the last occasion when the Germans were known to be advancing through the North Sea in strength, in the same month twenty-two years earlier, we had been able to deploy thirty-five capital ships, twenty-six cruisers, and eighty-five destroyers.'[1] Small wonder that the only surface contact on the 8th came about by accident. The destroyer *Glowworm*, after a running fight with two German destroyers, rammed the heavy cruiser *Hipper* and tore a hole forty metres wide in her side, an exploit for which Lt.-Commander G. Broadmead Roope was posthumously awarded the Victoria Cross.

About midday on 8 April the Polish submarine *Orzel* sank the German transport *Rio de Janeiro* off Lillesund. Survivors told the Norwegians that they had been on their way to 'protect' Bergen.

At 4 a.m. on the 9th *Renown* had an hour's duel with *Scharnhorst* and *Gneisenau* in snow squalls and very heavy weather about 50 miles west of the Norwegian coast and damaged the latter. The same evening the submarine *Truant* torpedoed the light cruiser *Karlsruhe* off Kristiansand. But nowhere had the British succeeded in bringing a German force to a general action. So, by the night of 9 April the Germans had seized Oslo, Bergen, Trondheim and Narvik. The main Norwegian towns and mobilization centres were all in their hands. But the German plan was not one hundred per cent successful.

At Oslo the Norwegians got considerable warning of the German attack, for at 11.6 p.m. on the 8th the Norwegian patrol boat *Pol III*, a 214-ton whaler, rammed a German torpedo boat and managed to raise the alarm before she was sunk. Later the minelayer *Olav Tryggvason* gallantly attempted to defend the naval base at Horten. But it was the fortress at Oscarsborg, built at the time of the Crimean War, which did most damage. 'Here the Norwegian batteries, armed with three 28-cm. guns (Krupp model of 1892), some 15-cm. guns, and torpedo tubes, and manned with particular enthusiasm, scored a success of some significance to the naval war at large as well as to the time-schedule for the occupation of Norway. Germany's latest cruiser, the *Blücher*, was set on fire, torpedoed, and sunk with the loss

[1] Derry: *The Campaign in Norway*, p. 29.

of about 1,000 men, including most of General Engelbrecht's staff for the occupation of Oslo.'[1] The pocket battleship *Lützow*[2] was damaged, and the expedition was compelled to land on the east bank of the fjord and continue the advance on foot.

The capital, with its 250,000 inhabitants, fell to six companies of airborne troops who landed, despite anti-aircraft fire, at Fornebu[3]. But the Norwegian Government had just time enough to escape to Hamar, 70 miles inland, and to order mobilization. Quisling, who soon gained control of the broadcasting station, caused some confusion by ordering its cancellation.

Kristiansand was taken with little resistance. Stavanger fell to 120 paratroops. At Bergen, the second largest town, fighting lasted only an hour, though the forts did serious damage to the cruiser *Königsberg*. The Germans took Trondheim, opposed only by the forts, which caused a destroyer to be beached.

At Narvik the Germans were opposed only by two 4,000 ton ironclads, *Norge* and *Eidsvold*, 1900 vintage. General Dietl permitted the action of the German flotilla leader who torpedoed the *Eidsvold* at 100 yards range, on a signal from his ship's boat which was returning from a parley. *Norge* got off 17 rounds before suffering a similar fate. The garrison, only 450 strong, was being reinforced, but the commander, Colonel Sundlo, declined to fight.

With all the main ports in enemy hands it would have been difficult for the Allies to fight back, even if they had had a corps already in being and earmarked for such a purpose: No such reserve existed. It was only with the greatest difficulty that a few brigades could be scraped together to oppose a well-found force of seven German divisions. At sea the British struck back with vigour and in two actions at Narvik, on 10 and 13 April, wiped out ten German destroyers for the loss of two.

Landings were made at Namsos and Aandalsnes in Central Norway with the object of recapturing Trondheim, and at Bodø, Mo and Mosjøen to deny those places to the enemy. Lacking air support and consisting to a great extent of partially-trained Territorials these forces were quite inadequate.

Aandalsnes and Namsos were evacuated on 2 and 3 May respectively. Only at Narvik did the Allies meet with any substantial

[1] Derry: p. 36.

[2] The *Deutschland* had been renamed *Lützow* in November, 1939, the Führer being concerned lest the loss of a ship called after the Fatherland might be an ill omen.

[3] The civil airport of Oslo.

success. A force consisting of British, French and Polish troops took the town on 28 May, the first clear Allied land victory of the war. But by this time events in France and Flanders had compelled the Allies to abandon the struggle in Norway. The successful evacuation of Narvik was marred by the loss of the carrier *Glorious* on 8 June.

By this campaign Hitler had acquired naval and air bases flanking the British Isles, and had loosened Britain's grip on the northern approaches to the Atlantic. It was now much easier for the Germans to attack Allied commerce either with warships or submarines.

From an economic point of view Norway was of value to Hitler, although her merchant navy, the fourth largest in the world, did not fall into his hands. The iron-ore route to Sweden via Narvik was working again by January 1941. Heavy water was another Norwegian product which might have proved vitally important.

Outside Scandinavia the moral effects of this campaign were quickly overshadowed by the German triumphs in France and the Low Countries.

The casualties on land were not very heavy. The Allies lost 1,869 British, 1,335 Norwegians and about 530 French and Polish. The Germans admitted a loss of 5,296.

The Germans lost 242 planes, of which about 80 were transport aircraft. While British losses were fewer, no loss of Allied planes at that time could be afforded.

The Royal Navy, despite its chronic lack of air support, had done well. Its losses, especially the *Glorious*, had been severe, but the German Navy had been very hard hit. By the end of June her cruisers had been reduced to three and her destroyers to four. Her losses in merchant shipping had also been heavy, and they were never made up. The Germans had no surface ships for operations in the Channel or for *Operation 'Sealion,'* the invasion of Britain. The British were left with an increased margin of superiority which enabled them to reconstitute the Mediterranean fleet, and that at a critical moment.

The Germans were to occupy Norway for five years, and at first it was of great value to them as a base. The campaign, so far from breaking the spirit of the Norwegian people, nerved them to resist. Had they not, led by their wise and steadfast General, Ruge, held out for two whole months against the army that struck down Poland in 18 days? Thanks to their spirit and to British raids, such as those on the Lofoten Islands (4 March 1941) and Vaagso (27 December 1941), Hitler became convinced that the Allies would attempt to reconquer Norway. He built up the garrison until at the end of the war it numbered 300,000 men. By that time they could hardly have been less use to him had they been in Allied prison camps. In the long-term Hitler's Norwegian campaign turned out to be the strategic blunder that Winston Churchill declared it was in the House on 11 April 1940. In the short term, the British people, not without reason, showed themselves very ill-satisfied with the conduct of the campaign. This feeling led to the fall of Chamberlain, and the assumption of power, in the nick of time, by Churchill.

The British troops were well led in Norway by commanders who included Generals Auchinleck, Paget and Carton de Wiart. The troops, to be frank, were of mixed quality. General Auchinleck, who had recently returned from long years with the Indian Army, considered their morale 'had often been lower than that of other troops working under comparable conditions'. While emphasizing the effects of inferiority of equipment and, above all, of the absence of adequate air support he concluded, with justice, 'that our existing methods of training lacked realism and did not do enough go inculcate habits of self-reliance'. General Carton de Wiart found that his soldiers in their fur coats and winter clothing 'were scarcely able to move at all and looked like paralyzed bears.'

It is only fair to say that some units, for example the 1st Scots Guards and the 1st Irish Guards, lived up to their ancient traditions. To a great extent it was to be the task of General Paget, as G.O.C. Home Forces, to remedy the defective training of the British army.

The campaign in Norway emphasized the need for special landing craft and special training in Combined Operations. It was as well that this lesson was re-learnt early in a war, where seaborne landings were to be a feature of operations in every theatre.

CHAPTER SIX

SITZKRIEG

1939

3 Sep.	Great Britain declares War on Germany.
6 Sep.	First German air raid on Britain.
8 Nov.	Bomb explosion in Bürgerbraukeller at Munich after a speech by Hitler.

1940

10 May	Germans invade the Low Countries.
11 May	Churchill forms a National Government.

'Nothing doing yet.'
'Looks like another bloody hundred years' war.'
(Heard in a Blackpool pub)

FOR six months after the fall of Poland the armies on the Western Front remained practically motionless. The French, who during the Polish campaign had advanced a few miles into Germany, retreated into the Maginot Line as soon as the main German army moved back from Poland.

The Maginot Line was the real key to Allied land strategy during these months. It had been begun in 1929 and called after the War Minister, André Maginot. France had lost 1,500,000 killed in the First World War, many of them victims of the *offensive à outrance* school of military thought. Except for a few months of 1914 and of 1918, the war on the Western Front had been a business of trench systems and the slow methods of siege warfare. But the trench systems had been improvised. Techniques forgotten since the days of Vauban and Marlborough had had to be re-learnt. It seemed logical to have a perfect defensive system carefully devised beforehand. Fortifications would redress the balance of manpower if France, with her population of 42,000,000, should find herself facing the German nation of 78,526,000.

The fortresses of the Maginot Line contained every feature that the generals of Verdun could have wished for. Underground barracks, ammunition dumps, cookhouses, hospitals, telephone exchanges and power stations: miniature railways, ammunition hoists, drainage systems – everything had been thought of. Elaborate charts showed fire plans covering every square foot of terrain in front of the line.

All this had cost something like £160,000,000,000. Yet, incredible as it may seem, the Line covered only that part of the French frontier from Switzerland to Montmédy. It is true that there were pill-boxes along the rest of the frontier to the sea, but these[1] were not to be

---

[1] They were not difficult to find. Their positions were clearly indicated by notices: 'Defence de photographier les ouvrages militaires'.

compared with the Maginot Line proper. It was as if Schlieffen had never been. Against an enemy who had violated Belgian neutrality in 1914, the French had put their serious defences only on that part of their frontier which actually marched with Germany.

The Line required a garrison of some 300,000 men, but since the French could put 2,776,000[1] in the field this was not necessarily a disadvantage. So long as their dispositions elsewhere were sound, all might yet be well. This is not to say, however, that the money would not have been better spent on tanks and planes, especially the latter.

Despite their new *Blitzkrieg* tactics, the Germans too made use of fortifications – the Siegfried Line. This was by no means as elaborate as the Maginot defences: some indeed have described it as a gigantic bluff, and it had certainly been built in a hurry. A labour corps of half-a-million workers, toiling under the supervision of Dr Fritz Todt, had built three lines of fortifications and anti-tank defences. This effort had served its turn by enabling Hitler to hold the Western Front with 23 of his 75 divisions while he concentrated against Poland. General von Mellenthin, who first saw this West Wall after the bluff had worked, was unimpressed. 'The second-class troops holding the Wall were badly equipped and inadequately trained, and the defences were far from being the impregnable fortifications pictured by our propaganda. Concrete protection of more than three feet was rare, and as a whole the positions were by no means proof against heavy calibre shelling. Few of the strong points were sited to fire in enfilade, and most of them could have been shot to pieces by direct fire . . . the West Wall had been built in such a hurry that many of the positions were sited on forward slopes. The anti-tank obstacles were of trivial significance, and the more I looked at the defences the less I could understand the completely passive attitude of the French.'[2] It was indeed an attitude hard for a general in Hitler's army to comprehend, for Hitler was nothing if not a leader, and it was precisely in this quality of leadership that the Allied statesmen and politicians were lacking. They found themselves saddled with a war which they did not want, and did not know how to go about winning. The French were the senior partners on the Western Front, but it is too easy to lay all the blame on the weak governments of Daladier and Reynaud. The British contribution was unimpressive. A nation of 45 million could find only ten infantry

[1] In front line units. Another 2,224,000 were mobilized in the interior.
[2] Von Mellenthin: *Panzer Battles.*

divisions to put into the field beside her French allies. The 33 million Poles had produced thirty. And Chamberlain did not know where he was going any more than his allies did. Montgomery has recorded how the Prime Minister visited his division on 16 December, 1939: 'He took me aside after lunch and said in a low tone so that no one could hear, "I don't think the Germans have any intention of attacking us. Do you?". '

Despite their triumph in Poland, the German High Command approached the problems of the Western Front without either enthusiasm or originality. But Hitler spurred them on. Their first inspiration was to revive the Schlieffen Plan of 1914. General von Manstein, with the technical advice of the tank expert, Guderian, and the approval of his superior, Colonel-General von Rundstedt, produced a far deadlier plan. This 'involved a strong tank thrust through southern Belgium and Luxembourg towards Sedan, a breakthrough of the Prolongation of the Maginot Line in that area and a consequent splitting in two of the whole French front'. This memorandum was ill-received. The High Command wanted to use only one or two of the nine panzer divisions for this attack, and in consequence of the row that followed, Manstein, the Germans' 'finest operational brain,' found himself commanding an infantry corps. But as luck would have it, the Schlieffen Plan was hopelessly compromised when a *Luftwaffe* officer-courier who, contrary to standing orders, was flying by night with papers referring to it, came down in Belgium.[1]

Hitler heard Manstein's views when the latter reported to him on taking command of his corps. The upshot was that the Manstein Plan was tried out in War games in February 1940. Halder, the Chief of the Army General Staff, was present on both occasions. Guderian records that neither he nor even Rundstedt 'had any clear idea about the potentialities of tanks'. The idea of driving a wedge deep and wide into the French front so that they need not worry about their flanks did not appeal to them. It was not only French and British generals who conceived this new war in terms of 1916. It takes a strong-minded commander to reject or improve upon the methods of his early campaigns. Those who can build on their experience are the true masters of war.

On the Home Front the phoney nature of the war was a gradual growth. Not without reason Government and people alike expected immediate air attack. The film of H. G. Well's *Shape of Things to*

[1] Guderian: *Panzer Leader*, pp. 89-90.

Come had done more than any one thing to influence the thinking of ordinary British people as to the nature of a future war. It is to the credit of the Government that they were prepared, with over 250,000 beds for air-raid casualties in the first few days of the war. Within three days of the declaration of war 600,000 children and adults had been evacuated from the capital. A strict blackout was enforced – tripling the rate of road accidents – and for a time, despite the protests of George Bernard Shaw, theatres and cinemas were closed. Servicemen and civilians alike carried their gas-masks with them wherever they went. The London Zoo sent its elephants to Whipsnade and destroyed its poisonous snakes.

'The Air Ministry had, in natural self-importance, greatly exaggerated their [air raids'] power. The pacifists had sought to play on public fears, and those of us who had so long pressed for preparation and a superior Air Force, while not accepting the most lurid forecasts, had been content they should act as a spur.'[1]

The fear of German air attack, though it gradually diminished, had a very real effect in curbing RAF bombing activities at a time when no other obvious means of striking at Germany existed. The bombing of German cities might have relieved the pressure on Poland to some extent. But even Churchill took the view that American opinion would be alienated if Britain began to bomb German cities before the Germans had bombed Britain. The RAF had to content itself with dropping millions of leaflets over enemy territory.[2] Hugh Dalton, a Socialist, urged Kingsley Wood, the Air Minister, to have incendiary bombs dropped on the Black Forest, saying that 'the smoke and smell of German forests burning would teach the Germans, who were very sentimental about their own trees, that war was not always pleasant and profitable, and could not be fought entirely in other peoples' countries'. Very properly the Minister pointed out that to burn the Black Forest would be contrary to the laws of war and the Hague Convention. When Leo Amery, a former Conservative Minister, told Kingsley Wood that in a few weeks it might rain and the opportunity would be lost, the latter asked: 'Are you aware that it is private property?', adding with a fine disregard for military logic 'Why, you will be asking me to bomb Essen next.'

There was another excellent reason for not bombing Germany.

[1] Churchill: Vol I, p. 319.

[2] John Gunther, the American author, was denied the text of certain leaflets for the excellent reason that this 'would convey information to the enemy'.

The French war factories were unprotected and their Government requested us to refrain from air attack for fear of retaliation.

The defeat of Poland led some people into the paths of defeatism. Lloyd George, the aged politician who had led the nation in 1916–18, suggested that if Chamberlain reckoned the chances of victory to be less than 50–50 he should ask Roosevelt to pave the way for Anglo-German negotiations. Neville Chamberlain was not the man to inspire that nation with a sense of purpose in such a situation. How shall a man of peace lead a nation to war? Chamberlain wrote: 'While war was still averted, I felt I was indispensable, for no one else could carry out my policy . . . Half a dozen people could take my place while war is in progress.' What six men he would have named had he been asked, we shall never know. But there was one man in his Government who – though he did not enjoy the Prime Minister's full confidence – was soon to show the *joie de combattre* which had so far been lacking in the Cabinet. Three weeks after he joined the Government, Winston Churchill made a speech in the House of Commons which struck a new note. After the war he wrote: 'I had a good tale to tell. In the first seven days our losses in tonnage had been half the weekly losses of the month of April, 1917, which was the peak year of the U-boat attack in the first war. In the previous week we had only lost 9,000 tons.

'One must not dwell upon these reassuring figures too much, for war is full of unpleasant surprises. But certainly I am entitled to say that so far as they go these figures need not cause any undue despondency or alarm.'[1] He told how British world trade was continuing 'without interruption or appreciable diminution. Great convoys of troops are escorted to their various destinations. The enemy's ships and commerce have been swept from the seas. Over 2,000,000 tons of German shipping is now sheltering in German, or interned in neutral, harbours . . .' Britain had taken 67,000 tons more German merchandise than had been sunk of its own.

'It is not going beyond the limits of prudent statement if I say that at that rate it will take a long time to starve us.'

This 25-minute speech, in which the First Lord recorded the failure of the first U-boat attack upon British trade, was very well received by the House. It was Mr Churchill's first speech since he had joined the Government, and was a worthy beginning to the great series of his wartime utterances. Coming, as it did, soon after a

[1] Churchill: Vol. I, p. 342.

singularly uninspired performance by the Prime Minister, this factual account had an effect beyond anything even the First Lord's friends had hoped for. His cheerful – not to say humorous – enthusiasm sparked the same mood in his hearers. Excited members began to think that the British had found a leader at last. But his time was not yet.

CHAPTER SEVEN

BLITZKRIEG, 1940

1940

10 May	5.30 a.m. The Germans invade Holland, Belgium and Luxembourg.
	Winston Churchill becomes Prime Minister.
14 May	Fall of Rotterdam. Surrender of the Dutch Army.
	The Germans cross the Meuse.
18 May	Reynaud becomes Minister of National Defence.
19 May	Weygand replaces Gamelin.
	Gort reports that retreat to Dunkirk may become inevitable.
20 May	Fall of Amiens. Germans reach the Channel at Abbeville.
21 May	Counter-attack at Arras.
24 May	Rundstedt halts German armour before Dunkirk.
25 May	Fall of Boulogne.
27 May	Fall of Calais.
28 May	Belgium surrenders.
27 May – 4 Jun.	Dunkirk.
29 May	Fall of Lille, Ostend and Ypres.
10 Jun.	Mussolini declares war.
12 Jun.	Surrender at St Valery-en-Caux.
14 Jun.	Fall of Paris.
22 Jun.	France accepts Hitler's terms.
23/24 Jun.	First British commando raid near Boulogne.
25 Jun.	Hostilities in France end.
1 Jul.	Germans occupy the Channel Islands.
3 Jul.	Oran. British destroy French naval squadron.
14/15 Jul.	British Commandos raid Guernsey.

'Le printemps rappelle aux armes.'

'Les parfums du printemps le sable les ignore!
Voici mourir le mai dans les dunes du Nord.'
LOUIS ARAGON

WHEN Hitler invaded Norway there was no lack of military experts
to proclaim this to be his spring offensive. Yet a casual acquaintance
with the remarkably accurate Intelligence Summaries then distributed in the BEF showed that the German force sent to Scandinavia
had subtracted nothing from their Order of Battle on the Western
Front.

On 10 May the *Sitzkrieg* came to an abrupt end, with the German
invasion of the Low Countries and France. This was almost a complete surprise to the victims, though why this was so is not clear,
since from about 7 May onwards German aircraft had been flying
over the Lille area at night, unmistakable from the interrupted buzzing
of their engines.

Surprise or no surprise the Germans were going to be hard to
beat. Little that had happened so far in the war, still less during the
months that led up to it, had fostered the morale of the Allies. The
German soldier was rapidly becoming a superman in the eyes of his
opponents. *'Ils ne passeront pas,'* said the French soldiery with ever
diminishing conviction, while a surprising number would confess
without shame to having *'frousse'*, which could be translated 'cold
feet'. 'The rather inactive behaviour of the French during the
winter of 1939–40 seemed to indicate a limited enthusiasm for the
war . . .' wrote General Guderian, in one of the great understate-
ments of all time.

'Le matériel est bon' the French would say enviously as the vehicles
of the BEF rolled by. Their own, for the most part, would not have
been out of place on the battlefields of 1870.

The problems of morale and *matériel* should not, however, be
overstressed. The BEF which had endured a particularly cold, dull

57

and cheerless winter in Northern France, doing the maximum of digging and the minimum of training and shooting, cheered up with the promise of spring. Its most obvious weakness was its very small proportion of tanks. That a major power should field an army of but ten divisions was unimpressive; to provide it with no more than one armoured brigade was pitiful. This was not a balanced force.

The French did not lack tanks; they seem to have had about 3,000 to the Germans' 2,700. The imbalance of their forces was due to the almost incredible state of their aviation.

But when all is said and done it was leadership, in which must be included military thinking, that lost and won the campaign of 1940. In England Mr Churchill took the reins on the very day the fighting began, and for the rest of the war onwards, at the highest level, the British were unusually well led. But the BEF also was, on the whole, well commanded. Lord Gort was a man with the courage to take decisions which many a cleverer soldier would have shirked. The other generals included Brooke (II Corps), Alexander (I Div.), Montgomery (III Div.), Johnson (IV Div.), Barker (10 Bde.), Dempsey (13 Bde.) and many other stout-hearted and war-wise soldiers.

Of the French war cabinet none can deny that Reynaud and Mandel had some fight in them, or that the much-maligned Admiral Darlan was a man of courage. As to the rest, the less said the better. The real weak point in the Allied set-up was little General Gamelin,[1] who as a Staff Officer in 1914 had followed the massive figure of Marshal Joffre through the anxious days of the Marne. If ever a man had had a chance to learn his trade it was Gamelin. But what do we find? In 1940 he assigned all but a fraction of his tanks to the infantry divisions spread out along the whole length of his front. Not only was there little armour in reserve, there was no reserve at all – no *masse de manoeuvre*. Without a reserve, especially when the enemy has the initiative and can strike where he wills, a commander cannot hope to influence the battle. In general the Allied commanders, as Guderian puts it, 'were preoccupied with the concepts of positional warfare'.

Their experiences in the First World War had taught the French the value of fire, but not the value of movement. Their doctrine, based on the idea of methodical positional warfare, was well-known to the Germans. And it was clear from their dispositions that they not only

[1] Ironside described Gamelin as – a 'nice little man, with a well-cut pair of breeches'.

expected the Germans to try the old Schlieffen Plan once more, but scarcely considered any other possible.

On the German side the generalship was highly professional, but perhaps less impressive than it appeared at the time. Except for Hitler himself, and for Manstein, Guderian and Rommel, it cannot be said that the generals had any real understanding of modern mobile warfare, or that they had learned the lessons of Poland. Like the French, even able men like Rundstedt were inclined to think in terms of the previous war. At the higher echelons they too were to have their moments of *frousse*.

The *Luftwaffe*, which had been built up by Hermann Göring, was as impressive over France as over Poland, though as time went by its head was to prove one of the Allies' chief assets, largely because he took on too many different jobs, and so did none well.

At the tactical level some of the BEF were to learn the elementary lessons that if you shot at a German he took cover like anyone else, and if you hit him he bled.

The campaign falls neatly into two parts, which one can call the battle of the Low Countries and the battle of France.

The line-up for the battle of the Low Countries was:

	Allies	Germans
Divisions	146[1]	126
Armoured divisions	3+[2]	10
Armoured vehicles	c.3,000	c.2,700[3]

'Tomorrow at dawn. Hold tight!' Dutch agents warned their masters on the evening of 9 April. At 4 a.m. the Germans struck. Parachutists, some in Allied uniforms, descended on airfields and bridges. Dive bombers, with their unnerving scream, plummeted out of the morning sky. The dozen squadrons which made up the Dutch air force were soon shattered.

At 6 a.m. the German minister at The Hague blandly delivered the customary Nazi ultimatum. The German action had been forced on them by irrefutable evidence that Britain and France, with the knowledge of the governments of Holland, Belgium, and Luxembourg, were about to invade the Netherlands. Instant submission or annihilation were the alternatives.

[1] 103 French, 20 Belgian, 13 British (including three incomplete Territorial divisions), 10 Dutch.

[2] 3 French and one British brigade.

[3] Excluding armoured reconnaissance cars and carriers.

Now that it was too late, Holland and Belgium appealed to France and Britain for help. But at least they fought on. The Dutch relied in vain on flooding and demolitions. The Germans penetrated 'Fortress Holland' in a matter of days.

On 14 May the centre of the open city of Rotterdam was blitzed to rubble by *Stukas*, and 40,000 civilians were killed. This the Inspector-General of the Bundeswehr explained in 1964 was 'a tragic misunderstanding owing to the failure of the Dutch and the Germans to appreciate that they were not using the same time, so that readiness to declare it an open city had not been received before the deadline expired'. The attack against the city, which was defended and occupied by troops, was, however, fully justified militarily, General Trettner said. He was good enough to add that German aggression against the Netherlands and Poland was morally unjustified.[1] Such a delicately adjusted sense of values can only excite our admiration. Many a German city was to 'Remember Rotterdam' before the war was done.

On 14 May 1940 the Dutch Army surrendered. Its casualties numbering 100,000, 25 per cent of its strength, attest the courage of its resistance. Queen Wilhelmina and her government escaped to England in a British destroyer, and under their guidance the Dutch colonies remained in the war.

Meanwhile the Germans were pouring into France and Belgium, and the Allies, in pursuance of Plan D, were pivoting forward to cover Brussels, a move which to their astonishment was accomplished without interference from the *Luftwaffe*. Despite this bonus, disaster dogged the Allies from the outset. To command the bridges of the Meuse and Albert Canal the Belgians had built the seemingly impregnable fortress of Eben Emael, which lasted a mere 36 hours. Thoroughly trained on a full-scale model, a combat team of parachutists and assault engineers descended on the position. In vain the commander called down on himself the fire of neighbouring forts. At 12.30 a.m. on 11 May the garrison, still 1,100 strong, surrendered. It had suffered only 100 casualties. The attackers' losses, such is the value of briefing and training, were even lighter.

This setback was bad, but not fatal. The Belgians fell back to the line Antwerp-Louvain and joined hands with the BEF who by the 15th had a division at Louvain, and another covering Brussels – the only time in the campaign that they were to be deployed in such depth.

[1] *The Times*, 14 April 1964.

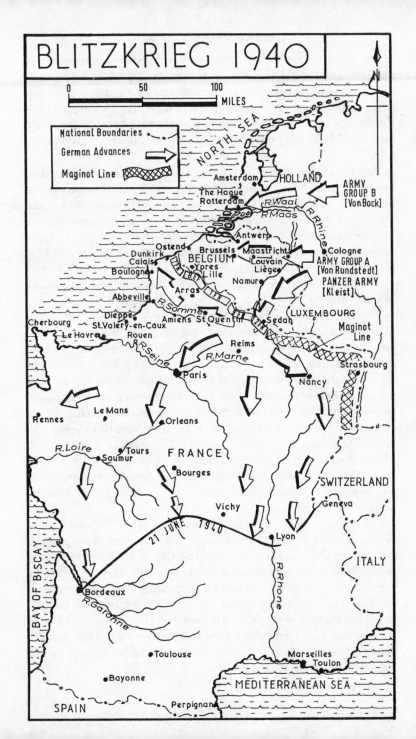

But already Gamelin's strategy had received a mortal blow. On the 13th Lt.-General von Kleist, advancing through the Ardennes, which were well-known in military circles to be impassable, had crossed the Meuse. A breach 50 miles wide was appearing in the French line between Namur and Sedan, the very hinge of the Allied position. The 14 May was for the Allies one of the black days of the war.

Von Kleist now wished to halt and consolidate the Meuse bridge-head, but this did not suit his subordinate, Guderian. 'I neither would nor could agree to these orders, which involved the sacrifice of the element of surprise we had gained and of the whole initial success that we had achieved.' Heated exchanges followed during the night 15/16 May and von Kleist reluctantly approved a further advance for the next 24 hours. Captured orders told the Germans that the French High Command was seriously concerned as to the defensive capability of their infantry.

Events were moving too fast for the Allies. With this breach in the Meuse front it was now imperative that the forces in Belgium, where General Billotte was supposed to be co-ordinating operations, should withdraw. But the French command set-up was not functioning smoothly and it was only at Gort's insistence that the decision was taken. On the morning of the 16th orders were given to withdraw to the Escaut.[1] Brussels and Antwerp had to be abandoned.

Gort had little enough up his sleeve, but there were three Territorial divisions, without artillery and with little in the way of signals and administrative units, which had been sent out to work in the rear areas. These were hastily provided with guns from reserve stores and sent to hold the Canal du Nord between Peronne and Douai: a timely piece of improvisation.

The evening of the 16th found Guderian's corps 55 miles beyond Sedan. It was a complete breakthrough. So far from being pleased, early on the 17th von Kleist berated Guderian violently for disobeying orders. It was OKH itself that had ordered the halt. However, with the connivance of Army Group (von Rundstedt) 'reconnaissance in force' was now permitted, though Corps HQ was under no circumstances to move. The wily Guderian got over this difficulty by having a telephone laid from corps to his advanced HQ. This had the added advantage that his orders could not be monitored by the wireless units of the OKH and OKW.

[1] Scheldt.

Opposition from the French was a lesser obstacle and by the evening of 17 May the Germans had a bridgehead across the Oise near Moy. On the 18th they reached St Quentin and next day they were pouring across the Somme battlefields of 1916.

In this desperate situation the French made a belated effort to take a grip on affairs. On 18 May the Premier, Reynaud, assumed the office of Minister of National Defence. The aged hero of Verdun, Marshal Pétain, became Vice-President of the Council, and Monsieur Mandel went to the Ministry of the Interior – an excellent appointment. Gamelin was dismissed and General Weygand, who had flown home from Syria, was appointed Chief of the General Staff of National Defence and Commander-in-Chief. But the time when such resolute measures might have had effect had already passed. Weygand, like his predecessor, knew nothing of armoured warfare, besides being too old. He had been a brilliant staff officer, but this appointment at the height of the battle was probably a mistake. The French and Belgian divisions were already so shaken by the pounding they had received that their power to resist was ebbing away. The BEF was giving a good account of itself, but the British Government was justifiably concerned lest it should be cut off.

Amiens fell on the 20th. 'Along the whole front the enemy is in retreat in a manner that at times approaches rout,' wrote Guderian in his Corps Order for the next day. It was a sober estimate. And every major move the Allies made was dogged by an army of refugees. In Albert the 2nd Panzer Division had captured a British battery, 'drawn up on the Barrack square and equipped only with training ammunition, since nobody had reckoned on our appearance that day.' Although somewhat short of fuel Guderian goaded his men into renewed activity and by 7 p.m. had them in Abbeville. Nobody could believe the German armour had got so far. Indeed the *Luftwaffe* actually bombed Guderian's HQ. 2nd Panzer Division reached the Atlantic coast that night (20 May).

The Germans wasted the 21st because Panzer Group von Kleist had received no instructions.

On this day the Allies made a hurriedly mounted thrust near Arras in which two battalions[1] and 74 tanks,[2] with some supporting

[1] 6th and 8th Durham Light Infantry.

[2] By this time the 1st Army Tank Brigade, which had travelled long distances with no time for maintenance, could only muster 58 Mark I and 16 Mark II tanks. The Mark I had heavy armour, was very slow, and had only one 7·9-mm. machine-gun. The Mark II was much bigger, and had a 2-pounder as well as the machine-gun.

troops, attacked part of the German 7th Armoured and SS *Totenkopf* Divisions. French tanks of General Prioux's Cavalry Corps co-operated. A confused day's fighting followed. The operation was conducted with sufficient vigour to convince the Germans that there were five British divisions round Arras, and it delayed the advance of the leading German divisions. British casualties were heavy, but they took 400 prisoners and destroyed a number of tanks and vehicles. Rommel himself was persuaded that his men were engaged in a 'very heavy battle against hundreds of enemy tanks and following infantry'. The staff of Panzer Group von Kleist became remarkably nervous.

Even so the Germans began their advance on the Channel ports next day and by that evening, despite much activity on the part of the RAF, had fought their way into Boulogne, which held out until the 25th, most of the garrison (20th Guards Brigade) being evacuated by sea.

Guderian tells us that the German tanks could not 'penetrate the old town walls. By the use of a ladder from the kitchen of a nearby house, and with the powerful assistance of an 88-mm. flak gun, a breach was at last made in the wall near the cathedral . . .'

At this juncture (23 May) Colonel-General von Rundstedt gave orders to the Fourth Army for a halt. Hitler, who appeared on the 24th, agreed with this arrangement, but – despite the assertions of German generals since the war – it was not his idea in the first place. When on 25 May OKH authorized the passage of the Canal front by the armour, Rundstedt still did not send it over. The Dunkirk area is not favourable for tanks and his decision may well have been correct, though Brauschitsch and Guderian did not agree with it. There was still much for the tanks to do in the South.

Calais fell to 10th Panzer Division on the 26th. 'We took 20,000 prisoners, including 3-4,000 British, the remainder being French, Belgian and Dutch, of whom the majority had not wanted to go on fighting and whom the English had therefore locked up in cellars.'[1] The resistance of Brigadier Nicholson's 30th Brigade was in the best traditions of the Rifle Regiments of which it consisted. They did not fight in vain, for they contained a German force of several divisions.

Meanwhile it had been decided to withdraw the BEF to England. Lord Gort had the courage to take this decision, so foreign to his nature, in good time.

The Royal Navy was not taken by surprise by the events of this

[1] Guderian: 118.

campaign. The Naval Staff had laid its plans soon after the outbreak of war and in the opening fortnight of the campaign a variety of unusual but not unexpected tasks were carried out. The rescue of the Dutch Royal family; the removal of the gold reserves and diamonds from Amsterdam; the withdrawal of merchantmen, barges and tugs from Antwerp; the movements by destroyer of the garrisons to Boulogne and back and to Calais.[1] In all these operations losses of warships had not been light.

A far more difficult task had now to be faced. At 6.57 p.m. on 26 May the Admiralty sent out the order: 'begin Operation "Dynamo" ' – the evacuation of the BEF. A sober view of the prospects was taken. It was thought that the operation might possibly last two days before the *Luftwaffe* and the German artillery made conditions impossible for Admiral Ramsay's force. It was hoped that 35,000 soldiers might be saved. Had this been the total it is difficult indeed to see how the British army could have been rebuilt to avenge the blow. But the operation was to last nine days, and 338,226[2] men were to be rescued.

Numbers rescued	TOTAL
26/27 May	7,669
28 May	17,804
29 May	47,310
30 May	53,823
31 May	68,014
1 June	64,429
2 June	26,256
3 June	26,746
4 June	26,175
	338,226

The peoples Hitler had crushed watched the operation, hardly daring to hope that the BEF would survive to play its part in their liberation. To any reasonable minded continental soldier it must have seemed that the world was about to witness the most humiliating defeat in the long history of the British Army: the surrender of a quarter of a million men. Such a defeat, followed as already seemed inevitable, by the fall of France, must surely kill all Allied hopes stone dead. That the 'nine days' wonder' of Dunkirk seemed well-nigh miraculous is the measure of the relief it brought to the free peoples of the world – to those of the United States as well as to the peoples already in the fight.

[1] The Cabinet forbade their evacuation for the sake of Allied solidarity, although Admiral Ramsay had organized a flotilla for this purpose.

[2] Including 120,000 French.

In Britain the success of Operation *Dynamo* was greeted, it is true, with heartfelt thanks, but perhaps with something less of wonder. ' "How, then," asked the foreigner, "could the British Army survive?" Happily the British government and people knew the answer to that question – almost instinctively – and the enemy did not.'[1] In these words the Royal Navy's Official Historian comes to the heart of the business. Only a power with salt water in the veins could have brought off *Dynamo*. For it was an operation whose success depended not only on the Royal Navy and the Merchant Navy, but upon the voluntary efforts of the owners of every type of small craft. Although a swell on 31 May made boat-work impossible off the beaches, the weather was 'almost miraculously favourable'[2] during practically the whole operation.

The cost was not light. Six destroyers were lost[3] and nineteen seriously damaged. Nine personnel ships were sunk, and eight seriously hit. Numbers of the launches and smaller craft never returned. But Dunkirk was not all loss. If the campaign on land had gone to the devil it was not the British line that broke.[4]

But it was sea-power that baffled Hitler at Dunkirk.

Göring had expressed his confidence that the *Luftwaffe* could smash the forces holding Dunkirk,[5] and the shipping and the beaches were heavily bombed. But the RAF, operating from home bases, intervened

[1] Roskill: *The Navy at War.* p. 79.

[2] Roskill: p. 79.

[3] The concentration of destroyers in the Channel was followed by a great increase in our losses from submarines in the Atlantic.

[4] A German evaluation is not unflattering to the men Gort had commanded:

'*The English soldier* was in excellent physical condition. He bore his own wounds with stoical calm. The losses of his own troops he discussed with complete equanimity. He did not complain of hardships. *In battle he was tough and dogged.* His conviction that England would conquer in the end was unshakable ...

'The English soldier has always shown himself to be a *fighter of high value*. Certainly the Territorial divisions are inferior to the Regular troops in training, but where morale is concerned they are their equal.

'In defence the Englishman *took any punishment that came his way*. During the fighting IV Corps took relatively fewer English prisoners than in engagements with the French or the Belgians. On the other hand, casualties on both sides were high.'

Ellis: *Victory in the War.* p. 326. The words in italics were underlined in the original.

[5] 'When Fourth Army ... were told that on Göring's order Dunkirk was being attacked by the *Luftwaffe* "in a such manner that further embarkations are reported to be impossible" the Fourth Army Chief of Staff retorted, "the picture in the Channel ports is as follows: big ships come alongside the quays, plank's are run up, and the men hurry aboard. All material is left behind. But we do not want to find these men, newly equipped, up against us again later." ' Ellis: *Victory in the West*, p. 214.

with great effect and between 27 May and 30 May shot down 179 German aircraft for the loss of 29.

Dunkirk gave the French to the South some respite. General Weygand now attempted to organize a system of defence in depth on the Somme and the Aisne. But by this time the remains of the French army, outgunned and bewildered, was in no condition to offer a prolonged resistance. Here and there individual formations distinguished themselves, notably the staff and students of Saumur, and de Gaulle's armoured division, but the majority had lost all confidence, not only in their leaders but in themselves. Nor were their allies in any condition to aid them. The 51st Highland Division serving under French orders was trapped at St Valery-en-Caux, and, after a dogged resistance, was compelled to surrender on 12 June. The 52nd Division and the 1st Canadian Division, which were sent out under Lt.-General Sir Alan Brooke, via Cherbourg, had to be evacuated.

The Germans were across the Seine by 10 June, and on that day Mussolini declared war. On the 12th the French Government declared Paris an open city and departed to Tours. Three days later it moved on to Bordeaux. Winston Churchill now made an offer of complete union between Britain and France, but this remarkable gesture came too late to affect the issue. Reynaud resigned and his successor, Marshal Pétain, lost no time in asking for an armistice. The German terms were accepted on 22 June, at Rethondes in the Forest of Compiègne. The scene was the railway carriage in which Marshal Foch had dictated the Allies' terms in 1918.[1]

All France North and West of a line from the Swiss Frontier at Geneva, via Bourges to St Jean Pied de Port (about 35 miles S.E. Bayonne), was to be occupied. France was to pay the cost of the occupation. Her forces were to be disarmed and demobilized. Her shipping was to stay in harbour, to be recalled, or to make for neutral ports. German prisoners of war were to be released, but French prisoners were to remain in German hands until the conclusion of peace.

The French Government now set up its capital at Vichy in the unoccupied zone.

General de Gaulle, who had distinguished himself in command of an armoured division, arrived in London, denounced the surrender, and set up a Provisional National Committee to work for the

---

[1] The campaign had cost the Germans 156,556 casualties.

recovery of his country's independence and the maintenance of her alliances. This was a brave and welcome initiative. But with or without Allies Britain now prepared to fight on.

On 4 June Winston Churchill spoke for his countrymen.

'Even though large tracts of Europe and many old and famous states have fallen or may fall into the grip of the Gestapo and all the odious apparatus of Nazi rule, we shall not flag or fail. We shall go on to the end. We shall fight in France, we shall fight in the seas and oceans, we shall fight with growing confidence and growing strength in the air; we shall defend our island, whatever the cost may be. We shall fight on the beaches, we shall fight on the landing-grounds, we shall fight in the fields and in the streets, we shall fight in the hills; we shall never surrender; and even if, which I do not for a moment believe, this island or a large part of it were subjugated and starving, then our Empire beyond the seas, armed and guarded by the British Fleet, would carry on the struggle, until, in God's good time, the new world, with all its power and might, steps forth to the rescue and the liberation of the old.'

CHAPTER EIGHT

THE BATTLE OF BRITAIN

1940

22 Jun.	The French armistice.
2 Jul.	Operational instructions issued to the *Luftwaffe*.
10 Jul.	Attacks on British convoys in the Channel. The beginning of the Battle of Britain.
10 Aug.	Hitler postpones *Sealion*.
15 Aug.	The *Luftwaffe* loses 76 aircraft.
7 Sep.	Severe daylight air attack on London.
15 Sep.	Biggest daylight attacks. *Luftwaffe* loses 56 aircraft.
c. 5 Oct.	End of daylight bombing.
12 Oct.	*Sealion* cancelled.
3 Nov.	Night. No air-raid on London.
14 Nov.	Coventry heavily bombed. Cathedral destroyed.
2 Dec.	Bristol heavily bombed.
29 Dec.	Incendiary bombing of City of London. Guildhall and eight Wren churches destroyed.

> '*Hitler knows that he will have to break us in this island or lose the war. If we can stand up to him, all Europe may be free and the life of the world may move forward into broad, sunlit uplands. But if we fail, then the whole world, including the United States, including all that we have known and cared for, will sink into the abyss of a new dark age, made more sinister, and perhaps more protracted, by the lights of perverted science. Let us therefore brace ourselves to our duties, and so bear ourselves that, if the British Empire and its Commonwealth last for a thousand years, men will still say: "This was their finest hour".*'

WITH these words, declaimed in the House of Commons on 18 June 1940, Winston Churchill steeled his countrymen for the great ordeal which now began: the Battle of Britain.

This chapter tells the story of Hitler's attempt to invade England – Operation *Sealion*. He planned to clear the way for a seaborne invasion by breaking the back of the RAF, especially Fighter Command. When their casualties mounted the Germans lost sight of their target and indulged in the attack on London and other cities known as 'the Blitz'.

The Germans set aside an army of some 20 divisions for the operation. It may be questioned whether the flotilla which they assembled was adequate to transport them. The German navy, as we have seen, had been roughly handled during the Norwegian campaign, and was in no condition to escort the force even by the shortest sea passage – which we now know was the one they had selected. Clearly their safe arrival depended on the *Luftwaffe* rather than the small German Navy. If Göring's men could destroy the Royal Air Force and drive the Royal Navy out of the English Channel, the invaders had a good chance of landing without unacceptable casualties.

Once ashore they would have had to deal with some 25 divisions, all more or less up to strength, but woefully short of modern weapons, transport and tanks. Though morale was very high, this army was neither as experienced nor as well-trained as the Germans. It was, moreover, spread out from Kent to Cromarty, with no means of knowing where to expect the landing. For a long time the East coast seemed the likeliest place. It was, of course, possible that there would be several landings at once. The possibility of airborne landings had to be taken into account, but there was no likelihood that para-chutists would cause the dismay and confusion they had spread in the Low Countries. The Local Defence Volunteers (soon to be re-christened the Home Guard) had sprung to life one May evening and, though armed at first with shotguns and even pikes, they were invaluable for guarding vulnerable points. Their ranks were full of determined veterans of 1914–18 who would, no doubt, have given a good account of themselves.

Britain and her Empire now stood virtually alone.[1] Furthermore it was impossible for her to deploy the whole of her meagre resources in defence of the British Isles, for it was necessary to maintain her position abroad, and especially in the Mediterranean.

But if we lacked allies we still had a good friend in President Roosevelt. There was at this time no want of Americans to proclaim that 'Britain was finished'. But the President 'scraped the bottom of the barrel in American arsenals'[2] and provided:—

500,000 rifles,
80,000 machine-guns,
130,000,000 rounds of ammunition,
900 75-mm. guns
100,000,000 shells.

And we still had some 200 tanks of our own.

The British Army exerted itself to prepare against invasion. Officers of proved ability, Generals Sir John Dill and Sir Alan Brooke, held the key positions of Chief of the Imperial General Staff and Commander-in-Chief Home Forces.

It would be a long time before the army could take the offensive, but, as an earnest of better things to come, the Commandos were formed with the object of carrying out raids anywhere from Narvik to Bayonne.

---

[1] The Emir Abdullah of Transjordan, an independent sovereign, remained our staunch ally.

[2] *The White House Papers of Harry L. Hopkins.* Ed. R. E. Sherwood, Eyre and Spottiswoode, 1948–9.

None need doubt that in the mood of 1940 the British would have met German invasion with stubborn fury. Still it was just as well that the British army was not invited to take on the Wehrmacht in the fields of Kent.

Keitel and other senior officers of the German Armed Forces Supreme Headquarters were convinced, after the French armistice, that England was prepared to sue for peace. So little did they understand the temper of the British people.

German air power was now at its height.

11 fighter groups	–	1,300 Messerschmidt 109s.
2 fighter-bomber groups	–	180 Messerschmidt 110s[1]
10 bomber groups	–	1,350 (Heinkel 111s[1]
		(Junkers 88s[1]
		(Dornier 17s[1])

2,830

With skilled and experienced crews who had tasted victory, the *Luftwaffe* entered the Battle of Britain confident of success.

Two air fleets took part: Second, under Field-Marshal Kesselring (HQ: Brussels); and Third, under Field-Marshal Sperrle (HQ: Paris).

On 2 July the German High Command issued orders designed to pave the way for the invasion of Britain. Two aims were laid down:

'(1) The interdiction of the Channel to merchant shipping, to be carried out in conjunction with German naval forces, by means of attacks on convoys, the destruction of harbour facilities, and the sowing of mines in harbour areas and the approaches thereto.

(2) The destruction of the Royal Air Force.'

To frustrate this plan Fighter Command had (8 August) some 600 or 700 fighters, organized in 55 operational squadrons, including six of night-fighters (Blenheims), which took no part in daylight operations. The great majority of the planes were Hurricanes, about one-fifth were Spitfires, and there were two squadrons of Defiants. Thanks to the efforts of Lord Beaverbrook, Minister of Aircraft Production, our strength in aircraft was growing all the time, and by 30 September we had 59 Squadrons (eight being night-fighters). Pilots were, of course, more difficult to replace than aircraft, but many naval pilots volunteered, and a large number were brought in from other commands.

[1] Twin-engined.

The Battle of Britain began when on 10 July German bombers attacked merchant convoys in the Channel. A week later (16 July) Hitler issued his instructions for Operation *Sealion*. Preparations were to be completed by the middle of August. Among them was the appointment by Heydrich of S.S. Colonel Professor Six as Representative of the Security Police (Gestapo) in Great Britain.

Intense German attacks on merchant convoys in the Channel took place between 8–12 August. Thereafter the enemy turned his attention to fighter airfields in the South and South-East. But though they did much damage, things were not going quite to plan. In the first ten days of their August campaign the *Luftwaffe* lost several times the RAF loss of 153 planes.[1] The British losses were single-seater fighters. The enemy lost many bombers, with crews of five, and many two-seater fighters. In the severe fighting of 15 August the Germans lost 76 aircraft. The Spitfire was consistently better than the Messerschmidt 109, while the two-seater Messerschmidt 110 was faster than the Spitfire but less manoeuvrable. The slower Hurricane was proving its worth against the German bombers. It would be absurd to underrate the skill and valour of the *Luftwaffe* pilots, who included such aces as Galland and Moelders. The fact remains that the British fighter pilots, knowing how much depended on their courage and tenacity, showed even more initiative and *élan* than their opponents. Not once but many times a pilot was shot down, escaped by parachute, and went into action again the same day. There was an advantage in 'playing at home', for many RAF pilots who came down – even those who fell into the sea – were rescued. The organizational control of Fighter Command under Air Vice-Marshal Sir Hugh Dowding and No. 11 Fighter Group under Air Vice-Marshal Park left little to be desired. The development of radar had given them an advantage in that they were able to discern which German attacks were feints and which were genuine, and to deploy their resources accordingly.

The Germans now increased the proportion of fighters to bombers, and, after a brief lull, made eleven major attacks between 1 and 5 September. This time the targets were inland fighter airfields and aircraft factories. Casualties were beginning to make the Germans lose sight of their true objective, the destruction of the RAF. Once they began to shift their targets they were beaten, though it may not have seemed so at the time. On 7 September came the first mass attack on

[1] The pilots of 60 were saved.

London. 'This', quoth Göring, 'is the historic hour when our air force for the first time delivered its stroke right into the enemy's heart.'

The attack came between 5 and 6 p.m. About 320 bombers, escorted by more than 600 fighters, came in up the Thames and bombed Woolwich Arsenal, Beckton Gas Works, Dockland, West Ham power station, the City, Westminster and Kensington. Tremendous fires were started, and the population of Silvertown had to be evacuated by water.

At 8.10 p.m. another 250 bombers came in. The attack continued until 4.30 a.m. The civilian casualties were 430 killed and about 1,600 seriously injured.

The London Fire Brigade fought all day to master the fires. At 7.30 p.m. on the 8th 200 more bombers appeared and, guided by the flames, carried on the Blitz. That night 412 people were killed and 747 badly hurt.[1]

For 23 days the *Luftwaffe* kept up the pressure. American observers were impressed by the way the Londoners took it. 'It is pretty incredible . . .' reported Helen Kirkpatrick of the Chicago *Daily News* (9 September) '. . . to find people relatively unshaken after the terrific experience. There is some terror, but nothing on the scale that the Germans may have hoped for and certainly not on a scale to make Britons contemplate for a moment anything but fighting on. Fright becomes so mingled with a deep almost uncontrollable anger that it is hard to know when one stops and the other begins.'

Serious though the casualties were, they proved by no means as severe as the disciples of Douhet must have expected. The biggest daylight attacks took place on 15 September, and fierce fighting between London and the Straits of Dover cost the Germans 56 planes. This was the climax of the struggle. The mounting toll of casualties was beginning to take the sting out of the *Luftwaffe*. The bombers stopped coming over in the daytime about 5 October. Raids, by heavily escorted fighter-bombers (ME 110s), flying at about 30,000 feet and carrying two bombs apiece, were not very formidable. By the end of the month the Battle of Britain was at an end.

On 12 October Hitler had cancelled Operation *Sealion*, because the *Luftwaffe* had failed to establish conditions in which the Germans

---

[1] In the first three months of the Blitz 12,696 Londoners were killed. The Germans are thought to have dropped 12,222 tons of bombs on London during the war, killing 29,890 and injuring 120,000. Among the targets they hit were Buckingham Palace and St Paul's Cathedral.

dared hazard a Channel crossing.[1] The attempt had cost the *Luftwaffe* 1,733 aircraft. It was a great British victory; one of the decisive battles of the war.[2]

It was not easily won. The loss of planes and pilots left Fighter Command exhausted, a fact which it contrived to conceal from friend and foe alike. Anti-aircraft artillery, searchlights, balloon barrages, observer corps and machine guns all played their part in the defence.

The sound of Ack-Ack fire was music in the ears of Londoners. The idea that he is hitting back – however illusory – has a tremendous effect on the Briton in battle! On 10 September General Pile, O.C. Anti-Aircraft Command, ordered that every gun was to fire every possible round. 'Fire was not to be withheld on any account. Guns were to go to the approximate bearing and elevation and fire. Searchlights were not to expose. RAF fighters were not going to operate over London, and every unseen target must be engaged without waiting to identify the aircraft as hostile.'

'The result was as astonishing to me as it appears to have been to the citizens of London – and, apparently, to the enemy as well. For, although few of the bursts can have been anywhere near the target, the heights of aircraft steadily increased as the night went on, and many of them turned away before entering the inner artillery zone' ... 'It was in no sense a barrage, though I think by that name it will always be known.'[3] The brave and steady work of the ARP, firemen and the Observer Corps deserves a better tribute than this brief

---

[1] On 19 September the German invasion armada seems to have consisted of:

Shipping previously available		*Lost or damaged*
Transports	168	21
Barges	1,697	214
Tugs	360	5

Whether such a flotilla would really have sufficed for the invasion may be doubted.

[2] *AIRCRAFT LOSSES*

	BRITISH	GERMAN	
		Admitted by the Germans	Claimed by the RAF
JULY (from 10 July)	58	164	203
AUGUST	360	662	1,133
SEPTEMBER	361	582	1,108
OCTOBER	136	325	254
	915	1,733	2,698

[3] General Sir Frederick Pile: *Ack-Ack: Britain's Defence Against Air Attack During the Second World War.* (Harrap, 1949).

account can give. Still it was to all intents and purposes a straight fight between the Royal Air Force and the *Luftwaffe*, a battle of a sort that the world had never before seen. It was a struggle in which the rival navies and armies played but little part.

Though the battle was really over, the night bombing continued. London, Southampton, Plymouth, Bristol, Liverpool, Coventry, Birmingham, and Exeter were among the cities that suffered. Many civilians were killed, yet the attack on the cities merely emphasized that the Germans had failed to achieve their real aim – the destruction of the RAF.

The RAF struck back against the Ruhr, against synthetic oil plants in Western Germany and against Berlin. Göring's boast that no British plane would ever appear over the Reich was proved false. Nor did the Italians escape scot free. In the autumn the RAF flew over the Alps to bomb Milan and Turin. Fantastic claims were made as to the results of this bombing and counter-bombing, 'the clumsiest, most brutal, and most wasteful of all forms of warfare'.[1]

It cannot be said that the bombing carried out in this phase brought the end of the war one day nearer. The relatively small amount of damage done to war industry was rapidly repaired by both sides. Civilian morale was nowhere sufficiently affected to cause concern to the Government. The Churchill Government, by the Emergency Powers Act, had given itself a control over the lives and property of the British people, which was none the less formidable for being more subtle than the iron grip of a Nazi or Fascist dictator.[2]

And so the year 1940, which had seen Hitler's greatest triumph, drew to a close. People everywhere perceived, however dimly, that his forces had received a defeat even more marked than the check to Napoleon's ambitions at Trafalgar.

It was no longer heresy to question the myth of German invincibility. It is true that Senator Burton K. Wheeler opined at Christmas that the USA was 'doing Great Britain a great disservice in urging her to go and fight until she is exhausted . . .' There was no sane officer, he said, who thought that England could land troops on German soil. 'And even if our own warmongers get us into the war . . . I doubt that the joint efforts of Great Britain and the United States could succeed in that project.'[3]

[1] Cyril Falls: *The Second World War.* p. 69.

[2] In December Parliament voted on a motion to consider peace. The motion was lost by 341:4.

[3] Flower and Reeves, p. 160.

But the President spoke to the American People on 29 December in a totally different sense.

'. . . The British people and their allies today are conducting an active war against this unholy alliance. Our own future security is greatly dependent on the outcome of that fight.'
'. . . We must be the great arsenal of democracy . . . We must apply ourselves to our task with the same resolution, the same sense of urgency, the same spirit of patriotism and sacrifice as we would show were we at war.'

President Roosevelt was way ahead of public opinion in America. In Britain Mr Churchill put into words what every inarticulate Briton was thinking. And for Fighter Command he had one of the happiest tributes that ever came from that silver tongue: 'Never in the field of human conflict was so much owed by so many to so few.'[1]

And far away the Russian poet, Nikolai Tikhinov, with a sympathy born of a sense of foreboding wrote:

'Through the night, through sheets of rain, and
    the wind cutting his cheeks,
Learning his lesson as he goes along,
The man of London winds his way to the shelter,
Dragging his rug along the watery pavement.
There's the cold steel key in his pocket,
A key to rooms now turned to prickly rubble.
We still are learning lessons at our school desk,
But at night we dream of the coming exam.'[2]

I am inclined, however, to quit this great battle on a lower note. That summer *The Times* Cricket Correspondent had this to say of daylight raids. 'Interruptions such as occur these days make it quite impossible for a captain to declare his innings closed at a moment even approximate to that which would normally allow a reasonably close finish.'

[1] 20 August. Churchill: Vol II, p. 300.
[2] Werth: *Russia at War*, p. 100.

CHAPTER NINE

WAVELL AND THE ITALIANS

1940

5 Aug.	The Italians invade Somaliland.
19 Aug.	The British evacuate Somaliland.
20 Aug.	Mussolini announces the 'total blockade' of British possessions in the Mediterranean and Africa.
13 Sep.	The Italians advance into Egypt.
28 Oct.	Italian invasion of Greece.
11/12 Nov.	Taranto.
21 Nov.	Greeks take Koritza.
9 Dec.	Major General O'Connor takes the offensive.

1941

5 Jan.	Bardia captured.
mid-*Jan.*	The Italians evacuate Kassala.
16 Jan.	Battle of the Juba river.
22 Jan.	Australians take Tobruk with 25,000 prisoners and 50 tanks.
29 Jan.	British enter Italian Somaliland.
30 Jan.	Derna.
31 Jan.	Battle of Agordat.
6 Feb.	Australians storm Benghazi.
7 Feb.	The British take Mogadishu, capital of Italian Somaliland. Italian surrender at Beda Fomm.
9 Feb.	The Royal Navy bombards Genoa.
12 Feb.	German troops under General Rommel arrive in Libya.
5 Mar.	British troops reach Greece.
16 Mar.	British reoccupy Berbera.
24 Mar.	Axis offensive in North Africa.
27 Mar.	Fall of Keren.
28 Mar.	Battle of Cape Matapan.
1 Apr.	Fall of Asmara.
3 Apr.	Rommel takes the offensive.

6 Apr.	Surrender of Addis Ababa.
8 Apr.	Surrender of Massawa.
11 Apr.	Tobruk besieged.
27 Apr.	The Germans enter Athens.
30 Apr.	End of resistance in Greece.
5 May	The Emperor of Abyssinia regains his throne.
16 May	The Duke of Aosta capitulates at Amba Alagi.

'I need a few thousand dead to justify my presence at the peace table.'   MUSSOLINI *to* GRAZIANI (17 June 1940).

WITH France out of the war splendid opportunities seemed to beckon Mussolini. Surely the Mediterranean would now become the *Mare Nostrum* of Fascist propaganda. Surely his African armies, half a million strong, could expel the British, and rival Nazi achievements with Fascist victories. Hitler, for his part, preoccupied as he was with *Sealion*, could safely leave these sideshows to his ally.

But were they sideshows? In a war with the sea power of Great Britain the control of Suez counted for something. In the final showdown with Russia an advance which might bring the Germans within striking distance of the Caucasian oil-fields was a potential war-winner. We may be thankful that no such notion seems to have struck the *Führer*.

The Italian Army in Africa looked impressive on paper. In Libya Marshal Balbo commanded some 250,000 men. In Abyssinia and Eritrea the Duke of Aosta was at the head of 350,000 men. The Italian Navy seemed well placed to control both the Mediterranean and the Red Sea, and could therefore cut the British lines of communication with Egypt.

It fell to General Wavell to defend the British position in the Middle East. His forces numbered no more than:

Egypt	36,000
Palestine	27,000
Sudan	9,000
Kenya	8,500
Aden	2,500
British Somaliland	1,500
Cyprus	800

In Egypt was the 7th Armoured Division of two brigades.

Thanks to the destruction of so much of the German surface fleet off Norway the Churchill Government had been able to build up two small fleets in the Mediterranean: one under Vice-Admiral Sir Andrew Cunningham based on Alexandria, the other under Vice-Admiral Sir James Somerville based on Gibraltar. On paper they were no match for the powerful and modern Italian Navy with its 10 battleships.

In Egypt the RAF had a few squadrons equipped with the obsolescent Gladiator.

Wavell's lines of communication, as we have seen, were insecure. The capture of Malta, garrisoned as it was by a mere five battalions, should not have been an unduly difficult operation.

Fortunately the British forces were not impressed by the opposition. General Wavell was well versed in military history. Like Robert E. Lee he knew that if he got to 'cipherin' ' he would be beaten. There is much to be said for the old adage that 'attack is the best defence'. The British determined to make up for their lack of numbers by audacity. They were instructed to 'make one man appear to be a dozen, make one tank look like a squadron, make a raid look like an advance.'[1] War is to some extent a business of credit – you've got as many men as the enemy is prepared to believe you've got! An active raiding policy confused the Italians. 'Soon from prisoners we learned extraordinary stories were going the round behind the Italian lines. There were two ... three ... five British armoured divisions operating, they said. A large-scale attack was imminent. Balbo drew in his horns, cut down his own patrols and called for more reinforcements from Rome.'

Balbo was killed on 28 June in an air raid on Tobruk, and was succeeded by Marshal Graziani 'who during the Italo-Abyssinian War had proved himself to be a veritable snail.'[2] Prodded by his master he moved up to the Egyptian frontier in mid-September and began to build a chain of seven forts. Reconnaissance showed that these works were neither mutually supporting nor prepared for all-round defence.

It might reasonably have been expected that Graziani would have made a forward movement to coincide with his master's invasion of Greece (28 October). Since he made no move the British decided to make a five day raid on his forts. The arrival in September of 50 'I' (Infantry) tanks from England enabled them to do so with some prospect of success. Italian defeats in Greece (11 November) and the

[1] Alan Moorehead: *African Trilogy* pp. 22–3.
[2] Fuller: *The Second World War*, p. 94.

Fleet Air Arm's damaging blow at Taranto were evidence that all was not well in Mussolini's war-machine, and doubtless encouraged the advocates of a forward policy. Even so the odds looked unhealthy enough. G.H.Q. credited Graziani with 80,000 men, 120 tanks and three times as many planes as the RAF. Major-General R.N. O'Connor's Western Desert Force consisted of:

31,000 men.
275 tanks.
120 guns.

A No Man's Land of 70 miles separated the armies. Transport was short and it was decided to dump supplies 20 or 30 miles *in front* of the British lines. General O'Connor made his approach march in two stages, advancing 30 miles on the night of 7 December, halting in the open during the 8th, and advancing by night to attack at dawn on the 9th. He had got the measure of his enemy, who thanks to particularly skilful security precautions remained blissfully ignorant of the gathering storm.

Meanwhile the Royal Navy was bombarding Meiktila, Sidi Barrani and the coastal road; the Royal Air Force was attacking Italian airfields with the object of destroying planes on the ground.

The Italians had obligingly left a 20-mile gap in their line of forts between Nibeiwa and Sofafi East and Sofafi West. By 7 a.m. on 9 December the British were in rear of Nibeiwa. The guns opened up and 35 minutes later the tanks went in followed by infantry. They made short work of the Italian tanks. The enemy anti-tank gunners found to their dismay that their 37-mm shells would not penetrate the 'I' tanks. Within an hour the garrison of 3,000 had been overrun. The commander, General Maletti, died fighting. Tummar West and most of Tummar East fell the same day. By nightfall the British had cut the coast road between Buq Buq and Sidi Barrani, which was taken next day. By the 11th General Wavell estimated that five Italian divisions were already *hors de combat*.

Despite Wavell's designs on Eritrea and Abyssinia the raid now turned into a campaign. The fortified towns of Bardia and Tobruk were assaulted, using methodical techniques not unlike those of the First World War: mine clearance, filling the anti-tank ditch, wire-cutting and artillery preparation.

The enemy in Cyrenaica was now intent only on flight. Generals Wavell and O'Connor, to whom taking risks was by this time second

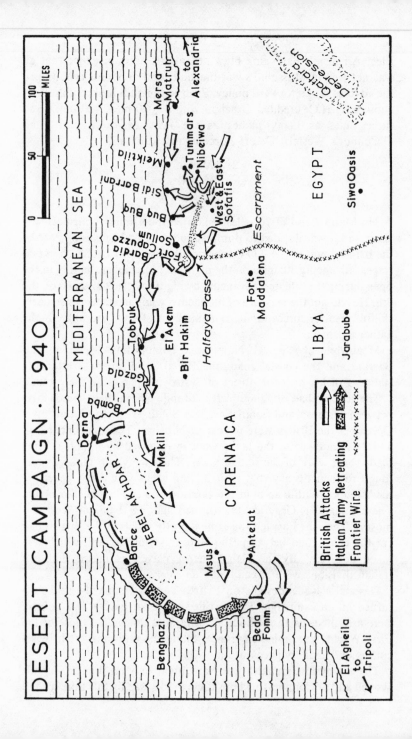

DESERT CAMPAIGN · 1940

MEDITERRANEAN SEA

to Alexandria

Mersa Matruh

Meiktila

Tummars
Nibeiwa

Sidi Barrani

West & East Sofafis

Buq Buq

Escarpment

Sollum

Fort Capuzzo

Bardia

Halfaya Pass

Tobruk

El Adem

Bir Hakim

Fort Maddalena

Gazala

Bomba

Derna

Mekili

JEBEL AKHDAR

CYRENAICA

LIBYA

EGYPT

Siwa Oasis

Jarabub

Barce

Msus

Antelat

Benghazi

Beda Fomm

El Agheila
to Tripoli

Qattara Depression

	British Attacks
	Italian Army Retreating
××××××	Frontier Wire

MILES
0   50   100

nature, decided to move across the desert without waiting for all their troops and supply echelons to come up. On 5 February a detachment of 7th Armoured Division cut the coast road at Beda Fomm 50 miles south of Benghazi. That evening a column of 5,000 Italians ran into the 4th Armoured Brigade, and, being taken by surprise, promptly surrendered. Next day the main enemy column came on the scene. Though they fought hard, General ('Electric Whiskers') Berganzoli made the classic mistake of putting his men into action piecemeal. He lost 84 tanks, and next day capitulated.

In 62 days a force which never exceeded two divisions had utterly destroyed ten enemy divisions, taking 130,000 prisoners of war; 380 tanks; 845 guns. The British lost 500 killed, 1,373 wounded and 55 missing.

The first German troops arrived in Libya in February, in time perhaps to have saved Tripoli had Wavell now attempted to take it. That he made no such attempt was due to events in Greece which have yet to be described.

History does not record another campaign like this of General O'Connor. Inter-service co-operation, audacity, mobility, offensive action, and the 'I' tank were its most striking features.

This campaign is often called 'the Wavell offensive'. This is in-accurate, as Field-Marshal Lord Harding, who was then O'Connor's Brigadier, General Staff, has shown:

'Although he had the invaluable support and wise advice of Field Marshals Wavell and Wilson to aid him, the plan of battle was hatched in General O'Connor's brain, the tactical decisions on which success or failure depended were his, the grim determination that inspired all our troops stemmed up from his heart; it was his skill in calculating the risks, and his daring in accepting them, that turned what might have been merely a limited success into a victorious campaign with far-reaching effects on the future course of the war.'[1]

Besides supporting General O'Connor's operations the Royal Navy had struck the Italian Navy two crippling blows.

On 11 November Admiral Cunningham took a force into Taranto Bay. Twenty ancient Swordfish from the *Illustrious*, made one of the most successful torpedo attacks of the war. There were six battleships in Taranto Harbour: three were sunk. In addition two cruisers and

[1] C. N. Barcley: Foreword, *Against Great Odds*, p. 5.

two auxiliaries were sunk by bombing. The British lost two planes, one officer killed and three men taken prisoner.

The Royal Navy made a good job of whittling down the Italian Navy – on 15 October 1940, for example, the British announced the sinking of three enemy destroyers. The bombardment – in broad daylight – of Genoa, on 9 February 1941, added something more than insult to injury. Docks, railway stations, power plants and stores all suffered.

But the second crippling blow to the Italian Navy came on 27 March when an Italian force, hoping to intercept a British convoy to Greece, ran into Cunningham's battle fleet off Cape Matapan. First the Italians were slowed down by air attack. The Admiral himself has described[1] the dramatic moment when, at 10.25 on the night of 28 March, Commodore Edelsten, his new Chief of Staff, who

'had come to gain experience . . . calmly reported that he saw two large cruisers with a smaller one ahead of them crossing the bows of the battle-fleet from starboard to port' . . . Commander Power, an ex-submarine officer and an abnormal expert at recognizing the silhouettes of enemy warships at a glance, pronounced them to be two *Zara* class 8-inch gun cruisers with a smaller cruiser ahead.

'Using short-range wireless the battle-fleet was turned back into line ahead.'

The British opened fire at point-blank range (3,800 yards), simultaneously illuminating the targets with searchlights.

'The Italians were quite unprepared. Their guns were trained fore and aft. They were helplessly shattered before they could put up any resistance.'

In a few minutes the Italian cruisers 'were nothing but glowing torches . . .' The battleship *Vittorio Veneto*, damaged by the earlier air attack, got away, but the Italians lost the 8-inch cruisers *Zara*, *Pola* and *Fiume* and two big destroyers. Despite the attention of some German JU.88s the victors rescued 900 Italian sailors, but some 2,400 were killed. The British lost two aircraft, but not a single sailor. With the exception of Tsushima (1905) it would not be easy to cite another instance of a battle between fairly equal fleets in which heavy losses were inflicted on the one and the other escaped unscathed.

[1] Cunningham: *A Sailor's Odyssey*.

The battle of Cape Matapan demonstrated with horrid force the superiority of the Royal Navy over their Italian opponents.

EAST AFRICA

The campaigns in East Africa began with the conquest of British and French Somaliland, which gave the Italians the opportunity to tighten their control of the southern entrance to the Red Sea. The garrison of British Somaliland, 1,500 British and native troops, was simply overwhelmed between 5 August and the 19th, when the survivors evacuated Berbera by sea. Mussolini followed up this 'magnificent victory' with the announcement of a 'total blockade' of British possessions in Africa and the Mediterranean. This was to prove the high-water mark of Italian military achievement in the Second World War.

On 2 December General Wavell held a conference in Cairo with Lt.-Generals Sir William Platt and Sir Alan Cunningham, the commanders of the British forces in the Sudan and in Kenya. Platt was to stir up rebellion in Abyssinia and to retake Kassala in February. For these tasks he was allotted 4th and 5th Indian Divisions. Cunningham was to maintain pressure on Meyale, and once the rains were over, in May or June, was to advance on Kismayu, near the mouth of the River Juba. He was given the 1st South African Division and the 11th and 12th African Divisions. These two campaigns, working from bases (Khartoum and Nairobi) 1,200 miles apart, have been described as 'the most rapid pincer movement ever carried out'.[1]

Thus while Wavell was planning his great raid on Graziani he was also laying the foundations of two ambitious campaigns, which, if all went well, might eventually clear one of his lines of communication – the long route round the Cape and up the Red Sea.

ERITREA

The Italians, so far from advancing on Khartoum as might have been expected, permitted themselves to be bluffed by pinprick raids into thinking they were opposed by much stronger forces than General Platt commanded. Rather unexpectedly they evacuated Kassala in the middle of January, and Platt was therefore able to begin his offensive sooner than planned. Crossing the Eritrean border on 20 January he caught up General Frusci and beat him at the battle of

[1] Fuller: p. 99.

87

Agordat on the 31st. The Italians took refuge in their mountain fortress of Keren, where the Kassala-Asmara road runs through a tremendous ravine. Here the Italians put up a good fight. They had 30,000 infantry, including the pick of the Italian Army, Alpini, Bersaglieri and the Savoy Grenadiers, with 144 guns. Fort Dologorodoc proved the key, and when it fell the Italians counter-attacked eight times, suffering heavy losses among their crack troops. The death of General Lorenzini, a brave and popular commander, discouraged the garrison. The fortress fell on 27 March. The siege had cost the British 4,000 casualties and the Italians 3,000 killed. The fall of Keren broke the back of resistance in Eritrea. Asmara fell with 10,000 prisoners on 1st April and the vital port of Massawa three days later. Still the Italians in Eritrea had put up a much better fight than Graziani's army in Libya.

ABYSSINIA

Meanwhile, rains or no rains, Cunningham had begun his advance on 24 January and beat the Italians on the Juba river on 16 February. Wavell now gave his permission for a further advance. Cunningham's army, though small in numbers, was extremely mobile. His reserve transport consisted of 40 companies, each of 75 two or three-ton lorries. Between 6 a.m. on 23 February and 5 p.m. on the 25th, a motorized African brigade group made a 275 mile advance to Mogadishu in Italian Somaliland, an astonishing performance. And there they found 350,000 gallons of petrol and 80,000 of aviation spirit.

The feebleness of the Italian resistance encouraged Cunningham to ask Wavell's permission to advance on Harar, via Giggiga, which is 774 miles from Mogadishu by road.

Cunningham moved off on 1 March and advanced 590 miles before he made contact with the enemy at Dagabur (10 March). Pushing on he took Giggiga on 17 March. Meanwhile a small force from Aden had retaken Berbera on 16 March, thus shortening Cunningham's line of communications. Giggiga is 1,600 miles from Kenya, but only 204 from Berbera. Pushing on up the Madar pass Cunningham captured Harar on 25 March. 'Thus, in thirty days, his advance had covered 1,054 miles at an average of 35 miles in the day, the last sixty-five miles of which had in 1935-36 hung up Graziani for nearly six months.'[1]

[1] Fuller: p. 101.

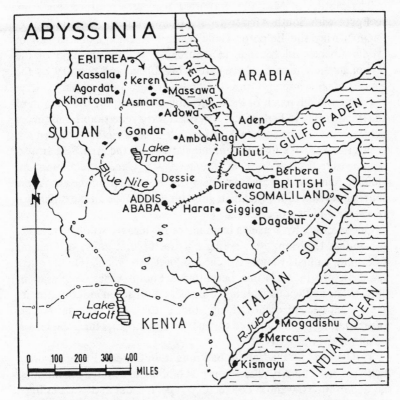

The Italians abandoned Addis Ababa on 4 April. After some fighting in the Combolcia Pass, Cunningham took Dessie (20 April). The Duke of Aosta entrenched the remnants of his army at Amba Alagi. But now the pincers began to nip, with Cunningham closing in from the south, and Platt from the north. Aosta, whose water-supply had been damaged, surrendered unconditionally on 18 May, but was granted the honours of war. The Duke was a man of honour and, delighted with this concession, gave the strictest orders that the battlefield should be handed over clean of mines and that all guns, equipment and stores should be handed over intact. His orders were scrupulously carried out.

In Gondar province hostilities continued until November 1941, but the campaign was virtually at an end. Skilfully conducted guerilla warfare in Western Abyssinia, in which Colonel Orde Wingate distinguished himself, had contributed to the result.

The capture of Massawa permitted Wavell to reinforce his army in Egypt with South African troops from southern Abyssinia.

On 5 May the Emperor Haile Selassie re-entered his capital of Addis Ababa and became, in Churchill's words, 'the first of the lawful sovereigns to be driven from his throne and country by the Fascist-Nazi criminals,' and 'the first to return in triumph.'

Feeble though much of the opposition had been, the destruction of the Italian army in Eritrea and Abyssinia was a remarkable and timely achievement. It came when Allied morale needed victories to feed on. It cleared Wavell's line of communications up the Red Sea. It also demonstrated the power of the RAF, for Gèneral Cunningham suffered remarkably little from enemy interference from the air. A few Hurricanes sent to the Sudan in good time had made all the difference to General Platt's operations.

One is struck by Wavell's handling of his meagre strategic reserve. 4th Indian Division, after taking part in the first phase of General O'Connor's offensive, was switched to Platt's command. On the other hand victory in Abyssinia permitted a South African build-up in Egypt. The audacious retaking of Berbera, only seven months after its fall, was a neat piece of strategy. Indeed the value of audacity and breath-taking mobility pitted against mere numbers is the great lesson of all these campaigns.

The British and the Italians had fought, in General Fuller's words, 'with marked chivalry. There was no bombing of the civil inhabitants, no deportations, wanton destruction, rape, murder and plundering.'[1] The Abyssinian war of 1935-6 had been fought in a different spirit.

Italian sacrifices in Africa were never to justify Mussolini's presence at any peace table. The few dead he had thought he needed now numbered many thousands; to which must be added countless prisoners.

Wavell's strategy was about to be put to yet sterner tests; but he had given the Allies their first big victory in the land fighting of World War Two.

[1] Fuller: p. 102.

CHAPTER TEN

CAMPAIGN IN THE BALKANS

1940

15 Aug.	Italian submarine sinks the Greek cruiser *Helle*.
7 Oct.	German troops enter Roumania.
28 Oct.	Greece rejects Italian ultimatum.
	Italians invade Greece.
1 Nov.	Greeks repel Italian attacks.
11 Nov.	The Fleet Air arm raids Taranto.
22 Nov.	Greeks take Koritza (Albania).
9 Dec.	British offensive in Libya.

1941

Jan.	German build-up in Roumania.
21 Jan.	British take Tobruk.
29 Jan.	Death of General Metaxas.
24 Feb.	The Greeks agree to accept a British army.
1 Mar.	Bulgaria joins the Tripartite Pact of Germany, Italy and Japan.
9 Mar.	Italian offensive in Greece.
24 Mar.	The Yugoslav Government joins the Tripartite Pact.
26 Mar.	Serbian nationalist officers overthrow the Regent and set up a Government in the name of King Peter.
27 Mar.	Hitler issues Directive No. 25 for the crushing of Yugoslavia.
28 Mar.	Battle of Cape Matapan.
6 Apr.	Germans attack Yugoslavia and Greece.
8 Apr.	Fall of Salonika.
13 Apr.	Occupation of Belgrade.
17 Apr.	Capitulation of Yugoslavia.
21 Apr.	Suicide of Count Teleki, the Hungarian Prime Minister.
24 Apr.	The Greek Government surrenders.
24 Apr./ *2 May*	The British evacuate Greece.

25 Apr.	Hitler issues his Directive for the capture of Crete.
26 Apr.	German airborne troops seize the bridge over the Corinth Canal.
27 Apr.	The Germans enter Athens.
5 May	General Freyberg, V.C., takes command in Crete.
20 May	Germans invade Crete.
1 Jun.	British evacuate Crete.
18 Jun.	Germany and Turkey sign treaty of friendship.
22 Jun.	Germans invade Russia.

'Are we again going to have "Salonika supporters" as in the last war? Why will politicians never learn the simple principle of concentration of force at the vital point and the avoidance of dispersal of effort.' GENERAL SIR ALAN BROOKE.

BETWEEN 28 October 1940 and 1 June 1941 the Axis Powers took the Balkans in an iron grip. Roumania and Bulgaria were peacefully occupied, Yugoslavia and Greece resisted and were supported by Great Britain. Between them they put into the field some 50 divisions, about 28 Yugoslav, 20 Greek and 3 British. On paper this looks a formidable force, but it was not properly co-ordinated, and was particularly weak in aircraft and tanks, the weapons of the *Blitzkrieg*. For the most part these considerable forces were armed with obsolete weapons, and depended for transport on horses and even oxen. Still they fought with tenacity and not entirely without success. Only at sea did the Allies have the advantage and here too losses were severe whenever ships were exposed within range of shore-based aircraft.

In November 1940 Mussolini needed a victory and a cheap one. Greece seemed the most suitable victim. Not unreasonably he considered that a nation of 45,000,000 ought to be able to crush one of 6,936,000.

In August 1940 Mussolini had demanded that Greece renounce the guarantee of her independence made in 1939 by Great Britain. When King George II and his premier, General Metaxas, refused, Mussolini denounced Greece for her 'un-neutral' attitude. The Italian army in Albania, 150,000 strong, began to concentrate on the frontier. The Greeks could oppose them with some 75,000. On 28 October an ultimatum was presented in Athens. It listed the 'wrongs' Italy had suffered at Greek hands, and demanded the occupation of strategic positions in Greece for the duration. In true Nazi-Fascist style the Italians then proceeded to invade Greece without awaiting a reply.[1]

[1] Indeed the Italian ambassador in Athens did not even know the terms of the ultimatum he was presenting!

Great Britain immediately promised her support to the Greeks and established RAF squadrons in Crete, but with 200,000 Italians pouring down the valleys of Northern Greece the prospects of resistance seemed bleak. Moreover, the Metaxas Line faced not Albania but Bulgaria.

It was not particularly prudent of Mussolini to choose the rainy month of November for this march through the mountains. But the Italian fiasco that followed was due not so much to weather and terrain as to the classic military fault of underrating the enemy. The Greeks were sustained by patriotism and indignation.

The Italian plan was to push up the valley of the Vojusa and, by taking Metsovo, cut off the Greeks in Thessaly and Macedonia from those in the Epirus. At first they made rapid progress up the Vojusa, though another column advancing towards the Kalamas river soon got stuck. The RAF had flown in a consignment of obsolescent Boys anti-tank rifles which knocked out nine Italian tanks. On the Albanian front the Greeks, who had mobilized with creditable speed, astonished the Italians by taking the offensive and thrusting towards the supply base of Koritza. At the same time they reinforced the Pindus front and fell upon the flanks of the column on the Vojusa. Between 8 and 10 November the 3rd Alpini Division, composed of some of the best Italian troops, was caught in the Pindus gorges and lost 5,000 men. The Greeks took Koritza on 22 November with a great quantity of equipment which they sorely needed. By the end of December a quarter of Albania was in Greek hands. The RAF bombed Valona, the principal port, as well as raiding Brindisi.

Taranto, Koritza and Benghazi all came as a rude shock to the Italian people, so long accustomed to Fascist vauntings. But 'the croaking bullfrog of the Pontine Marshes' was not done yet. 'We'll break the backs of the Greeks', Mussolini declared 'and we don't need any help!' But Hitler thought things had gone quite far enough, and on 13 December issued Directive No. 20 for 'Undertaking Marita'. . . . 'In the light of the threatening situation in Albania it is doubly important to frustrate English efforts to establish, behind the protection of a Balkan front, an air base which would threaten Italy in the first place and, incidentally, the Roumanian oilfields.' He intended to build up a force of some 24 divisions in Southern Roumania and then, when the weather was favourable, probably in March, to move across Bulgaria and occupy the northern coast of the Aegean, and if necessary the whole mainland of Greece. 'English bases in the Greek Islands' were to be seized by airborne troops.

On the completion of the operation the troops were to be withdrawn for 'new employment', because the denial to the British of any foothold on the continent of Europe was merely to clear the way for Hitler's ultimate aim 'the winning of living-space in the East'.[1]

On 11 January 1941 Hitler issued his orders[2] for supporting the Italians. 'The situation in the Mediterranean area, where England is employing *superior forces*[3] against our allies, requires that Germany should assist for reasons of strategy, politics, and psychology.'

X Air Corps was already operating from Sicily against British naval forces in the Mediterranean. Now a corps was to be moved into Albania. Meanwhile the Twelfth German Army under Field-Marshal List was assembling in Bulgaria for the attack on Greece. Operations *Sonnenblume*[4] and *Alpenveilchen*[5] were to save Tripoli and Albania respectively. But Mussolini wanted the credit of the victory in Albania for himself, and at a conference on 19 and 20 January persuaded Hitler to modify his instructions. German troops, the germ of the *Afrika Korps*, were to cross to Tripoli in mid-February, but the Albania offensive was to be left to the Italians.

Early in March Germany began to tighten her net round Greece. First she compelled Bulgaria to agree to the Tripartite Pact[6] and to the passage of her troops. Similar pressure made Yugoslavia join the Pact on 24 March. But 'the Jugs', despite their unfavourable strategic position, with hostile forces all along their frontier except in the south where it joined Greece, did not receive this pact in any docile spirit. A military *coup d'état* led by General Simovitch overthrew the government of the Regent, the young King's uncle Prince Paul (26 March). This move, which had general support in the country and was welcomed with enthusiasm in Britain, compelled the Germans to change their plans. Instead of invading Greece via Bulgaria they now determined to strike down both Yugoslavia and Greece at a blow. There was a certain amount of delay while this campaign was mounted.

[1] Directive No. 21 for 'Case Barbarossa' – the invasion of Russia – was issued only five days later on 18 December.

[2] Directive No. 22.

[3] Author's italics. If Hitler really believed this, all the more credit to Wavell and Cunningham.

[4] Sunflower.

[5] Alpine violet.

[6] Signed in Berlin by Germany, Italy and Japan on 27 September, 1940.

Meanwhile a British force was landing in Greece. These troops were badly needed in North Africa, and it was undoubtedly a grave strategic error to send them to Greece; a violation of the principle of concentration. It may be argued that the support of Greece, an ally, was a matter of honour, but this argument would have more force had the Greeks themselves not been extremely reluctant to receive this reinforcement. De Guingand has described[1] the way in which Mr Anthony Eden persuaded them to agree, and the shameless exaggeration of our available strength upon which he insisted.

It is said, by Guderian among others, that British intervention in Greece delayed the German invasion of Russia, but since this may equally well be explained by the weather, the question must remain an open one. But if it could be shown that the Greek episode really had this effect it would in large measure justify the adventure.

The capture of Tripoli and the successful termination of the campaign in North Africa seems now a prize far more worth while than anything that could have been hoped for in Greece. But in fact Wavell was very far from thinking in terms of taking Tripoli, and although it is often assumed that the expedition to Greece was prompted by Mr Churchill, it is evident that the Prime Minister left the ultimate decision to his General, and that the latter expected great things from his campaign in the Balkans.

On 6 April the Germans invaded Yugoslavia with 33 divisions, six of which were armoured. The Jugoslavs could oppose them with 28 divisions, three being cavalry. They were all strung out along the frontiers, only one being in strategic reserve. Though good fighting men, the Jugoslavs were no match for the Germans in training or armament. In the air the *Luftwaffe* had everything its own way. While Belgrade and other towns were ruthlessly bombed, six strong German columns were carving through the Yugoslav defences and breaking the army into fragments. The campaign lasted a mere 10 days. On 17 April Yugoslavia surrendered.

The main body of the Greek army, 14 divisions, was facing the Italians in Albania. The British army and three Greek divisions were deployed on a line between the Aegean Sea and the Yugoslav frontier, with part of the 1st Armoured Brigade, watching the Monastir Gap. Three and a half Greek divisions manned the Metaxas Line covering Macedonia and watching the Rupel pass. It was a long and mountainous front thinly held by a largely immobile army.

[1] In *Operation Victory*, p. 57.

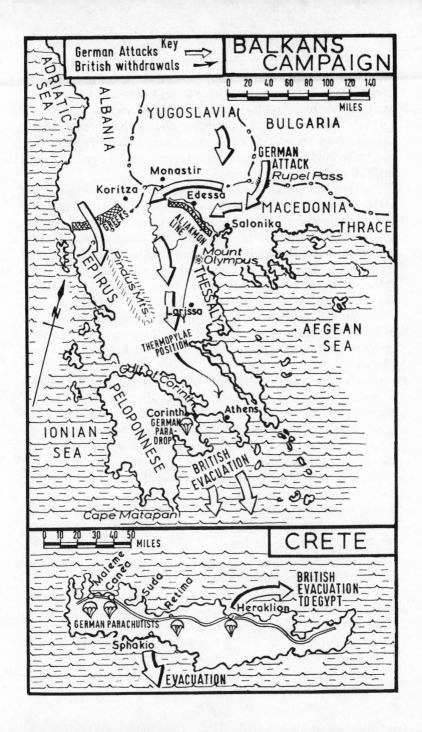

BALKANS CAMPAIGN

Key

German Attacks →
British withdrawals →

ADRIATIC SEA

ALBANIA

YUGOSLAVIA

BULGARIA

0 20 40 60 80 100 120 140
MILES

Monastir

Koritza

GERMAN ATTACK
Rupel Pass

Edessa

GREEKS

ALIAKMON LINE

MACEDONIA

THRACE

Salonika

Pindus Mts.

EPIRUS

Mount Olympus

THESSALY

AEGEAN SEA

Larissa

THERMOPYLAE POSITION

Gulf of Corinth

PELOPONNESE

Corinth
GERMAN PARA-DROP

Athens

IONIAN SEA

Cape Matapan

BRITISH EVACUATION

---

0 10 20 30 40 50
MILES

CRETE

Maleme
Canea
Suda
Retima

BRITISH EVACUATION TO EGYPT

Heraklion

GERMAN PARACHUTISTS

Sphakio

EVACUATION

Field-Marshal List determined to cut the Allies in two by piercing their centre and isolating the army in Albania. At the same time he intended to force his way through the Rupel Pass and by breaking the Metaxas Line to cut off the Greeks in Eastern Macedonia. Another column, moving down the Strumitza and Vardar, would attack Salonika from the east. For political reasons General Papagos had decided to hold the Metaxas Line, but from a military point of view this had nothing to recommend it.

The Germans crossed the Greek frontier at the same time as they invaded Yugoslavia. The dispositions of the Greeks holding the Metaxas Line and the British forces were unhinged from the outset by the rapid collapse of the Yugoslavs. The Greeks had prudently withdrawn from Thrace, but the enemy swiftly broke through the Rupel Pass and the Monastir Gap, which was not sufficiently strongly defended, and took Salonika from the west as planned (8 April). The Greeks east of the Vardar were now compelled to surrender.

The onslaught was accompanied by heavy air bombing. In the harbour of Piraeus a ship full of T.N.T. blew up, and another with a cargo of Hurricanes was sunk. The airfields at Larissa were overwhelmed.

General Sir Henry Maitland-Wilson's army, 56,657 strong,[1] consisted of the 1st Armoured Brigade, the 2nd New Zealand Division, and the 6th Australian Division. He now withdrew with great skill from the Vardar front and under appallingly difficult circumstances got back to a position round Mount Olympus and along the river Aliakmon.

Major Seton-Watson's description of a night withdrawal, when his battery managed a mere fifteen miles in twelve hours, conjures up the chaotic conditions of this retreat – and may serve to typify many such a night spent by British units from the Dunkirk days onwards during the first three years of the war.

'After dark we started on a nightmare drive. Grevena was full of burning dumps and houses, bewildered Greek troops and confused columns of mules and bullock carts. The road on to the Venetikos was narrow and twisting, sometimes with steep ravines or precipices on both sides. We were a mixed cavalcade. Vehicles were jammed nose to tail for miles, double – and even treble-banked whenever the road was wide enough. Buses and private cars, Greeks on

[1] 24,000 British. The remainder were mostly Australians and New Zealanders, though there was a Polish Brigade.

horseback and foot, were all jumbled in between our guns. Halts were interminable and we crawled forward a few hundred yards at a time. Weary drivers fell asleep in the cabs and had to be roused by cursing officers and N.C.Os. Our route was strewn with all the litter of a retreat: discarded clothing, ammunition and harness, dead mules and horses, sodden papers and office files, and dozens of abandoned vehicles – ramshackle requisitioned lorries from every province of Greece, British three-tonners side by side with Italian tractors and mobile workshops captured by the Greek Army in Albania and now waiting for their original owners; some bogged down in the ditches, some tipped at crazy angles into bomb craters, others burnt out or shattered by machine-gun bullets. All the time dawn was getting nearer and we could look forward to being caught by the first air sortie like rats in a trap, unable to disperse off the narrow road. But at first light the miracle occurred and the column began to move. As we twisted down into the Venetikos valley, a single Messerschmitt flew along the bottom of the gorge below us. But we were safely in action across the river and well camouflaged before the first air attacks began.'[1]

By 13 April General Wilson had completed his difficult withdrawal, but by that time the Greeks, worn down by continual bombardment, were collapsing, and the single British armoured brigade had practically shot its bolt. The Olympus line was too long for the troops Wilson had available, and he was compelled to withdraw to the Thermopylae line, though this uncovered the passes over the Pindus mountains and exposed the flank of the main Greek army retreating into the Epirus.

By 20 April the British were ensconced in the Thermopylae position, with 6 Australian Division emulating Leonidas and his Spartans[2] in the famous pass 'where the main bitumen road zigzagged up nearly three thousand feet of mountain wall.'[3] Unfortunately by this time the RAF had been driven from its airfields in Greece, and the Germans were thrusting for Corinth. The Greek army, which had put up a truly heroic struggle, was forced to surrender on 21 April.

It seemed highly improbable that any substantial part of the British expeditionary force could escape. The situation was even worse than

[1] W. E. Duncan, (Ed.): *The Royal Artillery Commemoration Book* 1939–45, (Bell, 1950)
[2] 480 BC
[3] Clifton: The Happy Hunted.

Dunkirk, for there was no fighter cover. And on 26 April by a bold stroke the Germans seized the bridge over the Corinth Canal with airborne troops, and cut off the Peloponnese from the rest of Greece.

Temperamentally General Wilson was just the man for a crisis of this sort. With magnificent skill and *sangfroid* he succeeded, despite the total lack of air cover, in evacuating the great majority of his troops. The work of the Royal Navy was beyond praise.

The Greeks too bore themselves nobly in this tragic hour. A British officer wrote: '. . . when we drove through Athens the Greeks lined the streets in thousands, many of them in tears, yet cheering and throwing flowers and shouting, "You will be back; we'll be waiting for you." Few retreating armies can have had such a send-off.'[1]

The Germans entered Athens on 27 April. The Swastika flew from the Acropolis.

Between 24 April and 2 May 43,000 British troops were evacuated, mostly to Crete, but all the *matériel* of the expeditionary force and 11,000 men were left behind.

Most of the Greek destroyers and all their submarines escaped. The King of Greece removed his seat of government to Crete. The King of Yugoslavia and his chief Ministers also succeeded in evading the Germans.

CRETE

Crete is an island about 160 miles long and varies in width from about $7\frac{1}{2}$ to 35 miles. Its garrison of three infantry battalions was reinforced by 27,000 of the troops from Greece, including the 2nd New Zealand Division and part of the 6th Australian Division. A detachment of Royal Marines was landed to hold Suda Bay. There were in addition two weak and ill-equipped Greek divisions. This force had to support it no more than 35 planes and nine tanks.

On 4 May Major-General Freyberg, V.C., the famous commander of the New Zealand Division, took command in Crete. With so resolute a leader there were high hopes that the island could be held. Already on the 28th Mr Churchill had signalled to Wavell, 'It seems clear from our information that a heavy airborne attack by German troops and bombers will soon be made on Crete. Let me know what forces you have in the island and what your plans are. It ought to be a fine opportunity for killing the parachute troops.' This was not

[1] Major C. I. W. Seton-Watson in Duncan.

an unreasonable view. But unfortunately the garrison was, in its commander's words (1 May), 'totally inadequate to meet attack envisaged'. It was the old tale of the balanced force – or rather the unbalanced force. 'Unless fighter aircraft are greatly increased', went on Freyberg, 'and naval forces made available to deal with sea-borne attack, I cannot hope to hold out with land forces alone, which, as result of campaign in Greece, are now devoid of any artillery, have insufficient tools for digging, very little transport, and inadequate war reserves of equipment and ammunition.' He urged that if the necessary support from the other services was not available the question of holding Crete should be reconsidered.

There were good reasons for holding on to Crete, quite apart from the importance of blunting the edge of the German airborne corps. The triangle of naval bases, Suda Bay, Alexandria, Benghazi, might give Admiral Cunningham a grip on the Eastern Mediterranean such as he had not previously enjoyed.

Meanwhile in a room in the Hotel Grande Bretagne in Athens General Student was briefing his commanders. 'It was his own, personal plan. He had devised it, had struggled against heavy opposition for its acceptance, and had worked out all the details . . . the plan had become a part of him, a part of his life. He believed in it and lived for it and in it.'[1]

Freyberg worked hard at his defences and by 16 May could report to Wavell that morale was high. He had 45 field guns well sited, with adequate ammunition dumped, and two infantry tanks on each aerodrome. 'I do not wish to be over-confident, but I feel that at least we will give excellent account of ourselves. With help of Royal Navy I trust Crete will be held.'

The Germans bombed the three airfields very severely and on 19 May the few RAF fighters that remained were withdrawn. On the 20th Student struck.

The first task of the *Luftwaffe* was to silence the anti-aircraft artillery, and in this the Germans were very successful. Next came the parachutists,[2] supported by waves of troop-carrying gliders, landing between Canea and Maleme. Many of these first 3,500 were slain, but 3,000 more men were landed at Retimo and Heraklion, and gradually the Germans succeeded in establishing a foothold. Their capture of Maleme airfield on 21 May was the turning-point of the

[1] Baron von der Heydte, C.O. 1/3rd Parachute Regiment, quoted in Flower and Reeves, p. 189.
[2] Including Max Schmeling, the former heavyweight champion of the world.

struggle. Aircraft began to pour in at the rate of 20 an hour. But a German attempt to follow up with a flotilla of Greek caiques met with calamity. A squadron consisting of three British cruisers and four destroyers got among them and sank almost every one either by gunfire or by ramming, including the Italian destroyer which was escorting them. A second convoy was attacked on the same day (22 May) but this time German aircraft from the Dodecanese sank the British cruisers *Gloucester* and *Fiji*, and three destroyers.[1] Even so the Germans made no further attempt at seaborne invasion.

Although the garrison was reinforced from Egypt (350 miles away) it was clear by the 28th that the battle was lost, and once again the Royal Navy was faced with the task of evacuating a British army. They succeeded in bringing away 14,967, though some 13,000 British and 5,000 Greek troops were left behind. Crete cost the Germans 12-17,000 men and 170 troop-carrying aircraft. Never again were they to risk the Seventh Air Division troops in so hazardous an operation. General Student visited Baron von der Heydte's battalion immediately after the fall of Canea. 'He had visibly altered. He seemed much graver, more reserved, and older. The cost of victory had evidently proved too much for him. Some of the battalions had lost all their officers, and in several companies there were only a few men left alive.'[2] If Freyberg's men were beaten they had at least blunted one of Hitler's most effective weapons, and the Royal Navy had demonstrated once more that, however desperate the situation, it was never prepared to abandon a British expeditionary force. Three cruisers, six destroyers and 29 smaller craft were lost. A battleship, four cruisers and seven destroyers were damaged. Naval casualties amounted to 2,000 men.

And so in the span of a few short weeks the Germans had crushed both Yugoslavia and Greece. Once again it was a question of air power, mobility and superior weapons rather than greater numbers. The Allies had fought with courage and determination, but the *Blitzkrieg* technique, so effective in 1939 and 1940, had not yet lost its magic. Allied armies, which would have been at home on the battlefields of 1914-18, were simply outclassed by the modern German *Wehrmacht*.

[1] Including the *Kelly* commanded by Lord Louis Mountbatten.
[2] Von der Heydte (Flower and Reeves, p. 196).

CHAPTER ELEVEN

ENTER ROMMEL

1941

12 Feb.	German troops in Libya.
31 Mar.	Rommel attacks in Cyrenaica.
3 Apr.	Revolt in Iraq.
4 Apr.	British take Addis Ababa.
8 Apr.	Fall of Massawa.
13 Apr.	Bardia evacuated. Tobruk holds out.
24 Apr./	
2 May	British evacuate Greece.
2 May	Siege of Habbaniya.
15 May	British attack on Sollum.
20 May/	
1 Jun.	Germans invade Crete.
8 Jun.	British invade Syria.
15/17 Jun.	British offensive towards Tobruk begins. Operation *Battleaxe*
18 Jun.	Treaty of friendship between Germany and Turkey.
21 Jun.	Free French take Damascus.
3 Jul.	Allies take Palmyra.
14 Jul.	Armistice signed at Acre. The Allies occupy Syria and Lebanon.
25 Aug.	British and Russian troops enter Persia.
13 Nov.	The *Ark Royal* sunk.
18 Nov.	Eighth Army's offensive in Libya.
23 Nov.	British take Bardia and Fort Capuzzo.
9 Dec.	Relief of Tobruk.

1942

2 Jan.	Bardia stormed by 2nd South African Division.
17 Jan,	Surrender of Halfaya Pass.
21 Jan.	Rommel advances to the Gazala Line

'Detachments of a German expeditionary force under an obscure general, Rommel, have landed in North Africa.'
From a British Intelligence Summary of March 1941.

AT THE same time that General Wavell was sending 56,000 men and 8,000 vehicles to Greece, Hitler was reinforcing his ally in Tripolitania with a Light Armoured Division under General Erwin Rommel. The brilliant strategical situation brought into being by General O'Connor's campaign was being sacrificed on the altar of Allied Solidarity. With the benefit of hindsight the Greek campaign appears a very forlorn hope indeed. To many, particularly at the lower staff levels, it seemed so at the time. The advantages of finishing off a beaten enemy in one theatre before switching to another should have carried more weight with General Wavell.

At the end of March the British had a thin covering force under General Philip Neame, V.C., in a position near El Agheila, 150 miles south of Benghazi. It consisted of the 2nd Armoured Division, which had one of its brigades in Greece; the 9th Australian Division, with a brigade in Tobruk; and an Indian Motor Brigade Group at Mekili. The Armoured Division was below establishment in tanks, and many of those it had were in bad condition. Some of the units were not fully trained in the special techniques of desert warfare.

On 31 March Rommel struck. Besides his German division, he had two Italian divisions, one armoured and one motorized. He gave orders to his air force to destroy British petrol-carrying transport.

Neame fell back according to plan and on 2 April was near Agedabia. On the 3rd it was reported that a strong German armoured column was approaching Msus, the main British petrol dump. The detachment guarding the place lost no time in setting fire to the petrol, and so depriving Neame's armour of its mobility. Benghazi was abandoned and Neame fell back to Tobruk, which was occupied by the Australians. The Armoured Division, harassed by air attacks on its wireless and petrol-carrying vehicles, did not reach Mekili until the 6th. The 3rd Armoured Brigade got into Derna, only to be

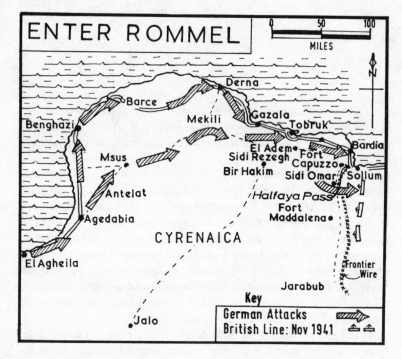

ENTER ROMMEL

MILES

Derna

Barce

Mekili

Gazala

Tobruk

Benghazi

El Adem   Fort

Sidi Rezegh   Capuzzo

Msus   Bir Hakim   Sidi Omar   Bardia

Sollum

Antelat   Halfaya Pass

Fort

Agedabia   Maddalena

CYRENAICA

El Agheila

Frontier
Wire

Jarabub

Key

Jalo

German Attacks
British Line: Nov 1941

captured there. The remainder of the 2nd Armoured Division was attacked at Mekili on the 7th, and was ordered to fall back to El Adem, south of Tobruk. At dawn next morning the 1st Royal Horse Artillery and some Indian troops broke out, but the rest of the division was taken.

To complicate matters still more on the night 6th–7th March, Generals Neame and O'Connor were captured near Derna by an enterprising German patrol. General Gambier-Parry had already been taken.

The question now was whether to hold the port of Tobruk with the thousands of tons of supplies which had been accumulated there. Wavell decided to do so, and sent in the 7th Australian Division and a few tanks by sea. They arrived on 7 March and four days later the place was besieged. The G.O.C., General Morshead, made his intentions perfectly clear: 'There'll be no Dunkirk here. If we should have to get out, we shall fight our way out. There is to be no surrender and no retreat.' Winston Churchill too was strongly in favour of holding Tobruk: '. . . a sally port; that is what we want. . . The further he advances the more you threaten, the more he has to fear. That is the answer, a sally port'. During the siege the garrison was to average some 23,000 men, about 15,000 being Australian, few enough for a perimeter of 25 miles. From April to November their spirited defence tied up one German and four Italian divisions.

By destroying the 2nd Armoured Division, Rommel had deprived the British of their offensive power. By defending Tobruk Wavell deprived Rommel of a forward base for his further advance into Egypt. The Germans reached the Sollum escarpment, but their attack had now lost its momentum. Thus in 12 days Rommel had robbed Wavell of much of the territory won in O'Connor's campaign and had inflicted severe losses on the British. But he could not give back to Mussolini his lost legions. Had Rommel's force been in the desert in December 1940 O'Connor's great success would not have been possible, but such an 'if' is not very helpful, because Mussolini was too proud to have accepted such help *before* Graziani had come unstuck. Still, the British may be thankful that Hitler sent Rommel to North Africa four months too late to have any real chance of taking Alexandria.

The disaster which overtook Neame's army can be directly attributed to the absence in Greece of the RAF squadrons required to give it something like air parity, and of the vehicles necessary to ensure the mobility of its supplies – especially of petrol. Without sufficient transport the British resorted to dumping, a World War I technique. That this was inappropriate to conditions in the Western Desert is forcibly demonstrated by the calamity at Msus. To a lesser extent the absence of 1st Armoured Brigade accounts for the defeat. Had Maitland-Wilson's army been in Cyrenaica instead of Greece Rommel would hardly have progressed beyond El Agheila.

Greece, Cyrenaica, East Africa: Wavell had plenty on his plate when on 3 April there came a revolt in Iraq. The new Prime Minister, Rashid Ali el-Gailani, immediately affirmed that he intended to fulfil Iraq's treaty obligations, which permitted the presence of British troops in his country in time of war or the threat of war. This good resolution was short-lived, for on 2 May the Iraqis laid siege to the British cantonment and RAF base at Habbaniya. The situation was alarming, because in addition to the threat to the oilfields and pipelines upon which Britain so much depended, there was the risk that the Germans would establish themselves in the

Middle East. Wavell's problem was to find the troops for a relief force. But Britain still had one staunch ally in those parts, Transjordan, which even in the blackest days of 1940 had remained pro-British. The Arab Legion under Glubb Pasha,[1] was a small but mobile force, wise in the ways of the desert. It provided 250 of the men under Major-General J. G. W. Clark, who relieved Habbaniya and took Baghdad (31 May).

Meanwhile, with the connivance of General Dentz, the French High Commissioner, the Germans and Italians had established air bases at Damascus, Rayak and Palmyra in Syria. They had bombed Habbaniya. On 8 June, with the agreement of General de Gaulle, a force under General Wilson invaded Syria and Lebanon. It had been hoped that resistance would be no more than formal, but the French fought stubbornly. As the campaign developed, the force from Iraq came in from the east and took Palmyra, where the Arab Legion once more distinguished itself (3 July). An armistice, giving the Allies the right to occupy Syria and Lebanon, was signed at Acre on 14 July.

This difficult campaign was followed in August by the Anglo-Russian occupation of Persia, which put an end to the danger of German penetration, and was executed practically without bloodshed. In order to supply Russia with vital war material the occupation of Persia was absolutely necessary.

Despite his losses in Greece, Crete and Cyrenaica, Wavell had successfully cleared up the situation in Iraq, Syria and Persia. Only in the Western Desert did his generalship still meet with ill-success. An abortive attack on Sollum (15 May) was followed by a more serious offensive intended to relieve Tobruk (15 June). Some progress was made at first but Rommel counter-attacked and drove back the 7th Armoured Division at Sidi Omar. Wavell withdrew on the night of 17 June. This was the ill-fated Operation *Battleaxe*.

The Panzer IV with the new 50 mm. gun was too much for the British armour. Skilful use of the 88 mm. anti-aircraft gun in the anti-tank rôle contributed to Rommel's success.

Mr Churchill was not pleased at this setback, though he himself had prodded Wavell into attacking before his army had recovered from its recent losses, and was therefore partly to blame. The Prime Minister now decided that it was time for a change in the Middle East. He was probably right. As a successor to Wavell he chose an

[1] Now Lt.-General Sir John Glubb, K.C.B., C.M.G., D.S.O., O.B.E., M.C.

excellent general – but the wrong one. General Sir Claude Auchinleck, Commander-in-Chief in India, was taken from a command for
which his career had best prepared him, and brought to the Middle
East. Wavell, whose whole career had been in the British Army, was
sent to Delhi. By mid-1941 it needed no seer to prophesy that the
Far East would soon be a theatre of war. The removal of Auchinleck
was, therefore, particularly unfortunate. If Wavell had to go, Auchinleck was not the only possible successor. Sir Harold Alexander, one
of Churchill's favourite generals, would have been a very suitable
choice. (And, if you like historical 'ifs', Alexander *might* have asked
for Lt.-General Montgomery to command his main striking force.)

The newly-formed Eighth Army was now given to Lt.-General
Sir Alan Cunningham, who had made his name in Abyssinia.

At this period Rommel's army was larger than Cunningham's, but
about two-thirds of it was Italian, and, therefore, on the whole, the
two armies were not altogether ill-matched when on 18 November
the British boldly and confidently embarked upon yet another
offensive. But though Rommel was short of Germans, in the weapons
of the *Blitzkrieg* – tanks and aircraft – he had the advantage in
quality.

	Rommel	*Cunningham*
Tanks	412	455
Anti-tank Guns	194	72

General Fuller has stressed Rommel's 'ballistical' advantage.[1]
'Rommel's tank and anti-tank guns were of 50 mm. ($4\frac{1}{2}$-pdr) and
75 mm. calibre, whereas Cunningham's were 2-pdrs, and the effective
armour-piercing range of this gun was from eight hundred to one
thousand yards less than that of the 50 mm. gun. Besides, the armour
of the British "I" tank (Matilda) was not proof against the 50 mm.
shell, let alone the 75 mm."

Rommel

German.
> 2 Panzer Divisions (15 and 21).
> 1 Light Division (90).
> 1 Infantry Division.

Italian.
> 1 Armoured Division (Ariete).
> 6 Infantry Divisions.

[1] Fuller: pp. 156, 20.

Lt.-General Sir Alan Cunningham.
XIII Corps. Lt.-General A. R. Godwin-Austin.
    4th Indian Division.
    New Zealand Division.
    1st Army Tank Brigade.

XXX Corps. Lt.-General Sir Willoughby Norrie.
    7th Armoured Division.[1]
    4th Armoured Brigade.
    1st South African Division.
    201st Guards Brigade Group.

Tobruk Garrison. Lt.-General Sir R. Scobie.
    70th Division.
    32nd Army Tank Brigade.
    A Polish Regiment.

Army Reserve.
    2nd South African Division.
    29th Indian Infantry Brigade Group.

RAF Component. Air Vice-Marshal A. Coningham.

	Squadrons
Light Bombers	9
Fighters	12
Medium Bombers	6

XXX Corps took the dominating ground at Sidi Rezegh on the 19th and engaged the Ariete Division, which put up a good fight. German armour was drawn into the battle, and attacked Sidi Rezegh on the 21st, but was held.

Meanwhile XIII Corps was working round the enemy's position on the frontier at Sidi Omar. Throughout 22 and 23 November a tremendous tank battle raged around Sidi Rezegh which eventually fell. Meanwhile the 4th Indian Division had taken Sidi Omar, and 70th Division from Tobruk was threatening Rommel's rear.

The Germans still had considerable garrisons holding Halfaya Pass and Bardia, 40 miles East of the Sidi Rezegh battlefield. In a gamble to save them, Rommel led 15 and 21 Panzer Divisions right through the back area of XXX Corps to the frontier at Bir Sheferzen. The chaos that this bold stroke caused has been well described by Alan Moorehead, the famous war correspondent: 'All day for nine

[1] 7th and 22nd Armoured Brigades and 7th Support Group.

hours we ran. It was the contagion of bewilderment and fear and ignorance. Rumours spread at every halt, no man had orders. Everyone had some theory and no one any plan . . . I came to understand something of the meaning of panic in this long nervous drive. It was the unknown we were running away from . . . Had there been someone in authority to say, "Stand here. Do this and that" – then half our fear would have vanished.'[1]

To Cunningham the situation looked black. The HQ of XIII Corps was split up and out of touch; the HQ of XXX Corps had taken refuge in Tobruk. The New Zealanders had made a brief contact with the garrison at El Duda, but the Germans had reacted violently and the place was now invested once more. Its twenty-five pounder ammunition had fallen dangerously low. Most of the British tanks seemed to have been lost, and Cunningham thought the best course was to retreat into Libya and re-group. In war if you can make the enemy think he's beaten, you win. But Rommel had not won, for at this juncture the man to say 'Stand here' flew up to the desert from Cairo. Auchinleck absolutely forbade withdrawal. Cunningham was replaced by Major-General N. M. Ritchie.

Meanwhile, for all the confusion, the two British corps had stood firm and the RAF had battered Rommel's transport, and he, realizing that his opponents were determined to fight it out, withdrew to his supply bases between Bardia and Tobruk. XXX Corps attacked the two German divisions as they went back, but they broke through to the West nearly cutting off the New Zealand Division as they went.

The British had not yet shot their bolt, and they attacked again on 26 November, and again on 2 December. Rommel now withdrew, leaving the battlefield and 400 tanks to the victors. The British had lost 18,000 men, but they had caused 24,500 casualties and taken 36,500 prisoners. They had cleared Cyrenaica, and relieved Tobruk. It was a notable achievement against a well-led and well-equipped enemy.

The Japanese offensive in the Far East now robbed Auchinleck of expected reinforcements and Rommel, in greater strength than ever, advanced once more from El Agheila in January, driving the Eighth Army back to the line Gazala-Bir Hakim. The campaign ended with the fall of Rommel's frontier garrisons at Bardia and Halfaya Pass.

There followed a lull of some four months.

[1] Alan Moorehead: *A Year of Battle, August* 1941 – *August* 1942. p. 65.

Meanwhile the people and garrison of Malta were winning the island her George Cross.[1]

After the fall of France Britain had little enough to spare for the defence of this base. In the autumn of 1940 the garrison consisted of five infantry battalions supported by ten ancient aircraft. The best of these were three sea-Gladiators, known as Faith, Hope and Charity, which held their own very well against the Italians for some time. With great difficulty Hurricanes were flown in, and serious attacks both by submarines and aircraft were made on Italian convoys to North Africa. In August 1941 Rommel lost 35 per cent of his supplies and reinforcements and 63 per cent in October. The Germans eventually felt compelled to send a strong force of the *Luftwaffe* to Sicily, and in October 25 U-boats, one of which sank the *Ark Royal* in the following month, were diverted to the Mediterranean from the Atlantic.

The sufferings of the inhabitants from hunger were very serious, for the island had long depended on seaborne supplies. Continual pounding from the air was their lot for 18 months. Many were compelled to live in the huge caves beneath Valletta.

The Governor, General Sir William Dobbie, was a deeply religious old soldier cast in the mould that produced Cromwell's Ironsides. He regarded the struggle as a crusade. He was succeeded by Field-Marshal Lord Gort, V.C., another inspiring leader. It is typical that in those days they both lived on the lowest ration scale so as to share the privations of the people in their care. They were ably supported by Air Vice-Marshal Lloyd, who inspired the RAF to prodigies of valour and energy.

Early in 1942 Hitler stepped up the air offensive, and by the beginning of April only six British aircraft remained. Forty-seven Spitfires were flown in one morning, but 30 were destroyed on the ground before they could be refuelled.

By the beginning of May the end seemed near. Food, fuel and ammunition were all nearly exhausted. But at the end of the month 62 more Spitfires were flown in, and this time the ground staff got them into the air just before the bombers came over.

Tremendous efforts were made to fight convoys through from Alexandria and Gibraltar. In June two freighters out of six got through from Gibraltar, and in August five out of 11. The last in was the American tanker *Ohio*, full of fuel and practically disabled. By

[1] Awarded in April, 1942.

112

the Autumn of 1942 the worst was over, and the island had survived an ordeal unequalled even by the famous siege of 1565 when Jean Parisot de la Vallette and the Knights of Malta had held out for four months against the Turks.

CHAPTER TWELVE

BARBAROSSA

1941

22 Jun.	Germans invade Russia.
24 Jun.	Germans take Brest-Litovsk.
3 Jul.	Stalin orders a 'scorched earth' policy.
16 Jul.	German advanced guard reaches Smolensk.
25 Jul.	Fighting around Smolensk.
27 Aug.	Russians blow up the Dnepropetrovsk dam.
18 Sep.	Germans cut off the Crimea.
	Fall of city of Kiev.
26 Sep.	Russians surrender near Kiev.
6 Oct.	German attack on Moscow.
16 Oct.	Panic in Moscow. The Soviet Government leaves. Germans and Roumanians occupy Odessa.
19 Oct.	Germans take Taganrog on the Sea of Azov.
26 Oct.	Fall of Kharkov.
Oct.	Leningrad beleaguered.
7 Nov.	Stalin's Holy Russia Speech.
17 Nov.	Russians evacuate Kerch.
30 Nov.	Russians retake Rostov.
6 Dec.	Zhukov's counter-ofiensive starts.
14 Dec.	Germans retreat from before Moscow.

'When Barbarossa opens, the world will hold its breath.'

ADOLF HITLER.

'Comrades, Red Army and Red Navy men, officers and political workers, men and women partisans! The whole world is looking upon you as the power capable of destroying the German robber hordes! The enslaved peoples of Europe are looking upon you as their liberators . . . Be worthy of this great mission! The war you are waging is a war of liberation, a just war. May you be inspired in this war by the heroic figures of our great ancestors, Alexander Nevsky, Dimitri Donskoi, Minin and Pozharsky, Alexander Suvorov, Michael Kutuzov! May you be blest by great Lenin's victorious banner! Death to the German invaders! Long live our glorious country, its freedom and independence! Under the banner of Lenin – onward to victory!'

STALIN. 7 November 1941.

ON 22 June, 1941, Germany attacked her ally, Russia. The news that Hitler, like Charles XII and Napoleon I before him, had invaded Russia, certainly made the world hold its breath, but it came as a tonic to his other enemies. Now surely he was undone. Churchill lost no time in declaring Britain's full support for Russia. The people of Britain, at least since Churchill had assumed control, had never expected to be beaten. The war might go on for years but eventual victory now seemed certain. Yet Hitler's armies came within an ace of putting Russia out of the war. And unwise though it seemed to his enemies, the invasion of Russia was inherent in all Hitler's long-range plans to give Germany *Lebensraum*. The invasion may have been a blunder, but it was not one made on the spur of the moment. It was part of a deep-laid long-term scheme.

On 14 June Hitler assembled his generals in Berlin, and explained his intentions and the change of his line of operations. According to Guderian he said that he could not defeat England. Therefore in order to bring the war to a close he must win a complete victory on the Continent. Germany's position on the mainland would only be unassailable when Russia had been defeated. The audience dispersed in silence and some at least with heavy hearts. Many no doubt shared the Panzer leader's opinion. 'So long as the war in the West was still undecided, any new undertaking must result in a war on two fronts; and Adolf Hitler's Germany was even less capable of fighting such a war than had been the Germany of 1914.'[1]

The German Army was nevertheless extremely formidable.

	Divisions.
West	38
Norway	12
Denmark	1
Balkans	7
Libya	2
Eastern Front	145[2]
	———
	205

The garrison of Norway, then and throughout the war, was unnecessarily high, and, moreover, in 1941 there was no threat of invasion to warrant the retention of 38 divisions in the West. It would have been possible for Hitler to have employed at least 155 German divisions on the Russian front at the outset. He evidently underrated his enemy, and both OKW and OKH were confident of victory.

The Chief of the Army General Staff, Halder, calculated that the Russian campaign would require no more than 8 – 10 weeks. It was to be carried out by three roughly equal army groups, which would attack simultaneously, but with diverging objectives. Apparently it was not until 30 August 1941 that OKH awoke to the need for winter clothing. The *Luftwaffe* and the *Waffen-SS*, it seems, were more far-sighted and had laid in ample stocks.

It was on 22 June 1812 that Napoleon had crossed the Niemen. It is odd that a man so superstitious as Hitler should have chosen the 129th anniversary as the day to begin his own Russian campaign. But it was also the first anniversary of the signature of the French Armistice in the Forest of Compiègne.

[1] Guderian: *Panzer Leader.*
[2] Including 19 armoured and 12 motorized.

Stalin, whose forces had last shown their paces in Finland, was far from courting a trial of strength with Nazi Germany. He had taken care to honour the agreement of January 1941 by which Russia was to deliver food and raw materials to Germany, and this despite many German violations of Soviet air space, among other provocations.

It is estimated that Russia, including her reserves, had an army of 12,000,000 men, organized in 160 infantry and 30 cavalry divisions. There were, in addition, 35 motorized and armoured brigades. But while Hitler still depended on the *Blitzkrieg* technique, which had served him so well in the early years of the war, the Russians relied on their traditional assets: numbers, space, scorched earth, January and February. Their huge army seriously short of motor transport, was as yet quite unattuned to the pace of modern warfare Nazi pattern. And in the air, though they may have had as many as 7,500 planes, they were no match for the *Luftwaffe*, which was not only experienced but well armed.

There were a variety of reasons for the Russians' unpreparedness. The purges of 1937[1] had shaken the Red Army to its very soul. It did not compare with the German Army either in experience or in training. Armament too left much to be desired. Although there were perhaps 20,000 tanks, many were obsolescent. The KV and T-34 tanks only began to be produced in really significant numbers by early 1941. The Red Air Force suffered from the lack of a proper network of airfields, and from a shortage of trained pilots. Strategically the Russians, like the Poles and the Yugoslavs before them, made the mistake of concentrating too near their frontier.

But if the Russians were ill-prepared, not everything was perfect with the Germans. The vehicles of the new divisions were French and unsuitable for warfare in eastern Europe. Although the old Panzers I and II had been almost completely replaced by Panzers III and IV, the number of tanks in the panzer division had been cut down. At this time the Germans were producing 1,000 tanks a year. On the Eastern front they had 3,200 tanks but even their heaviest, the Panzer IV, was not as good or as heavy as the Russian T-34, which first appeared at the front in July 1941. Incredible though it may seem, the Army Ordnance Office had failed to re-equip the Panzer III with the mark of 50 mm. cannon which Hitler personally had ordered them to provide.

[1] 15,000 officers eliminated.

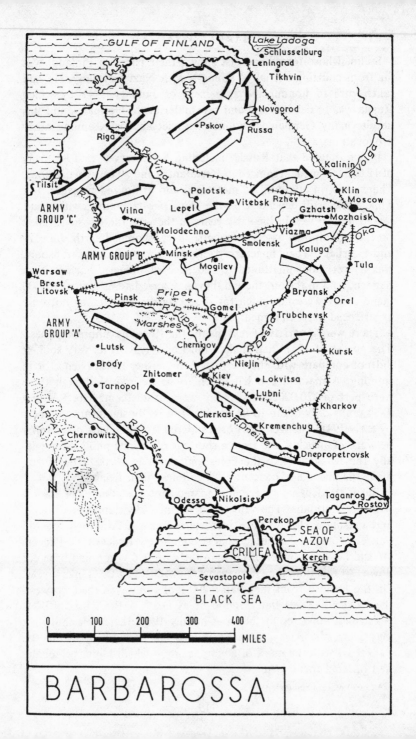

BARBAROSSA

The *Blitzkrieg* began with successes comparable, at least in terms of prisoners and booty, with those of 1940. In the first weeks of the campaign the Soviet air force suffered fearful losses, many of them on the ground. Göring actually claimed that 3,000[1] planes were destroyed in the first week. By the beginning of July the Germans estimated that their fast-moving columns, piercing into the Russians, breaking them up into fragments and encircling them, had taken 150,000 prisoners, 1,200 tanks and 600 guns. By 10 July the Germans were attacking Smolensk, where at last the *Blitzkrieg* met with a decided check. So far the Nazis had covered 400 miles in 18 days. Moscow itself lay only 200 miles ahead.

At this juncture Goebbels' propaganda machine put out one of its more charming effusions: 'the eastern continent lies, like a limp virgin, in the mighty arms of the German Mars'.

But in fact it was at this very time that the Russian resistance was becoming more effective. The appearance on the battlefield of the famous *Katyusha* mortars, first used near Smolensk on 15 July, had something to do with it. Moreover, the Russians were now using a few modern planes, and the *Luftwaffe* was no longer having everything its own way. The dogged rearguard action at Smolensk gave the Russian High Command a breathing space. Drastic measures were taken against Generals who failed. Dismissal or imprisonment were not enough. Army General G. D. Pavlov, who had lost his grip on the Western Front, was court-martialled along with his Chief of Staff and commander of signals. They were sentenced to death.

And successful though their tactics were, all was not well within the German High Command, nor was there the universal doctrine that one might have expected after two years of successful *Blitzkrieg*. Guderian records that on 27 July he anticipated orders to push on towards Moscow or at least Bryansk, but learned to his surprise that Hitler had ordered that his 2nd Panzer Group was to go for Gomel in support of Second Army. This meant a swing to the South-West – in fact towards Germany. 'We were informed that Hitler was convinced that large-scale envelopments were not justified: the theory on which they were based was a false one put out by the General Staff Corps, and he believed that events in France had proved his point.

---

[1] Göring's figures may be suspect. It is certain, however, that Lt.-General Kopels of the Russian Military Air Power, committed suicide on the second day of the campaign. He had lost 600 planes and had not inflicted more than a dozen casualties on the enemy.

He preferred an alternative plan by which small enemy forces were to be encircled and destroyed piecemeal and the enemy thus bled to death. All the officers who took part in this conference were of the opinion that this was incorrect: that these manoeuvres on our part simply gave the Russians time to set up new formations and to use their inexhaustible man-power for the creation of fresh defensive lines in the rear area; even more important, we were sure that this strategy would not result in the urgently necessary, rapid conclusion of the campaign.'[1]

On 4 August 1941 Hitler held a conference at Novy Borissov, the HQ of Army Group Centre. He designated the industrial area about Leningrad as his primary objective. He had not yet decided whether Moscow or the Ukraine would come next. He seemed to incline towards the latter target for a number of reasons: first, Army Group South seemed to be laying the groundwork for a victory in that area: secondly, he believed that the raw materials and agricultural produce of the Ukraine were necessary to Germany for the further prosecution of the war: and finally he thought it essential that the Crimea, 'that Soviet aircraft-carrier operating against the Roumanian oil-fields', be neutralized. He hoped to be in possession of Moscow and Kharkov by the time winter began.

On 21 August Hitler issued orders for the Battle of Kiev. He asserted that: 'Of primary importance before the outbreak of winter is not the capture of Moscow but rather the occupation of the Crimea, of the industrial and coalmining area of the Donetz basin, the cutting of the Russian supply routes from the Caucasian oilfields, and, in the north, the investment of Leningrad and the establishment of contact with the Finns . . . The capture of the Crimean peninsula is of extreme importance for safeguarding our oil supplies from Roumania.' Such thinking tended to lead to a dangerous dispersion of effort.

The greatest German successes came in the Kiev area. The city itself fell on 18 September. The veteran Marshal Budienny was relieved of his command, and probably owed his life to his popularity in the army. His successor, Timoshenko, could not stop the rot, and on 26 September the encircled forces surrendered, leaving 665,000 prisoners in German hands.

This was a tremendous victory, yet by the beginning of October things were not looking so bright for the Germans. The roads,

[1] Guderian: pp. 182 and 183.

which were appalling, were pocked with bomb craters. The Russians were making much better tactical use of their tanks. The short-barrelled 75 mm. gun of the Panzer IV could only knock out a T-34 if it attacked it from the rear. 'The Russians attacked us frontally with infantry, while they sent their tanks in, in mass formation, against our flanks. They were learning. The bitterness of the fighting was gradually telling on both our officers and our men. General Freiherr von Geyr brought up once again the urgent need for winter clothing of all sorts. In particular there was a shortage of boots, shirts and socks.'[1]

Notwithstanding the success of their initial thrusts, it was early October before the Germans began their final advance on Moscow. 'Today begins the last great decisive battle of the year!' Hitler proclaimed on 2 October, and certainly at this stage it was still possible for Germany to win the war.

Despite an unwise dispersal of the German armour, this offensive began well for the Nazis. In three weeks von Bock was within 30 miles of Moscow, and the capital was in danger of encirclement. In the south von Rundstedt had overrun the Crimea, where resistance continued only in Sevastopol.

In this crisis the Soviet government and the *corps diplomatique* removed themselves to Kuibyshev, some 500 miles to the east. There was something of a panic in the capital. But Stalin – resolute, enigmatic, cruel, but nothing if not a leader – stayed on in the Kremlin. In speeches which he made on 6 and 7 November, on the occasion of the 24th anniversary of the Revolution, he galvanized his countrymen. His Holy Russia speech ranks with some of Churchill's of 1940. It is worth noting that his references to the recent Moscow Conference, when Harriman and Beaverbrook had agreed to supply the USSR with planes, tanks and raw materials as well as a US loan of one billion dollars, were greeted with storms of applause. 'All this shows', said Stalin 'that the coalition between the three countries is a very real thing which will go on growing in the common cause of liberation.'

And as Russian reserves massed behind Moscow in preparation for a counter-attack, the 'Napoleon weather' came. In 1941 as in 1812 the weather broke early in November. The weather which had demoralized the *Grande Armée*, brought the Germans to a halt. Of course, the weather affected both sides, but the Russians were

[1] Guderian: p. 235.

accustomed to their winter and had prepared for it with proper foresight. Mud dominated the next few weeks, and then came the snow. Anti-freeze for the water coolers of the German tanks was not to be had any more than warm clothing. By 13 November the cold was making the telescopic sights of the tanks useless. One of Guderian's brigades was down to some 50 tanks.

But if his armies were exhausted, Hitler was not. The fate of Napoleon was insufficient to make him agree to send his frost-bitten legions into winter quarters. On 15 November the Germans launched yet another great offensive towards Moscow. Despite the weather, by 2 December they had fought their way into the suburbs, but the thermometer was below zero and by 6 December the German attack on Moscow had broken down. As Guderian puts it: 'I would never have believed that a really brilliant military position could be so b . . . d up in two months.' A prompt withdrawal to a properly pre-pared defensive position was the only sensible move. Far away in East Prussia the Supreme Command had other ideas.

Up to the end of November the Germans had lost about 750,000 men on the Russian Front, that is 23 per cent of their average total strength of 3,500,000 men. Of these 200,000, including 8,000 officers, were dead.

In Berlin Dr Goebbels, with characteristic efficiency, organized the collection of furs and warm clothing for the troops – an appeal to which the civilian population responded with a patriotism worthy of a better cause.

On 6 December Marshal Zhukov launched a great counter-attack against his semi-paralysed foe.

Still Hitler forbade any major withdrawal. He insisted that Rzhev, Viazma, Yukhnov, Kaluga, Orel and Bryansk must be held, and of these only Kaluga was retaken. The German commanders, many of whom advised withdrawal, were threatened with the direst penalties should they disobey. There followed a wholesale shake up in the German High Command. Generals Höppner (4 Panzer Group) and Guderian were sacked, the former being deprived of his rank and forbidden to wear uniform. General von Bock, who had been held up before Moscow, fell ill as did von Leeb, who had failed to take Leningrad. He was replaced by Küchler, a more ardent Nazi. The Russian recapture of Rostov led to the dismissal of von Rund-stedt. Most important of all von Brauschitsch, the Commander-in-Chief, was relieved in his command by Hitler himself. In the long term the *Führer* was doing the Allies a great service, but in the short term he rode the storm. The Russians retook Kaluga and Kalinin, but the Dictator compelled his wretched, freezing soldiers to hold fast and gradually the front solidified leaving the Germans well-placed to begin a new offensive in the spring. In the north Leningrad had been invested since October. In the south they had overrun the best corn-lands of the Ukraine. Though their losses had been terrible, those of the Russians had been much worse. Moreover the German armies were reinforced by Hungarian, Italian, Roumanian and Finnish contingents, until the Russians, for all their enormous manpower, were actually outnumbered.

The Russian counter-offensive achieved a great deal, but very much less than the Soviet High Command had hoped. Rostov was recaptured at the end of November; in the Crimea Sevastopol was still holding out. It was on the Moscow front that the counter-attack achieved its most spectacular success and liberated most territory. Leningrad remained beleaguered, but the recapture of Tikhvin had alleviated its supply position.

If the Russians failed to achieve more, it was because they had no advantage in numbers or *matériel* and were still very short of transport, arms and ammunition. One is astonished not that they did not achieve more but that, after the awful blows they had suffered, they had the resilience to go over to the offensive so soon.

Shortly before the invasion of Russia the OKW had sent out an order regarding the treatment of civilians and prisoners. It laid down that German soldiers committing excesses against them were not automatically to be tried by military law. Disciplinary action was only to be taken at the discretion of unit commanders, and for the preservation of discipline. A number of generals forbade the publication of this order, but even so it led to countless atrocities and reprisals, and in due course was to play its part in the trial of German war criminals. This policy, so far from terrorizing the Russians, convinced even the most lukewarm that the Germans were as unspeakable as Stalin told them. When in the second half of December the Soviet Army retook Volokolamsk they found a gallows in the main square. Eight 'partisans', one a woman, were hanging from it. Terrorism only steeled the hearts of the Russians against the invader.

CHAPTER THIRTEEN

THE WAR AT SEA, 1940–42

1940

May	Iceland occupied by the British.
3 Jul.	Oran.
17 Aug.	Hitler declares a total blockade of Britain.
2 Sep.	Transfer of 50 American destroyers to Britain.
5 Nov.	*Sheer* attacks Convoy HX 84.
24 Dec.	*Hipper* attacks Convoy WS 5A.

1941

23 Jan.	*Scharnhorst* and *Gneisenau* leave Kiel.
28 Mar.	Battle of Cape Matapan.
9 May	Capture of *U–110*.
24 May	HMS *Hood* sunk.
27 May	*Bismarck* sunk.
22 Jun.	Invasion of Russia.
7 Jul.	US forces land in Iceland.
12 Aug.	The Atlantic Charter drawn up by Churchill and Roosevelt.
27 Aug.	*U–570* captured.
4 Sep.	US destroyer *Greer* attacked by a U-boat.
17 Oct.	US destroyer *Kearny* torpedoed off Iceland.
30 Oct.	US destroyer *Reuben James* torpedoed.
13 Nov.	HMS *Ark Royal* sunk.
19 Nov.	Action between *Kormoran* and HMAS *Sydney*.
7 Dec.	Pearl Harbor.
10 Dec.	HMS *Repulse* and *Prince of Wales* sunk.

1942

mid-*Jan.*	The battleship *Tirpitz* arrives at Trondheim.
11/13 Feb.	*Scharnhorst* and *Gneisenau* dash up the English Channel.

'The English never yield, and though driven back and thrown into confusion, they always return to the fight, thirsting for vengeance as long as they have a breath of life.'

GIOVANNI MOCENIGO,
Venetian Ambassador to France, to the Doge, 8 April 1588.

THE Britain of 1940 was a moated fortress. Its inadequately armed defenders included a great many *bouches inutiles*, who could not just be banished as Montluc had banished the citizens of Siena long ago.[1] The fortress was far from being self-supporting. Not only arms but food had to be brought in from outside. Since the besiegers' best weapon, as in 1917, was the submarine, it is not too much to say that everything depended on the success of the Royal Navy and the Merchant Navy in combatting its menace. Terrible were the losses sustained in this struggle, yet few in Britain imagined that it could end in defeat, for here again the inspired leadership of Winston Churchill met its response. Confidence in a Navy which for hundreds of years had rendered invasion impossible was unbounded.

The loss of the French fleet was a grave setback, but fortunately the Home Fleet was superior to the German surface fleet and in June 1940 it was possible to assemble Force H (Vice-Admiral Sir James Somerville) at Gibraltar. This powerful squadron included the fleet carrier *Ark Royal*, a battle cruiser and two battleships. Its first task was its most difficult and unpleasant. It was to ensure that the French fleet at Oran did not go over to the Axis. The story of the tragedy that followed is a complex one. It is true that Somerville was told from London that if he did not 'settle matters quickly' he 'would have reinforcements to deal with' – not altogether an unreasonable view. But Admiral Gensoul signalled to his government that he had been presented with an ultimatum 'to sink his ships within six hours', which was woefully inexact. He had in fact been offered more honour-

[1] The old hypocrite's charming comment 'Dieu doit être bien miséricordieux vers nous qui font tant des maux' should be the prayer of every old campaigner! Blaise de Montluc: *Siège de Siena*).

able alternatives, of which he mentioned only that which his former allies least desired.[1]

At 6 p.m. on 3 July Somerville's squadron opened fire. A number of ships were seriously damaged and 1,297 Frenchmen died. The battleship *Bretagne* blew up. The battle cruiser *Strasbourg* and five destroyers, though attacked by *Ark Royal*'s obsolescent torpedo-bombers, got safely to Toulon.

Admiral Gensoul must certainly bear a share of the blame, but given time, a peaceful settlement could probably have been made. Cunningham's success in negotiating a peaceful solution with Admiral Godfroy's squadron at Alexandria strengthens this view.

At Dakar attempts to put the new battleship *Richelieu* out of action were unsuccessful. French ships in the West Indies were immobilised by lack of oil and by diplomatic pressure. The French naval commanders in Algerian ports and at Toulon honoured their undertaking not to allow their ships to fall into enemy hands. All in all Oran can hardly be justified and its effect on Anglo-French relations was deplorable. Even so it was evidence to America, and indeed to Britain, that the Churchill government was imbued with a resolution quite foreign to its fumbling predecessors.

While this was going on Hitler was preparing to invade England. Since Operation *Sealion* was never launched it is easy to underrate its menace. An essential factor for its success was the defeat of the Royal Air Force, and it was the opinion of Admiral Forbes (C.-in-C. Home Fleet) that 'the correct strategy was to keep our main strength based at Scapa, whence Ireland as well as the southern coast of England could be covered; to conduct offensive sweeps in the North Sea to impress upon the enemy the extent of our control of those waters, and to continue to employ all the light forces we could spare on Atlantic escort duties. Although such a strategy had behind it the authority of centuries of experience, it was rejected both by the naval authorities in their southern commands and by the British government.'[2] It seems now that Forbes was right. The rejection of his plan condemned the Fleet to a passive role and increased our losses in the Western Approaches, while bombardment of the German invasion flotillas, whether from the sea or the air, inflicted no crippling damage upon them.

[1] The alternatives were: (a) to join British naval forces; (b) to sail with reduced crews to either a British port, or to the French West Indies; (c) to scuttle his ships within six hours.

[2] Roskill: p. 87.

For all their resolution it may be supposed that the British people were relieved that the Germans never ventured to launch their 13 assault divisions. Yet there are those who regret that they did not, feeling that Britain would have won a decisive victory comparable with Barfleur or Quiberon Bay.[1] Historical 'ifs', though fascinating are not very profitable. But in this case speculation is illuminated by the fate of the German surface fleet off Norway under conditions far less favourable to the Royal Navy than those prevailing in the English Channel, where land-based air cover was within easy reach. Captain Roskill points out with justice that 'of all the factors which contributed to the failure of Hitler's grandiose invasion plans, none was greater than the lack of adequate instruments of sea power and of a proper understanding of their use on the German side.'[2]

It is easy to forget that throughout the summer, when all eyes were fixed on the Battle of Britain, the long drawn-out and deadly Battle of the Atlantic was also going on. As yet the British, instead of using the maximum number of vessels in the escort role, wasted much effort in hunting for submarines either in the open ocean or where it was thought that they might lurk, as it were, in ambush. The German tactics of the 'wolf-pack,' hunting on the surface at night like torpedo-boats, met with considerable success. Most of the escorts had not yet got radar and were in any case too slow to catch a surfaced U-boat. Asdic[3] was only designed to detect the *submerged* submarine. Grand-Admiral Dönitz had forecast these tactics in a book published in 1939, but even so the Admiralty was taken by surprise.

On 17 August Hitler declared a total blockade of Britain and, with his usual disregard for international law, announced that neutral as well as British shipping would be sunk on sight. In these circumstances the agreement (2 September) by which America agreed to transfer 50 ancient destroyers to Britain in return for the lease of bases in the western hemisphere was a Godsend.

Astonishingly enough the factor which did most to turn the tide of success against the Germans was their own lack of foresight. Despite their tremendous success in World War I, Hitler had given U-boat construction a very low priority. Incredible though it may seem, by the end of 1940 the Germans had lost 31 U-boats and had

[1] Roskill: p. 88.
[2] Underwater detecting equipment.

22 left! These factors, taken with the improvement both of British tactics and their production of escort vessels, eased the situation.

In addition to submarines the Germans employed a number of converted merchantmen as armed raiders, a perfectly legitimate form of warfare.[1] They operated mostly in the South Atlantic. During 1940 they accounted for 54 ships (370,000 tons) and caused much confusion and delay, being a match for any warship less powerful than a cruiser. It was not until 5 May, 1941 that the *Cornwall* caught one of them, the *Pinguin*, and sent her to the bottom of the Indian Ocean.

The remaining German major warships were a further menace. On 5 November the pocket-battleship *Scheer* attacked the Convoy HX 84 (37 ships), which was escorted by a single Armed Merchant Cruiser, *Jervis Bay*. Captain E. S. F. Fegan sacrificed his ship to cover the dispersal of the convoy, and his courageous action was rewarded, since only five merchantmen were lost.

Hipper also made a sortie into the Atlantic via the Denmark Strait, attacked a troop convoy west of Finisterre, and, having done very little damage, got safely into Brest (27 December). Her presence there was a constant threat.

Bombers from bases in France and Norway caused the British serious losses, second only to those suffered from U-boats. They operated not only off the west coast of Ireland but in coastal waters.

Admiral Lütjens left Kiel with *Scharnhorst* and *Gneisenau* on 23 January 1941 and during a two-months cruise sank or took 22 ships (115,600 tons) before escaping into Brest. There Admiral Tovey[2] blockaded him much as Cornwallis had blockaded Ganteaume in 1805. Both battle cruisers were to be severely damaged in air raids, and as things turned out their commerce-raiding was over.

In a five months' cruise (October-1 April) the pocket battleship *Scheer* accounted for 16 merchantmen (99,000 tons) besides the *Jervis Bay*. This was a somewhat modest haul, but her foray into the Indian Ocean caused a good deal of dislocation on the convoy routes. The heavy cruiser *Hipper* made a brief sortie from Brest in February and sank seven of a convoy of 19 unescorted merchantmen homeward-bound from Sierra Leone.

The convoy system and the sinking of their supply vessels gradually

[1] One ruthless captain, von Rukteschell, was tried as a war criminal, but the rest conducted their operations in accordance with the accepted rules of civilized warfare – if one may use such an expression!

[2] He had succeeded Admiral Forbes in command of the Home Fleet in December 1940.

put an end to the successes of surface raiders and after the middle of 1941 they did very little harm.

With the spring the U-boat war flared up once more. In March they sank 41 ships but lost five submarines and several 'aces', including Prien, who had torpedoed the *Royal Oak*. But they were still sinking merchantmen far more quickly than these could be replaced. In April and May, with 40 U-boats operational, sinkings remained very heavy, but the Royal Navy scored some notable successes. On 9 May U-110[1] was captured intact, a tremendous advantage for British intelligence.

Admiral Lütjens now reappeared on the scene with the formidable new battleship *Bismarck*[2] and the heavy cruiser *Prinz Eugen*. He sailed from Gdynia on 18 May 1941. The Germans had hoped that *Scharnhorst* and *Gneisenau* would be able to sally forth from Brest at the same time, but the RAF had already cancelled that part of the German plan.

After leaving Bergen on 21 May Lütjens was not sighted until his squadron was seen by the heavy cruiser *Suffolk* at the northern entrance to the Denmark Strait, steering SW. Vice-Admiral L. E. Holland, with the battle-cruiser *Hood*, the battleship *Prince of Wales*, and four destroyers, was about 220 miles away, SW of Iceland. *Hood* and *Prince of Wales* were the fastest of Tovey's heavy ships, but the former was over 20 years old and had not been properly modernized, while the latter had not had time to work up to full fighting efficiency. During the night contact with the enemy was lost; Admiral Holland detached his four destroyers, presumably for reconnaissance, and they lost contact with him. At 0247 *Suffolk* again sighted Lütjens still on the same course. Admiral Holland now began to close at full speed, but, doubtless in order to obtain surprise he would not let the *Prince of Wales* send off her reconnaissance plane, or allow his ships to use their radar. By maintaining wireless silence he deprived himself of the support of the two heavy cruisers and perhaps of his four destroyers.

At 0535 *Hood* sighted the enemy. Holland gave the Germans a distinct tactical advantage by taking his ships into action in close order. Had he allowed his captains freedom to manoeuvre they might have been able to bring more guns to bear. As it was they were

---

[1] Its commander, the notorious Lemp, who sank the *Athenia* on the day war was declared, was killed.

[2] She had eight 15-inch and 12 x 5·9-inch guns. Her displacement was 42,500 tons, and her maximum speed 28 knots.

outgunned. At 0552 all four ships opened fire, *Hood* engaging the *Prinz Eugen* which was leading and which she mistook for the *Bismarck*. The British missed with their opening salvos, but *Bismarck* hit *Hood* hard with her second or third, and at 0600 she blew up. No doubt one of her inadequately armoured magazines had been hit. Of her crew of 1,419 only three survived. The *Prince of Wales* was hit by four 15-inch and three 8-inch shells and turned away making smoke. She had, however, hit *Bismarck* twice and damaged some of her fuel tanks. Lütjens was compelled to abandon his foray and make for France.

Admiral Holland's disaster may be attributed to his sticking to the letter of the Admiralty's 'Fighting Instructions' (1939). It has been suggested that he had in mind this passage:

> 'Prior to deployment the Admiral will control the movements of the Battle Fleet as a whole. He will dispose the guides of divisions on a line of bearing at right angles to the bearing of the enemy battle fleet . . .'[1]

These tactics may have been appropriate to a great fleet action like Jutland – though Nelson had been far less rigid at Trafalgar. Military history does not lack illustrations of the danger of sticking too closely to 'the book'. *En passant* one wonders what would have happened if Harwood had fought the Battle of the River Plate on these lines.

Meanwhile the Admiralty was trying to draw a net about the quarry. Admiral Somerville was summoned from Gibraltar (24 May), the battleships *Ramillies* and *Rodney* were released from convoy duty. Even so the net was full of holes, and nobody could tell where Lütjens was going.

Tovey, determined to try and slow him up, sent the aircraft-carrier *Victorious* ahead with an escort of four light cruisers. About midnight a Swordfish scored a torpedo hit on the *Bismarck*, but as it hit her main armour it did her little harm. That evening the two German warships had parted company. Meanwhile Admiral Dönitz had given orders to his U-boats to suspend operations against merchantmen, and had moved seven to positions south of Greenland in the hope of torpedoing important units of the Home Fleet.

Early on the morning of the 25th Lütjens altered course to make for western France, and in so doing shook off the shadowing British cruisers. Tovey, who at about 4 a.m. was some 110 miles ahead of

[1] Roskill: p. 132. fn.

Lütjens, was misled by signalling and plotting errors into believing that *Bismarck* was now steering NE. and at 1047 turned in the same direction. Fortunately the Admiralty acted on the assumption that Lütjens was making for Brest and disposed Somerville's Force H, the *Rodney* and other forces to cut him off. Tovey came to the same conclusion independently, but he was now 150 miles behind his quarry.

During the night 25–26 May the net tightened but nobody could tell whether there was anything in it. Everything now depended on Coastal Command's dawn patrols. It chanced that Air Chief Marshal Bowhill, its C.-in-C., had served at sea as a young officer. Lütjens, he said, would not steer direct for Brest but would make for Cape Finisterre. At his insistence one patrol was sent well to the south of *Bismarck's* direct course for Brest. At 1030 on the 26th a Catalina sighted her 690 miles west of the port, and only 30 hours steaming from safety.

In foul weather 14 Swordfish flew off from *Ark Royal*. They made a spirited attack on *Sheffield*, which was shadowing the *Bismarck*, but the cruiser was sufficiently skilful to avoid her colleagues' torpedoes. A second attack in the failing light of evening scored two hits on the *Bismarck*. One struck the armour belt, but the other damaged her propellers and jammed the rudder. Her speed fell.

Captain Vian's destroyers attacked during the night and may have scored two more torpedo hits.

At about 0845 on 27 May Admiral Tovey came up with *King George V* and *Rodney* and in less than two hours silenced *Bismarck's* guns and battered her into a blazing hulk. Finally, hit by yet more torpedoes, she sank at 1036 with her colours flying. Nearly all her crew of 2,000 perished with her.[1] Lütjens had fought a good fight, but the sinking of the *Bismarck* was a tremendous relief to the British, at a time when the war was going none too well. Morale rose accordingly.

While these exciting events were taking place, the U-boat campaign continued on its course. Heavy losses went on, but a new phase was beginning. Escorts were becoming stronger and in consequence the U-boats had to attack in force. Towards the end of June ten of them attacked convoy HX 133 south of Greenland. By throwing in the escorts of two outward-bound convoys the Admiralty was able to concentrate 13 warships to reinforce the threatened one. In

[1] There were only 110 survivors.

a battle which went on for five days and nights five merchantmen were lost, but the Germans lost two submarines. Thus was born the strategy of the 'support groups', which were to play a decisive part in the Battle of the Atlantic.

On 22 June the Germans invaded Russia, an event which had an immediate effect on the Atlantic campaign, for in July and August sinkings were much reduced. To the casual observer this may seem strange. But the explanation is straightforward. Bombers which had been doing considerable damage had been moved to the eastern front. The German Navy was busy supporting operations on the Baltic coast.

A curious episode took place on 27 August when the U-570 was captured intact by Squadron Leader J. H. Thompson in a Hudson. The submarine inadvertently surfaced immediately below the aircraft which attacked with such speed and skill that the Germans surrendered. This was no mean prize![1]

After the summer lull it was sad to find the sinkings getting worse again in September.[2] The U-boat strength was now nearly 150. Dönitz intended to send some of his larger submarines to prey upon the distant trade routes, but the sinking by cruisers of their supply ships *Kota Pinang* (13 October) and *Python* (1 December) put paid to this. On 22 November the cruiser *Devonshire* ended the career of another predator, the disguised *Atlantis*, which had sunk 22 ships (146,000 tons) during a cruise of some 20 months. About the same time a strange fight took place off Western Australia. The light cruiser HMAS *Sydney* came upon the raider *Kormoran* disguised as a Dutch ship. Suspicious, but not suspicious enough, *Sydney* closed to 2,000 yards. She was steaming parallel to the *Kormoran* when the latter suddenly discharged her torpedoes and opened up with everything she had got. *Sydney* returned the fire but she was hard hit, and 'finally disappeared over the southern horizon a mass of flames'.[3] She was seen no more, and it must be assumed that she blew up with all her crew. *Kormoran* too was seriously damaged and her crew had to scuttle her. Most of them reached Australia.

If the Russian campaign had brought temporary relief in the Atlantic battle it also brought the Home Fleet a serious new problem, escorting convoys of supplies to Murmansk and Archangel, often in

[1] U.570 continued her career as HMS *Graph*.
[2] 53 ships, about 200,000 tons.
[3] Roskill: p. 141.

appalling weather conditions and exposed to heavy attacks by U-boats, bombers and surface ships during most of the 2,000 miles voyage.

On 9 August Churchill and Roosevelt met in Placentia Bay, Newfoundland, and drew up the Atlantic Charter. Already in July American forces had arrived in Iceland to reinforce and later to replace the British. Now Roosevelt arranged for American warships and aircraft to 'patrol' the Western Atlantic and inform the British if they should sight any U-boats.

Congress and the American people still hoped to keep out of the war. The President was taking a more realistic view. The Germans were furious. On 4 September a U-boat attacked the US destroyer *Greer* off Iceland. Roosevelt retaliated by ordering US destroyers to attack any submarine on sight. On 17 October the US destroyer *Kearny* was torpedoed with 11 casualties, an incident which not unnaturally caused a tremendous outcry in the United States.

It is not easy, however, to see how the German commanders were to distinguish American destroyers from those which had been transferred to the Royal Navy under Lease-Lend.[1] German writers have made a great song and dance about the help the United States gave Britain in the days before she entered the war. It is easy to forget that in 1940 the raider *Komet* reached the Pacific via the Arctic route with the help of Russian ice-breakers, and that Japan permitted the *Orion* to refit in the Marianas so that she was able to go on operating until 1941. Spain allowed U-boats to refuel in the Canaries. It is true that these things were a drop in the bucket compared to the help Britain received from the United States. It is too much to expect a belligerent not to accept the help of a neutral if he can get it.

The co-operation of the Americans, the departure of U-boats to the Mediterranean, and the increasing efficiency of Coastal Command, all combined to reduce sinkings during the last three months of 1941.

In November the United States, though then still neutral, sent two battleships and two cruisers to Iceland to help watch the northern exits to the Atlantic. Losses in the Mediterranean and the menace of approaching war with Japan made this move doubly welcome.

[1] It may seem rather unlikely, but it so happens that the present writer, then a captain in No. 3 Commando, sailed to Iceland – for 'sea-experience' – in HMS *Amazon*, one of the destroyers escorting the convoy which *Kearny* was with when she was hit. It really was not easy to tell which warships were British and which were American!

In December a new type of warship came into the service. This was the escort carrier. The *Audacity*,[1] which helped to fight convoy HG 76 through from Gibraltar, proved her worth in closing the 'air gap' before she was sunk.

And now, just when at last the Allies seemed to be getting the upper hand in the Atlantic, the Japanese struck in the Far East. In the ensuing disasters shipping losses were heavy. Nor did the fact that America was now in the war ease the situation in the Atlantic. Quite the contrary. The Americans were compelled after Pearl Harbor to send many of their best ships to the Pacific. Dönitz's submarines had a field day from January to April 1942 off the eastern seaboard of the United States against unescorted merchantmen sailing singly as if in time of peace. Many of the ships lost were tankers which the Allies could ill afford to lose. The Americans were slow to profit by the hard-won experience of their Allies and adopt the convoy system. They had shown themselves generous friends. It is gratifying to be able to record that the British were able in some measure to respond in kind. 'At the height of the onslaught against shipping in the western hemisphere we lent two dozen anti-submarine trawlers to the Americans, we released two of our mid-ocean Atlantic groups to strengthen the escorts on the American eastern seaboard, we offered to turn over ten corvettes to the United States Navy, and we transferred an experienced squadron of Coastal Command aircraft to the west side of the Atlantic.'[2]

In the first six months of 1942 U-boats sank 585 merchantmen – over three million tons of shipping.

The best way to help the Royal Navy surmount this crisis would have been to strengthen Coastal Command at the expense of the bombing offensive against Germany, which – as we now know – had had very disappointing results thus far. However, the strategic views of 'Bomber Harris' carried a good deal of weight at this period, and when the matter was referred to the Prime Minister a compromise was made. Coastal Command was to be strengthened gradually, but there was to be no diminution in the bombing of Germany. Another year was to pass, and countless ships were to be sunk, before Coastal Command had the long-range aircraft needed to play a really decisive part. Although the Navy remained starved of air cover, it must not be assumed that the compromise made was unjustified.

[1] A German prize, the *Hannover*, which had been converted.
[2] Roskill: p. 195.

But the tide of Axis successes was reaching its highwater mark, and by the autumn of 1942 the Allied navies had at last gained the upper hand at sea, though in 1942 the loss of Allied ships was the heaviest of the whole war: 1,664 ships (7,790,697 tons), of which 1,160 were sunk by U-boats.

But the bald summary of losses is as cold as the winter Atlantic, and recalls nothing of the hardships of countless seamen who made that long, slow voyage time and again, waiting for the inevitable torpedo, the shuddering shock running through their stricken ship, the violent explosion, the screams of scalded shipmates trapped in the engine-room: flung about like dolls, staggering in the dark, trying to launch boats suspended at a crazy angle, as their ship foundered beneath them, taking its dreadful noises with her into the deep. And then long hours in the midnight sea hoping some corvette might see the little red lights bobbing in the water.

Not that the U-boats had it all their own way. Of 1,162 commissioned during the war 785 were sunk,[1] mainly by surface ships (246) and shore based aircraft (245). To be attacked by a group of efficient destroyers was an experience to bring the sweat to the brow of the most stolid Teuton – the sudden desperate crash dive, instruments shattering as depth-charges exploded near, water trickling through as the bulkhead supports buckled at 100 fathoms. In the gloom of the emergency lighting many a crew waited in its steel coffin for an end as terrible as any it had meted out.

[1] U-31 managed to get sunk *twice*!

THE HOME FRONT, 1939–45

1939
21 Aug.	German-Soviet non-aggression pact.
22 Aug.	The British Cabinet calls up the active defences against air attack.
24 Aug.	Parliament recalled.
31 Aug.	The Government orders evacuation to begin next day.
1 Sep.	General mobilization ordered. The Blackout enforced.
3 Sep.	War declared.
8 Sep.	The Ministry of Food set up.

1940
Jan.	Food rationing begins.
9 Apr.	Germans invade Denmark and Norway.
Apr.	Lord Woolton becomes Minister of Food.
7/8 May	Debate on the war situation.
19 May	Mr Churchill becomes Prime Minister and forms an all party administration. German plane drops bombs near Petham and Chilham, Kent.
14 May	The Local Defence Volunteers (Home Guard) formed.
18 Jun.	End of the Battle of France.
7 Sep / *May 1941*	The London Blitz.
14/15 Nov.	Coventry bombed.
27/28 Nov.	'The Fire of London'.

1941
11 Mar.	The 'Lease-Lend' Act becomes law.
21/28 Apr.	Plymouth severely bombed.
2 May	Rudolf Hess lands in Scotland.
10/11 May	The Chamber of the House of Commons destroyed.
13 May	Formation of the National Fire Service announced.

1 Jun.	Clothes rationing begins.
22 Jun.	Hitler invades Russia.
14 Jul.	Churchill reviews London's civil defence services in Hyde Park.
1 Dec.	Points rationing scheme in force in Britain.

1942

9 Feb.	Soap rationed.
Apr./Jun.	The 'Baedeker Raids'.
Jul./Jan. 1944	'Tip and Run' raids.

1944

Jan./Mar.	The 'Little Blitz'.
12/13 Jun.	The first flying bomb (V.1) lands in England.
Sep.	Dover heavily shelled.
8 Sep.	The V.2 campaign begins.

1945

27 Mar.	End of the V.2 campaign.
8 May	V.E. Day.
26 Jun.	United Nations Charter signed at San Francisco.
5 Jul.	Labour wins the General Election.
21 Aug.	Lend-lease terminated.
2 Sep.	The Japanese surrender.

'There will be many men, and many women, in this island who when the ordeal comes upon them, as come it will, will feel comfort, and even a pride – that they are sharing the perils of our lads at the front – and are drawing away from them a part at least of the onslaught they have to bear.'

WINSTON S. CHURCHILL 19 May 1940.

AT 11.28 a.m. on 3 September 1939, only a few minutes after the Prime Minister, Mr Neville Chamberlain, had completed the singularly uninspiring broadcast in which he told the British nation that it was at war with Germany, the dismal wailing of the air raid sirens broke out over London.

One has become so used to thinking that absolutely nothing had been done to prepare for war that it comes almost as a shock to learn that the Air Raid Precautions Committee of the Home Office had been set up as early as 1924.

It is often forgotten that there was a considerable amount of bombing during the First World War. Altogether the Germans made 103 bombing raids by airships and aeroplanes, in which they dropped about 300 tons of bombs and caused 4,800 casualties, of which 1,413 were fatal. These raids had an important influence on the planning carried out by the ARP Committee.

It was to be many years before any positive steps were taken. In the days when pacifism and disarmament were hailed as the solution to international problems it was 'war-mongering' even to talk of defence. As an example of the well-meaning yet wrong-headed and somewhat dishonest way in which pacifist propaganda was put about we may quote a broadcast made by Professor Philip Noel-Baker in February 1927. In a talk on 'Foreign Affairs and How They Affect Us' he made an attempt to enlist the support of the British public for the disarmament negotiations at Geneva by emphasizing the horrors of a future war. 'The Professor quoted Mr Baldwin's speech to the Classical Association in the Middle Temple hall, "Who in Europe does not know that one more war in the West and the civilisation of

143

the ages will fall with as great a shock as that of Rome?" He painted a picture of gas attack from the air in another war and claimed, "all gas experts are agreed that it would be impossible to devise means to protect the civil population from this form of attack." As a matter of fact the Chemical Warfare Research Department was very far from agreeing with Noel-Baker's remarks. On the contrary it "emphatically disputed the accuracy both of the details of the picture and of this statement".'[1]

In April 1933 Major General H. L. Pritchard (1871–1953) was appointed Air Raids Commandant (Designate). He prepared a long but realistic 'Memorandum on the Preparation of a Scheme for the Passive Defence of London against Aerial Bombardment'. He appreciated that the success of ARP depended upon morale and forecast that

'In organizing the whole civilian population to protect themselves they must be organized on a civilian basis . . . the ARP Service must create and maintain its own honourable status and prestige and not lean upon some other Service. It would be contrary to the principle of this civilian organization to resist attack upon civilians if it were to be incorporated in the Territorial Army or any other military organization.'[2]

It was not until early in 1935 that the Cabinet approved an expenditure on ARP services of some £100,000, a great sum then, but trifling compared with the £1,026,561,000 which Civil Defence is estimated to have cost during the six years of war. A more important step was taken when by the Air Raid Precautions Act 1937 local authorities were compelled to prepare measures of defence, much of the cost of which was to be met from national funds.

Even after the Italians had gassed Abyssinians from the air, and after the outbreak of the Spanish Civil War, it was difficult to arouse much popular interest in ARP. But the Munich crisis of 1938 brought a change of mood. A million feet of trenches were dug; public buildings were protected by hastily erected sandbag walls; 38 million civilian gas-masks were distributed. The Munich Agreement, which Mr Chamberlain described as meaning 'peace in our time', though greeted with relief when it was announced, was soon seen to do no more than put off the evil day, and from this time onwards serious

[1] O'Brien: *Civil Defence*, p. 31.
[2] O'Brien, p. 45.

preparations were made to deaden the knock-out-blow with which it was anticipated that Hitler would attempt to start his war.

In the 'twilight between peace and war' that prevailed during the summer of 1939 there was a new sense of urgency in the ARP world. Nearly 1,500,000 Anderson[1] shelters were delivered to householders in the most vulnerable parts of the country.

The Government ordered the evacuation of women and children from London and other cities on 31 August and this began next day, two days before the declaration of war. The world was bound to regard evacuation as a sign that the Government had given up hope of a peaceful solution. Moreover this mass movement would seriously impede military movement for some days. Although no massed bombing attacks followed, the Government's measures were certainly justified.

Mobilization began before war was declared.

'Arrangements were completed to set up a censorship, to disperse foodstocks from threatened areas, to protect vulnerable points all over the country from sabotage and to bring passive defence into a state of final readiness for action.'[2]

The ARP schemes were put into force, and while every bulletin brought reports of the bombing of Polish towns, thousands of wardens reported for duty, and hospital beds were cleared. Vehicles were requisitioned for ambulance and rescue work. More gas-masks were issued, public shelters were opened and the public warning system was manned. The use of factory sirens and hooters for any other purpose was forbidden. From sunset on 1 September the Blackout was enforced. 'The statement of Britain's Foreign Secretary[3] when the First World War broke out that "the lamps are going out all over Europe" was, in a way he could not have imagined, being fulfilled.'[4]

Immediately after the declaration of war the BBC broadcast a number of announcements. Cinemas and theatres were closed; gatherings such as football matches were forbidden. It was stated that the London Underground, being needed for traffic, was not available for air-raid shelters. Everyone was to take his gas-mask wherever he went.

[1] Sir John Anderson, who had long been head of the ARP Committee, was now Lord Privy Seal.
[2] O'Brien: p. 292.
[3] Sir Edward Grey.
[4] O'Brien: p. 293.

Six weeks passed before the Germans dropped a bomb on British soil, and eight months before an attack was made on the civilian population. The people were right behind the Government in its declaration of war. They were well aware of the barbarity of Hitler's régime and though far from enthusiastic for war accepted it calmly. The anticlimax when no German attack came bred a mood almost of disappointment. The slogan 'turn on the lights and turn out the ARP workers' was heard on all sides. Optimism and apathy went hand in hand. This period of coma ended rudely on 9 April 1940, when the Germans invaded Denmark and Norway. The Chamberlain Government had never really been in tune with the people, and the disasters in Norway finally destroyed any confidence it may have enjoyed.

The Opposition pressed for a debate on the situation and this took place on 7 and 8 May. The Government was attacked from all sides. In a splendid passage Churchill recalled the scene:

'Sir Roger Keyes, burning for distinction in the new war, sharply criticized the Naval Staff for their failure to attempt the capture of Trondheim. "When I saw", he said, "how badly things were going, I never ceased importuning the Admiralty and War Cabinet to let me take all responsibility and lead the attack." Wearing his uniform as Admiral of the Fleet he supported the complaints of the Opposition with technical details and his own professional authority in a manner very agreeable to the mood of the House. From the Benches behind the Government Mr. Amery quoted amid ringing cheers, Cromwell's imperious words to the Long Parliament: "You have sat too long here for any good you have been doing. Depart, I say, and let us have done with you. In the name of God, go!" These were terrible words, coming from a friend and colleague of many years, a fellow Birmingham Member, and a Privy Counsellor of distinction and experience.'

True though this is, Amery certainly spoke for the majority of his countrymen.

On the second day of the debate the Prime Minister appealed to his friends to stand by him.

'But today they sat abashed and silenced, and some of them had joined the hostile demonstrations. This day saw the last decisive intervention of Mr Lloyd George in the House of Commons. . .

After warning me not to allow myself to be converted into an air-raid shelter to keep the splinters from hitting my colleagues, Mr Lloyd George turned upon Mr Chamberlain: "It is not a question of who are the Prime Minister's friends. It is a far bigger issue. He has appealed for sacrifices. The nation is prepared for every sacrifice so long as it has leadership, so long as the Government show clearly what they are aiming at, and so long as the nation is confident that those who are leading it are doing their best." He ended: "I say solemnly that the Prime Minister should give an example of sacrifice, because there is nothing which can contribute more to victory in this war than that he should sacrifice the seals of office." '[1]

When the House divided, the Government had a majority of 81, but 60 Conservatives had abstained and 30 had voted with the Opposition. It was tantamount to a defeat and next day Chamberlain resigned.

On 10 May Mr Churchill, his political record unstained by pacifism or defeatism, formed an all-party Government and got down to the business of waging war. 'If necessary for years, if necessary alone.'

A new spirit began to breathe in the country. When on 14 May the Local Defence Volunteers (later the Home Guard) were formed, the response was tremendous. Within eight weeks this army numbered over 1,000,000. The deliverance of the BEF from Dunkirk and the inspired leadership of the new Prime Minister carried the country defiantly into the period when – except for Transjordan – Britain had no Allies left in the fight. In this upsurge of morale the ARP Wardens and Rescue Parties shared, and it is amusing to find Mr Noel-Baker, whom we have met before, stating in Parliament, 'this service is alive and inspired by a splendid spirit.'[2]

It was the same spirit that induced the public to put up with the other trials and tribulations, which gradually closed in on them as the war years dragged by. Everyone realized that the disasters of 1940 meant that it would take an immense effort to fend off the Germans, let alone beat them. The shortage of shipping was bound to reduce imports and the amount of food available. Gradually the standard of living fell as rationing was introduced: beginning with butter, sugar, bacon and ham in January 1940.

[1] Churchill: Vol I, p. 521.
[2] O'Brien, p. 373.

In May there were widespread, though comparatively light, bomb-attacks. Once more the complex problem of evacuation reared its head. By 1 August some 213,000 children had been moved to safer areas.

As the Battle of Britain reached its peak the Battle of London or 'London Blitz' began (7 September). For the next 57 nights, until 2 November, the city was bombed every night by about 200 planes. On the night 18/19 September, the enemy dropped 350 tons of bombs, more than they had dropped on Britain in the whole of the First World War. There was heavy damage to houses, especially in the poorer districts in the East End, but the disruption of war production was less than had been anticipated. The King, his Ministers and the Members of Parliament visited the stricken areas. The Prime Minister was everywhere well received. 'In all my life', he said on 8 October, 'I have never been treated with so much kindness as by the people who have suffered most . . . On every side there is the cry, "We can take it," but with it, there is also the cry, "Give it 'em back".'

Though London remained the main target in November the Germans began to increase the scale of their attacks against other cities and towns. Liverpool and Birmingham both suffered heavy onslaughts.

The attack on Coventry on the night 14/15 November over-shadowed others at this time. It began early in the evening with the dropping of numerous incendiary bombs near the fourteenth-century cathedral. Then, guided by the fires, waves of bombers dropped 500 tons of bombs. Water ran short, the gas and electricity supplies were disrupted, telephone lines broken. Unexploded bombs added to the chaos. Two hospitals were hit and casualties had to be sent elsewhere. The killed numbered 554 and the seriously injured 865.

It is only fair to say that this town of 250,000 inhabitants was a centre of the motor, engineering and radio industries. About 100 acres of the city centre were demolished. The Germans, well-pleased with their success, coined the word *Coventrieren* to describe this type of attack. Air-Marshal Harris tells that this raid did enough damage 'to teach us the principle of concentration, the principle of starting so many fires at the same time that no fire fighting services, however efficiently and quickly they were reinforced by the fire brigades of other towns, could get them under control'.[1]

[1] Harris: *Bomber Offensive*, p. 83.

One of the worst raids of the London Blitz came on the night 27/28 November. The City of London was enveloped in flame. The scene resembled the great Fire of 1666, so vividly reported by Samuel Pepys. Eight of Wren's churches were burnt, the Guildhall was demolished and Guy's Hospital had to be evacuated, to mention only some of the more spectacular pieces of damage. This may have been the raid when 'Bomber' Harris and Portal 'watched the old city in flames from the roof of the Air Ministry, with St Paul's standing out in the midst of an ocean of fire'. As they turned to go Harris said 'Well, they are sowing the wind.'

Damage in London was widespread. But because of its very size the city could 'take it' better than a smaller city. Quentin Reynolds, the well-known American journalist, who had lived in London since September 1940, wrote: 'Nothing I had seen prepared me for the sight of Plymouth.'[1] In five nights of concentrated bombing by 100-150 bombers, 1,000 people were killed or wounded and 40,000 rendered homeless. The city centre of Plymouth was completely demolished.

In a very severe raid on the night of 10/11 May the Chamber of the House of Commons was destroyed, besides many other historic buildings. These were grievous casualties, but the ordeal was nearly at an end, for already the *Luftwaffe* was moving its squadrons to the East – whence few were to return. On 22 June Hitler's armies invaded Russia and gave Britain not only an ally but a breathing space.

There is no doubt that a watching world was impressed by Britain's survival. Churchill pointed this out when he reviewed London's civil defence workers in Hyde Park on 14 July:

'I do not hesitate to say that the enormous advance in United States opinion towards making their contribution to British resistance thoroughly effective has been largely influenced by the conduct of Londoners and of the men and women in our provincial cities in standing up to the enemy's bombardments.'

The story of the Blitz as told by men like the late Ed Murrow and Quentin Reynolds, who went through it all, was not exactly damaging to the British cause . . .

During the rest of 1941 the Germans still kept a sizeable bomber

[1] Quentin Reynolds: *Only the Stars are Neutral.*

force in the West, but although there were a number of severe raids the breathing space lasted until April 1942, when raids began to increase again. The notorious 'Baedeker raids' against inland cathedral cities were probably intended as reprisals for Bomber Command's effective raids on Lübeck (28 March) and Rostock (23 April).

Early in 1942 the enemy began their series of 'Tip and Run' raids, usually made by single fighter-bombers making use of cloud cover. The targets were often South coast towns.

The 'Morrison' indoor shelter was invented towards the end of 1942. They were more in demand than the 'Andersons', because instead of having to depart up the garden, you could take refuge under your own dining room table – warmer. It was a rectangular steel framework 6 ft. 6 in. long, 4 ft. wide and 2 ft. 9 in. high. Its sides were filled in with wire mesh, the bottom was a steel mattress and the roof was made of steel plate an eighth of an inch thick, and capable of withstanding the collapse of two upper floors. It was meant to be placed on the ground floor where the walls would protect the people in it from lateral blast. It was easily erected and could accommodate two adults, or two or three children. The 'Anderson' shelters if properly covered with earth or sandbags gave rather better protection, but the 'Morrisons' could be moved, and 400,000 were ordered – enough for nearly 1,000,000 people.

The disasters of early 1942 – Singapore and Burma – stiffened the resolution of the country. Had this not been so the great transfer of resources from civilian to direct war purposes would not have been possible. Sacrifices could be made simply because they had the approval of the people. Under these circumstances abolition of the basic petrol ration was now accepted, as were minor burdens of war such as the rationing of soap, sweets and chocolate – all of which dated from 1942. Despite the heavy losses of merchantmen, essential food supplies were maintained, and in the interests of morale imports of tobacco were kept at the level of demand. The general clothing ration for 1942–3 was cut by a quarter.

By this stage in the war the housing situation had become very bad, and at the end of the year 300,000 people were living in houses that by peacetime standards should have been condemned as slums. Another 2,500,000 were living in bombed houses, which had received 'first-aid'. Military requisitioning had increased the shortage of civilian accommodation and there was serious overcrowding.

The 'Little Blitz' of January-March 1944 was a reprisal campaign, laid on when the Allied Bomber Offensive was hitting the Germans hard. By taking every long-range bomber they could from the Russian and Mediterranean fronts they were able to muster about 150 planes. Not a single German long-range bomber was left in Italy. The weight of bombs dropped on England rose sharply and 2,350 tons were dropped during the period 21 January – 31 March 1944.

The invasion of Normandy was only six days old when on the night 12/13 June the first of the flying bombs (V.1) landed in England. In the next two weeks casualties were as heavy as in September 1941 and damage too was very severe. This new bombardment imposed a great strain on people living in the area under attack. A story was current of a woman who was bombed out of her house:

The Air Raid Warden: 'Where's yer 'usband?'

Woman (bitterly): 'In Normandy – the coward!'

But though this campaign caused the Government grave concern, the morale of the people, wearied by years of war, stood up remarkably well under the menace of this pilotless 'buzz-bomb' which came at random at any hour of the night or day. The successful conclusion of the Normandy campaign more or less put an end to this threat, since the V.1 bases were in France.

Meanwhile the Germans had been preparing the V.2, a long-range rocket. Very disturbing reports reached the War Cabinet as to the characteristics of this weapon, but by the beginning of September a more optimistic view was prevalent. On 7 September Mr Duncan Sandys told the Press that he felt able to speak of the Battle of London being over 'except possibly for a last few shots'. The following day the first of more than 1,000 long-range rockets arrived! This campaign was to last seven months. Arnhem (17 September) brought a week's lull while the German rocket troops trekked eastwards.

The campaign continued, despite fighter-bomber retaliation, until 17 March 1945. There was a particularly bad incident on 8 March 1945 when a rocket caused 233 casualties in Smithfield Market.

In all 5,823 Flying Bombs and 1,054 Long-Range Rockets landed in England. In addition 271 bombs and four rockets fell in the sea. One of the bombs contrived to get as far west as Shropshire. London received 41 per cent of the bombs and 49 per cent of the rockets. It is calculated that over 64,000 tons of bombs fell on the British Isles, a figure which with bombs and rockets goes up to more than 71,000.

The statistics that follow this chapter (Appendix A) give some idea, however inadequate, of the suffering and loss which ordinary people endured in this long ordeal.

A man or woman who was in the civil defence services for three years was entitled to the Defence Medal. The ribbon is green, signifying the fields of Britain, and orange – for the flames of the Blitz – and has two black bars to symbolize the blackout. No soldier earned his medals better than the legion of ARP workers, firemen, policemen, doctors and nurses, who struggled with such notable success against the midnight horrors of the Blitz and the unpredictable hazards of Hitler's secret weapons.

APPENDIX A

Civilians killed and injured by enemy action against Great Britain.

	Killed	Seriously injured
3 Sep. 1939 – 6 Sep. 1940	1,698	2,289
7 Sep. 1940 – 31 Dec. 1940	22,069	28,240
1941	19,918	21,165
1942	3,236	4,148
1943	2,372	3,450
1944	8,475	21,989
1945	1,860	4,223
Northern Ireland	967	678[1]

Civilians killed, missing and seriously injured[2]

Men	Women	Children under 16	Unidentified
67,661	63,221	15,358	537

London suffered over 80,000 casualties.
Birmingham and Liverpool both had more than 5,000.

The casualties were caused by:

	Killed	Seriously injured	Total
Bombs	51,509	61,423	112,932
Flying bombs	6,184	17,981	24,165
Long-range rockets	2,754	6,523	9,277
Cross-Channel bombardment	148	255	403
	60,595	86,182	146,777

[1] See O'Brien: *Civil Defence*, p. 677, for a more detailed breakdown.
[2] Including Civil defence workers, Police, Firemen &c. of whom 2,379 were killed and 4,459 seriously injured. Of these 618 were women.

APPENDIX B

Night attacks between 7 September 1940 and 16 May 1941 in which over 100 tons of bombs were dropped.

Target	Attacks	Tons
London	71	18,291
Liverpool-Birkenhead	8	1,957
Birmingham	8	1,852
Glasgow-Clydeside	5	1,329
Plymouth-Devonport	8	1,228
Bristol-Avonmouth	6	919
Coventry	2	818
Portsmouth	3	687
Southampon	4	647
Hull	3	593
Manchester	3	578
Belfast	2	440
Sheffield	1	355
Newcastle-Tyneside	1	152
Nottingham	1	137
Cardiff	1	115

APPENDIX C

1944	*Flying bombs*	*Long-Range Rockets*
June	1,435	—
July	2,453	—
August	1,450	—
September	87	34
October	131	91
November	101	144
December	74	121
1945		
January	33	220
February	—	232
March	59	212
	5,823	1,054

CHAPTER FIFTEEN

RAIDING, 1940–42

1940

23/24 Jun. The first commando raid.

17 Jul. Sir Roger Keyes becomes Director of Combined Operations.

1941

4 Mar. Raid on the Lofoten Islands.

Aug. Raid on Spitzbergen.

27 Oct. Lord Louis Mountbatten becomes Chief of Combined Operations.

27 Dec. Raid on Vaagso.

1942

18 Mar. Raid on St Nazaire

19 Aug. Dieppe

*'What are the ideas of C.-in-C. H.F., about Storm Troops?
We have always set our faces against this idea, but the
Germans certainly gained in the last war by adopting it, and
this time it has been a leading cause of their victory. There
ought to be at least twenty thousand Storm Troops or 'Leop-
ards' drawn from existing units, ready to spring at the throats
of any small landings or descents. These officers and men
should be armed with the latest equipment, tommy guns,
grenades, etc.'* WINSTON CHURCHILL. 18 June 1940.

FIVE days after the Prime Minister penned these words the first
commando raid took place.

Offensive action ranked high among the eight Principles of War
which, according to British Army doctrine current in 1940, governed
the conduct of operations. With the *Wehrmacht* ensconced along
the coasts of Europe from Narvik to Bayonne it was not altogether
clear how Home Forces were to make themselves felt until that
distant day – still four years ahead as it turned out – when the
Allies should return to France.

The troops had scarcely left Dunkirk when Lt.-Colonel Dudley
Clarke, RA, Military Assistant to the Chief of the General Staff, Sir
John Dill, a man well versed in military history and with experience
of guerrilla warfare in Palestine, had the idea that led to the formation of the commandos. Dill spoke to Mr Churchill on 5 June and
Clarke was given a free hand on condition that no unit should be
diverted from its most essential task, the defence of Britain, which
might very soon have to face invasion; and secondly, that this force
of amphibious guerrillas would have to make do with the minimum
quantities of arms. Clarke was ordered to mount a raid across the
Channel at the earliest possible moment.

The shortage of arms – there were then only 40 Thompson sub-
machine guns in the country – was as nothing compared to the
complete lack of raiding craft. The only two landing craft had been
lost off Norway. The best available was the fast RAF crash boat,

reliable and seaworthy, but very high out of the water, and, of course, totally without armour.

The early raids near Le Touquet (23/24 June) and on Guernsey (14/15 July) were not remarkable as operations of war, but at least they were evidence that the British Army was still in business.

The Commandos, each of which was about 550 strong, were formed from volunteers, selected by the officers who were to train them and to lead them in battle. Those who failed to measure up to the most exacting standards of training, discipline and conduct under fire could be Returned to Unit without more ado – and were.[1]

In July Admiral of the Fleet Sir Roger Keyes was appointed Director of Combined Operations. The Commandos hoped that with the old hero of Gallipoli and Zeebrugge in charge of things they would see plenty of action. They were disappointed. Frustrated by the shortage of landing craft and weapons, the Admiral unfortunately abandoned the policy of launching frequent small raids and set his heart on building up his force for an operation on a big scale. At first the target was the Azores, but later he planned to take Pantelleria, whose occupation at that stage would have been an embarrassment to us, while doing the Axis no harm at all. Perhaps he thought that if he kept 4,000 men idle long enough the 'powers-that-be' would eventually be moved to action. If so he was mistaken.

It was not until 4 March 1941 that an important raid took place. Then Nos. 3 and 4 Commandos raided four small ports in the Lofoten Islands, blew up a large number of fish oil factories, took 225 prisoners, sank an armed trawler, a 10,000 ton German fish factory ship; and brought away 315 Norwegians volunteers, without suffering any casualties themselves. 'In this raid,' wrote the Official Historian of the Royal Navy, 'we may find the genesis of the great combined operations of the later years of the war.'[2]

In August a force of Canadians and Norwegians raided Spitzbergen, unopposed, and destroyed 450,000 tons of coal.

A few small raids were made on the French coast during 1941, but none of any great significance.

On 27 October Admiral Keyes, who had long been at loggerheads not only with the Chiefs of Staff but also with the Cabinet, was succeeded by Lord Louis Mountbatten, who had made a great name for himself as a destroyer captain.

[1] The US Ranger battalions were formed on the same lines.
[2] Roskill: p. 120.

Keyes, who was a member of the House of Commons, fired his parting shots in that august assembly. 'After fifteen months' experience as Director of Combined Operations, and having been frustrated in every worthwhile offensive action I have tried to undertake, I must fully endorse the Prime Minister's comments on the strength of the negative power which controls the war machine in Whitehall.' Keyes reminded the House how in 1915 Churchill had 'tried to deliver an amphibious stroke' at Turkey, only to be frustrated by 'inter-Service committees and sub-committees' which had 'become almost a dictator of military policy instead of the servants as they should be of those who bore all the responsibility.' By emphasizing every hazard they succeeded in delaying or thwarting every amphibious enterprise. 'Great leaders of the past have always emphasized the value of time in war . . . time is passing and so long as procrastination, the thief of time, is the key-word of the war machine in Whitehall, we shall continue to lose one opportunity after another . . .[1]

Young, energetic, forthright Lord Louis Mountbatten was not the man to be frustrated by quill-pushers. He lost no time in mounting the sort of raid that really hurt. The first took place exactly two months after he took over, when on 27 December 1941 No. 3 Commando[2] fell upon South Vaagso and the little island of Maaloy, and practically annihilated a garrison of 150 men in four hours street fighting. A battery was destroyed, and many fish-oil factories, besides some 16,000 tons of shipping. It was of course, a very small-scale battle, but it proved that the British soldier, given proper training, was still a match for the German. It was refreshing for the public to read of a British operation that had gone according to plan.[3]

Hitler was sensitive to any threat to Norway, and built up the garrison to such an extent that by June 1944 he had 372,000 soldiers there. It was well for the Allies that they were not on the Russian Front or in Normandy.

Next came the raid on St Nazaire by No. 2 Commando (28 March 1942). This was as desperate a business as Zeebrugge itself, for the objective lay six miles up the River Loire, and the flotilla was exposed to the fire of numerous shore batteries during the run-in. At St Nazaire was the only dry dock on the Atlantic coast big enough to take the German battleship *Tirpitz*. The main object of the raid was

---

[1] Hansard.
[2] Reinforced by part of No. 2 Commando.
[3] A film taken by the Army Photograph Staff and widely shown was a valuable fillip to morale at a time when victories were in short supply.

achieved when the ancient destroyer *Campbeltown*[1] rammed the great gates of the Forme Ecluse and put it out of action for the rest of the war. The secondary aim was to damage U-boat pens and the docks and here also some measure of success was gained. Casualties were heavy, but the *Tirpitz* was compelled to remain in Norwegian waters, where in September 1944 RAF Lancasters sent her to the bottom.

The biggest British raid of the Second World War was Dieppe. The port was attacked at dawn on 19 August 1942 by the 2nd Canadian Division and three commandos, a raiding force nearly 6,000 strong.

Despite meticulous planning the operation did not go well, and No. 4 Commando, which stormed the coast defence battery at Varengeville, was the only major unit to capture its objective.

It had been decided not to bomb the town the previous night, partly because rubble might stop the tanks, which as it turned out were unable even to negotiate the stony beach. Naval gunfire support proved inadequate, for the Royal Navy had declined to risk a 6-inch cruiser in the Channel. The Canadians, who had never been in action before, found themselves confronted by carefully sited strongpoints tunnelled into the chalk cliffs and ensconced in buildings. All but three of the men of the Royal Regiment of Canada who landed at Puys stayed there, either killed or captured. Only the two battalions at Pourville made any real progress. Instead of supporting them, Major-General Roberts chose to send his single reserve battalion into Dieppe itself – reinforcing failure, with the usual result.

During the afternoon the force withdrew having suffered some 3,670 casualties.[2] Other losses included a destroyer, 29 tanks and numerous landing craft. Overhead a costly air battle had been fought. The British lost 106 planes and the Germans admitted the loss of 48.

The raid did nothing to persuade Stalin that his Allies were trying to help him. Nor did it please the Canadians, although their troops, who had been clamouring for action for two years, had fought with determination. The Germans, whose losses amounted to 591 men, were far from being distressed.

Even so the officers concerned with planning the invasion of Europe learned a great deal from Dieppe. One thing above all was

---

[1] Originally the US destroyer *Buchanan*, one of the 50 handed over to Great Britain by order of President Roosevelt in 1940.

[2] In addition the Royal Navy lost 550 and the R.A.F. 153 officers and men.

clearly shown, and that was that when at length the time should come to re-enter the continent the Allies were not likely to take a port on D Day.

Admiral Mountbatten was to remain at Combined Operations Headquarters until 23 October 1943, by which time the tide of war had turned, and the British, who for so long had had to content themselves with amphibious pinpricks, had already played their part in three major invasions. But the raiding period had helped to revive the long neglected art of amphibious warfare, and had induced the enemy to commit strong forces to coast defence in France and Norway – forces which could otherwise have been employed against the hardpressed Russians. At a time when the British could only hit back at Germany with the Bomber Offensive, which did not get into its stride until 1942, raiding was the only form of offensive action open to a Government whose policy was to wage war by every means in its power.

CHAPTER SIXTEEN

FROM PEARL HARBOR TO SINGAPORE

1941

7 Dec.	Japanese attack Pearl Harbor.
8 Dec.	Japanese land in Malaya.
10 Dec.	HMS *Repulse* and *Prince of Wales* sunk off Malaya.
	Japanese invade the Philippines.
11 Dec.	Japanese repulsed at Wake Island.
17 Dec.	Japanese invade Sarawak.
23 Dec.	Japanese capture Wake Island.
26 Dec.	Surrender of Hong Kong.
31 Dec.	Admiral Nimitz takes over as Cincpac.

1942

1 Jan.	The 'United Nations' declaration.
2 Jan.	Japanese take Manila and Cavite.
3 Jan.	Japanese land in Borneo.
21 Jan.	Alliance concluded between Japan and Thailand.
23 Jan.	Japanese land in New Guinea, and the Solomon Islands.
1 Feb.	American aircraft attack Kwajalein.
15 Feb.	Surrender of Singapore.
20 Feb.	Air battle over Rabaul.
27 Feb.	Battle of the Java Sea.
9 Mar.	Surrender of Java.
17 Mar.	General MacArthur arrives in Australia.
31 Mar.	Japanese break through the Bataan position.
9 Apr.	American surrender in Bataan.
18 Apr.	Colonel Doolittle's raid on Tokyo.
6 May	Fall of Corregidor.
7 May	British invade Madagascar.
7 May	US forces sink 11 Japanese warships off the Solomon Islands.

> '*We, by the grace of heaven, Emperor of Japan, seated on the Throne of a line unbroken for ages eternal, enjoin upon ye, Our loyal and brave subjects:*
> *We hereby declare war on the United States of America and the British Empire. The men and officers of Our Army and Navy shall do their utmost in prosecuting the war, Our public servants of various departments shall perform faithfully and diligently their appointed tasks, and all other subjects of Ours shall pursue their respective duties; the entire nation with a united will shall mobilize their total strength so that nothing will miscarry in the attainment of our war aims.*'
> Imperial Rescript: the 8th day of the 12th month of the 16th
> year of Shava.

THE Japanese did not await this pronouncement before beginning their war in a somewhat less formal way. Like their Nazi and Fascist allies they struck the first blow without warning.[1]

At dawn on 7 December 1941 350 Japanese planes flew off from their carriers and attacked the US Pacific Fleet in Pearl Harbor, in the Hawaiian island of Oahu. They also attacked the Army Air Force planes on Hickham and Wheeler airfields. For the loss of 29 planes and five midget submarines they had sunk three battleships, capsized another and damaged four more. In addition 3 light cruisers and 3 destroyers, among other vessels were seriously damaged. The Americans lost 188 planes and suffered 3,389 casualties. All this was achieved within half an hour, most of it within 10 or 15 minutes. The Japanese concentrated on the aircraft first, and then on the 'sitting ducks' in Battleship Row.

> 'The bursting bombs, the rattle of the enemy machine-guns, and the red ball insignia on the wings were the first intimation of war that anyone had at Wheeler. In a few moments the parked aircraft, many with their fuel tanks filled, were blazing; great clouds of oily

[1] The Japanese had not declared war on China in 1895 or on Russia in 1904.

smoke were rolling up on the still air to obscure everything and hamper the frantic efforts to pull the planes apart and get them armed.'[1]

The Americans managed to get about a dozen aircraft into the air, but out of 126 modern or fairly modern fighters on the field only 43 survived the attack. At Hickham Field it was the same story. Within five minutes of the beginning of the attack the place was a shambles.

The Pacific Fleet lying at anchor off Fort Island received equally short shrift.

'Every one of the five outboard battleships took one or more torpedo hits in the first five minutes, and the two inboard ships, *Maryland* and *Tennessee*, were hit by bombs.'[2]

Only one thing marred for the Japanese their tactical success at Pearl Harbor; they neither damaged nor sank a single carrier, for the simple reason that they were out on an exercise. And it was the carrier, not the battleship, that was to be the vital warship of the Pacific War, for deprived of their battleships the Americans made a virtue of necessity and fought a new kind of war.

From the point of view of grand strategy Pearl Harbor was a disastrous blunder. The Americans could take hard knocks, but they did not care to be the victims of low cunning. They had not wanted war. However anxious Roosevelt may have been to aid the victims of Nazi and Fascist aggression, they did not wish to become involved. The aftermath of Isolation was still strong. But now at a blow the Japanese put the nation right behind their President, and that far-seeing statesman lost no time in denouncing 7 December as 'a date which will live in infamy', and in declaring that the war was all one, whether against the Japanese or against Hitler and Mussolini. Congress voted for war against Japan without a single speech or one dissentient voice.

Far away in Berlin the German Foreign Minister, von Ribbentrop, was jubilant. Mussolini too was happy. Count Ciano, more intelligent than either, saw that America would now enter the European conflict, which would be so long that she would be able to bring all her potential forces to bear. On 11 December Germany and Italy declared war on the United States, which returned the compliment.

[1] Walter Millis: *This is Pearl*, (quoted in Flower and Reeves, p. 283).
[2] Walter Millis: (quoted in Flower and Reeves, p. 285).

Latin America was thoroughly aroused by these events, and within the next few days Costa Rica, the Dominican Republic, Haiti, Honduras, Nicaragua, El Salvador, Cuba,[1] Guatemala and Panama all declared war on the Axis.

It is no more than realistic to recognize that 7 December 1941 was one of the most significant days in British history: the day that put the United States squarely in the war as an ally. The war had now been going on for more than two years, years during which Britain had won few enough victories to set off against a multitude of German triumphs. It is true that the British had always been confident of ultimate victory; this conviction was certainly an asset but it was not altogether logical. And it is true that Hitler had dealt himself a deadly blow on the day he invaded Russia. But now by their attack on Pearl Harbor the Japanese ranged the most powerful of all possible allies on the British side. Whatever disasters lay in store – and there were plenty – the most pessimistic of Britons could no longer suppose that the Allies could lose.

But the way ahead was still a long one, and the United States, like Britain, were to pay a sorry price for years of pacifism and isolationism.

It is in no sense to excuse the conduct of the Japanese that one attempts to explain the causes that led them to make war. In the days before 1853, when Admiral Perry forcibly awoke Japan from her long sleep of isolation, that country was self supporting. In the process of Westernization she rapidly became industrialized and as swiftly became aware of her basic lack of economic resources. It may be remarked that a similar realization was coming to the Germans at much the same time.

Japan had set out on her empire-building course during the last quarter of the nineteenth century, when she acquired the Kurile, Bonin, Kyuku and Volcano islands. Her war with China (1894–95) gave her Formosa, the Pescadores and, temporarily, Port Arthur, which Russia, Germany and France soon compelled her to relinquish. She recovered it as a result of the Russo-Japanese war, when she also won control of Korea, which she annexed in 1910, and the southern half of the island of Sakhalin. She joined the Allies in the Great War and in 1919 was granted a mandate over the Mariana, Caroline and Marshall Islands, with the exception of Guam.

Japan was hard hit by the slump of 1929, and it was partly to

[1] It is odd to recall that 'Sergeant' Batista was our ally!

distract her peoples' attention from home affairs that in 1931 she invaded Manchuria, which, as Manchukuo, she added to her empire. Perhaps she thought of this as a short cut to prosperity. However that may be, it provoked the antagonism of China.

Japan, like Hitler's Germany, sought *Lebensraum* – 'The Greater East Asia Co-Prosperity Sphere'. On 7 July 1937 she invaded China. The war was long and bloody but indecisive. China was financed by the United States and also received supplies through the ports of Indo-China and via the Burma Road from Lashio to Chungking. On 21 July 1941 Vichy France, unable to protect Indo-China, agreed to its temporary occupation by Japan. Roosevelt reacted swiftly by freezing Japanese assets in the USA, some £33,000,000. Great Britain followed suit, and put an end to her commercial treaties with Japan. The Netherlands, though practically powerless to defend her Far Eastern empire, acted with America and Britain.

General Fuller sees this as 'a declaration of economic war', and 'the actual opening of the struggle', but it is more realistic to date this from the invasion of China in 1937, if not from the wanton aggression against Manchuria in 1931.

Japan now considered that she was faced with either war or economic ruin. When in October 1941 Prince Konoe's cabinet, which had favoured agreement with the United States, resigned, the new government of General Tojo determined to cut the Gordian Knot. Unfortunately for her Japan did not appreciate that by taking the initiative she was uniting America against her. But it is not easy to see how she could have provoked Roosevelt, far less Churchill, into attacking *her*.

In the short term Japan enjoyed certain advantages, for although she was taking on the world's two greatest maritime and industrial powers, and although their homelands were virtually beyond her reach, many of their possessions were extremely vulnerable.

The strength of the Japanese Navy lay in its carrier fleet. Vice-Admiral Nagumo had under his command ten fast modern carriers, each carrying about 75 aircraft. Japan's early successes were in large measure due to her superiority at sea and in the air.

It had been calculated that she had 2,625 aircraft, integrated with her navy and army, and earmarked for operations:

Malaya	700
Philippines	475
China	150
Manchuria (in reserve)	450
Japan	325
Marshall Islands	50
Pearl Harbor raid	400
Fleet (seaplanes)	75
	2,625

Against this the Allies had in the Far East only 1,290 planes, many of them obsolete, widely scattered and lacking unified control.

US Navy and Army Air Forces
Philippines	182
Wake	12
Midway	12
Hawaii	387

Royal Netherlands East Indies Air Force
East Indies	200

RAF
Malaya	332[1]

Royal Australian Air Force
Australia, Solomons and Malaya	165
	1,290[2]

The Japanese were swift to exploit their success at Pearl Harbor. In the Central Pacific they overwhelmed the small US garrison of Guam (10 December) and on 23 December, after one bloody repulse (11 December) and a long and heavy bombardment, invaded Wake Island, where some 500 United States Marines under Major James Deveraux put up a magnificent resistance.

Next the Japanese struck at the Philippines, where General Douglas MacArthur was in command. MacArthur, who had been Chief of the US Army Staff, had no illusions as to the likelihood of war with Japan, and had done all that lay in his power to prepare his

[1] 141 fit for war.
[2] Fuller: *The Second World War*, p. 132.

171

command. He had at his disposal about 200 aircraft, including 35 Flying Fortresses, 19,000 American troops and 11,000 Philippine Scouts. The newly-raised Philippine Army, which was as yet of little military value, numbered about 160,000.

The 7,083 islands of the Philippine Archipelago had been annexed by the United States after Admiral Dewey's victory over the Spanish Fleet in Manila Bay during the Spanish-American War (1898). The biggest islands are Luzon and Mindanao. The Americans had promised to give independence to this considerable part of their empire by 1946.

The preliminary air bombardment destroyed many of the American planes. On 10 December the Japanese began to land on the north coast of Luzon, following up with yet another landing on the east coast.

On 27 December General MacArthur reported to Washington:

'Enemy penetration in the Philippines resulted from out of weakness in the sea and in the air. Surface elements of the Asiatic Fleet were withdrawn and the effect of submarines has been negligible. Lack of airfields for modern planes prevented defensive dispersion and lack of pursuit planes permitted unhindered day bombardment. The enemy has had utter freedom of naval and air movements.'

On the same day Manila was declared an open city. This did not save it from a destructive air bombardment which lasted two days. On 2 January the Japanese occupied the city and the naval base of Cavite.

In January MacArthur now withdrew some 40,000 men into the Bataan Peninsula where he had always intended to make his last stand. Bataan, which is about 25 miles long by 20 miles wide, juts out from Luzon. The Americans attempted to supply MacArthur by blockade-runners, but none got through. In February he was ordered to Australia, and much against his will went to take over the South West Pacific Area. The Japanese broke through the Bataan position on 31 March, and on 9 April 35,000 Americans laid down their arms. The prisoners were treated with bestial cruelty in the notorious death march that followed. Lt.-General Jonathan Wainwright held out in the old Spanish island fortress of Corregidor until 6 May, denying the enemy the use of Manila Bay, one of the best natural harbours in the East.

By their conquest of the Philippines the Japanese had destroyed an army of at least 90,000 men.

Meanwhile on 8 December the Japanese had landed in Malaya, where it must be said the British resistance lacked the epic quality of the American defence of the Philippines. There were several reasons for this. Nobody need be surprised if the British lacked a leader of the calibre of MacArthur. In the early years of the war Britain had needed her best generals in Europe and the Middle East. The same applies to her troops, for few regular battalions could be spared for Malaya. The Americans, on the other hand, attached more importance to the Japanese menace than to the war in Europe, and had deployed good troops there.

The morale of the civilian population was an important factor. The population of 5,250,000 was Malayan, Chinese and Indian. Of the 700,000 inhabitants of Singapore itself 75 per cent were Chinese. The Malayans resented the presence of the Chinese and blamed the British for allowing them to establish themselves in their country. The people of the Philippines knew that they were due to become independent in 1946. Malayan independence lay far in the future.[1] But in fact, in the early days of the campaign, especially at Penang, the native population, contrary to popular belief, stood up fairly well to merciless air bombardment, although it caused complete confusion. To be honest the morale of the white population was not altogether satisfactory. The root of the trouble was that they thought that, wherever else World War II went, it would keep away from Singapore. Men whose main concern in life was the production, in an enervating climate, of tin and rubber were not anxious to assume other responsibilities. Nevertheless one observer,[2] writing on 13 December, recorded: 'Raffles Hotel still has dancing every night, but there are not as many dancers.

'A good deal of the apathy about war has gone. In any event it is true that the certainty that war would not come to Singapore has disappeared.'

The training of the troops was vitiated by the pre-war attitude of all too many commanders, who considered that thick jungle and mangrove swamp would be 'Out of Bounds'. With the single exception of the 2nd Battalion of the Argyll and Sutherland Highlanders, none of the garrison were trained in jungle warfare. The Japanese are not accustomed by nature to work in jungle: but they had trained for it.

Even more important was the fact that the defenders were not steeled by their training against the horrors of air attack. The fate of the French in 1940 should have given the High Command notice of this problem. Later in the war German morale stood up to the complete loss of air cover. At the minor tactical level, the Japanese, travelling light, were very mobile, while the British, burdened with all the paraphernalia of European warfare, including steel helmets and gas-masks, were loaded like donkeys.

When tension in the Far East began to grow, Mr Churchill and his advisers, with admirable prescience, sent out the new battleship *Prince of Wales* and the battle-cruiser *Repulse* to strengthen our forces there. Unhappily there was no aircraft carrier available to support them. At the very outset of the campaign these two fine ships, venturing on a sortie in which for various reasons they did not have

---

[1] It finally achieved in 1957.
[2] Brown: *Suez to Singapore*.

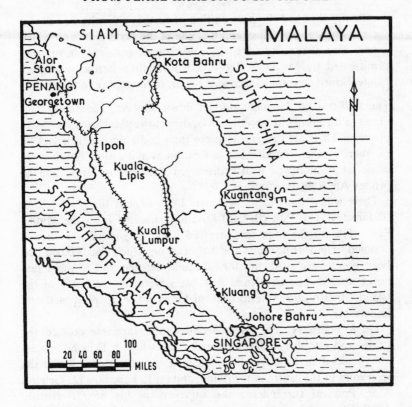

the support of shore-based aircraft, were sunk by Japanese planes from the neighbourhood of Saigon. Their daring commander, Vice-Admiral Tom Phillips, went down with his ship. It is easy to say that unwise risks were taken. The fact is that nothing in their experience against the Germans prepared the officers of the Royal Navy for the truly astonishing skill of the Japanese pilots. But by 1942 it should have been clear that capital ships should only venture within range of enemy air power with a proper air screen. A calculated risk led to unprecedented castastrophe. Far away in Britain it seemed one of the most unnerving events of a war which had not lacked black moments.

In Malaya the effect on morale was deadly. Ian Morrison writes:

'I still remember the chill sense of calamity which was caused by the loss of these two ships. It was worse than calamity. It was calamity that had the premonition of further calamity . . . Blown clean away at one fell swoop was one of the main pillars on which our sense of security rested. Nor was our despondency in any way mitigated by Mr Duff Cooper's Churchillian heroics and well-intentioned attempt to reconcile people in Singapore to the news.'[1]

The well-trained Japanese pushed down Malaya, seconding their thrusts with a series of amphibious landings to outflank each successive position. Their air superiority more than made up for their lack of numbers on the ground. As time went on even a 250-lb. bomb could cause panic in towns with a dismayed Asiatic population and no proper Air Raid Precautions.

There was a short stand at Kuala Lumpur, but the place fell on 10 January. The 18th (British) Division, diverted from the Middle East while on the high seas, arrived when Singapore was already doomed. The fortifications and batteries on which £60,000,000 had been spent were sited, not for all-round defence, but to resist sea-borne attack. The naval and RAF bases were on the north of the Island. British and American naval losses made supply practically impossible.

On 8 February, after bombardment, the Japanese crossed the straits and established a bridgehead, from which a British counter-attack failed to dislodge them. Pushing on, the enemy seized the reservoirs in the centre of the island, and on 15 February Lt.-General A. E. Percival surrendered the survivors of his 85,000[2] British, Australian and Indian troops, by far the largest British army ever to lay down its arms.

In Britain's long military annals there is no more dismal chapter than the fall of Singapore. It is a sort of anthology of all that is worst in British military history. It is a tale of complacency, unpreparedness, and weakness, relieved only by isolated tactical successes and the firmness of a handful of units and individuals. Defeat is something not unknown in the history of any martial race. But seldom indeed has an army capitulated to one which it actually outnumbered. Lt.-General Yamashita and his men had, from the tactical point of view, literally run rings round the defenders. Once more in this war the better balanced force had won. Yamashita may have had fewer soldiers, but he had air and sea power.

---

[1] Ian Morrison: *Malayan Postscript* (Faber, 1942). Mr Duff Cooper was Resident Minister for Far Eastern Affairs at Singapore.
[2] Some 15,000 being non-combatant.

Allied leaders meet at Yalta; Winston S. Churchill, President Roosevelt,
Marshal Stalin

Field Marshal Viscount Montgomery   Field Marshal Viscount Slim

Admiral Sir Andrew
Cunningham

General Dwight D. Eisenhower

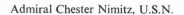

Admiral Chester Nimitz, U.S.N.

Adolf Hitler

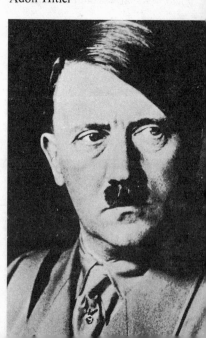

General George C. Marshall General Douglas MacArthur

Field Marshal von Manstein Generaloberst H. Guderian

Field Marshal von Rundstedt   Benito Mussolini

General Tojo   General Zhukov

German troops in Warsaw, 1939

The 4th Battalion Border Regiment in France, 1940. They held the whole of a large sector of the Somme during a vital stage in the German advance

Dunkirk, June 1940. From a painting by Charles Cundall, R.A.

Spitfires on patrol

The sinking of the *Graf Spee*

Russian Convoy (P.Q. 18), September 1942. HMS *Eskimo* in the foreground

A gun bombarding Bardia, 1940

The blitz on London. Flames surrounding St. Paul's Cathedral

The attack on Pearl Harbor. U.S. *California* settles slowly into the mud, with the hulk of the capsized battleship *Oklahoma* on extreme right of picture

The surrender of Singapore, February 1942

An RAF Halifax over its target in the Pas de Calais area, July 1944

Street fighting in Stalingrad

The Central Front, west of Rzhev; a heavy Soviet gun shelling enemy positions

The Arakan, Spring 1944

The Pacific. U.S. Navy Hellcat fighters about to take off on a mission against the Japanese

Monastery Hill, Cassino, after its capture by Allied troops

The U.S. Marine Corps on Iwo Jima

Operation Overlord. Royal Marine Commando Troops making their way ashore at St. Aubin sur Mer, June 1944

East of Chambois. Wrecked
German transport as the
enemy retreats

Winter offensive in Russia,
1941

German offensive in the
Ardennes, December 1944

German photograph of a
V2 long-range rocket just
before launching

Atom bomb at Nagasaki

Belsen Concentration Camp
Germans forced to remove
the dead at rifle point

Percival assumed command nearly seven months before the Japanese invaded Malaya. Entering the army in 1914 he had won the D.S.O. and the M.C. in the First World War and had commanded a battalion with distinction. In 1939 he was a Brigadier. It cannot be pretended that his selection to command was unreasonable. It is easy to say that a more dynamic commander could have achieved more in the time. Perhaps a man as ruthless and logical as Montgomery might have done, but Montgomerys, like MacArthurs, don't grow on bushes. Surrender is an odious thing to a soldier, and it is never easy to justify. One must judge every case on its own merits. Once the reservoirs had gone the situation in Singapore was evidently hopeless, but 85,000 is a lot of soldiers, and it should not have been beyond the wit of man to have killed off a few more Japanese with an army of that size.

But when all is said and done, it is probably no exaggeration to say that the one thing that could have saved Malaya was an adequate fighter force. Had the defence disposed of, say, 300 fighters, it may be doubted whether the Japanese landings would have succeeded in the first place.

The Japanese now turned their attention to Java. The Netherlands East Indies were garrisoned by 120,000 European and Indonesian troops, but without naval and air support they were to be an easy prey.

The Allies had hastily scraped together a heterogeneous squadron, the Combined Striking Force,[1] of five cruisers and nine destroyers, under a Dutch Rear-Admiral, K. W. F. N. Doorman. The squadron had had no opportunity to train together and had no properly coordinated communications system, or secure base. All had been working for a long period under severe strain and Doorman considered that they had reached the limit of their endurance.

On the afternoon of 27 February Doorman attacked a Japanese force of four modernized cruisers and 14 destroyers north of Sourabaya. The fighting was indecisive, though the *Exeter* was hit and the *Kortenaer* blown up. About 9 p.m. the *Jupiter* was mined and in a second encounter about 10.30 p.m. the flagship *De Ruyter* and *Java*

---

[1] Doorman's Combined Striking Force comprised:
        8-inch cruisers: *Exeter* (British) and *Houston* (American).
        6-inch cruisers: *Perth* (Australian; *De Ruyter* and *Java* (Dutch)
        destroyers: *Electra*, *Encounter* and *Jupiter* (British); *Witte de Witt* and *Kortenaer* (Dutch); *John D. Edwards*, *Alden*, *Ford* and *Paul Jones* (American).

were both torpedoed. The gallant Doorman went down with his ship.

Early next morning *Houston* and *Perth*, rounding a headland, suddenly came upon a line of anchored Japanese transports. They attacked at point-blank range sinking two and damaging others before Admiral Kurita came on the scene with three cruisers and nine destroyers and, after a hard fight, sank them both.

The damaged *Exeter* put to sea on the evening of the 28th, escorted by the *Encounter* and *Pope*. Sighted by aircraft, they were intercepted next day by four heavy cruisers and three destroyers. The *Exeter*, of River Plate fame, fought well for an hour and a half before she was torpedoed. Both the destroyers were sunk as well.

Of the Allied ships engaged in the Battle of the Java Sea, only four American destroyers survived. They reached Freemantle, Western Australia, on 4 March. Despite their heavy losses in men and ships the Allies had only managed to delay the invasion of Java for 24 hours.

On the night of 28 February the Japanese effected three landings on the north coast of Java. The Dutch, who had generously spent their aircraft to help in the defence of Malaya, held out as best they could with the aid of small British and American forces. Once again mere numbers counted for little against the balanced force. On 9 March, 98,000 men surrendered at Bandoeng. The Japanese proceeded to mop up the other islands at their leisure, but in Sumatra and elsewhere, as in the Philippines, small bands of stout-hearted men hung on in the hills and forests.

The Japanese had now built up a brilliant strategic situation. Malaya, Java, Sumatra, Bali, Samba and Timor formed their outpost line. It appears to have been their intention to consolidate their position in Burma, Siam, Malaya, China and the East Indies. Although it was open to them to thrust outwards against Australia or India, and although to the Allies both these offensives seemed imminent, it does not now appear that the Japanese originally had any such intentions.

The first six months of their war had gone so well for the Japanese that they were seriously misled as to its future course. The victories of their Nazi allies and their contempt for democracy alike led them to undervalue their enemies. Russia seemed unlikely to survive; Britain, on the defensive against Germany, could do Japan no harm; America, crippled by Pearl Harbor and politically decadent, would eventually come to terms.

But grave though the situation was, the Americans were already striking back. Admiral Chester W. Nimitz, who had succeeded Admiral Kimmel on 31 December 1941, had lost no time in restoring the morale of his command.

'He had the prudence to wait through a lean period; to do nothing rash for the sake of doing something. He had the capacity to organize both a fleet and a vast theater, the tact to deal with sister services and Allied commands, the leadership to weld his own subordinates into a great fighting team, the courage to take necessary risks, and the wisdom to select, from a variety of intelligence and opinions, the correct strategy to defeat Japan.'[1]

Nimitz saw that for the time being hit-and-run raids, similar to those that the British were making on the coasts of Europe, were the only form of offensive action he could take. In the Pacific the aircraft carrier took the place of the commando. On 1 February 1942 Admiral Halsey's group, built up round the carrier *Enterprise*, attacked Kwajalein in the Marshall Islands, and besides killing the Japanese commander sank a transport and damaged nine other vessels.

Admiral Wilson Brown's *Lexington* group raided Rabaul and brought on an air battle in which the Americans won the upper hand (20 February). On 10 March this force, with the *Yorktown* added, raided Lae and Salamaua on the North coast of Papua.

But the raid which really puzzled the Japanese came on 18 April, when Lt.-Colonel James H. Doolittle and 16 B-25 Mitchells flew 668 miles from the carrier *Hornet*, bombed Tokyo, and flew on to land in China.[2] The actual damage inflicted was not very great, but the effect on American morale was tonic. Moreover the Japanese now allotted hundreds of planes to the defence of Tokyo, for they could not guess where the planes had flown from. President Roosevelt's announcement that the aircraft had come from Shangri-La was unhelpful.

---

[1] Morison: *The Two-Ocean War*, p. 138.
[2] The Japanese executed two of the pilots who fell into their hands.

CHAPTER SEVENTEEN

RETREAT IN BURMA

1942

15 Jan.	The Japanese invade Burma.
15 Feb.	Surrender of Singapore.
17/19 Feb.	Battle of the Sittang River.
5 Mar.	General Alexander assumes command.
9 Mar.	Fall of Rangoon.
13 Mar.	Lt.-General Slim arrives.
23 Mar.	Japanese occupy the Andaman Islands.
24/30 Mar.	Japanese capture Toungoo.
1 Apr.	British evacuate Prome.
14 Apr.	Destruction of Yenangyaung oilfields ordered.
29 Apr.	The Japanese cut the Burma Road at Hsipaw. Japanese enter Lashio.
30 Apr.	Burma corps back across the Irrawaddy; Ava Bridge blown.
1 May	Mandalay evacuated.
4 May	British evacuate Akyab.
6 May	Surrender of Corregidor.
8 May	Japanese occupy Myitkyina.
8 May	Battle of the Coral Sea.
10 May	Rearguard action to cover the crossing of the Chindwin at Kalowa.
15 May	General Stilwell reaches Assam.
20 May	Chinese reach Imphal.
4 Jun.	Battle of Midway.

For Map of Burma see Chapter 32, p. 369.

'We took a hell of a beating.'
LT.-GENERAL JOSEPH W. ('Vinegar Jo') STILWELL.

ON 16 January the Japanese invaded Burma, and by mid-May they had taken Rangoon (9 March), cut the Burma Road (29 April) and driven the Allies across the Chindwin to the borders of India. The wonder is not that the Japanese won, but that the Allies were not utterly destroyed.

The defenders laboured under practically every possible disadvantage. The Japanese had command of both sea and air. When the invasion began there were only five RAF squadrons in Burma[1] and they were equipped with the obsolete Buffalo fighter. The morale of the troops suffered gravely in consequence of the lack of air cover, and the commanders were hampered by lack of air reconnaissance. The shortage of artillery and transport, and their inexperience in jungle warfare, contributed to this sad state of affairs. The almost total lack of reinforcements was most discouraging.

The invasion of Burma offered the Japanese three possibilities. Firstly the capture of Rangoon, the capital; secondly the cutting of the Burma Road by which the Allies were sending supplies to China; and thirdly the opportunity, if all went well, to push on and invade India.

Shortly before the invasion began, General Sir Archibald Wavell, Commander-in-Chief, India, had sent his Chief of Staff, Lt.-General T. J. Hutton to take command. The task he set him was to defend Burma, and particularly Rangoon, and to make plans for offensive operations against Siam.

Hutton considered that Rangoon was the key to Burma, since it was his only adequate channel of supply, for as General Fuller has pointed out,[2] the British had been in Burma for over 100 years but 'so little attention had they paid to its strategic defence that but

---

[1] Two fighter, one bomber, and two army co-operation squadrons. The Third Squadron of Colonel Chennault's excellent American Volunteer Group was sent by Chiang-Kai-Shek to help in the defence of Rangoon.

[2] Fuller: p. 145.

three mule tracks – frequently impassable during the monsoon – traversed the Indo-Burmese frontier.'

Even so, Hutton realized how vulnerable Rangoon was, and with commendable foresight set up a number of supply depots in Upper Burma so that if the worse came to the worst his army could retreat into Assam. He decided that he could only defend Burma by blocking the routes from Siam, but for this purpose his forces were totally inadequate, since he had at his disposal only two divisions, 17th Indian and 1st Burma. The former was deployed initially on a front of 400 miles!

Wavell had arranged with Generalissimo Chiang-Kai-Shek for the assistance of the Fifth and Sixth Chinese Armies, under General Lo-Cho-Ying, and the American General Stilwell. These Chinese armies consisted of veteran troops, but their organization was totally different from that of a European army.[1]

The Japanese crossed the frontier on 15 January and compelled the British to withdraw. The defenders fought delaying actions on the Salween and the Bilin, before making a serious stand on the Sittang (17–19 February) where 17th Indian Division was attacked in front and on the flank by two Japanese Divisions, and lost heavily, many men being cut off on the wrong side of the river when the bridge was prematurely blown. The Japanese had quickly captured airfields from which they could give fighter cover to their bombers attacking Rangoon.

General Wavell, partly because of his successes against the Italians in North Africa, had a strong belief in offensive action. He also underrated the Japanese, whom he considered to be second-rate troops. The Viceroy of India, the Marquis of Linlithgow, now stuck

---

[1] 'A Chinese "Army" corresponded to a European Corps and consisted usually of two or three divisions. The division itself was not only much smaller than its British or American equivalent, having a strength of from seven to nine thousand, but only two-thirds of the men were armed; the other third replaced the absent animal or motor transport and acted as carriers. As a result the rifle power of a Chinese division at full strength rarely exceeded three thousand, with a couple of hundred light machine guns, and a few 3-inch mortars. There were no artillery units except a very occasional anti-tank gun of small calibre, no medical services, meagre signals, a staff car or two, half a dozen trucks, and a couple of hundred shaggy, ill-kept ponies. Nevertheless the Chinese soldier was tough, brave and experienced – after all, he had already been fighting on his own without help for years. He was the veteran among the Allies, and could claim up to this time that he had held back the Japanese more successfully than any of the others. Indeed, he registered his arrival in the forward areas by several minor but marked successes against enemy detachments.' Field Marshal-Slim, *Defeat into Victory*. 17.

his oar in. Though in New Delhi he was necessarily remote from the fighting in Burma, he had come to the conclusion that uninspired leadership at the top accounted for the poor performance of the troops, and informed the Prime Minister of his view. In consequence Churchill sent General the Hon. Sir Harold Alexander to take over the command.

On 1 March Wavell held a conference with the Governor of Burma, Sir Reginald Dorman-Smith, and General Hutton, and decided that every effort must be made to hold the capital. The Chinese were advancing on Toungoo, 7th Armoured Brigade[1] and other reinforcements were on their way by sea. Alexander arrived in Rangoon on 5 March and immediately decided to evacuate the city. It was none too soon, and the British troops only got clear because the Japanese removed a vital road-block – an unaccountable tactical error.

The Governor's optimistic prophecy that the Burmese would rise up in their wrath and fight the invaders had been proved nonsense. The Burmans were a peace-loving people. Most European civilians regarded the war as an unwarrantable interference with the comfortable routine of their lives. Conditions in Rangoon, which had been heavily bombed, became chaotic, partly as the result of the decision of an officer of the Indian Civil Service to release the occupants of gaols and institutions, thereby leaving the city a prey to 5,000 convicts and an assortment of lunatics and lepers.

It was now decided to form the British troops in Burma into a corps, and the command of this formation was given to Lt.-General W. Slim[2] who arrived at Prome on 13 March.

Every kind of problem confronted him. Intelligence was extremely bad; the population were unhelpful; his troops were neither trained nor equipped for jungle warfare; his units were below strength and sickness was on the increase. His two divisions were 80 miles apart. Worst of all morale, not only in the Burmese units, was shaken. This is how Slim saw the situation when he took over:

> The troops had fought well, but they had had no success. Constant retreats, the bogy of the road-block, the loss of Singapore and

---

[1] An experienced formation which had fought well in the Western Desert.

[2] Oddly enough he and his two divisional commanders, Major Generals Bruce Scott (1st Burma Division) and 'Punch' Cowan (17th Indian Division) had all served together in the 1st Battalion, 6th Gurkhas, for about 20 years. Their mutual confidence and friendship in this testing time were assets of incalculable value.

Rangoon, and the stories of Japanese supermen in the jungle, combined with the obvious shortages of every kind, could not fail to depress morale. At this stage, the effects of the Sittang disaster on the fighting troops were evident but not irremediable, but morale in the administrative areas in our rear did not impress me as good. There were a lot of badly shaken people about.'[1]

The new commander set about putting matters right.

Despite its losses 17th Division was not prepared to let the Japanese have things all their own way. On 17 March Major Calvert with a party of commando men and Royal Marines made a bold river raid on the Irrawaddy port of Henzada and cut up a force of dissident Burmese under Japanese officers. At about the same time the 1st Gloucesters surprised and routed a Japanese battalion billeted at Letpadan, 80 miles south of Prome, driving it into the jungle and inflicting heavy casualties. These flashes of spirit gave promise of better days to come.

Thus far, against heavy odds, the Allied Air Force in Burma had done well, having destroyed 291 Japanese planes for a loss of 97. But now the Japanese, using about 250 planes, made concentrated attacks on the airfields of Magwe (21 March) and Akyab (23 and 27 March), as a result of which the RAF was driven out of the country. The cities of Burma – Mandalay, Pegu, Prome, Meiktila, Lashio, crumbled in ruins as the Japanese pattern-bombed them at their leisure,

On 24 March the Japanese attacked the Chinese Fifth Army at Toungoo on the Sittang. The 200th Division defended itself well, but Stilwell could not induce the reserves to counter-attack. At Stilwell's request Alexander agreed (28 March) to attack on the Irrawaddy front in order to relieve pressure on the Chinese. This led to confused fighting around Shwedaung in which a striking force from 17 Division was cut off for a time, losing many vehicles.

The Chinese 200th Division managed to extricate itself from Toungoo on 30 March. The loss of the place uncovered the British left and made it practically impossible to hold Prome, which was evacuated (1 April).

By the end of April the Japanese had completed the conquest of central Burma. On the 29th they overran Lashio, the terminus of the Burma road. Thus they had cut the only land route to China, which was now completely blockaded.

[1] Slim: p. 40.

On the 30th the British withdrew across the Irrawaddy and at midnight blew up the Ava bridge. Still hard-pressed, the Burma Corps crossed the Chindwin at Kalewa, losing its tanks and much of its transport. There is no space here to recount the story of the rearguard action (10 May), which Field-Marshal Slim has told so well. It must, however, be recorded that even in those days of adversity some of the troops, among them 1/7 Gurkhas and 7 Armoured Brigade, still had some fight left in them. The survivors of the corps were back across the river, but very little of its equipment remained.[1]

Meanwhile what was left of the Fifth Chinese Army was retreating to the north. Their conduct left something to be desired. 'They seized trains, ejecting our wounded and refugees, women and children, took all supplies on evacuation routes, and looted villages. Their necessities knew no law and little mercy.'[2] Lt.-General Sun Li Jen, a graduate of Virginia Military Academy, who commanded the rearguard, fought his way out, starving and in rags, it is true, but with his 38th Division still a fighting formation.

On 12 May the monsoon broke:
'On that day our rearguard was leaving Kalewa and our main body toiling up into the hills. From then onwards the retreat was sheer misery. Ploughing their way up slopes, over a track inches deep in slippery mud, soaked to the skin, rotten with fever, ill-fed and shivering as the air grew cooler, the troops went on, hour after hour, day after day. Their only rest at night was to lie on the sodden ground under the dripping trees, without even a blanket to cover them. Yet the monsoon which so nearly destroyed us and whose rain beat so mercilessly on our bodies did us one good turn – it stopped dead the Japanese pursuit. As the clouds closed down over the hills, even their air attacks became rare.'[3]

So ended the 900 mile retreat. By 20 May all Burma was in the hands of the Japanese.

---

[1] 'Of the 130 guns of all kinds that Burma Corps had possessed at one time, 74 had reached the Chindwin, but of these only 28 had crossed into India. The total mechanical transport of the corps on arrival at Imphal was 50 lorries and 30 jeeps. Our casualties had been some 13,000 killed, wounded, and missing, besides, of course, those evacuated sick. The Japanese losses had been only a third of this – 4,600 killed and wounded.' (Slim: p. 119).

[2] Slim: p. 115.

[3] Slim: p. 109.

CHAPTER EIGHTEEN

THE DESERT, 1942

1942

15 Apr.	Malta awarded the George Cross.
5 May	British landings in Madagascar.
26 May	Rommel attacks.
4/5 Jun.	British attack the 'Cauldron'.
10 Jun.	French withdraw from Bir Hakim.
12 Jun.	Ritchie decides to withdraw.
14 Jun.	The Guards are withdrawn from Knightsbridge.
21 Jun.	Rommel storms Tobruk.
23 Jun.	Rommel crosses the Egyptian frontier.
25 Jun.	Auchinleck takes over from Ritchie.
1 Jul.	Rommel held up at El Alamein. 'Ash Wednesday' in Cairo.
6 Aug.	Alexander selected to command the Middle East. Gott chosen for Eighth Army.
7 Aug.	Death of Gott. Montgomery chosen to replace him.
11 Aug.	Malta convoy action.
13 Aug.	Montgomery assumes command of the Eighth Army.
15 Aug.	Alexander takes over from Auchinleck.
30 Aug./ 7 Sep.	Battle of Alam el Halfa.

'Well, Freddie, you chaps seem to have been making a bit of a mess of things. Now what's the form? . . . I was only told I was coming out here in London forty-eight hours ago, but I have been doing a lot of thinking since. Yesterday I spent at GHQ, Cairo, and worked out with Harding[1] how I want this Army organized. You'll never win a campaign as it is at the moment.'

GENERAL B. L. MONTGOMERY to Brigadier F. de Guingand,

13 August 1942.

IN THE desert the year 1942 opened with a lull of four months, while both sides prepared for another bout.

Rommel's aim was to recapture Tobruk and drive the British back into Egypt. The British intended to win back Cyrenaica so as to re-establish the airfields without which they could not cover convoys from Egypt to Malta. Auchinleck was under pressure from London to attack in mid-May, but did not think much of the prospects, for he had lost two Australian divisions, the British 70th Division and 7th Armoured Brigade which, with squadrons of the Desert Air Force, had been sent to the Far East. From that quarter came nothing but tidings of woe – Corregidor, Singapore and Burma had fallen; India and Ceylon were threatened.

Auchinleck thought it might be better to send reinforcements to India and to remain on the defensive in Libya. This infuriated the Prime Minister, who was on the point of recalling Auchinleck and replacing him with Alexander. General Brooke, the CIGS, succeeded in dissuading him, but, in view of subsequent events, may well have made a mistake in doing so. Brooke in his Diary gives an amusing glimpse of the Higher Direction of World War Two. He tells us that on 7 May he was on his way to a meeting of the Chiefs of Staff, when he was summoned to see the Prime Minister.

[1] Now Field-Marshal Lord Harding. He was then Deputy-Chief of General Staff in Cairo.

'That morning's meeting with Winston was typical of many others. He was a wonderful sight in bed, with large cigar in his mouth, hair somewhat ruffled, bed littered with papers and messages and alongside of the bed one of those large cuspidors to drop his cigar ends in. On this morning he was in one of his dangerous moods; the Auk had roused him properly with his proposed postponement of his attack. The situation required handling delicately; in his upset state he might well take some wild decision which it would then be very hard to wean him from.'[1]

Be that as it may, the War Cabinet ordered Auchinleck to open an offensive in May or at the latest in early June. Auchinleck declined to visit London to discuss the situation, but, although relations between him and Churchill were strained thereafter, he retained his command.

At this time the Eighth Army was holding the Gazala Line in front of its forward base at Tobruk, which had now been connected with Alexandria by railway. The defensive positions were covered by extensive minefields and included several large strongpoints or 'boxes', sited for all-round defence, but too far apart to be mutually supporting.

Rommel, who had watched these defences growing with some misgivings, determined to get his blow in first, before General Ritchie (Eighth Army) was strong enough to engage him frontally, while making a simultaneous 'left hook' at his lines of communications via Benghazi to Tripoli.

The British were relieved rather than otherwise when Rommel took the initiative. They would now be able to receive him on 'ground of their own choosing', instead of launching an offensive whose prospects they had always thought doubtful.

Rommel advanced on 26 May and by nightfall it looked as if he was making a strong push towards the 1st Free French Brigade at Bir Hakim. In the early hours of the 27th the mobile force of the Afrika Korps refuelled south of Bir Hakim, planning to thrust NE towards Tobruk, Acroma and El Adem. General Carver describes this as 'a bold plan and half successful, catching Norrie's 30th Armoured Corps unbalanced, its three armoured brigades separated by considerable distances, and 7th Armoured Division, east of Bir Hakim, still out of its battle positions.'[2]

[1] Bryant: *The Turn of the Tide*, p. 380.
[2] Carver: *El Alamein*, p. 23.

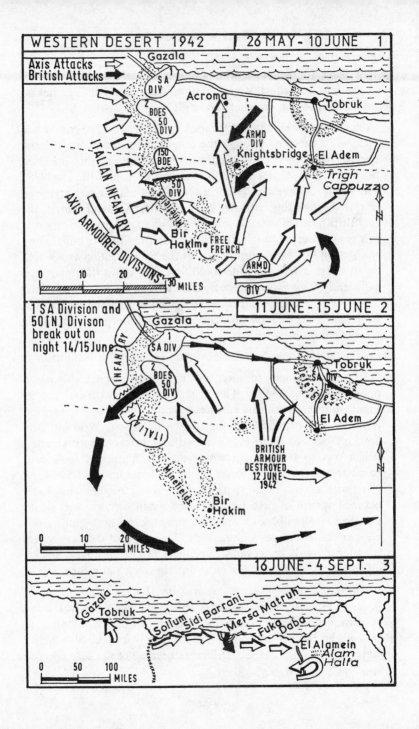

The British recovered quickly, however, and for a time things looked black for Rommel, who was east of the minefields, cut off from his base and short of ammunition. Captain Cyril Falls has an illuminating passage on what followed:

'A fierce armoured battle developed in this region. The enemy had meanwhile cut gaps through the minefields of the main position, overwhelmed a section of the troops holding it, and thus provided himself with a shorter supply line than that round Bir Hacheim. The Army Commander (Ritchie) conceived that he was trying to retreat through this corridor, but Lieutenant-General Norrie, the first British commander to grip the tactics of armoured warfare in this country, came to the true conclusion, that he was building up strength in his "bridgehead" east of the main position and would try to smash a way out if he could first wear down the opposition sufficiently. This was, indeed, typical German tactics, already fully described in a book, *Blitzkrieg*, published in England by a Czech student of war, Captain Miksche, and therefore should have been recognized for what it was.'[1]

On the night 1/2 June Rommel moved up to attack Bir Hakim:

'After our summons to surrender had been rejected, the attack opened at about midday. The Trieste from the north-east and 90 Light from the south-east advanced against the fortifications, field positions and minefields of the French defenders. With our preliminary barrage there began a battle of extraordinary severity, which was to last for ten whole days. I frequently took over command of the assault forces myself and seldom in Africa was I given such a hard-fought struggle. The French fought in a skilfully planned system of field positions and small defence works – slit trenches, small pill-boxes, machine-gun and anti-tank gun nests – all surrounded by dense minefields. This form of defence system is extraordinarily impervious to artillery fire or air attack, since a direct hit can destroy at the most one slit trench at a time.'[2]

The *Luftwaffe* flew 1,300 sorties against Bir Hakim.

A series of tank battles followed with heavy losses on both sides. A determined British attack (4/5 June) on the 'Cauldron', as Rommel's bridgehead was named, failed, partly for lack of sufficient infantry to press it home, but still more because of the very effective

[1] Falls: *The Second World War*, p. 122.
[2] *The Rommel Papers*.

German anti-tank guns. After inflicting heavy casualties on the Germans seething about in the Cauldron the British were driven back in considerable disorder by an armoured counterstroke.

The battered French brigade was withdrawn from Bir Hakim after a truly heroic resistance (10/11 June).

Once he had disposed of the 150th Infantry Brigade[1] at Dahar el Aslaq and the Free French, Rommel set about the task of destroying the Eighth Army's tank strength. By 12 June the British had only 70 tanks left, while Rommel had still about 100 German and perhaps 60 Italian tanks.

The Battle of Gazala was lost. Unable to support the Guards, who had beaten off every attack on Knightsbridge, Ritchie was compelled to withdraw them (14 June).

The fate of Tobruk now hung in the balance. As Carver puts it:

'The desire of all concerned to have their cake and eat it too undoubtedly led to misunderstandings over Tobruk. Auchinleck was determined that Tobruk should not become invested again, but also that it should not be surrendered to the enemy,'[2]

While Ritchie was reorganizing his army on the Egyptian frontier Rommel struck.

At dawn on 20 June Rommel stood with General von Mellenthin on the escarpment NE of El Adem, where Battle Headquarters had been set up, and watched the Stukas attack Tobruk.

'Kesselring had been as good as his word and sent hundreds of bombers in dense formations; they dived on to the perimeter in one of the most spectacular attacks I have ever seen. A great cloud of dust and smoke rose from the sector under attack, and while our bombs crashed on to the defences, the entire German and Italian army artillery joined in with a tremendous and well co-ordinated fire. The combined weight of the artillery and bombing was terrific . . . and had a crushing effect on the morale of the Mahratta battalion in that sector. The Stukas kept it up all day, flying back to the airfields at Gazala and El Adem, replenishing with bombs, and then returning to the fray.

'After a time the assault engineers released orange smoke as a signal that the range should be lengthened, and at 0635 the report

---

[1] From the 50th Northumbrian Division.
[2] Carver: *El Alamein*, p. 23.

came back that the wire had been cut in front of Strong Point 69. Group Menny, and the infantry of the Afrika Korps, now attacked the forward line of bunkers and made rapid progress against feeble resistance. At 0703 Group Menny reported that a whole company of Indians had been taken prisoner; and by 0745 a wide breach had been made and about ten strong points had been taken. Bridges were laid across the anti-tank ditch and the way was prepared for the tanks to enter the perimeter.

'The weak resistance . . . was due primarily to the bombardment, and paradoxically to the excellent concrete shelters built by the Italians. Under the crushing weight of bombs and shells the Indians were driven below ground, where they were relatively secure, but could not bring any fire to bear on our attacking troops, who followed closely the barrage. Another important factor was the weakness of the defenders' artillery fire.'[1]

The German armour poured in through the gap torn in the front of the Indian brigade, and, beating off a counter-attack, began to wreak havoc in the back area which was full of 'soft-skinned' vehicles. That evening General Klopper (2nd South African Infantry Division), who had not the necessary communications to organize a break-out, surrendered the fortress with some 25,000 men and enormous quantities of stores. Part of the Coldstream Guards under Major Sainthill refused to capitulate and broke out in their transport that night.

The moral effect of the capture of Tobruk was very great. In Germany morale reached a peak that it had not touched since the fall of France. Rommel, the man of the hour, was immediately promoted Field-Marshal, while his followers celebrated 'with captured tinned fruit, Irish potatoes, cigarettes and canned beer'.[2] In Britain the shock was the more bitter for being unexpected. Nobody realized that the fortress had been allowed to fall into disrepair since its splendid defence the previous year.

Rommel, swift to follow up his victory, crossed the frontier on 23 June with 44 tanks, and during the next few days dispersed Gott's 13 Corps near Mersa Matruh. The Eighth Army, tired, scattered and

[1] Mellenthin: *Panzer Battles*, 1939-1945.

[2] Lieutenant Heinz Werner Schmidt tells what a pleasure it was 'to snuffle round the field-kitchens, where pork sausages and potatoes, so long a rarity, were being fried. There was British beer to drink, and tinned South African pineapples for dessert'. Australian bully beef was another delicacy. *With Rommel in the Desert*, (Harrap, 1951).

confused, was in desperate plight: Auchinleck decided to take command in person and on the 25th flew up from Cairo and relieved Ritchie. But even he could not rally the survivors until they had swept right back to the El Alamein position, where at last on 1 July Rommel was brought to a halt.

It was not a moment too soon. In Cairo much of the 'bumf' of the British Embassy, the Headquarters of Middle East and British Troops Egypt, was committed to the flames on 1 July, the celebrated Ash Wednesday – a good 'flap' is not without its benefits. It was rumoured that the Navy had left Alexandria in haste. But, as so often in war, things were not quite as bad as they seemed.

The so-called Alamein Line – miles of empty sand, indistinguishable from the rest of the desert, but with its flanks on the sea and on the virtually impassable Qattara Depression – was thinly enough held at first, but Rommel's men were as weak and as exhausted as Eighth Army. All through July there was fighting, but neither side could summon the strength for a knockout blow. At the end of the month Auchinleck sent a telegram to London in which he said: 'It is unlikely that an opportunity will arise for resumption of offensive operations before mid-September.' This was not music in the ears of his masters in London, who had long since come to the conclusion that it was time for a change in the direction of the desert war. In every battle since mid-1941 we had outnumbered the enemy both on the ground and in the air, and now the bewildered Eighth Army on which equipment had been lavished when it could least be spared was back on its start line.

Early in August the Prime Minister and the CIGS descended on Cairo to feel the situation for themselves. Churchill wanted Gott to command the Eighth Army, but Brooke felt that Montgomery was the man and that Gott, though the best of the old hands, was tired. Moreover he had risen from battalion to corps commander since 1939 and possibly required more experience before commanding an army. It is impossible to say whether his great qualities would have sufficed to win us an Alamein. General Carver, himself a veteran of the desert days, speaks of:

'His clarity of mind, his rock-like imperturbability and common sense, his readiness always to propose a course of action when others faltered or were in doubt, all these qualities combined with a truly Christian character had made him the oracle to whom all, both high and low, turned for advice and reassurance at all times, but especially in bad.'

In short Gott had many of the qualities that distinguished Auchinleck himself.

On 6 August Churchill decided to give Alexander command of the Middle East and Gott the Eighth Army, but the very next day the latter was killed when two German fighters attacked a transport aircraft. It was under these circumstances that Montgomery was selected for the command of the Army with which his name will always be linked.

Alexander reached Cairo on 9 August and was given a brief directive by the Prime Minister, in which his prime duty was defined:

'to take or destroy at the earliest opportunity the German-Italian army commanded by Field-Marshal Rommel, together with all its supplies and establishments in Egypt and Libya'.

Montgomery flew out from England with all speed and after conferring with Alexander went up to the desert on 13 August to look round. He did not like what he saw, and decided to assume command without more ado, though this was contrary to Auchinleck's orders. He made a good beginning by cancelling all plans for any withdrawal; by deciding to form a Reserve Armoured Corps; and by giving his Chief of Staff, de Guingand, complete authority over the headquarters and all branches of the staff. Like Allenby in the days before Third Gaza his presence was 'a strong reviving wind'. Even as hardbaked an officer as Brigadier Kippenberger, the New Zealander, felt stimulated.

And on the other side of the hill all was not well. In mid-July an ADC[1] had written to tell Frau Rommel that the Field-Marshal, who had not spared himself during his 19 months in Africa, was suffering from 'digestive disturbances'.

In Rome as early as 6 July grave anxiety was felt. Ciano wrote:

'There is in the air a vague concern on account of the lull before El Alamein. It is feared that after the impact of the initial attack is spent Rommel cannot advance further, and whoever stops in the desert is truly lost. It is enough to think that every drop of water must come from Mersa Matruh, almost two hundred kilometres of road under bombardment of enemy aviation. It is

[1] Lieutenant Alfred Ingemar Berndt.

reported to me that in military circles there is violent indignation against the Germans because of their behaviour in Libya. They have grabbed all the booty. They thrust their claws everywhere, place German guards over the booty and woe to anyone who comes near.'[1]

Montgomery had been in the saddle for but 17 days when Rommel struck once more. But by that time the desert fox was too late. In a famous and characteristic passage in his memoirs Montgomery drily sums up the situation, 'I understood Rommel was expected to attack *us* shortly. If he came soon it would be tricky, if he came in a week, all right, but give us two weeks and Rommel could do what he liked; he would be seen off and then it would be our turn.' Montgomery had made good use of his 17 days. He knew, for example, that 44 Division had arrived in the Delta, but GHQ had said that it would not be available until the end of August at the earliest.

One evening Montgomery told de Guingand to phone Cairo and say that he required the Division *at once*. 'I got on to the staff at GHQ', de Guingand writes, 'and was told that this was quite impossible, but that they would try and get elements of the Division moving in a few days' time. I reported this to the Army Commander. He seized the phone and had a few minutes talk to Alexander. Later that night I was rung up and told that the division would start moving that night . . .'[2]

Montgomery had pondered deeply over the previous battles with Rommel and with his keen tactical insight he had seen 'that what Rommel liked was to get our armour to attack him; he then disposed of his own armour behind a screen of anti-tank guns, knocked out our tanks, and finally had the field to himself.'[3] Montgomery was determined not to let this happen:

'I would not allow our tanks to rush out at him; we would stand firm in the Alamein position, hold the Ruweisat and Alam Halfa Ridges securely, and let him beat up against them. We would fight a static battle and my forces would not move; his tanks would come up against our tanks dug-in in hull-down positions at the western edge of the Alam Halfa Ridge.'

And this is exactly what he did.

[1] *Diary*, pp. 504–5.

[2] De Guingand: *Operation Victory*, p. 141.

[3] Montgomery: *Memoirs*.

On the night of 30 August the German and Italian columns began to move forward in a 'right hook' designed to out-manoeuvre Montgomery by getting round behind his main defensive position. It just did not work, and in consequence Alam el Halfa is one of the most straightforward battles of the whole war. There was no surprise on the first night, because the RAF had spotted the enemy in their forming-up areas 24 hours earlier. Deep minefields and heavy bombing delayed the Germans, who did not seem to be coming on with their old verve. Rommel thrust at the Alam el Halfa ridge, probably not realizing that 13 Corps (Lt.-General Horrocks) was strongly ensconced there, and that Montgomery regarded it as the key to his position. The battle lasted a week, but Rommel could have pulled out several days earlier for all the good he was doing. He attributed his repulse to the weight of British artillery fire, the intricacy and depth of their minefields and his own shortage of supplies, especially petrol. Most of his losses he put down to air attack.

Major-General Freyberg (2nd New Zealand Division):

'attributed the enemy's failure, in a situation in which they could not find room for manoeuvre, to their inability to carry out a proper infantry attack in co-operation with artillery. He accused them of having become tank followers.'[1]

If the Germans were getting cautious, the British were becoming cunning. Montgomery fought with his tanks dug-in, and refused to be tempted. In consequence the old Rommel magic did not work. The shortage of petrol which deprived the German of freedom of manoeuvre, was largely due to the havoc wrought to their lines of communication by the RAF.

[1] Carver: p. 73.

CHAPTER NINETEEN

THE CORAL SEA AND MIDWAY

1942

3 May	Japanese take Tulagi, unopposed.
4 May	*Yorktown's* aircraft bomb Tulagi.
6 May	Surrender of Corregidor.
7 May	*Shoho* sunk.
8 May	Climax of the battle of the Coral Sea.
3 Jun.	Japanese bomb Dutch Harbor.
4 Jun.	Midway.
7 Jun.	Japanese occupy Attu and Kiska.

> *'Heard the heavens fill with shouting,*
> *And there rained a ghastly dew*
> *From the nations' airy navies*
> *Grappling in the central blue.'*
> TENNYSON.   Locksley Hall, 1842.

BY NOW Imperial General Headquarters was suffering from the form of megalomania which, after the war, a Japanese admiral named 'Victory Disease'. New conquests beckoned. They would capture Tulagi in the Solomons and Port Moresby in Papua. This would give them air control of the Coral Sea. Then their main fleet would seek out and destroy the remains of the United States Pacific Fleet in an operation, with Midway and the Western Aleutians as their rewards. The capture of New Caledonia, Fiji and Samoa would follow and would cut off Australia from American support.

Japanese strategy was certainly correct in seeking to try conclusions with the Pacific Fleet before American war production could make it too powerful.

By mid-April CINCPAC Intelligence was already aware of the Japanese threat to the Coral Sea and Admiral Nimitz sent Task Force 17 (Rear-Admiral Fletcher) to take a hand.

Friction de guerre – 'Grit in the works' might serve as a rough translation – is a concept well-known to military commentators since the days of Clausewitz. If you have a warped sense of humour, or like illustrations of how the right thing often happens for the wrong reason, a study of the Battle of the Coral Sea may be recommended.

On 2 May 1942 a Japanese invasion force was detected approaching Tulagi. The small Australian garrison withdrew to the New Hebrides. The Japanese landed unopposed next day and began to convert the island into a seaplane base. Fletcher made for Tulagi in the carrier *Yorktown*.

Early next morning he sent his planes in to attack Tulagi harbour, but they did only minor damage. The *Yorktown* withdrew and rejoined the *Lexington* and the rest of the force on 5 May. She

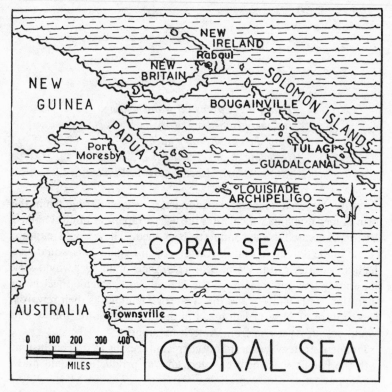

had escaped unscathed because the Japanese carriers, *Shokaku* and *Zuikaku* were delayed for two days delivering *nine* fighters to Rabaul, and so on the 4th were too far away to counter-attack! This mission was a false economy if ever there was one.

On the 6th Fletcher, leaving the destroyer *Sims* and the fleet oiler *Neosho* behind at his refuelling point, made for the Louisiade Archipelago. Early on the 7th Japanese aircraft sighted these two vessels and reported them as a carrier and a cruiser. Vice Admiral Takagi, not unnaturally, ordered an all-out bombing attack and sank them both. The American carriers were still unscathed.

Meanwhile an aircraft from *Yorktown* had reported two carriers and four heavy cruisers 175 miles NW and Fletcher had sent every plane he could to attack what he assumed to be the main enemy force. When they had gone it was discovered that the report should have read 'two heavy cruisers and two destroyers'.[1] But as luck would

[1] In fact it was two light cruisers and three gunboats escorting a seaplane tender.

have it the American fliers sighted the light carrier *Shoho* and sank her in ten minutes, as well as a light cruiser. They lost five planes.

Vice-Admiral Inouye (Commander in Chief Fourth Fleet), who was directing operations from Rabaul, was so discouraged by this loss that he ordered the Port Moresby invasion group to alter course and move around at a safe distance north of the Louisiades.

Meanwhile Fletcher had sent Rear-Admiral Crace, RN, with two Australian cruisers, the USS *Chicago* and some destroyers, to seek out the invasion group. He was attacked by 31 Japanese bombers from Rabaul and three American B-17s from Townsville (Queensland), but managed with great skill to dodge the lot. The Japanese pilots claimed to have sunk two battleships and a heavy cruiser . . .

That evening Japanese aircraft tried once more to find the American carriers. Nine were shot down by fighters. After dark six did eventually find the *Yorktown* but taking her for a Japanese carrier they were lost while trying to land on her! During the night eleven others met a similar fate on their own carriers.

The 8 May saw the climax of the fighting, when the carrier groups finally located each other. They were well-matched.

	Americans	Japanese
Planes	122	121
Carriers	2	2
Heavy cruisers	5	4
Destroyers	7	6

The weather favoured the Japanese. The *Yorktown* sent out 41 planes which missed *Zuikaku* in a rain squall and concentrated on *Shokaku*. They only hit her twice, but one bomb bent the flight deck so badly that she could no longer get her planes off. Half *Lexington*'s group failed to find the Japanese under their umbrella of cloud. The other half scored one more hit on *Shokaku*.

Meanwhile 70 Japanese planes had put in a determined attack on the American carriers, which were clearly visible in brilliant sunshine. They scored only one hit on the *Yorktown*, though it killed 66 men. *Lexington* was hard hit – two torpedoes and two bombs. Internal explosions compelled the crew to abandon ship, and she was finally torpedoed by American destroyers.

At noon on 8 May Takagi believed that both American carriers were sinking, and decided to send the damaged *Shokaku* back to Truk.

Admiral Inouye now recalled the Port Moresby Invasion Fleet to

Rabaul. He was unwilling to risk it South of Papua without air cover. 'Thus the battle was really won by the Americans owing to their biggest mistake, the sighting and bombing of *Shoho*; her loss led Inouye to throw in the sponge.'[1] The Americans lost 66 planes, the Japanese considerably more. In point of tonnage sunk the Japanese were the winners, but it took them more than a month to replace *Zuikaku's* plane losses, and two months to repair the *Shokaku*, and so neither was available for the attack on Midway.

But one cannot judge the results of a battle purely by the casualties. The strategic result of the Coral Sea was that the Japanese gave up their attempt on Port Moresby, the key to New Guinea, which could itself have proved the gateway to Australia.

Moreover, though the battle was by no means a decisive one, from this time forwards the Americans were no longer on the defensive. Coming immediately after the fall of Corregidor (6 May) the victory was a splendid fillip to American morale.

The battle was remarkable as the first in which no surface warships engaged. The Americans had got the better in the first battle of a new era of naval warfare.

If the Coral Sea was a fantastic chapter of accidents and blunders the battle of Midway was one of the most brilliant ever fought, and a decisive turning point in the Pacific War. Once again the predominant factor was air power.

On 5 May Imperial Headquarters ordered the occupation of the Western Aleutians and Midway Island. Midway would be valuable as a base for air raids on Pearl Harbor, and all the islands would form part of the 'ribbon defence' that was to secure the Japanese conquests. But the main object was to bring the US Pacific Fleet to battle and to annihilate it before new construction could make up for its losses at Pearl Harbor.

The operation was the biggest ever mounted by the Japanese Navy. Admiral Yamamoto's armada consisted of 162 warships and auxiliaries without counting patrol craft. The main components were:

Advanced Force:	16 submarines.
Nagumo's Pearl Harbor Striking Force:	4 big carriers.
Midway Occupation Force:	12 transports.
	5,000 men.
	2 battleships.

[1] Morison: *The Two-Ocean War*, p. 147.

	6 heavy cruisers.
	Many destroyers.
Yamamoto's Main Body:	3 modern battleships.
	4 older battleships.
	1 light carrier.
Northern Area Force:	2 light carriers.
	2 heavy cruisers.
	4 big transports.

The object of the last force was to bomb Dutch Harbor and to occupy Adak, Attu and Kiska.

To meet this formidable armada Nimitz had only 76 ships, including the North Pacific Force. These included three carriers, *Enterprise, Hornet* and, incredibly enough, *Yorktown,*[1] besides an 'unsinkable aircraft carrier' in Midway itself – she carried 115 planes. Nimitz had one great asset. The Americans had broken the Japanese naval cipher and he knew when and where they planned to attack. He could take his measures with a certainty which is denied to most commanders.

The battle began on the Aleutian flank. On 3 June the Japanese bombed Dutch Harbor and on 7 June they occupied Attu and Kiska. The operations are chiefly of interest as an object lesson to 'clever' commanders. CINCPAC Intelligence had given warning of the Japanese intentions as early as 28 May, but Rear-Admiral ''Fuzzy' Theobald, as usual, thought he knew better – that the enemy was going to seize Dutch Harbor. Consequently he deployed the main body of his force about 400 miles south of Kodiak, instead of trying to break up the Western Aleutians invasion force.'[2] The Japanese slipped past between him and the land and were able to bomb Dutch Harbor twice. They could indeed have taken the place for all Theobald could have done about it.

Meanwhile Nagumo's carriers, protected by heavy cloud were approaching Midway unseen. On 3 June a Catalina sighted the Occupation Force, but the island-based aircraft only managed to hit one oiler in the early hours of the 4th. Before sunrise that day Nagumo sent off 108 planes to attack Midway, keeping back 93, armed with bombs and torpedoes, in case any American ships should appear.

Radar picked up the Japanese when they were 93 miles away, but the Americans had not enough fighters to stop them. The bombing

[1] *Yorktown* had been 'repaired at Pearl Harbor in two days, when by peacetime methods it would have taken ninety'. Morison: p. 149.

[2] Morison: p. 151.

began at 0630 and lasted 20 minutes. Though much damage was done the runways were not put out of action. About one-third of the Japanese planes were shot down or hard hit by planes or anti-aircraft fire. The Americans lost 15 fighters. Meanwhile the Midway-based bombers had taken off to counter-attack the Japanese carriers.

Fletcher had heard soon after 0600 that a Catalina from Midway had seen two Japanese carriers moving SE, and had promptly ordered Rear-Admiral Spruance with *Enterprise* and *Hornet* 'to proceed southwesterly and attack enemy carriers when definitely located'. He would follow with *Yorktown* as soon as his search planes were recovered.

Nagumo had not expected to encounter American carriers and had, therefore, sent out only a few reconnaissance planes. By 0700 these had spotted nothing. At this juncture the Admiral heard from the commander of his striking force that Midway required further attention. The point was proved almost at once when the bombers from the island started coming over. Nagumo ordered that his 93 reserve aircraft should be rearmed with incendiary and fragmentation bombs.

A quarter of an hour later one of the reconnaissance planes reported 10 American ships to the NE, where no American ship should have been. The unfortunate Nagumo pondered his problem for another 15 minutes, and then decided to rearm his reserve with torpedoes. Before the planes could be got ready his striking force began to return from Midway.

Spruance launched an all-out strike (116 planes) when, at 0700, he was about 175 miles from the Japanese estimated position.

At 0905 Nagumo altered course 90 degrees and began steaming ENE to seek out the American Task Force. In consequence the dive-bombers and fighters from *Hornet* missed him. But her 15 torpedo-bombers saw him and went in without fighter cover. Only one survived the Zekes and the anti-aircraft fire. They were followed by the torpedo-bomber squadrons of *Enterprise* and *Yorktown*. All but eight of their Devastators were shot down. Not a single hit had been scored when, about 1024, the third attack ended.

In the words of the official historian of the United States Navy 'for about one hundred seconds the Japanese were certain they had won the Battle of Midway, and the war'.[1]

Then at 1026 the 37 Dauntless dive-bombers from *Enterprise* came

[1] Morison: p. 156.

on the scene. One squadron went for the *Kaga*, the other for Nagumo's flagship *Akagi*. They struck before the Zekes, which had been dealing with the Devastators, had time to climb, and while the planes were still changing their armament. Two bombs hit the *Akagi* and Nagumo was compelled, most reluctantly, to transfer from his blazing flagship to the cruiser *Nagara*. Four bombs made an inferno of the *Kaga*.

Yorktown's 17 dive-bombers fell upon *Soryu* as she was about to launch planes, scoring three hits. She was sunk, after she had been abandoned, by the US submarine *Nautilus*.

Nagumo still had one carrier, the *Hiryu*, and he now sent 40 planes to attack *Yorktown*. American fighters and anti-aircraft fire accounted for most of them, but at least seven got through. About 1445 *Yorktown* received three bombs and two torpedoes. Admiral Fletcher was compelled to shift his flag to the cruiser *Astoria*, but not before he had ordered a search mission to find the fourth Japanese carrier. At 1540 Spruance sent off 24[1] dive-bombers from the *Enterprise*. At 1700 they plummeted down on *Hiryu* and sank her with four hits.

Mitsuo Fuchida gives a vivid picture of the fate of the Japanese carriers.

'When the attack broke, deck parties were busily preparing the carrier's planes for take-off, and their first awareness of the onslaught came when great flashes of fire were seen sprouting from *Kaga*, some distance off to port, followed by explosions and tremendous columns of black smoke. Eyes instinctively looked skyward just in time to see a spear of thirteen American planes plummeting down on *Soryu*. It was 1025.

'Three hits were scored in as many minutes. The first blasted the flight deck in front of the forward elevator, and the next two straddled the amidship elevator, completely wrecking the deck and spreading fire to petrol tanks and munition store rooms. By 1030 the ship was transformed into a hell of smoke and flames, and induced explosions followed shortly.

'In the next ten minutes the main engines stopped, the steering system went out, and fire mains were destroyed. Crewmen, forced by the flames to leave their posts, had just arrived on deck when a mighty explosion blasted many of them into the water. Within

---

[1] Ten were refugees from the *Yorktown*.

twenty minutes of the first bomb-hit the ship was such a mass of fire that Captain Ryusaku Yanagimoto ordered "abandon ship!"'

The captain himself remained on the bridge. 'No ship commander in the Japanese Navy was more beloved by his men.' They were determined to save him, and sent Chief Petty Officer Abe, a Navy wrestling champion to rescue him. He found Yanagimoto 'standing there motionless, sword in hand, gazing resolutely towards the ship's bow'. The Petty Officer's entreaties were met with silence. 'Abe guessed the Captain's thoughts and started towards him with the intention of carrying him bodily to the waiting boat. But the sheer strength of will and determination of his grim-faced commander stopped him short. He turned tearfully away, and as he left the bridge he heard Captain Yanagimoto calmly singing *Kimigayo*, the national anthem.'[1]

At first Yamamoto intended to renew the battle, but the news that he had lost all four of his fast carriers, with their 250 planes and 2,200 men, compelled him to withdraw.

Whether to save face or to cover his withdrawal he ordered a bombardment of Midway. The cruisers *Mogame* and *Mikuma* managed to collide with each other while trying to avoid an American submarine. As they made off they were attacked by aircraft from the *Hornet* and the *Mikuma* was sunk.

The price the Americans paid for their victory was the *Yorktown* and 147 aircraft.[2]

It is significant that once more a great naval battle had been fought without any action between surface ships. The day of the battleship was done. The battle left the Japanese with five carriers, including only one large one, fit for action. Six more were on the stocks or under repair. The US still had three large carriers with the Pacific Fleet, with 13 more building as well as 15 escort carriers. The Japanese were quite incapable of keeping up with the American rate of construction. It is not too much to say that from the time of Midway onwards the Japanese Navy could only take on the US Navy at night or when supported by land based aircraft. It was a splendid achievement that within six months Admiral Nimitz could truly say 'Pearl Harbor has been partially avenged'.

---

[1] Mitsuo Fuchida and Masataka Okumiya: *The Battle that Doomed Japan* (Hutchinson, 1951).

[2] Of these 109 were carrier-borne and 38 shore-based.

CHAPTER TWENTY

EL ALAMEIN TO TRIPOLI

1942

13 Aug.	Montgomery assumes command of the Eighth Army.
30 Aug./ *7 Sep.*	The Battle of Alam el Halfa.
23 Sep./ *25 Oct.*	Rommel on leave.
6 Oct.	Montgomery changes his plan.
23 Oct/ *4 Nov.*	The Battle of El Alamein.
8 Nov.	Operation *Torch*. The landings in French North Africa.
13 Nov.	Fall of Tobruk.
20 Nov.	Fall of Benghazi.
24 Nov.	Rommel halts at El Agheila.

1943

23 Jan.	Eighth Army enters Tripoli.

'When I assumed command of the Eighth Army I said that the mandate was to destroy Rommel and his Army, and that it would be done as soon as we were ready. We are ready NOW!'
LT.-GENERAL MONTGOMERY.   23 October, 1942.

WITH characteristic thoroughness Montgomery had seen to it that this was no idle boast. He had refused to be prodded into action before he was ready. He had weighed up not only his enemy but his own army, for he knew well that its defects in training limited the scope of his tactical plans.

The morale of the Eighth Army which had carried it triumphantly through the Crusader battles against considerable odds, had slumped after Gazala. Churchill had found it 'brave but baffled'. Montgomery's confident attitude and his firm control of the Battle of Alam el Halfa had done much to put things right.

The Axis army, so long accustomed to swift armoured thrusts and a practically continuous offensive, found itself in a novel situation. It no longer enjoyed anything like air parity. Starved of petrol at the limit of an extended and vulnerable line of communications, it was so immobile that it was condemned to act on the defensive. And Rommel himself was in hospital in Germany.

The balance of forces was now about two to one in Montgomery's favour. The Axis army, temporarily under the command of the 56 year old General Stumme, was 108,000 strong, and included 53,000 Germans. It had about 600 tanks, but 300 of them were of the type known as 'the self-propelled coffin' – the Italian M.13. Only the 38 German Mark IVs, with their 75 mm. guns, were really a match for the Shermans. The enemy had 345 aircraft (216 being Italian) against some 900 British planes. There were only 24 of the powerful 88 mm. guns available.

The Axis defensive position, which was very heavily mined, was five miles deep and about 40 miles long. They had about 2,000 men to a mile of front, which was not much by desert standards. The shortage of fuel meant that the armour would have to fight where it was – 21st Panzer and Ariete in the south; 15th Panzer, 90th Light and Littorio in the north; Trieste was in reserve south of 90th Light.

Montgomery had 220,000 men and 1,351[1] tanks. Of the 1,196 in the forward area, 1,021 were fit for action on the evening of the 23rd. The British had 1,400 anti-tank guns, (550 two-pounders and 850 six-pounders). They also had 884 pieces of artillery, including 52 medium and 832 field guns.

For once a British Army was going into battle with a clear-cut numerical advantage and, of all things, a well-balanced force! And for once the commander, like a modern Wellington, was a man of iron will, a master tactician, bold yet prudent, a far-sighted administrator. In short he was that rarest of animals in the British military hierarchy, a thoroughgoing professional.

Eisenhower understood him well:

'General Montgomery has no superior in two most important characteristics. He quickly develops among British enlisted men an intense devotion and admiration – the greatest personal asset a commander can possess. Montgomery's other outstanding characteristic is his tactical ability in what might be called the "prepared" battle . . . He is careful, meticulous and certain.'

Montgomery was severely critical of the state of training in his army. 'Most commanders', he writes, 'had come to the fore by skill in fighting and because no better were available: many were above their ceiling, and few were good trainers . . . The Eighth Army had suffered some eighty thousand casualties since it was formed, and little time had been spent in training the replacements.'

On 6 October, only a fortnight before the battle was due to start, he altered his plan.

'My initial plan had been based on destroying Rommel's armour; the remainder of his army (the un-armoured portion) could then be dealt with at leisure. This was in accordance with the accepted military thinking of the day. I decided to reverse the process and thus alter the whole conception of how the battle was going to be fought. My modified plan now was to hold off, or contain, the enemy armour while we carried out a methodical destruction ·of the infantry divisions holding the defensive system. These un-armoured divisions would be destroyed by means of a crumbling

[1] Shermans – 285; Grants – 246; Crusaders – 421; Stuarts – 167; Valentines – 223; Matildas – 6; Churchills – 3.

process, the enemy being attacked from the flank and rear and cut off from their supplies. These operations would be carefully organized from a series of firm bases and would be within the capabilities of my troops.'[1]

Large-scale rehearsals were carried out, and careful briefing was a notable feature of the preparations. Major-General de Guingand, Montgomery's Chief of Staff, has described the addresses which the Army commander gave to all officers 'right down to lieutenant-colonel'.

'Clear and full of confidence. I warrant there were no doubters after he had finished. He touched on the enemy situation, stressed his weaknesses, but was certain a long "dog-fight" or "killing match" would take place for several days – "it might be ten". He then gave details of our great strength, our tanks, our guns and the enormous supplies of ammunition available. He drummed in the need never to lose the initiative, and how everyone – *everyone* – must be imbued with the burning desire to "kill Germans". "Even the padres – one per weekday and two on Sundays!" '[2]

If doubts remained, they were in the minds of some of the more senior officers. The three divisional commanders of 30 Corps, Freyberg, Morshead and Pienaar, had little confidence in any early breakout by the armour.

In the open desert it was impossible to conceal the signs of a coming offensive. For this reason the British laid on a deception plan calculated to make the enemy expect the attack on the desert flank, which had tended to be the tactical pattern in early battles. 'All the "armour" in the staging areas, the "guns", the "dumps", and the "pipeline", in the south were stick and string, tin and canvas.'[3] Not since Megiddo had a British offensive been so thoroughly prepared.

For the infantry crouching in their slit trenches 23 October passed slowly. Captain Grant Murray (5th Seaforth), whose patrol was covering the start line, describes the scene as the battle began:

'The hands of my watch seemed to creep round as we lay listening and watching. To our front all was quiet apart from a Verey light or two and some machine-gun fire. As zero drew near I twisted round

[1] Montgomery: *Memoirs*.
[2] De Guingand: *Operation Victory*, p. 160.
[3] Geoffrey Barkas: *The Camouflage Story: From Aintree to Alamein* (Cassell, 1952).

and looked back towards our own lines. Suddenly the whole horizon went pink and for a second or two there was still perfect silence, and then the noise of 8th Army's guns hit us in a solid wall of sound that made the whole earth shake. Through the din we made out other sounds – the whine of shells overhead, the chatter of the machine-guns . . . and eventually the pipes. Then we saw a sight that will live for ever in our memories – line upon line of steel-helmeted figures with rifles at the high port, bayonets catching in the moonlight, and over all the wailing of the pipes . . .'[2]

This opening attack won considerable success, for during the night 30 Corps fought its way on to Miteiriya ridge, and on the southern sector 13 Corps made some progress. The two deep belts of mine-fields and stubborn, if uneven, resistance caused a good deal of delay.

There was no quick enemy reaction, for General Stumme had little idea what was happening. He drove, unescorted, to 90th Light to try and find out, was fired on – probably by the Australians – and died of heart failure while his driver was trying to get away. His body was not found for 24 hours. And so at a critical moment of the battle the *Panzer Armee* was leaderless. It defended itself with obstinacy, but there was no counterstroke.

The crisis of the battle came swiftly. Although Montgomery could not as yet be certain exactly how much progress had been made, it seemed that things had gone well; the problem was to get the armour forward through the narrow lanes in the minefields.

During the night of 24/25 October Gatehouse's 10th Armoured Division tried to push forward. There was considerable confusion among the gapping parties, and vehicles became double-banked nose to tail. About 10 o'clock a German bomber set fire to about 25 vehicles carrying petrol and ammunition, and started a blaze which went on all night. Gatehouse wanted to call off the attack and Lumsden (10 Corps) rather agreed with him. This was the moment when the battle could be lost and won. Fortunately de Guingand, realizing this, summoned Lumsden and Leese to be at Army Head-quarters at 3.30 a.m., and woke up Montgomery – an act of cool courage, for his Spartan master did not like having his slumbers disturbed. Montgomery made it abundantly clear that his original plan was to be carried out, and told Gatehouse this on the telephone. After the conference he detained Lumsden and warned him 'that, if

[2] Quoted by Carver: p. 109.

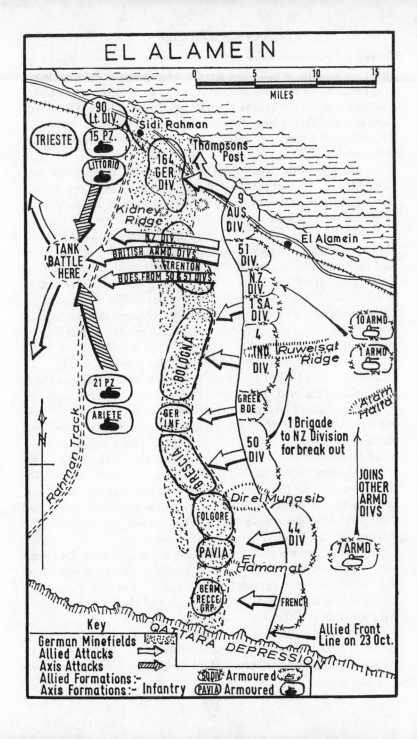

EL ALAMEIN

0   5   10   15
MILES

90 Lt. DIV.
Sidi Rahman
TRIESTE
15 PZ.
Thompsons Post
LITTORIO
164 GER DIV.
Kidney Ridge
9 AUS DIV.
El Alamein
TANK BATTLE HERE
NZ. DIV.
BRITISH ARMD. DIVS.
TRENTON
BDES. FROM 50 & 51 DIVS.
51 DIV.
N.Z. DIV.
1 S.A. DIV.
10 ARMD
1 ARMD
21 PZ
ARIETE
BOLOGNA
4 IND. DIV.
Ruweisat Ridge
Aram Halfa
GER. INF.
GREEK BDE.
1 Brigade to NZ Division for break out
BRESCIA
50 DIV.
JOINS OTHER ARMD DIVS
FOLGORE
Dir el Munasib
PAVIA
44 DIV.
7 ARMD
El Hamamat
GERM. RECCE. GRP.
FRENCH
Rahman Track
N
Key
QATTARA DEPRESSION
Allied Front Line on 23 Oct.

German Minefields
Allied Attacks
Axis Attacks
Allied Formations :-
Axis Formations :- Infantry
50DIV. Armoured
PAVIA Armoured

he and his divisional commanders were not determined to break out, others would be found who were'.[1] Montgomery himself rightly regarded this as the real crisis of the battle. Before 8 o'clock that morning one of Gatehouse's brigades was reported to be 2,000 yards west of the minefield area. The New Zealand Division had also fought its way clear. Counter-attacks by 15 Panzer Division were repulsed with loss.

In the south 7th Armoured Division had got through the first minefield on the night 23/24 October, but had then been halted. Montgomery wanted to use this formation later in the battle and called off the attack before the casualties should become too serious.

By the morning of the 26th Montgomery's first onslaught had lost its momentum, casualties were mounting, about 200 British tanks had been knocked out, but 30 Corps had taken most of its objectives. The Eighth Army had taken 2,000 prisoners, 600 being German. It was estimated that the enemy had lost about 30,000 men and some 250 tanks besides a number of guns, but it now seems that intelligence was being over-optimistic. Montgomery spent the day pondering and planning.

Meanwhile Rommel had reappeared the previous evening (25 October) and had taken over from General Ritter von Thoma, who had replaced Stumme. The situation he found was not encouraging. 15 Panzer had only 31 tanks left, petrol was short, constant bombardment from the air as well as the artillery had caused heavy casualties; morale was affected. Rommel determined to throw in his reserves, drive the British out of his main position and retake the feature known to him as Hill 28, and to the British as Kidney Ridge. His attack went in on the evening of the 27th, but was baffled by the combination of bombing, heavy armour and anti-tank guns. The 2nd Rifle Brigade, whose commanding officer, Lt.-Colonel Vic Turner, won the Victoria Cross, knocked out at least 37 enemy tanks.

Meanwhile Montgomery had thought out a new plan. Lumsden was to push on west and north-west of Kidney Ridge, while Leese was regrouping for his next major attack. The 7th Armoured Division was brought up from the south and the New Zealanders were taken out of the line.

On 29 October the Australian Division launched a diversionary attack in order to make Rommel commit his remaining reserves. Advancing from the northern flank of the Kidney Ridge salient they

[1] Carver: p. 135.

made for the coast, threatening to cut off 164 Infantry Division. Rommel, who had already expressed his doubts as to the outcome in a letter written to his wife the previous day, reacted as Montgomery had hoped. He struck back at the Australians with his reserves, including 31st Panzer and 90th Light Division. The Australians held firm and by so doing paved the way for Operation *Supercharge*, the *coup de grâce*.

Rommel was already contemplating a withdrawal to Fuka, for he had only 90 tanks left, while the British still had some 800.

Supercharge began on the night 1/2 November and was held up by the German anti-tank screen. But this was a Pyrrhic victory for the enemy, whose tanks were further reduced. The German retreat had already begun when on 3 November orders came from Hitler expressly forbidding any retirement. Thus Montgomery was granted another 24 hours in which to maul his enemies before the *Führer* changed his mind and permitted Rommel to withdraw.

The British finally broke through on 4 November, but the pursuit got off to a slow start and when heavy rain began to fall on 6 November 'the bottom fell out of the desert'. Rommel, with a metalled road behind him, was able to save something from the wreck. Considering their enormous armoured superiority at the end of the battle the British might well have destroyed the Afrika Korps. The long battle had exhausted the victors and for this reason a complete triumph eluded them.

Rommel's losses cannot be accurately assessed. Of his 108,000 men, some 30,000 (including about 10,000 Germans[1]) were taken prisoner. The immobile Italians suffered particularly heavily in this respect. The Germans gave their other losses as:

	Killed	Wounded	Total
Germans	1,100	3,900	5,000
Italians	1,200	1,600	2,800
	2,300	5,500	7,800

General Carver,[2] however, thinks it probable that they really lost 20,000 killed and wounded.

In addition Rommel lost 1,000 guns and 450 of his 600 tanks.

[1] Among them General von Thoma, commander of the Afrika Korps.
[2] Carver: p. 195.

During the retreat the Italians abandoned another 75 tanks for lack of fuel. By 15 November Rommel had no more than 80 tanks left.

Montgomery's casualties numbered 13,500 (8 per cent of his force). Although 500 tanks had been put out of action, only 150 were damaged beyond repair; 100 guns had been destroyed.

The tonic effect that the resounding victory of El Alamein had in Britain can hardly be believed by those who were not there to follow its course during those ten days – waiting impatiently for each succeeding BBC bulletin. At first the news was good, but then the Eighth Army seemed to get stuck. Was it to be the old desert story of hope deferred? When the breakthrough came, with the magnificent bag and the beginning of the long pursuit to Tripoli, a feeling of immense relief and indeed pride was everywhere prevalent. And the news that Britain had found a great general was not the least of it. Well might Churchill say:

'The Battle of El Alamein was the turning point in British military fortunes during the World War. Up to Alamein we survived. After Alamein we conquered'.

or as he put it – with pardonable inaccuracy – 'Before Alamein we never had a victory. After Alamein we never had a defeat.'

CHAPTER TWENTY-ONE

NORTH AFRICA

1942

Jun.	General Eisenhower takes command of American forces in the United Kingdom.
Jul.	The Allies decide to invade French North Africa.
23 Oct.	The Battle of El Alamein begins.
5 Nov.	General Eisenhower sets up his Headquarters at Gibraltar.
8 Nov.	The Landings in North Africa. Operation *Torch*.
9 Nov.	German troops begin landing at El Aouana airport, Tunis.
10 Nov.	Admiral Darlan orders the French in North Africa to cease all resistance to the Allies.
11 Nov.	Patton takes Casablanca.
12 Nov.	The British take Bone.
20 Nov.	Rommel quits Benghazi.
25 Nov.	British take Medjez el Bab.
27 Nov.	The Germans enter Toulon. French fleet scuttled.
29 Nov.	Rommel visits Hitler's HQ.
29 Dec.	Darlan assassinated.

1943

14/24 Jan.	The Casablanca Conference.
23 Jan.	Montgomery takes Tripoli.
2 Feb.	German surrender at Stalingrad.
14 Feb.	Germans attack the Kasserine Pass.
6/7 Mar.	The Battle of Medenine.
20/26 Mar.	Montgomery attacks the Mareth Line.
5 Apr.	Allied attacks on airfields in Sicily and Tunisia.
6 Apr.	The Wadi Akarit position broken.
7 Apr.	Americans contact the Eighth Army near Gafsa.
9 Apr.	The Fondouk Pass forced.
20 Apr.	Battle of Enfidaville.
6 May	The final advance in Tunisia.
7 May	Tunis and Bizerta fall.
13 May	Marshal Messe surrenders.

'This must not be considered as the end; it may possibly be the beginning of the end, but it certainly is the end of the beginning.'

WINSTON S. CHURCHILL, at the Lord Mayor's Luncheon Banquet at the Mansion House, 10 November 1942.

ON THE night of 8 November 1942 a great Allied amphibious expedition consisting to a great extent of American troops descended upon the coasts of French North Africa, with the object of seizing the widely separated ports of Casablanca, Oran and Algiers.

It was hoped that the effect of this operation would be to trap Rommel between the Eighth Army and the forces advancing from the West, in a giant nutcracker. Once occupied, North Africa would serve as a base for future operations against Europe. A success here was bound to confirm Franco in his policy of neutrality, and would forestall any designs the Axis might have in the same area.

Command of this expedition was given to an unknown American officer, Lt.-General Dwight D. Eisenhower. General Eisenhower, who came of a family of German Mennonites which had emigrated in the 1730s, was born at Denison, Texas, on 14 October 1890. He graduated from West Point in 1916, but saw no fighting in the First World War. He served on MacArthur's staff in the Philippines from 1935–9 and during the early years of the Second World War held high staff appointment. A man of great charm and impartiality, he had the gift of being able to get Allies to work harmoniously together with the minimum of friction and mistrust. One has only to compare his team with the Axis partnership to appreciate his gifts in that field. But he was far more than a high-powered liaison officer. Though he had never previously commanded in the field he was well versed in the history of his profession, in staff-work and in administration. Though no great tactician he has been somewhat underrated as a commander, for he was to prove on occasion that he had the power to take decisions, and to make the right ones. British history shows the value of a loyal and trusted ally, General Eisenhower was one to rank with Prince Eugène and Marshal Blücher.

The naval commander was Admiral Sir Andrew Cunningham, who, because of his successes at Matapan and elsewhere, enjoyed the confidence of the Americans as well as the British. He had 500 warships and 350 transports and cargo ships under his orders.

Operation *Torch* was not launched without grave misgivings. As late as September 1942 such prominent British generals as Sir John Dill (who had just been succeeded as Chief of the Imperial General Staff by Sir Alan Brooke), and Sir Bernard Paget, the Commander-in-Chief Home Forces, were still worried about the security of the United Kingdom. They feared that without the *Torch* forces it might be impossible to repel a possible German invasion in the spring. But the Prime Minister saw that the time for invasion was passed, and backed the preparations with all his tremendous energy. By the end of the month it was clear that the Americans too were backing the operation and the planners began to believe that it had a good chance of success.

As early as 9 October Ciano had prophesied 'that the Anglo-Saxons are preparing to land in force in North Africa, whence, later on, they intend to launch their blows against the Axis. Italy is geographically and logically the first objective'.[1] And on 4 November the Italians heard from Gibraltar that a great convoy was being prepared. This suggested the possibility of a landing in Morocco. But the Germans saw in it an operation for 'the provisioning of Malta or an attempt at landing in Tripolitania in order to fall upon Rommel's rear'.[2] Their chief reaction was to station U-boats off Dakar.

The Allies, hoping that there would be no resistance from the French, tried to ensure their co-operation by diplomatic means and by sending an American, Major-General Mark Clark, by submarine to contact General Mast and others in Algiers. This cloak and dagger affair did not achieve its aim, and the landings provoked a certain amount of resistance—two destroyers were sunk at Algiers – though it proved uneven in quality and ferocity. Still there were 14 French divisions in the theatre and unfortunately the pro-Allied Commander-in-Chief, General Juin, was arrested. However, it chanced that Admiral Jean Darlan, Marshal Pétain's heir-apparent, was visiting

[1] Ciano: *Diary*, pp. 528-9 and 538.
[2] Ciano: p. 540.

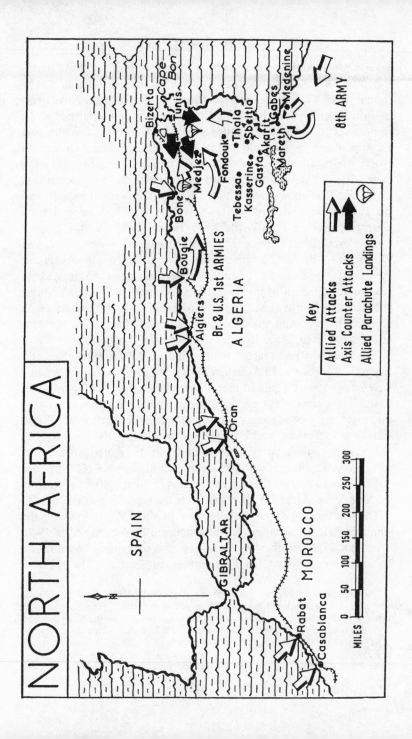

NORTH AFRICA

SPAIN

GIBRALTAR

MOROCCO

Rabat

Casablanca

Oran

ALGERIA

Algiers

Br. & U.S. 1st ARMIES

Bougie

Bone

Medjez

Fondouk

Bizerta

Cape
Bon

Tunis

Tebessa

Kasserine

Gafsa

Thala

Sbeitla

Akarit

Gabes

Mareth

Medenine

8th ARMY

Key

Allied Attacks

Axis Counter Attacks

Allied Parachute Landings

MILES

0   50   100   150   200   250   300

his sick son in Algiers. Eisenhower, who neither wished to kill Frenchmen nor to lose his own men to no purpose, convinced Darlan that he should order a cease fire, and this the Admiral did on 10 November. In vain Pétain repudiated his action. Eisenhower was criticized on ideological grounds for using the anti-British Darlan[1] in this way, and for appointing the ex-Vichy minister as French political chief in all North Africa. In war one cannot always be nice in the choice of one's instruments. This one was not to be available for long because at Christmas Darlan was assassinated by a young French patriot, and the gallant General Henri Giraud, a man who had escaped from German prisons in both World Wars, reigned in his stead.

Once established in their three main objectives, Algiers, Oran and Casablanca – the last had proved the most stubborn – the Allies cast their eyes upon Tunis. Eisenhower decided upon an immediate advance, and troops of the British First Army swiftly occupied Bone (12 November). But already on 15 November there were clashes with German patrols, and the advance was finally checked on the 25th at Medjez el Bab, some 30 miles south-west of Tunis.

The Germans had reacted swiftly, and on 9 November their first troops had landed at El Aouana airport, Tunis. Soon reinforcements were coming in at a rate of more than 1,000 a day. On 9 November Ciano had a conversation with Hitler in Munich. Laval was arriving that night. Hitler was going to insist on the total occupation of France, a landing in Corsica, and a bridgehead in Tunisia. 'Hitler is neither nervous nor restless, but he does not underrate the American initiative and he wants to meet it with all resources at his disposal. Göring does not hesitate to declare that the occupation of North Africa represents the first point scored by the Allies since the beginning of the war.'[2]

The Germans lost no time in overrunning 'Vichy France', the southern half of the country, which had not been occupied in 1940. When on 27 November the Germans entered Toulon, Admiral de Laborde ordered that the French fleet be scuttled. The splendid

---

[1] Ciano, who had a meeting with Darlan on 10 December 1941, formed this impression of him. 'He is a small man, energetic, wilful, and rather boastful, who talks without reticence, and calls a spade a spade. He is a military man, who is beginning to develop a taste for politics, and because he is French, he does it with a certain finesse. Is he sincere? I can't say, except for one thing: he hates the British.' (*Diary*, pp. 416–7 and 559).

Later Ciano was struck by the 'cold indifference' with which the English press commented upon his death.

[2] Ciano: p. 541.

battle-cruisers *Dunkerque* and *Strasbourg* were among the ships that went down.

At Hitler's Headquarters, the *Wolfschanze*, far away in East Prussia, the staff were preoccupied with the worsening situation at Stalingrad. (See Chapter 22). Nevertheless there was a good deal of anxiety about North Africa. In mid-November General Alfred Jodl, Head of the Armed Forces Operational Staff, wrote in an appreciation:

> 'North Africa is the glacis of Europe and must therefore be held under all circumstances. If it is lost we must expect an Anglo-Saxon attack against south-eastern Europe via the Dodecanese, Crete and the Peloponnese; we must therefore pacify and secure the Balkans.'[1]

General Messe had told Ciano as early as 14 November 1942 that the loss of Tripolitania was inevitable and that the attempt to establish a bridgehead in Tunisia could have no lasting success.[2] But Mussolini, despite stomach pains probably brought on by worry, had recovered something of his old spirit by the 22nd.

The effect of this swift arrival of German troops, taken with the heavy rains of early winter, and problems of supply, was to bring about a stalemate. The British First Army (Lt.-General K. A. N. Anderson) hung on to Medjez el Bab, but lost Jebel el Ahmera (Longstop Hill) to the north. It may be, as General Brooke thought at the time,[3] that Eisenhower was far too preoccupied with political matters and was not paying enough attention to the Germans. However that may be there was deadlock from Christmas until mid-February.

On the other side of the hill everything was not going as smoothly as the Allies, burdened with their own cares, may have thought. For one thing the Axis had a cumbersome command set-up: '. . . authority ran from Hitler and Mussolini, through the two high-level Defence Staffs, to Kesselring (Commander-in-Chief South) and thence to the German Army Commanders, of whom there were now two, side by side'. (Rommel and von Arnim).[4]

Then at the end of November there was friction in the Axis camp when Rommel secretly left Libya to see the *Führer*. The Italians said

---

[1] Warlimont: *Inside Hitler's Headquarters*, p. 282
[2] Ciano: pp. 544 and 547.
[3] Bryant: *The Turn of The Tide*, p. 534.
[4] Warlimont: p. 309.

that if one of their generals had behaved in this way he would have been court-martialled and Göring was sent to soothe them. The root of the trouble was that Rommel did not think it possible to hold Tripolitania and wanted to withdraw into Tunisia. The Italian general, Bastico, and some of the Italian General Staff, disagreed with his views. The officers of Göring's suite promised to send three armoured divisions to Tunisia and talked big about reaching Morocco in three months. The Italians – rightly as it turned out – were not impressed.

Moreover, by this time Rommel had lost the confidence of both Hitler and Mussolini. On 7 December 1942 the German Operations Staff War Diary has the acid comment that: 'just now the *Führer* considers it a positive advantage that for the moment Rommel's Army has insufficient fuel to enable it to withdraw further'.[1] While on 5 January 1943 Mussolini spoke harshly not only of his own Chief of Staff, the shifty and dishonest toady Marshal Cavallero, but of 'that madman Rommel, who thinks of nothing but retreating in Tunisia'.[2]

In mid-January General Messe was made commander of the broken Italian forces retreating into Tunisia. So far from being pleased he was convinced that Cavallero had appointed him in the hope that he would lose his reputation in a desperate gamble and end up in a prison camp. In fact Cavallero was the first to go. On 30 January he was succeeded as Chief of Staff by General Ambrosio, an honest and respected patriot, but no thunderbolt. The Germans were not pleased at the dismissal of the obsequious Cavallero.

But despite the growing friction within the Axis, and what Ciano calls (19 January) 'the prudent but inexorable advance of Montgomery',[3] Mussolini still had his attacks of ill-founded optimism, as on 21 January when he declared: 'Our Libyan forces are entering Tunisia and we still have many trump cards to play.'[4] To the more realistic among his followers, however, the loss of Tripoli, which Montgomery entered in triumph two days later, was a bitter blow.

If Mussolini had run out of trumps, Rommel still had a card up his sleeve. At this time his army was facing Montgomery in the old French frontier position known as the Mareth Line. His communications with von Arnim in Tunisia were threatened by two American divisions

[1] Warlimont, 308.
[2] Ciano: p. 566.
[3] Ciano: p. 572.
[4] Ciano: p. 573.

(1st and 34th) in the Sbeitla-Gabes area. Rommel had the advantage of interior lines and, while part of his army guarded the Mareth position, he rushed a strong force north and fell upon the Americans (14 February), broke through the Kasserine Pass (20 February) and sent columns towards Thala and Tebessa, thus threatening the communications of the British First Army. He was eventually checked after fierce fighting and fell back on the 23rd.

The Kasserine battle had been a rude jolt to the Allies. General Alexander, who had just become Eisenhower's deputy, made a three-day tour of the American and French fronts and was 'frankly shocked by the situation'. He found the Americans required experience and the French required arms. To the Prime Minister he signalled: 'Hate to disappoint you, but find victory in North Africa is not just around the corner.'

It was now Rommel's turn to be disappointed. Having struck his fierce blow at the Americans he turned on the Eighth Army only to get a bloody nose at Medenine, a few miles east of the Mareth Line (6–7 March). Even after this repulse Hitler remained optimistic. 'Tunis was a strategic position of the first order' and all available resources must be used to hold it.[1]

Rommel managed to hold on to his strong position on the Mareth Line until nearly the end of March. Then Montgomery attacked. He made a frontal attack with XX Corps and pinned the Germans down, and then did a left hook with 2nd New Zealand Division and the 8th Armoured Brigade. General Leclerc's French force, which had come all the way from Lake Chad, stormed 'Plum Pass' and fell on the Germans' rear. X Corps was kept in reserve. The attack was very well supported by the Desert Air Force (Air Vice-Marshal H. Broadhurst), who did a 'Blitz' with bombs and cannon of the sort the Germans had so often employed. It was a fine piece of 'Army Co-operation' by bombers accustomed to give their support by attacking airfields, headquarters and supply dumps.

The attack on 'Plum Pass' was to be heralded by a 'crump' from 40 light bombers, operating on a very narrow frontage. Sixteen Kittybomber squadrons were available and these, with Spitfires as top cover, were to range, two at a time, over the battlefield, shooting up everything in sight with bomb and cannon. A specially trained squadron of 'tank busters' was to seek out the German armour.[2]

[1] Warlimont: p. 312.
[2] De Guingand: *Operation Victory*, pp. 256–7.

50 Division made the frontal attack on the Wadi Zigzaou at 1030 on 20 March. It had the support of a tremendous artillery barrage and gained a foothold, only to be thrown out on the 22nd by the 15th Panzer and 90th Light Divisions.

Montgomery now reinforced his left hook with X Corps Headquarters and the 1st Armoured Division. The 7th Armoured Division reinforced XXX Corps and 50 Division was withdrawn to prepare for a fresh onslaught on the German centre.

The New Zealanders made their way through the Foum Tatahouine Pass, but were held up at 'Plum Pass'. 1st Armoured Division came on the scene, and following a heavy bombardment from the Desert Air Force and the artillery, broke through on the evening of the 26th. After a lull the advance was continued in the moonlight, until it was held up near El Hamma by anti-tank guns.

By this time Rommel was off and 'the desert fox' succeeded in getting his battered army away with the loss of only 2,500 prisoners. But if the bag was small, Mareth was one of Montgomery's most brilliant operations. It was Rommel's last battle in Africa. A few days later he was ordered home to Germany. The Italian, Messe, who now assumed command, fell back to Enfidaville.

The tempo of the campaign was rising. The Eighth Army captured Enfidaville on 20 April and the First Army at last took Longstop Hill. Alexander now regrouped his forces for the final assault of the Axis 'fortress'.

The battle opened on 6 May with heavy bombing which in the words of General Arnold 'blasted a channel from Medjez el Bab to Tunis'.[1] Meanwhile over 1,000 guns were pounding the defenders. At 3.30 a.m. sappers stole forward to clear mines and cut wire, to make way for the infantry, who overran the enemy outposts in the dark and by dawn had reached his main position. By 11 a.m. they were through, and casualties had not been heavy.

It was now the turn of the armour, and by the night of the 7th two divisions (6th and 7th) had occupied Tunis. The same day the Americans took Bizerta.

The Axis forces, still more or less intact, but in great confusion, were beating a hasty retreat into the Cape Bon Peninsula. This is well described by General Fuller as 'an exceedingly strong position and the natural citadel of the Tunisian fortress. Like a double wall, across its base ran two lines of hills, with two main gates, one in the north

[1] Quoted in Fuller: p. 248.

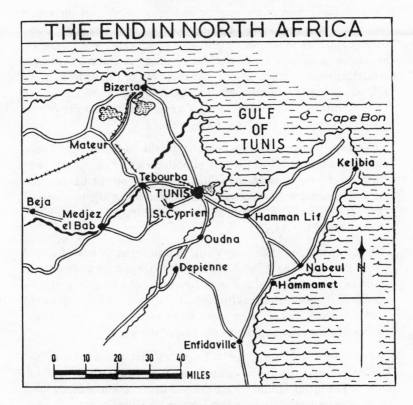

THE END IN NORTH AFRICA

and the other in the south at Hammam Lif and Hammamet respectively.'[1]

Alexander knew that if he did not strike at once the enemy would get set in this citadel. He sent in the 6th Armoured Division at nightfall on the 8th. Its moonlight advance from Hammam Lif to Hammamet in 10 hours is one of the strangest and most impressive feats of arms in the whole history of the Second World War. Without stopping to take prisoners they thrust on right through the heart of the enemy position, striking confusion into all who saw them. British tanks seemed to be everywhere. The German communications system had collapsed. There were plenty of generals and plenty of soldiers; the orders just weren't coming through. Every man was left to take counsel of his own fears. There was a wholesale surrender. On the 12th 250,415 German and Italian troops laid down their arms. The

[1] Fuller: p. 249.

Battle of Tunis, one of the swiftest and most decisive of the whole war, was over. The Tunisian campaign had cost the Allies some 70,000 casualties of whom 20,000 were Americans. From now on Eisenhower would be leading soldiers with some claim to consider themselves veterans. 'The troops that come out of this campaign,' he said, 'are going to be battle-wise and tactically efficient.'

The following July Hitler gave his version of the results of this disaster to senior officers on the Eastern Front:

'Naturally I have tried to reckon whether the undertaking in Tunis, which eventually led to the loss of both men and equipment, was justified. I have come to the following conclusion: by the occupation of Tunisia we have succeeded in postponing the invasion of Europe by six months. More important still, Italy is as a result still a member of the Axis.

'If we had not done this, Italy would almost certainly have defected from the Axis. The Allies would at some stage have been able to land in Italy unopposed and push forward to the Brenner and, as a result of the Russian breakthrough at Stalingrad, Germany would not have had a single man available to put in there. That would inevitably have led rapidly to the loss of the war.'[1]

It was an unconvincing argument. To put another quarter of a million Axis soldiers into the prison camps was a long step towards finishing the war. The campaign may have delayed the invasion of Sicily for a few months: it was still a very bad bargain on Hitler's part.

[1] Warlimont: p. 314.

CHAPTER TWENTY-TWO

STALINGRAD

1942

Mid-Feb.	Russian winter offensive loses its momentum.
5 Apr.	Hitler's Directive No. 41 for his summer offensive.
12 May	Timoshenko's Kharkov offensive.
30 May	RAF 1,000 bomber raid on Cologne.
21 Jun.	Rommel takes Tobruk.
28 Jun.	German summer offensive begins.
1 Jul.	Fall of Sevastopol.
6 Jul.	Germans take Voronezh.
13 Jul.	Von Weichs takes over Army Group B from von Bock.
21 Jul.	Directive No. 44.
23 Jul.	Germans take Rostov.
	Directive No. 45.
6 Aug.	Germans advance towards the Caucasus.
18 Aug.	Directive No. 46 deals with partisan activity.
6 Sep.	Germans halted at Stalingrad.
9 Sep.	Hitler dismisses List and takes over Army Group A.
24 Sep.	General Zeitzler replaces Halder as chief of OKH.
23 Oct.	The Battle of El Alamein begins.
8 Nov.	Operation *Torch*.
19/21 Nov.	Stalingrad encircled.
22 Nov.	Colonel-General von Kleist given command of Army Group A in the Caucasus.
16 Dec.	Eighth Italian Army smashed on the Don.
19 Dec.	Fourth Panzer Army within 35 miles of Stalingrad.
28 Dec.	Manstein orders the Fourth Panzer Army to withdraw south of Stalingrad.

1943

6 Jan.	Germans retreat from the Caucasus and the Don elbow.
14 Jan.	Hungarian Second Army disintegrates before a new Russian attack on the Don.

14 Jan.   German ring round Leningrad broken.
23 Jan.   Montgomery takes Tripoli.
31 Jan.   Germans surrender at Stalingrad.
6 Feb.   Hitler gives Manstein permission to withdraw

'Ich bleibe an der Wolga.'

ADOLF HITLER.

'For us, there is no land beyond the Volga!'
Slogan of the Russian 62nd Army.

BY THE end of 1941 the Russians, it is estimated, had already suffered about 4,500,000 casualties. It is idle to pretend that their long retreat was part of a subtle master-plan, though this myth was an article of faith to all good Bolsheviks while Stalin lived. Even so their heavy sacrifices had won the Russians time to organize new armies and by December 1941 the Germans had identified 280 rifle and cavalry divisions and 44 tank or mechanized brigades.

The great Russian winter offensive, designed to encircle the German Army Group Centre, had lost its momentum by mid-February. Fresh German divisions arrived to fill the gap torn by the Russians between Army Groups Centre and North, and the Germans, clad in the furs and winter clothing produced by Goebbels' appeal, made a gradual recovery. Then came the spring rains, and, both sides being stuck in the mud, there was a temporary halt.

On the ground the great Russian offensive had been indecisive, but in peoples' minds it had a tremendous importance. The veteran Russian generals, January and February, had lost none of their old skill; the new ones Zhukov and Koniev had also proved their worth. The myth of Teuton invincibility was exploded. Everywhere the men who were to face the German armies in the years ahead took heart.[1] But despite all this Hitler himself had strengthened his personal position. His will-power, he could boast, had saved the day, when his staff-trained generals had wanted to take refuge in retreat. The *Führer* was now his own Commander-in-Chief. General Halder,

[1] By 30 April 1942 the Germans had suffered 1,167,835 casualties in Russia. Ciano on a visit to Germany in May 1942 noted: 'Losses in Russia are heavy. Ribbentrop says two hundred and seventy thousand dead. Our General Marras raised it to seven hundred thousand. And between amputation, frostbite, and the seriously ill who will not recover by the end of the war, the figure rises to three million.' (*Diary*, 1 May 1942, p. 479.)

chief of the OKH, was no more than his personal chief of staff. By remote control this semi-educated former corporal conducted the operations involving millions of men, from his Headquarters, the *Wolfschanze*, at Rastenburg in East Prussia. On 5 April 1942 he issued Directive No. 41 in which he outlined his plans for his summer offensive. His aim was 'to wipe out the entire defence potential remaining to the Soviets, and to cut them off, as far as possible, from their most important centres of industry'. All available German and allied forces were to take part in this task, but the security of occupied territories in western and northern Europe, *especially along the coast*, was to be ensured in all circumstances.

The plan was for Army Group Centre to stand fast while the armies in the north were to capture Leningrad and link up with the Finns, while those in the south were to break through into the Caucasus. Hitler considered that these aims could only be achieved one at a time and therefore meant to begin in the southern sector by 'destroying the enemy before the Don'.

The Russians too were thinking in terms of the offensive and, as preliminary operations, meant to launch local attacks at Leningrad, Demyansk, Orel, Kharkov, in the Donetz bend, and in the Crimea. On 12 May Marshal Timoshenko (South-West Front) began with a thrust near Kharkov, only to find that he had run into the main German striking force. With the concurrence of his political commissar, Nikita S. Krushchev, he asked Stalin to let him call off the offensive. This permission was refused, and when on 17 May the Germans struck back his force in the Izyum bridgehead south of Kharkov was seriously compromised. On 19 May Stalin gave Timoshenko his belated permission to extricate his men, but the trap had sprung. In the fighting that followed 240,000 Russians were taken. And that was the end of Stalin's summer offensive.

For the Germans this was a great start to the campaigning season, but there was now a delay of two months while they overran the Crimea. Sevastopol, which had held out for eight months, fell to the Eleventh Army on 1 July.

It was not until 28 June that the main German summer offensive was begun by Army Group B. By 6 July the Second and Fourth Panzer Armies had taken Voronezh. Meanwhile on 30 June the Sixth Army had pushed eastward from Kharkov to act as the southern jaw of a giant pincer movement. The bag produced by this encirclement fell short of 100,000 prisoners, and Hitler, so far from being grateful for a respectable victory, sacked von Bock and on 13 July gave command of Army Group B to Field Marshal von Weichs. On the same day Hitler ordered Army Group A, with Fourth Panzer Army attached, to turn south, cross the lower Don and drive the Russians into a pocket round Rostov. The town fell on 23 July, but once again the Führer got less prisoners than he had bargained for. It was at this juncture that, most unwisely, he removed about half of the Eleventh Army for his Leningrad offensive. As in 1941 he was flouting the principle of concentration of force.

The early summer of 1942 had seen some revival of the old German successes – the rapid overrunning of the Crimea; the capture of Tobruk (21 June); the air offensive which seemed to be starving Malta into submission. Certainly Hitler had reason to be pleased with these successes, but they deluded him into believing that his strategic situation was rather better than was actually the case. On 21 July, in Directive No. 44, Operations in Northern Finland, he stated his view that:

'The unexpectedly rapid and favourable development of the *operations against the Timoshenko Army Group* entitle us to assume that we may soon succeed in depriving Soviet Russia of the Caucasus, with her most important source of oil, and of a valuable line of communication for the delivery of English and American supplies.

'This, coupled with the loss of the entire Donets industrial area, will strike a blow at the Soviet Union which would have immeasurable consequence.'

He went on to say that the time had come to cut the northern supply route, the Murmansk railway, by which the Anglo-Saxon powers were supplying Russia. He assumed that Leningrad would be captured 'in September at the latest . . .' In his next Directive (No. 45), which dealt with the Caucasus offensive,[1] he alleged that only weak forces from Timoshenko's Army Group had got back across the Don.

'We must expect them to be reinforced from the Caucasus.'

In a perceptive moment he added:

'A further concentration of enemy forces is taking place in the Stalingrad area, which the enemy will probably defend tenaciously.'

[1] Operation *Braunschweig* (*Brunswick*).

The German successes continued in August, but already the troops were showing signs of tiredness and their tactics were becoming stereotyped. Marshal Chuikov (64th Army), who had his Second World War 'baptism of fire' on the Don Front in July, has some comments on their performance.[1]

'Observing how the Germans carried out their artillery preparation against the 229th Infantry Division's sector, I saw the weak points in their tactics. In strength and organization this artillery preparation was weak. Artillery and mortar attacks were not coordinated or in depth, but only against the main line of defence. I saw no broad manoeuvre with artillery cover in the dynamic of battle.'

He goes on to say:

'I was expecting close combined operations between the enemy's artillery and ground forces, a precise organization of the artillery barrage, a lightning-fast manoeuvre of shell and wheel. But this was not the case. I encountered the far from new method of slow wearing down, trench by trench. . . .

'The German tanks did not go into action without infantry and air support. On the battlefield there was no evidence of the "prowess" of German tank crews, their courage and speed in action, about which foreign newspapers had written. The reverse was true, in fact – they operated sluggishly, extremely cautiously and indecisively.

'The German infantry was strong in automatic fire, but I saw no rapid movement or resolute attack on the battlefield. When advancing, the German infantry did not spare their bullets, but frequently fired into thin air.'

On the other hand the thoroughly efficient co-operation of the *Luftwaffe* showed the familiarity of the pilots with the tactics of both sides.

'In modern warfare victory is impossible without combined action by all types of forces and without good administration. The Germans had this kind of polished, co-ordinated action. In battle the different arms of their forces never hurried, did not push ahead alone, but fought with the whole mass of men and technical backing. A few minutes before a general attack, their aircraft would fly in, bomb

[1] Chuikov: *The Beginning of the Road*, p. 33.

and strafe the object under attack, pinning the defending troops to the ground, and then infantry and tanks with supporting artillery and mortar fire would cut into our military formations almost with impunity.'[1]

Meanwhile on the Leningrad front the Russians had made an unsuccessful attempt to break the German siege, but had at least forestalled the German attempt to capture the city.

In the south Army Group A (Field-Marshal von Kleist) had taken Maikop, but too late to prevent the complete destruction of the oilfield. German Jäger planted the Swastika on Mount Elbrus, but the Russians still held out in the passes of the Caucasus. By 21 August the *Führer* was already 'very agitated' by the lack of progress on that front.[2] The Sixth and Fourth Panzer armies closed in on Stalingrad, but being compelled to detach troops to guard their flanks, were gradually brought to a halt by 6 September. At last the Russians seemed to be getting the measure of the invaders. Their losses in men and territory, though grievous, had been far less serious in 1942 than in the previous year. In terms of attrition the German position was by no means brilliant. Hitler's armies on the Eastern Front numbered some 3,138,000, excluding the Finns, while Stalin had 4,255,000 men in the field. Behind the German front the partisans were active, as Hitler tells us in Directive No. 46 of 18 August:

'In recent months *banditry in the East* has assumed intolerable proportions, and threatens to become a serious danger to supplies for the front and to the economic exploitation of the country.'

By this time he had evidently resigned himself to the thought that the war was not going to be won that year;

'By the beginning of winter these bandit gangs must be substantially exterminated, so that order may be restored behind the Eastern front and severe disadvantages to our winter operations avoided.'

He expressed the pious hope that the confidence of the local population in German authority could be gained by handling them strictly but justly – a notion that would probably not have worked in the summer of 1941, and was certainly unrealistic in the autumn of 1942.

As the situation worsened, Hitler resorted to his old remedy of sacking generals. List was the first to go (9 September), and for two

[1] Chuikov: p. 34.
[2] Warlimont: p. 256.

and a half months the Dictator actually commanded Army Group A in person: an extraordinary arrangement. The fact that his HQ, Vinnitsa in the Ukraine, was 700 miles in the rear of his front might have daunted a more professional soldier, but in Hitler's fantasy world such considerations went for little. On 24 September, after a series of fearful scenes, Halder was relieved as chief of OKH by General Zeitzler. Warlimont, whose position as Deputy Chief of the OKH staff gives his evidence considerable weight, assesses the *Führer*'s state of mind at this period. He tells us of a briefing conference:

'Hitler fixed me with a malevolent stare and suddenly I thought: the man's confidence has gone; he has realized that his deadly game is moving to its appointed end, that Soviet Russia is not going to be overthrown at the second attempt and that now the war on two fronts, which he has unleashed by his wanton arbitrary actions, will grind the Reich to powder. My thoughts ran on: that is why he can no longer bear to have around him the generals who have too often been witnesses of his faults, his errors, his illusions and his day dreams; that is why he wishes to get away from them, why he wishes to see people around him who he feels have unlimited and unshakable confidence in him.'[1]

Colonel-General Halder was a typical German General Staff officer of the old school, a thorough professional soldier. Dismissed by Hitler he wrote in his diary 'My nervous energy is used up and his is not as good as it was. We must part.' No doubt it was a relief to go. Hitler now prepared to run the army on his own lines. It was 'necessary to educate the General Staff in fanatical belief in an ideal'. The Army 'rather than relying on technical competence ... must be inspired by the fervour of belief in National-Socialism.'[2]

For a time the new chief of staff, Zeitzler, enjoyed great popularity with Göring and the rest of Hitler's courtiers. He certainly began well, with an address to the officers of OKH in which he said:

'I require the following from every Staff Officer: he must believe in the *Führer* and in his method of command. He must on every occasion radiate this confidence to his subordinates and those around him. I have no use for anybody on the General Staff who cannot meet these requirements.'[3]

[1] Warlimont: p. 258.
[2] Halder, quoted by Warlimont, p. 258.
[3] Warlimont, p. 260.

This was to be the atmosphere at HQ during the siege of Stalingrad, in that winter when the tide of war had at last reached the turn.

November was a black month for Hitler. The news of El Alamein, followed by that of *Torch*, made it clear that sooner or later the Axis forces in North Africa were going to be crushed. This news came when Hitler was on his way to address the 'old comrades' of the Nazi party in the Munich Beer Cellar. By way of offsetting the bad tidings he could think of nothing better than to assure the veterans that he was now master of Stalingrad, where the doubtful battle had been raging since early September. On 19 November the Russian Fifth Tank Army broke through the Roumanian Third Army North of that city. By the 22nd the Sixth German Army and about half of General Hoth's Fourth Panzer Army were encircled; 280,000 men were in mortal peril.

This was indeed a reversal of fortune, for in the September days there had been desperate fighting at Stalingrad, and the Russians had barely clung to the west bank of the Volga. Marshal Chuikov, who bore much of the responsibility, had decided, as a result of his experiences against 'the Whites' in the Civil War and his study of enemy tactics,

'that the best method of fighting Germans would be close battle, applied night and day in different forms.[1] We should get as close to the enemy as possible, so that his air force could not bomb our forward units or trenches. Every German soldier must be made to feel that he was living under the muzzle of a Russian gun, always ready to treat him to a fatal dose of lead.'[2]

They reduced No-man's-land to the throw of a grenade. Strong-points were fortified in the centre of the city and garrisoned by 50 or 100 men. Buildings changed hands not once but many times. From 17–20 September, for example, there was a fierce struggle for an enormous building on the southern outskirts of the town, the grain elevator. Colonel Dubyanski (O.C. Guards Infantry Division) reported by telephone to Chuikov:

'The situation has changed. Before, we occupied the upper part of the elevator and the Germans the lower part. Now we have driven them out of the lower part, but German troops have penetrated upstairs and fighting is now going on in the upper part.'[3]

Stubborn fighting marked the resistance of improvised fortresses without number. Archetype of these was the defence of 'Pavlov's House', a key strongpoint in the central district held by a handful of men belonging to Rodimtsev's 13th Guards Infantry Division. Sergeant Jacob Pavlov and two of his men, Alexandrov and Afanasiev, were Russians. The rest of his garrison were Subgayda and Gluschenko from the Ukraine; Mosiyashvili and Stepanashvili, both Georgians; Turganov, an Uzbek; Murzayev, a Kazakh; Sukba, an Abkhazian; Turdiev, a Tajik; and Ramazanov, the Tartar. It was a roll call of the nationalities of the USSR! Chuikov tells us that the Germans 'unleashed a torrent of bombs and shells on to the house', which was held for more than fifty days, without sleep and rest, and remained

---

[1] As early as 26 June 1942 Mussolini had told Ciano that the Bolshevists had 'put into action the tactics of Lenin, who instructed the proletariat to fight house by house against the armies of the bourgeois, thus obliging them to abandon their artillery and aviation, to use only guns and bomb'. (Ciano: *Diary*, p. 502).

[2] Chuikov: p. 72.

[3] Chuikov: p. 98.

impregnable to the end. For his dogged defence Pavlov became a Hero of the Soviet Union.

All through October the struggle went on. Those were the darkest days. But somehow the Russians hung on. Reserves were fed in across the Volga as they reached the front and eventually Paulus' seemingly inexhaustible reserves could do no more. On 29 October the battle began to die down and the next day, apart from exchanges of firing, there was no action. On the 31st the 62nd Army counter-attacked from its narrow strip of land along the banks of the Volga. Advances were measured in yards, but the attack was a great success and retook part of the Krasny Oktyabr factory.

Early in November the temperature dropped sharply and ice began to appear on the river. On 11 November Paulus launched a new attack, but this too was held in two days of stubborn fighting. The *Luftwaffe*, which in October had been flying as many as 3,000 sorties a day, could no longer manage more than 1,000.

And thus it came about that when on 19 November the Russians counter-attacked on three fronts at once a trap closed behind the Germans which cost them 22 divisions.

Hitler entrusted to Field Marshal von Manstein the task of rescuing Sixth Army, but he refused Paulus permission to try and break out. The supply difficulty became acute. Petrol, shells, and firewood were hard to come by. After Christmas the bread ration was cut by half to 50 grammes a day. Many of the men existed on watery soup fortified with the bones of horses they dug up. Colonel Dingler tells us that 'As a Christmas treat the Army allowed the slaughtering of 4,000 of the available horses.'[1] This was no help to the armoured and motorized Divisions.

The cold was bitter in December and the ground was too hard to dig. Aeroplane tyres stuck to the runways. If a position was abandoned the soldiers found themselves without dugouts or trenches when they got back to their new line. Without petrol the armour could not manoeuvre to repulse the Russian attacks. The apertures of tanks became blocked with ice. Men froze to death in their vehicles.

But all hope was not yet gone. On 9 December it was announced that Fourth Panzer Army, which had been reinforced, would start its relieving attack next day, and by 16 December distant gunfire could be heard. Plans were made to break out as soon as Colonel-General Hoth's spearhead should be within 20 miles.

---

[1] Quoted by von Mellenthin: *Panzer Battles*.

The plans for the relief were carefully examined by Field-Marshal von Manstein. It was decided that Hoth, himself 'an officer with an excellent reputation', should make his thrust from the direction of Kotelnikovski some 60 miles SE of Stalingrad. At Nizhna Chirskaya on the Chir the Germans were only 25 miles away, but an attack from this direction would involve a crossing of the Don, which von Manstein rightly rejected as too hazardous an operation.

From the first Hoth met with furious opposition from strong Russian forces of armour and infantry under General Vatutin. It took the Germans a week to fight their way forward 30 miles, but at the end of it they succeeded in capturing two crossings over the river Aksay by a *coup de main*. They were still 45 miles short of the beleaguered army.

At this moment Marshal Zhukov launched a massive offensive on the middle Don, tore a sixty mile gap in the front of the Italian Eighth Army, and thrust southwards towards Rostov, threatening the communications of Field-Marshal von Kleist's Army Group in the Caucasus. Von Manstein had nothing up his sleeve. To check the Russian flood he was compelled to take 6 Panzer Division from Hoth's army. On paper the latter still had two panzer divisions, though their tank strength was now down to 35. Desperate fighting during the next week brought no real progress, partly perhaps because Paulus himself remained inactive. Had he also attacked, the Russians might not have been able to concentrate against 57 Panzer Corps, Hoth's spearhead. Again lack of petrol may have been the key to the tactical situation.

On Christmas Eve the Russians counter-attacked the Aksay bridgehead in great force, and, keeping up the pressure night and day, had retaken both bridges by the 26th. The decimated Germans withdrew southwards.

'The characteristic features of this dramatic battle were mobility, quick reaction and utter perseverance on both sides. Tanks were the main weapon used and both sides realized that the main task of the armour was to destroy the opposing tanks.

'The Russians did not stop their attacks when darkness fell, and they exploited every success immediately and without hesitation. Some of the Russian attacks were made by tanks moving in at top speed: indeed speed, momentum and concentration were the causes of their success. The main effort of the attacking Russian armour was speedily switched from one point to another as the situation demanded.'

Von Mellenthin concedes that 'the tactical conduct of the battle by the Russians was on a high level'. By 26 December 57 Panzer Corps had 'literally died on its feet'.[1]

No power on earth could now save the Sixth Army, least of all the *Luftwaffe*, which Göring had promised would keep Paulus supplied.[2] On 15 January the Hungarian Second Army disintegrated, and far away in the north on that same day the German siege of Leningrad was broken. On the 22nd General Zeitzler, urged on by von Manstein, plucked up his courage to ask Hitler whether Sixth Army should now be authorized to capitulate, only to be told that the army should fight to the last man. But Sixth Army had reached the end of its tether. On 31 January Paulus, who had been promoted Field-Marshal only the previous day, surrendered. Hitler had lost 20 German divisions, of which three were armoured and another three motorized, besides two Roumanian divisions – whom their allies had struck off the ration strength a fortnight before the end!

The Germans lost 60,000 vehicles, 1,500 tanks and 6,000 guns. Of the 280,000 men encircled 42,000 wounded, sick and specialists were evacuated by air; 91,000 surrendered. Of these it is thought, only 6,000 lived to see their homes once more.

It has often been suggested that Hitler should have given Paulus permission to break out. But had this been attempted it is difficult to imagine it being successful. We know that petrol for the six mobile divisions was lacking. The remaining 16, with the possible exception of the Roumanian cavalry division, were comparatively slow-moving and had eaten most of their horses by the end of December. If Hitler and his entourage had withdrawn Sixth Army at the end of October, when it was clearly stuck, a large part of it might have made a reasonably orderly retreat. By the time von Manstein tried to break through, there was really very little hope of pulling Paulus back, even had Hitler consented to such an attempt. Mussolini, more clear-sighted about other people's troubles than his own, commented that Stalingrad 'makes clear to the minds of the masses the great attachment of

---

[1] Mellenthin: p. 192.

[2] It was calculated that 500 tons were required daily to maintain Sixth Army. This would require 250 JU. 52s with the necessary backing. The average amount delivered was only 100 tons. 300 tons on 5 December was the record.

the Russian people to the régime – a thing proved by the exceptional resistance and the spirit of sacrifice'.[1]

No disaster suffered by the Allies in a war where disasters had not been lacking could be compared with the blow Hitler received at Stalingrad. And he was soon (13 May) to receive another at least as costly in Tunisia. Truly the tide had turned in those November days of 1942 when Montgomery emerged victorious from the field of El Alamein; when Eisenhower's host set foot on the shores of North Africa; and when, after an epic defence, the Russians encircled their besiegers on the banks of the Volga.

[1] Ciano: *Diary*, 27 September 1942, p. 525.

CHAPTER TWENTY-THREE

GUADALCANAL

1942

3 May	Japanese seize Tulagi.
7 Aug.	American landings.
8 Aug.	Tulagi retaken.
9 Aug.	Battle of Savo Island.
24 Aug.	Battle of the Eastern Solomons.
12/14 Sep.	Battle of Edson's Ridge.
15 Sep.	*Wasp* sunk.
11/12 Oct.	Battle of Cape Esperance.
26/27 Oct.	Battle of the Santa Cruz Islands.
12/15 Nov.	Naval Battle of Guadalcanal.
30 Nov.	Battle of Tassafaronga.

1943

4 Jan.	Tojo decides to evacuate Guadalcanal.
30 Jan.	Battle of Rennell Island.
6 Feb.	Japanese evacuation completed.

'. . . an island that neither side really wanted, but which neither could afford to abandon to the enemy.'

SAMUEL ELIOT MORISON.

AS EARLY as February 1942 it occurred to Admiral Ernest J. King that it would be unwise to permit the Japanese to consolidate their gains in the Pacific. King was prepared to concede that the Allied strategic aim of defeating Germany first was correct. But at the same time he was convinced of the need for a 'defensive-offensive' strategy in the Pacific.

After the defeat at Midway, General Tojo began to build up a new Eighth Fleet in the South Pacific. A new offensive against Port Moresby was in the wind. King was aware of this design, and on 2 July, despite the objections of General Marshall, he obtained the Joint Chiefs of Staff directive for Operation *Watchtower*: the seizure, by a force based on New Zealand, of Tulagi and Guadalcanal in the Solomon Islands.

It was only three days later that American reconnaissance planes reported that the Japanese were building an airfield on Guadalcanal. Without more ado King ordered that *Watchtower* should begin within the month.

This was the Americans' first combined operation since the Spanish-American War of 1898, and it was laid on in great haste. The forces available were not numerous, and to many officers it was known by the code-name *Shoestring*. The 1st Marine Division, which was to do the assault landing, was under-trained, despite some rehearsals in the Fiji Islands, and lacked administrative backing.

Nevertheless the actual landings on Guadalcanal and Florida Island, though carried out in daylight, were a complete surprise and met but little opposition. The airstrip, where the Japanese just melted into the jungle, was captured by 1600 hours, and was renamed Henderson Field. There were not more than 500 Japanese soldiers and 1,500 pioneers in the island.

Now began a six months' campaign by land and sea. Ashore it was fought out in a dank and malarious jungle. Throughout August and September some 17,000 Marines, under Lt.-General Alexander A. Vandegrift, were only·strong enough to hold a narrow strip seven miles long and four miles wide and to protect the vital airstrip.

Both sides strove hard to reinforce their armies, and this set the pattern of the fighting afloat, with the Americans trying to intercept the 'Tokyo Express' bringing reinforcements down from Bougainville, and the Japanese striving to avenge Midway. Seven major sea-fights mark the course of the campaign.

News of the American landings reached Vice-Admiral Mikawa (Eighth Fleet) at Rabaul early on 7 August. He decided at once to reinforce the Japanese garrisons, and several hundred troops were embarked in the *Meiyo Maru*. About midnight on 8 August she was sunk off Cape St George by the submarine S-38.

Meanwhile Mikawa had concentrated seven cruisers and a destroyer. This force got among the Allied fleet on the night 8/9 August and in the battle of Savo Island, sank four heavy cruisers and a destroyer for the loss of 35 men killed and 57 wounded.

Ashore the US Marines were holding their own. Fortunately the Japanese thought that only 3,000 had been landed. With typical arrogance they considered that the 815 men under Colonel Ichiki, whom they landed on the night 18/19 August, should be sufficient to deal with such a force. Within two days this Japanese unit had been annihilated by the 1st Marines for a loss of 34 men killed, in the battle of Alligator Creek. The Japanese jungle-fighter had met his match at last.

The third week of August saw the inconclusive battle of the East Solomons. Yamamoto, with a strong force, including three carriers, was covering the passage of transports reinforcing western Guadalcanal with another 1,500 men. The Americans sank the light carrier *Ryujo* and several other vessels,[1] but failed to hit the *Shokaku* or the *Zuikaku*. The *Enterprise* was badly damaged and the *Saratoga*, which was torpedoed on 31 August, took three months to repair. It was not much of a victory, even though it taught the Americans a good deal about aircraft tactics and carrier construction.

In mid-September a powerful thrust by General Kawaguchi was repulsed by the Marines in the Battle of Edson's Ridge, the central feature of the American perimeter. The battle cost the Japanese 2,000 of the 9,000 men they then had on Guadalcanal. American

---

[1] A B-17 sank a destroyer – to the astonishment of all concerned.

casualties numbered only about 200, but the second Japanese assault had very nearly won the crest of the ridge. It had been touch and go.

At sea a curious battle had developed. The Americans ruled the waves by day and the 'Tokyo Express' – light cruisers and destroyers full of troops – by night. Both sides were still trying hard to build up their land forces and were paying a heavy price in warships. On 15 September the Americans lost the big carrier *Wasp*, torpedoed while covering six transports which succeeded in landing the 7th Marine Regiment on the 18th.

The next crisis at sea was the indecisive Battle of Cape Esperance (11–12 October), in which the Americans, under a brilliant young Rear-Admiral, Norman Scott, got rather the better of Admiral Goto. While the sea-fight was being fought out, both sides succeeded in putting still more men ashore.

By mid-October the Marine aviators at Henderson Field were desperately short of fuel.[1] Moreover, the Americans were constantly being subjected to heavy bombardment from the sea. Well might Nimitz say (15 October): 'It now appears that we are unable to control the sea in the Guadalcanal area. Thus our supply of the positions will only be done at great expense to us. The situation is not hopeless, but it is certainly critical.'

At this juncture Nimitz replaced the conscientious but uninspiring Admiral Ghormley with Vice-Admiral 'Bill' Halsey. 'The announcement that he was now COMSOPAC was received on board ships of that force with cheers and rejoicings.'[2]

Admiral King reinforced Halsey with the new battleship *Indiana* and a task group from the Atlantic, besides 24 submarines. It was none too soon, for the Japanese, who were planning to take Henderson Field, had fixed 22 October as the day when it should be theirs once more.

At this time the depredations of German U-boats in the Atlantic and the claims of Operation *Torch*,[3] were engrossing the attention of the Joint Chiefs of Staff, but on 24 October President Roosevelt himself came to the support of King and MacArthur, ruling that Guadalcanal must be reinforced, and that speedily.

The Japanese land offensive, which had opened on 20 October, had

---

[1] The Americans were reduced to fitting a submarine, *Amberjack*, to carry 9,000 gallons of gasoline and 10 tons of bombs.

[2] Morison: *The Two-Ocean War*, p. 190.

[3] The landings in North Africa.

been firmly met. The Marines, reinforced by Army units, beat off every attack on the airfield and gave Admiral Kincaid time to intervene. In the battle which takes its name from the malarious island of Santa Cruz,[1] the Japanese had the *Shokaku* put out of action for nine months and lost about 100 planes, but sank the new carrier *Hornet* and damaged the *Enterprise* at a time when the other American carrier in the Pacific, *Saratoga*, was under repair. Even so the Americans had gained time to make ready for the next crisis.

The opening round of the sea battle of Guadalcanal was fought on the night 12/13 November. It was a desperate and confused affair in which the Japanese lost a battleship (*Hiei*) and two destroyers, and the Americans two light cruisers, and four destroyers. Two Rear-Admirals, Daniel J. Callaghan, the commander of the US force and Norman Scott, were killed.

In round two, Vice-Admiral Tanaka reinforced the Japanese garrison by means of a super 'Tokyo Express' – 11 destroyers and 11 transports. American airmen from *Enterprise* and from Henderson Field sank six of the transports, but Tanaka pushed on with admirable *sang-froid* and actually landed the men from four of his transports by literally running the ships ashore! His destroyers picked up some 5,000 survivors from the others.

Meanwhile American aircraft had sunk the heavy cruiser *Kinugasa*.

Round three was yet another night battle, in which Rear-Admiral Willis Augustus ('Ching') Lee defeated Kondo[2] and sank the battleship *Kirishima*. Things were at last beginning to go rather better for the Americans, and indeed the Japanese Navy would now have given up Guadalcanal if Tojo would have let them.

Admiral Halsey calls this 'a decisive American victory by any standard'. His comments are significant.

'If our ships and planes had been routed in this battle, if we had lost it, our troops on Guadalcanal would have been trapped as were our troops on Bataan. We could not have reinforced them or relieved them. Archie Vandegrift would have been our "Skinny" Wainwright, and the infamous Death March would have been repeated ... Unobstructed, the enemy would have driven south, cut our supply lines to New Zealand and Australia and enveloped them.'[3]

---

[1] The site of 'Bali-Hai' in the musical comedy *South Pacific*.

[2] Kondo, a favourite of Yamamoto's, is described by the Japanese Admiral Hara as 'the British gentleman sort of man'.

[3] Admiral William Halsey and J. Bryan: *Admiral Halsey's Story*, (McGraw, 1947).

Halsey now created a new striking force, mainly heavy cruisers and destroyers.

Before this force, under Rear-Admiral Carlton H. Wright, had time to train together, it had to take on the tenacious Tanaka and another 'Tokyo Express' in the battle of Tassafaronga. It was yet another night fight, and this time the Japanese though badly outnumbered, came off best.

At 2316 hours the destroyer *Fletcher*, which had the latest kind of radar

'... picked up Tanaka's force, broad on the port bow, steaming slowly along the Guadalcanal shore toward the jumping-off place. The squadron commander in *Fletcher* asked permission for his four van destroyers to fire torpedoes. Wright hesitated for four minutes before granting it, and so lost the battle. For, by the time the torpedoes were launched, about 2321, the Japanese column had passed the Americans on a contrary course and the range was too great for American torpedoes to overtake them.'[1]

The Japanese lost one destroyer. The Americans had the heavy cruiser *Northampton* sunk, while the *Minneapolis*, *New Orleans* and *Pensacola* were all so badly damaged that they were out of action for the next nine months.

Morison, with his customary candour, describes this as 'a sharp defeat, inflicted on an alerted and superior cruiser force by a surprised and inferior destroyer force whose decks were cluttered with freight'.[2] But at least the Japanese had been prevented from landing their reinforcements, and for this the ungrateful Japanese higher command removed Tanaka shortly afterwards.

In December both sides continued to reinforce their garrisons. General Imamura, who had 60,000 men in Rabaul, was able to spare two divisions. But by the end of the month the Japanese on Guadalcanal were practically starving. On 19 January General Patch, who had succeeded General Vandegrift (9 December), began a two-division thrust towards Cape Esperance, driving the remnants of the Japanese before him and mopping up the island at the rate of about a mile a day.

The Japanese were still dangerous. On 22 January 1943, for example, the Inagaki unit made a suicidal attack:

[1] Morison: p. 209–10.
[2] Morison: p. 210.

'On the eve of the sortie, at midnight, all the assembled men sing the *Kimigayo*, the sad and solemn hymn to the Emperor, then give three *banzais* for his eternal prosperity. The company bows in the direction of the Imperial Palace. While the American loudspeakers, which are set up above the lines, continue to repeat in Japanese the invitation to capitulate, the two hundred men, including the sick and the wounded who have still survived, rush towards death in a supreme attack . . .'[1]

On 4 January Tojo at last decided to evacuate the island. On 23 January reconnaissance planes reported large numbers of warships and transports at Rabaul and Buin. Halsey deduced that this portended a further attempt at reinforcement. In the hope of luring Yamamoto out, he himself sent up four transports with a strong escort. The bait was not taken, but the covering group under Rear-Admiral Robert C. Giffen was severely attacked from the air and lost the heavy cruiser *Chicago* in the so-called Battle of Rennell Island.

By 6 February the Japanese had completed the evacuation of 11,000 men. Not until the 9th did the Americans realize that they had gone, proof of the skill with which the Japanese carried out their withdrawal.

Admiral Tanaka attributed the Japanese defeat to lack of an overall operation plan, committing forces piecemeal, terrible communications, unendurable relations with the Army, belittling the enemy, and inferiority in the air. 'We stumbled along from one error to another, while the enemy grew wise.'[2]

In this long, desperate and precarious struggle Japanese losses on land, perhaps 20,000 were far greater than those of the Americans, which were not severe. At sea both sides lost precisely 24 warships. Strategically the battle turned the tide of war in the South Pacific. The myth that in the jungle the Japanese soldier was invincible had been dispelled by the us Marine Corps.

[1] Flower and Reeves: p. 716 quoting the newspaper *Yomiuri*.
[2] Morison: p. 211 n., summarizing *Japan's Losing Struggle for Guadalcanal*, U.S. Naval Inst. Proceedings LXXXII (1956).

CHAPTER TWENTY-FOUR

THE BOMBER OFFENSIVE
AGAINST GERMANY

1939

18 Dec.	Unsuccessful raid on the Schillig Roads.

1940

Mar.	Raid on Sylt.
Apr.	Decision to confine Bomber Command mainly to night action.
11 May	British bomb Freiburg in Baden.
15 May	Raid on the Ruhr by 99 British bombers.
Sept.	In the Battle of Britain, Fighter Command defeats the daylight bombers.
Dec.	RAF bomb Mannheim. Their first concentrated bombing attack.

1941

Mar.	*Scharnhorst* and *Gneisenau* arrive in Brest.
Mar.	Crisis in the Battle of the Atlantic. Bomber Command diverted to targets of naval significance.
Aug.	The Butt Report on night bombing.
Dec.	Berlin bombed.

1942

Feb.	Escape of *Scharnhorst* and *Gneisenau*.
23 Feb.	Harris takes over as Commander-in-Chief, Bomber Command.
Mar.	*Gee*, a radar aid to navigation, comes into operational use.
Mar.	Successful raid on the Renault works at Billancourt.
Mar.	Area attack on Lübeck.
30 May	1,000 bomber raid on Cologne.
Aug.	Arrival of the American Eighth Air Force in Britain. The Pathfinder Force created.
Nov.	Attacks on Genoa, Turin and Milan.

Dec.   *Oboe*, a radar aid to bombing or marking, comes into service.

1943

Jan.   The Casablanca Conference.

Jan.   Attacks on Berlin.

Jan.   H25, a radar aid to navigation and bomb-aiming, comes into service.

Mar./Jul. The Battle of the Ruhr.

16/17 May Breaching of the Möhne and Eder dams.

20/21 Jun. Attack on Friedrichshafen.

24/30 Jul. Hamburg bombed.

17/18 Aug. Attack on V weapon factory at Peenemunde.

14 Oct.   USAAF's disastrous Schweinfurt raid.

18/19 Nov.
mid-Mar.
1944   The Battle of Berlin.

Dec.   Attacks on V.1 sites on the French coast.

Dec.   The P.51B (Mustang) long-range fighter comes into service.

1944

Feb.   German bombing raids on London.

Feb./Apr. Indecisive offensive against the German aircraft industry.

Mar.   German air defences get on top of the bombers by night, but not by day.

May/Mar. 1945 Successful offensive against German oil-production.

13 Jun.   V.1 attacks on London.

Jul.   Allied break-out from Normandy, overruns many German air bases and their early warning chain.

Aug.   The Allies win command of the air.
          The Russians take the Roumanian oilfields.

Sep.   V.1 sites in France overrun.

12 Nov.   Sinking of the *Tirpitz*.

1945

Jan./Feb. Bomber Command destroys the Leuna oil plant.

13/14 Feb. Bombing of Dresden.

'If a single bomb drops on Berlin you can call me Meyer!'
HERMANN GÖRING.

THERE were some to whom the experience of the First World War revealed 'the shape of things to come'. One of these was General Smuts, who wrote in 1917 that the air arm 'can be used as an independent means of war operations. Nobody who witnessed the attack on London on 11 July[1] could have any doubt on this point ... As far as at present can be foreseen there is absolutely no limit to the scale of its future independent war use. And the day may not be far off when aerial operations with their devastation of enemy lands and destruction of industrial and populous centres on a vast scale may become the principal operations of war, to which the other forms of military and naval operations may become secondary and subordinate.'[2]

The theories of the Italian Brigadier General Giulio Douhet, author of *The Command of the Air* (1921), had a very considerable influence – especially among airmen. While preoccupied with strategic bombing, he had no great opinion of aircraft as tactical weapons. He saw that command of the air must be won, but thought that this would be the result of offensive bombing rather than aerial combat. He considered that once the air force won command, superiority on the ground and at sea must follow automatically. A power that had once lost command of the air could not regain it, because the bombing of her aircraft industry would prevent any revival. Douhet considered that the rôle of armies and navies, at least initially, must be defensive, and that this should guide a nation in the deployment of its resources: 'resist on the ground in order to mass for the offensive in the air'. He saw too that an air force which has the initiative can seek out the enemy in his bases, where he is most vulnerable, and destroy his planes and installations on the ground.

[1] A formation of 14 Gothas dropped 118 high explosive bombs on London, scored a direct hit on Liverpool Street Station, and killed and wounded 588 people.
[2] Quoted by Harris: *Bomber Offensive*, p. 17.

It followed that the side that got its blow in first had an enormous advantage. 'Whatever its aims, the side which decides to go to war will unleash all its aerial forces in mass against the enemy nation the instant the decision is taken, without waiting to declare war formally. . .'

Douhet underrated the fighter as a defence against the bomber, and grossly underestimated the tonnage of bombs required to knock out a target. 'He considered 500 tons of bombs (mostly gas) quite sufficient to destroy a large city and its inhabitants.'[1] He gave little guidance on the vital subject of target selection, though he did point out that it is 'the most difficult and delicate task in aerial warfare'.

The beginning of the war found the RAF's Bomber Command with very little to back it in the way of reserves or training organization. It was fortunate indeed that there was no bombing campaign in the autumn of 1939 to use up the few trained crews available. In any case the 'Rules of Warfare' as agreed by the Washington Conference on the Limitation of Armaments (1922) laid down that:

> 'Aerial bombardment for the purpose of terrorizing the civilian population, of destroying or damaging private property not of a military character, or of injuring non-combatants, is prohibited.'[2]

Despite this prohibition, and its own inadequate resources, Bomber Command gradually began to make itself felt from 1940 onwards. The RAF inflicted considerable damage on the invasion barges when a German invasion seemed imminent. Later good work was done against French factories working for the enemy, but the main attack on Germany did not begin until 1943. As it mounted the *Luftwaffe* was compelled to use an ever increasing part of its strength for the defence of the Fatherland, with a decisive effect on the campaigns in Sicily and Italy and, later, Normandy as well as the Eastern Front.

After the fall of France Britain had three alternatives. One was to surrender – unthinkable; a second was to accept a stalemate which was tantamount to admitting defeat; the third was to attack Germany by a bombing offensive, for any army that Britain alone could raise was unlikely to be able to invade the continent in the teeth of the German Army. The War Cabinet, advised by the Chiefs of Staff, advised the build-up of a force of 4,000 heavy bombers – a number that was never in fact reached.

[1] Brodie: *Strategy in the Missile Age*, p. 89.
[2] Article 22, Part II.

In 1940 Bomber Command was still small, and its aircraft were obsolescent. It was not in its power to strike with any precision, as General Fuller has suggested should have been done, at the sources of German industrial power, oil and coal. However immoral it may be to measure the success of a bombing offensive by the acreage devastated, the Bomber Command of those days was not a sufficiently sophisticated weapons system to have any alternative. If Mr Churchill was compelled to use a bludgeon, it was for lack of a rapier.[1]

With only a very small bomber force it was good tactics to make concentrated attacks on one target at a time. It was not until December 1940 that Bomber Command first put this idea into action in an attack on Mannheim, which did considerable damage. Thus encouraged, they later made further concentrated attacks on Bremen, Wilhelmshaven, Kiel and other suitable targets.

With the arrival of the two German battle cruisers, *Scharnhorst* and *Gneisenau*, at Brest in March 1941, much of the British bomber force which might otherwise have been bombing Germany was tied up in attacking them. It was a relief to the RAF when, in February 1942, they made their escape up the Channel. Soon after that Sir Arthur Harris took over Bomber Command.

Harris found that he had at his command 69 heavy, about 259 medium and 50 light bombers, a total of no more than 378 serviceable aircraft with crews. The war had been going on for about two and a half years but Bomber Command had not really begun to expand. It was obvious that the Americans would not be able to develop their full strength for another year.

On the night 28/29 March 234 aircraft dropped 144 tons of incendiaries and 160 tons of high explosives on Lübeck, an industrial town of secondary importance, and destroyed about half of it by fire, for a loss of 13 aircraft. At this time Bomber Command was receiving only about 200 new aircraft a month, so that even such relatively light casualties were serious. This was followed by successful attacks on Rostock, with its Heinkel factory. Again casualties were light (12 aircraft lost from 521 sorties) and the morale of Bomber Command rose as they began to get results. Already Germany had suffered about as much bomb damage as England.

The first of the 'thousand bomber raids' took place at the end of

[1] 'After the extent of devastation in a number of towns had been compared with the loss of output in these towns over a period of months, a definite correlation was found between acreage of concentrated devastation and loss of man hours; ...' (Harris: p. 87).

May, when 1,101 assorted aircraft including 1,074 bombers took part in an attack on Cologne. The defences were saturated and 600 acres were devasted for the loss of 39 aircraft. The Prime Minister, who above all wanted to get on with the war, was convinced that we had now 'an immensely powerful weapon'.[1] This was the beginning of the real Bomber Offensive, and compelled the Germans to redeploy much of the *Luftwaffe*, which had been trained for army co-operation, to defend their industry. It has been estimated that when in 1941 the Germans invaded Russia, 50 per cent of their aircraft were available to help the army. By the end of 1943 this had fallen to 20 per cent.

In August a Pathfinder Force came into being, which led to more concentrated bombing. The introduction of efficient marker bombs gave a clearer aiming-point to the follow-up bombers.

By December 1942 the British had an average front-line strength of 78 medium and 261 heavy bombers. The introduction of four-engined aircraft, absolutely necessary though it was, had tended to slow down the process of expansion. The Lancaster, the best bomber the British had, was then the only aircraft in the world which could take the 22,000 lb. 'Grand Slam' bombs.[2] It is interesting to note that 37 per cent of the pilots were from dominion and colonial Air Forces, Canada contributing a particularly high percentage. Polish, French and Czech pilots also played an important part.

In January 1943 attacks were made on Berlin by 388 Lancasters. The weather was unfavourable with haze and snow, and the damage was scattered. To attack the German capital involved 4 hours' flying over very heavily defended country, and Bomber Command was still not really strong enough for the job.

In January and February, at the insistence of the Admiralty, the U-boat bases at Lorient and St Nazaire were severely attacked. The towns were devastated, but in vain, for the U-boat pens with their reinforced roofs proved too strong for any bomb then available.

The Casablanca Conference of January 1943 laid down the basic strategy for the Combined Bomber Offensive. The primary objectives were to be:

> 'The progressive destruction and dislocation of the German military, industrial, and economic system, and the undermining of the morale of the German people to a point where their capacity for armed resistance is fatally weakened.'

[1] Harris: p. 112.
[2] This and the 12,000 lb. *Tallboy* were Professor Barnes Wallis's 'specials'.

The Battle of the Ruhr began on the night 5/6 March 1943, with an accurate and successful attack by 442 aircraft on Essen, which hitherto had proved more or less invulnerable. Five more attacks were made during the following months and by the end of July Krupps' factories had been severely damaged. Duisburg, Bochum, Gelsenkirchen, Oberhausen, Mülheim, Wuppertal, Remscheid, München-Gladbach, Krefeld, Münster, Aachen, Düsseldorf and Cologne were all heavily bombed.

Wing Commander Guy Gibson with 19 Lancasters attacked two vital dams, supplying water to the Ruhr, on the night 16/17 May. A special mine designed by Barnes Wallis of Vickers Armstrong was used, and Gibson's No. 617 Squadron of No. 5 Group was raised and trained for this particular rôle. The lightly defended Möhne Dam was breached and 130,000,000 gallons of water were lost. The attack on the Eder Dam was also successful and 202,000,000 tons of water were released to flood parts of Kassel. Eight planes were lost. On the night of 20/21 June the RAF carried out a successful raid on the former Zeppelin works at Friedrichshafen on Lake Constance. This was a radar factory. The defences were light, as the place was not thought to be in danger on a short June night. The bombers flew on to North Africa to refuel and rearm, and bombed the Italian naval base at Spezia on the way home.

The devastation of Hamburg began on the night 24/25 July, when some 700 aircraft attacked and started terrible fires. Harris quotes[1] a German official document which describes the results when, two days later, the British added fuel to the flames with results 'beyond all human imagination'.

'The alternative dropping of block busters (4,000 lb. high capacity bombs) high explosives, and incendiaries, made fire-fighting impossible, small fires united into conflagrations in the shortest time and these in turn led to the fire storms ... Through the union of a number of fires, the air gets so hot that on account of its decreasing specific weight, it reaches a terrific momentum, which in its turn causes other surrounding air to be sucked towards the centre. By that suction, combined with the enormous difference in temperature (600–1000 degrees centigrade) tempests are caused which go beyond their meteorological counterparts (20–30 centigrades). In a built-up area the suction could not follow its shortest

[1] Harris: pp. 173–4.

course, but the overheated air stormed through the street with immense force, taking along not only sparks but burning timber and roof beams, so spreading the fire farther and farther, developing in a short time into a fire typhoon such as was never before witnessed, against which every human resistance was quite useless.'

When on the night 29/30 July Bomber Command attacked again, the water supply, gas and electricity failed. From the economic point of view the city was knocked out: nearly a million of the inhabitants fled. The dead numbered 40,000 and the injured nearly as many. Hamburg's four great shipbuilding yards, which had turned out many U-boats, had been severely damaged and 6,200 acres of the built-up area had been obliterated by 7,196 tons of bombs.

Bomber Command, which had thoroughly confused the defences by the use of 'Window',[1] had lost 57 planes, or 2·4 per cent of those employed.

Colonel Adolf Galland tells us that:

'A wave of terror radiated from the suffering city and spread throughout Germany. Appalling details of the great fires were recounted, and their glow could be seen for days from a distance of a hundred and twenty miles. A stream of haggard, terrified refugees flowed into the neighbouring provinces. In every large town people said, 'What happened to Hamburg yesterday can happen to us tomorrow.' Berlin was evacuated with signs of panic. In spite of the strictest reticence in the official communiqués, the Terror of Hamburg spread rapidly to the remotest villages of the Reich.

Psychologically the war at that moment had perhaps reached its most critical point. Stalingrad had been worse, but Hamburg was not hundreds of miles away on the Volga, but on the Elbe, right in the heart of Germany.

After Hamburg in the wide circle of the political and military command could be heard the words: 'The war is lost.'[2]

Speer, the German minister for war production, thought that six more attacks might bring Germany to her knees.

The attack on Hamburg was followed when the nights grew longer

---

[1] Metal strips dropped to confuse the defender's radar.
[2] Adolf Galland. *The First and the Last*, p. 220–1. (Methuen, 1955).

with another three bombings of Berlin, which was visited by 1,647 aircraft in 10 days. There was a considerable exodus of the inhabitants.

Meanwhile the Germans had been working at Peenemunde on a secret weapon. Their research establishment and factory were working on a rocket weighing 80 tons and with a warhead containing 10 tons of explosives. In an effective attack by 600 planes on the night of 17/18 August heavy damage was done and many of the scientists and staff were killed.

The American Eighth Air Force came to Europe believing in precision bombing in daylight by 'Flying Fortresses', with or without fighter escort. German fighters exacted a terrible toll, and in October 1943 the disastrous raid on Schweinfurt, coming after other heavy casualties, compelled them to call a halt. On 14 October 291 Flying Fortresses set off to attack the greatest centre of German ball-bearing production. Beyond Aachen they were outside the range of fighter cover. The Fortresses did severe damage, but 60 were shot down by German cannon and rocket-firing fighters. Of the 231 bombers that returned 130 had been damaged. The Americans retained their faith in daylight bombing, but realized the need for a long-range fighter. The P.51 Mustang, which the Americans had rejected in 1940 because of its unimpressive performance, was given a Rolls Royce engine, and, incredible though it may seem, was in service by December. It surpassed the German fighters in speed, range and manoeuvrability, and swiftly reversed an apparently disastrous situation. Before the end of the war 14,000 Mustangs were produced.

During the winter 1943–4, despite awful weather, Bomber Command made the 16 attacks on the German capital which are called the Battle of Berlin. Cloud hindered photographic reconnaissance and it was difficult to tell how much damage was being done. Berlin was not devastated as Hamburg had been, but about 5,000 acres of the city were obliterated, for a loss of 300 aircraft. By the end the German night fighters had got the better of the bombers.

On 9 February 1944 the Bishop of Chichester, speaking in the House of Lords, condemned the area bombing of Berlin, where it was reported that 74,000 people had been killed and 3,000,000 rendered homeless. 'The policy', he declared, 'is obliteration, openly acknowledged.' His remarks were in excellent taste, though it is just as well that he was not in the War Cabinet.

In January first priority had been given to bombing the German aircraft industry. The growing strength of the *Luftwaffe* 'threatened both the bomber offensive itself and the projected invasion of Europe'.[1] The Eighth USAAF was to attack airframe and other aircraft factories, while Bomber Command attacked industrial towns where aircraft component factories were located. Most of these were further afield than the Ruhr. In the period February to April 1944 the Allies spent most of their bomber effort against the aircraft industry. This was a good idea in theory, but it did not work very well in practice, because the Germans proceeded to disperse their plants. It may be that the Germans were deprived of as much as 20 per cent of their production by this offensive, but it was indecisive.

By April 1944 the Allies had a formidable striking force. On average 1,119 heavy bombers were available. But from April to September 1944 *Overlord* had priority and the strategic bombing offensive, which had lasted a year, had to be abandoned for the time being. This gave German industry a lull of six months in which to repair the ravages of the past year. The contribution of the air to the invasion of Normandy is discussed elsewhere: suffice it here to say that it was decisive.

On 8 June it was decided to make German oil production, which had previously been considered to be out of range, a top-priority target. Between the end of June 1944 and March 1945 the Allies made 555 attacks on 135 targets, which included every known synthetic-fuel plant and major refinery. The effect on German oil production is obvious from this simple chart:

	Average in tons
May, 1944	662,000
June	422,000
December	260,000
March, 1945	80,000

The production of aviation gasoline went down from 170,000 tons per month in mid 1944 to 52,000 in the following March. The effect on the operations of the *Luftwaffe* may be imagined. Training became practically impossible. A large number of aircraft were grounded simply for lack of fuel. Fewer and fewer fighters were available to meet the bombers that were doing all this damage.

The Army also suffered and 'in the last stages of the war huge

[1] Harris: p. 165.

numbers of German tanks were unable to reach the fighting areas, or were abandoned on battlefields, for lack of fuel. Before the end, wood or coal-burning gas generators, such as had been only moderately successful on buses and trucks, had been put on some fifty tanks.'[1]

Dresden because of its beauty, was still considered safe. Perhaps 200,000 refugees had swollen the number of the inhabitants which, pre-war, had been 630,000; and it was by far the biggest German city still intact. In February 1945 it was the main centre of communications for the German armies on the southern sector of the Eastern Front. It was in addition a centre of industry. On the night of 13/14 it was attacked by 800 bombers with results that recalled those at Hamburg in July 1943. The casualties have been variously estimated at 250,000 and 400,000.[2] The effect of Operation *Thunderclap* on morale throughout the Reich was grave in the extreme.

The losses of Bomber Command throughout the war were very heavy. It has been estimated that 7,122 aircraft were lost, and that 55,573 aircrew and 1,570 ground staff lost their lives. Some 22,000 were injured and another 11,000 were taken prisoner. USAAF losses were 23,000 planes and 120,000 battle casualties in over 2,300,000 sorties.

It has been said that German war production increased, despite the bombing, between mid-1942 and mid-1944. This is to ignore the fact that Allied bombing took a long time to get into its stride. In 1942 an average of only 6,000 tons a month was being dropped on Germany. By 1944 this had gone up to 131,000 tons. And there had been a corresponding improvement in operational techniques, notably the use of radio detection devices. Again, the German war economy did not really get going until mid-1942. Until that time few women were employed, and industry was operating largely on a single-shift basis, so that it is fair comment to say that 'judged by the standard of British industrial mobilization the German economy never attained anything like its full war potential.'[3]

The strategic bombing offensive brought the German war economy to the verge of complete collapse. It is true that this result was only achieved at the very end of the war. On the other hand the offensive was virtually halted for six months in order to support *Overlord*.

---

[1] Brodie: p. 112.
[2] c.f. Rumpf: *The Bombing of Germany*, p. 99, for the impossibility of calculating the number of dead.
[3] Brodie: p. 110.

There is no doubt that strategic bombing could have brought German industry to a halt much sooner, had the war leaders had more faith in its potential, and had the selection of targets been more intelligent.[1] That this would have shortened the war and saved Allied lives cannot be doubted.

The bombing of cities, although it could affect production temporarily, is generally held now to have been indecisive, but at the time when it was begun it was the most effective technique available.

The V.2, the submarine, the tank, and a multitude of other weapons, influenced the course of the Second World War, but none had a more dominating influence than the heavy bomber.

[1] For example there was no all-out attack on the German chemical industry, which might have brought very good results.

CHAPTER TWENTY-FIVE

RUSSIA, 1943

1943

23 Jan.	British take Tripoli.
31 Jan.	German surrender at Stalingrad.
14/16 Feb.	Russians retake Kharkov.
12 May	The Allies take Tunis and Bizerta.
5 Jul.	Operation *Citadel* begins.
10 Jul.	Allied invasion of Sicily.
15 Jul.	Russians counter-attack towards Orel.
25 Jul.	Overthrow of Mussolini.
3 Aug.	Russian offensive begins.
4 Aug.	Germans evacuate Orel.
5 Aug.	Russians take Belgorod.
22 Aug.	Germans abandon Kharkov.
3 Sep.	Allied invasion of Italy.
22 Sep.	Russians occupy Poltava.
25 Sep.	Russians retake Smolensk.
14 Oct.	Malinovsky takes Zaporozhe.
23 Oct.	Tolbukhin captures Melitopol.
25 Oct.	Malinovsky takes Dnepropetrovsk.
3 Nov.	Directive No. 51.
6 Nov.	Russians retake Kiev.

1944

Feb./Mar.	Koniev encircles Korsun Salient.
5 Feb.	Vatutin takes Rovno.
30 Mar.	Model takes over Army Group South.
	Manstein dismissed.

GUDERIAN: 'How many people do you think even know where Kursk is?... Why do we want to attack in the East at all this year?'

HITLER: 'You're quite right. Whenever I think of this attack my stomach turns over.'[1]

THE Allied victories of November 1942 brought a fundamental difference to the conduct of the war. Up to now Hitler had held the initiative; henceforth it was the Allies who would rough hew the shape of events.

The Stalingrad surrender had been a wounding blow to the Germans, Dictator and people alike. Hitler could not comprehend why Paulus had not blown his brains out rather than fall alive into the hands of the Russians. It was the first time a German Field-Marshal had ever surrendered. The nation lamented its loss in three day's mourning.

There was to be no spring offensive in 1943. Rather it was to be a question of warding off renewed Russian attacks. By this time the Italians were demoralized. The Hungarians and Roumanians were little use except for hunting down partisans in the back areas. The Bulgarians now appeared to be the most reliable of Germany's European Allies.

The story of the Eastern Front in 1943 is the story of the great Russian victories at Kursk, Orel and Kharkov, which sent the Germans reeling back along the whole front from Moscow to the Black Sea. On the Northern front things remained quiet while these great events were taking place.

It will be recalled that on 6 February Hitler had given Manstein permission to withdraw Army Group Don to the line of the rivers Mius and Donetz. The Russians followed up and took Kharkov (14–16 February). Through the gap of 100 miles between the flanks of Army Groups B and Don the Soviet armoured group under Colonel-General Popov wheeled south to cut Manstein's communications,

[1] Guderian: *Panzer Leader*, p. 309.

severing the railway from Dnepropetrovsk to Stalino (13 February) and reached the junction at Sinelnikovo (19 February).

In this situation Manstein displayed his talents to great advantage. On 18 February he turned on the Russians and in eight days' bitter fighting crushed the Popov Group between First Panzer Army and the re-created Fourth Panzer Army. The Germans reached Kharkov once more on 11 March. The end of this counter-offensive left their Army of the South holding the line of the Donetz as far as Belgorod, while to their north the Russians held a great salient west of Kursk. There followed the lull which the Russian spring, with the thaw and the mud, imposed on the combatants.

To the Germans, as Alan Clark[1] shrewdly observes

'The War meant the war in the East. The bombing, the U-boat campaigns, the glamour of the Afrika Korps, these were incidentals when over two million fathers, husbands, brothers were engaged day and night in a struggle with the *Untermensch*!'[2]

But some of these incidentals were beginning to hurt too. It was in January that U.S. Flying Fortresses first bombed the Reich in daylight. The Afrika Korps breathed its last in May. July saw the Sicily landings and the destruction of Hamburg. The tide that had turned in November 1942 was to flow with ever increasing power towards Germany throughout 1943; never again would Hitler's regiments see the Volga or the Caucasus. Yet the German position was far from hopeless. The retreat from the Don and the Caucasus and the withdrawal of Army Group Centre (February and March) had shortened the line and had allowed Hitler to build up a considerable reserve.

General Guderian had been recalled to active service and appointed Inspector-General of Armoured Troops with direct access to the *Führer* (28 February 1943). With the support of Albert Speer, the Munitions Minister, he set to work to reform the German armoured formations. In April the factories at Schweinfurt, Cassel and Friedrichshafen were turning out the Panzer IV at the rate of 1,955 a month, and the new Tigers and Panthers were beginning to come into production. The anti-aircraft defences of these towns were strengthened to protect them from the bomber offensive.

As spring turned to summer Hitler's generals put forward their plans for the 1943 campaign. Zeitzler and von Kluge were for a

---

[1] *Barbarossa.*
[2] Sub-human.

double envelopment of the huge Russian salient west of Kursk. Model opposed this on the grounds that the Russians had prepared a strong defence in great depth. Guderian was anxious to build up strength against the day of the Anglo-American invasion. At Berlin on 31 May a revealing scene took place:

'After the conference I seized Hitler's hand and asked him if I might be allowed to speak to him. He said I might and I urged him earnestly to give up the plan for an attack on the Eastern Front; . . . the great commitment would certainly not bring us equivalent gains; our defensive preparations in the West were sure to suffer considerably. I ended with the question: "Why do you want to attack in the East at all this year?" Here Keitel joined in, with the words: "We must attack for political reasons." I replied: "How many people do you think even know where Kursk is? It's a matter of profound indifference to the world whether we hold Kursk or not. I repeat my question: Why do we want to attack in the East at all this year?" Hitler's reply was: "You're quite right. Whenever I think of this attack my stomach turns over."[1] Well it might.'

The attack took place nonetheless. Hitler decided that he needed one more big victory in Russia that would 'shine like a beacon around the world'. Operation Citadel,[2] began somewhat late in the campaigning season, on 5 July, and followed Zeitzler's plan for a double envelopment, the Ninth Army (Model) striking down from the north and the Fourth Panzer Army (Hoth) thrusting upwards against the base of the Russian salient.

The attack came as no surprise to the Russians. Marshal Zhukov, whose command included more than five infantry armies (or 'Combined-Arms Armies') and a Tank Army, had made his preparations with great thoroughness. His artillery was particularly formidable and amounted to 20,000 pieces, including 920 Katyushas and 6,000 x 76 mm. anti-tank guns.

The training of the men and the construction of defences in depth left little to be desired. Clark quotes a Russian captain's description of the way in which his brigade took advantage of the long respite the Germans allowed them. They

'anticipated five possible places where they (the Germans) may strike and at each of them we know alongside whom we shall be

[1] Guderian: pp. 308–9.
[2] Zitadelle.

271

fighting, our replacements and command posts. The brigade is situated in the rear, but our trenches and shelters are ready up in front, and the routes by which we are to get there are marked out. The ground, of which we have made a topographical survey, has been provided with guide marks. The depths of fords, the maximum loads of bridges are known to us. Liaison with division has been doubled, codes and signals are arranged. Often alerted by day or night, our men are familiarized with their task in any eventuality . . .'[1]

Never before had the Russians had so much time in which to lay their plans and to get set before the storm. The days of improvisation were behind them.

The German Order of Battle was impressive and included 17 Panzer divisions, nine of which were with Hoth: these included such renowned formations as the *Gross Deutschland, S.S. Leibstandarte, S.S. Das Reich*, and *S.S. Totenkopf* divisions.

On 5 July this mighty force rode forth to do battle according to the well-tried *Blitzkrieg* formula of 1939–40; a formula by now as familiar to Muscovite as to Teuton. The German armour advanced in the wedge formation, known as the *Panzerkeil*. The *Tigers* at the sharp end were too well-armoured frontally for the standard Russian L.30 anti-tank gun (76·2 mm.) to do them much harm, and many got deep into the Russian position, only to find themselves unsupported. For behind them the Panzer IVs had been hard hit, by mines as well as guns, and the infantry had experienced the greatest difficulty in following-up to protect the armour from the tank-killing squads ranging the battlefield by night.

The Achilles heel of some of the new German monster tanks – the 90 Porsche Tigers which were with Model – was now exposed. They had no machine-guns, and without infantry or light tanks to support them were soon in trouble. Guderian criticises them bitterly.

'Once they had broken into the enemy's infantry zone they literally had to go quail shooting with cannons. They did not manage to neutralize, let alone destroy, the enemy rifles and machine-guns, so that the infantry was unable to follow up behind them. By the time they reached the Russian artillery they were on their own. Despite showing extreme bravery and suffering unheard-of

[1] Clark: p. 290.

casualties, the infantry of Weidling's division did not manage to exploit the tank's success. Model's attack bogged down after some 6 miles. In the south our successes were somewhat greater but not enough to seal off the salient or to force the Russians to withdraw.'[1]

Rain on 5 July held up Hoth's advance, when he was about to cross a stream. The German tanks found themselves stuck in a swamp of mud under the direct fire of the enemy tanks and guns. Heavy casualties were suffered before they got going again on the 8th. In desperate fighting Hoth's men had by 11 July hacked a salient 15 miles wide and nine deep in Vatutin's line. But there had been no breakthrough and Zhukov still had his reserve, the Fifth Armoured Army, intact.

On 12 July Hoth concentrated what armour he could, some 600 tanks, and sent it in to pierce the last Russian belt of defences. They ran head-on into the fresh Fifth Tank Army – Clark aptly names it 'The Death Ride of the Fourth Panzer Army.' It was a rude shock to troops who had expected nothing worse than anti-tank guns supported by a few independent tank brigades. For eight hours the battle raged in clouds of dust and smoke. Evening found the Russians masters of the battlefield and all its booty. Next day Hitler announced to his generals that Operation *Citadel* was cancelled. The greatest tank battle in history was over, and the weapon which Guderian had striven so hard to reforge was shattered. 'It is,' wrote General Fuller, 'in no way an exaggeration to say that the defeat at Kursk was as disastrous to the Germans as had been their defeat at Stalingrad.'[2]

Though foiled, the Germans hoped that they had done enough damage to the Russians to be able to count on a breathing-space. They were deceived. In consequence of this miscalculation they began to withdraw their surviving Panzer divisions from the Kursk front.

The Russians now advanced on a broad front towards the Dnieper and took Kharkov on 23 August. In the south von Kleist began to pull back into the Crimea.

In the centre too the Germans were going back, methodically perhaps, but nevertheless retreating. On 22 September the Russians retook Poltava, and on the 25th Smolensk. By the end of September

---

[1] Guderian: p. 311.
[2] Fuller.

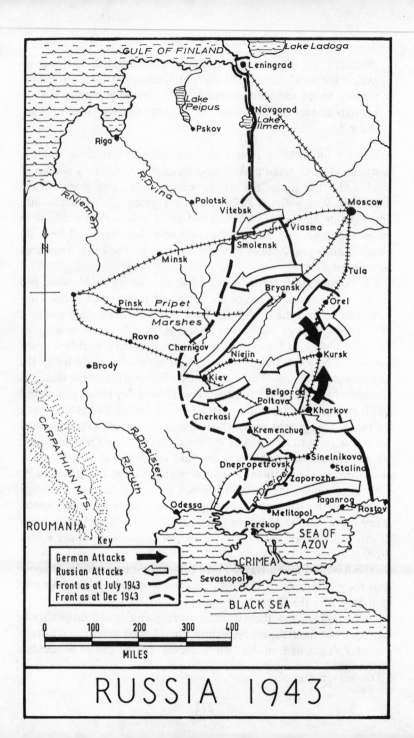

RUSSIA 1943

the Germans were back on their 'Winter Line' – the Dnieper – but the Russians kept up the pressure and early in October crossed the river north of Kiev, also taking Zaporozhe (14 October) and Melitopol (23 October). The pasage of the Dnieper was an astonishing feat.

'They had done it *s'khodu*, that is, 'on the march'. No sooner had they reached the Dnieper than thousands rowed or paddled across in small craft, on improvised rafts, on a few barrels strung together, or even by clinging on to planks or garden benches. The Germans, who had boasted of their impregnable *Ostwall* on the right bank of the Dnieper, were taken completely by surprise.'[1]

At this period the German army was dwindling away: it is estimated, for example, that in the three months after the end of *Citadel* Manstein's Army Group suffered 133,000 casualties and received only 33,000 replacements.[2]

The Russians on the other hand were well up to strength and were receiving a great deal of material from the Americans:

'from sheet steel to shoe leather; clothing, blankets, tents, radio sets; enormous quantities of tinned food, iron rations (even fruit juice!) and first-aid packs. Most important of all, perhaps, were the trucks – particularly the White half-track – which began to put the Red Army infantry on wheels for the first time in its history.'[3]

On 3 November Hitler issued Directive No. 51 in which he took a long and gloomy look at his future prospects.

'The hard and costly struggle against Bolshevism during the last two and a half years, which has involved the bulk of our military strength in the East, has demanded extreme exertions. The greatness of the danger and the general situation demanded it. But the situation has since changed. The danger in the East remains, but a greater danger now appears in the West; an Anglo-Saxon landing! In the East, the vast extent of the territory makes it possible for us to lose ground, even on a large scale, without a fatal blow being dealt to the nervous system of Germany.

'It is very different in the West! Should the enemy succeed in breaching our defences on a wide front here, the immediate

[1] Werth: *Russia at War*, p. 771.
[2] Clark: p. 320.
[3] Clark: p. 321.

consequences would be unpredicatable. Everything indicates that the enemy will launch an offensive against the Western front of Europe, at the latest in the spring, perhaps even earlier.'

He had decided to reinforce the defences of the West – 'particularly those places from which the long-range bombardment of England will begin.'[1] Weapons, manpower and materials were to be spent in an intensive effort to put the western defences from Denmark to France in good order. No units or formations were to be withdrawn from the West or from Denmark without his approval.

Early in November the First Ukrainian Front broke out from a bridgehead west of the Dnieper and liberated Kiev, the capital of the Ukraine (6 November), driving back the Fourth Panzer Army and gravely jeopardizing the left flank of Army Group South.

By this time some 5,700,000 Russians faced about 3,000,000 Germans on the Eastern Front, and the Soviets had great superiority in guns and tanks. Hitler's best strategy would probably have been to withdraw Army Group South to the line of the Bug, but he had not abandoned hope of recapturing Kiev and going over to the offensive in the Crimea.

Manstein managed to induce his master to provide him with a few fresh divisions, but it was beyond his power to repeat his exploits of the previous spring, though in a month's bitter fighting he won a temporary delay. About Christmas the Russians resumed the offensive and recovered the ground they had lost.

That winter brought no lull, for the Russians had sufficient reserves to keep up a continuous offensive.

On 15 January the Leningrad Front came to life and after a tremendous artillery barrage the Russians drove westwards in a two-pronged offensive. The German battle line, though strongly prepared with pillboxes and minefields, disintegrated after five days' fighting and by 19 January Leningrad was no longer beleaguered. Hitler's left flank was giving. The Finns could no longer be counted upon. On 13 February Hitler ordered Army Group North to fall back to the Panther Line on the borders of Estonia – the sector of the 'East Wall' running along the Narva River to Lake Peipus and Lake Pskov. Here they managed to hold the Russians (1 March). Thus after a 30 months' siege the Leningrad blockade was finally broken, to the indescribable relief of the 600,000 inhabitants who

---

[1] A reference to the V1 and V2 campaign. See Chapter 23.

still endured there. This was the first of the Russian triumphs of 1944 – the Year of the Ten Victories.

The second followed in February and March when Koniev, with the men of the 2nd Ukrainian Front, supported by Vatutin and his 1st Ukrainian Front, encircled the remnants of eight German divisions in the 'little Stalingrad' of the Korsun Salient on the Dnieper. Von Manstein broke through, but he could not keep open the escape corridor for long, and a frantic rout ensued as desperate men raced westwards. Perhaps 50,000 were killed or taken.

Meanwhile, in the centre, Vatutin took Rovno (5 February) and swung his tanks southwards to split Army Group South asunder in what the Russians called their 'Mud Offensive'. The crisis passed, for after eight months the almost continuous offensive lost its momentum. But the Russians were not held up until they had forced the Bug, the Dniester and the Pruth, and reached the northern frontier of Roumania. Ironically enough it was now, when a lull was about to develop, that Hitler dismissed von Manstein, who had weathered so many storms and had shown himself full of resource in the worst days. The *Führer* graciously decorated him and von Kleist, who fell at the same time, and said: 'All that counts now is to cling stubbornly to what we hold' . . . Hitler recognized in von Manstein a master of manoeuvre, but he felt that what was wanted now was someone who 'would dash round the divisions and get the very utmost out of the troops'. And the lot fell on that plain, blunt man, Field Marshal Walther Model.

CHAPTER TWENTY-SIX

SICILY AND ITALY (TO ROME)

1943

12 May	The end in Africa.
26 May	Air attack on Pantellaria begins.
11 Jun.	Surrender of Pantellaria.
3 Jul.	Heavy air attacks on the Sicilian airfields begun.
9 Jul.	*Night.* Airborne forces sieze Ponte Grande near Syracuse.
10 Jul.	Allied invasion of Sicily.
	Americans take Gela and Licata.
10/11 Jul.	British take Syracuse.
11 Jul.	Americans repel German armour at Gela.
13 Jul.	British take Augusta.
13/14 Jul.	British parachutists take Primosole Bridge.
16 Jul.	Churchill and Roosevelt make their joint appeal to the Italian people.
19 Jul.	500 US bombers drop 1,000 bombs on marshalling yards at Rome.
22 Jul.	Patton's troops take Palermo.
25 Jul.	Fall of Mussolini. General Badoglio forms a government.
28 Jul.	Fascist party dissolved.
13 Aug.	USAAF raids Rome.
14 Aug.	Italian Government proclaims Rome an open city.
Aug.	Eighth Army takes Catania.
17 Aug.	Capture of Messina.
3 Sep.	Invasion of Italy.
8 Sep.	Italy surrenders.
9 Sep.	Allied landing at Salerno.
10 Sep.	Germans occupy Rome.
12 Sep.	Mussolini liberated from the Gran Sasso.
1 Oct.	Americans capture Naples.
3/5 Oct.	Battle of Termoli.

1944

17/18 Jan.	Battle of the Garigliano begins.
23 Jan.	Anzio landing.
29 Jan./ *4 Feb.*	Offensive at Cassino.
15 Feb.	Cassino destroyed by bombing.
18 Feb.	Allies attack Cassino.
15/23 Mar.	Allied offensive at Cassino.
9 May	King Victor Emmanuel III of Italy abdicates in favour of his son, Prince Umberto.
4 Jun.	Fall of Rome.

The paramount task before us is, . . . using the bases on the African shore, to strike at the underbelly of the Axis in effective strength and in the shortest time.

WINSTON S. CHURCHILL. January 1943.

THE successful conclusion of the campaign in North Africa left the Allies with powerful forces available for some great offensive stroke. The time was not yet ripe for the invasion of France, but an attack on Sicily and Italy offered an attractive alternative. The loss of his African Empire had shaken Mussolini's Fascist régime, and had demoralized the Italian army. If one of the Axis partners, albeit the junior, could be driven out of the war, the morale of free people everywhere was bound to soar. Moreover, the capture of Sicily would secure the vital Mediterranean sea route to the Far East, which, even with the North African coast in Allied hands, was still vulnerable to Axis naval forces operating from Italian ports.

It was at the Casablanca Conference in mid-January that Roosevelt and Churchill agreed upon this strategy, besides fixing the date of the cross-Channel invasion of France for May 1944. It was intended to exploit the capture of Sicily in such a way as to tie down the maximum number of German divisions, but the object of the campaign was diversionary. It was, of course, never expected or intended that it would give the *coup de grâce* to Hitler's *Reich*.

It was at this Casablanca Conference that the Allied war leaders proclaimed their demand for the unconditional surrender of the Axis powers. This declaration has been roundly criticized by commentators from both sides, but although Goebbels made great play with it in his propaganda, it is doubtful whether it really prolonged the war. It is easy to say that it stiffened the resistance of the Germans, but this is to ignore the fact that the German people were, with the exception of a pitifully small band of anti-Nazi officers and idealists, solidly behind Hitler. While he was still in the saddle the penalties for any weakening were painfully obvious to his followers, and the pronouncements of Allied war leaders made very little difference.

On the other hand the Italians might have surrendered sooner had it not been for this declaration. The idea behind 'Unconditional Surrender' was not so black-hearted as some have pretended.[1] It is worth recalling what the Allied statesmen had in mind as expressed by Winston Churchill (30 June 1943):

'We, the United Nations, demand from the Nazi, Fascist and Japanese tyrannies unconditional surrender. By this we mean that their willpower to resist must be completely broken, and that they must yield themselves absolutely to our justice and mercy. It also means that we must take all those far-sighted measures which are necessary to prevent the world from being again convulsed,wrecked and blackened by their calculated plots and ferocious aggressions. It does not mean, and it never can mean, that we are to stain our victorious arms by inhumanity or by mere lust of vengeance, or that we do not plan a world in which all branches of the human family may look forward to what the American Declaration of Independence finely calls "life, liberty, and the pursuit of happiness".'

A great triangular rock of 10,000 square miles: that is the island of Sicily. On the north-east coast is the mighty volcano, Etna, 10,784 feet high, standing like a giant sentinel between Messina and the broad plain of Catania with its invaluable airfields. There are no navigable rivers, but Palermo, the capital, Catania, Syracuse, Messina and Augusta are all useful ports.

To defend the island, with its 600 miles of coastline, General Guzzoni had 12 divisions, two German[2] and ten Italian. Five of the latter were infantry and five were immobile coastal divisions. The garrison, though 350,000 strong, included only about 75,000 Germans. Even the German divisions were not fully mobile. The beach defences, pillboxes and barbed-wire, were not particularly formidable, and the defenders had few modern tanks. On the other hand the rugged, rolling country lent itself to defence.

For this expedition General Eisenhower was the supreme commander. Directly under him were three British commanders for sea,

---

[1] According to Ciano, the Italian press received the news of the Unconditional Surrender formula with 'easy ironies', though he himself thought it a serious thing (*Diary*, p. 575).

[2] 15th Panzer Grenadier, the remnants of the Afrika Corps, and Hermann Göring, which was still on its way to Sicily.

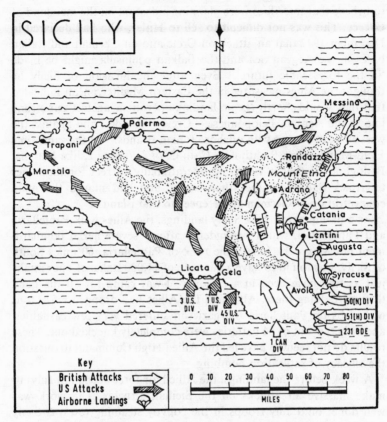

land and air: Admiral Sir Andrew Cunningham, General Alexander and Air Marshal Tedder.

The Allied land forces consisted of the US Seventh Army (General Patton) of two and a half divisions, and the British Eighth Army (General Montgomery) of four and a half divisions.

The naval side of the operation was extremely complicated, for convoys, totalling some 2,700 ships and craft, were to approach from practically every port between Gibraltar and Port Said.

The original Allied plan was to make two widely separate landings in the north-west and the south-east of the island. Montgomery rightly objected that this violated the principle of concentration of force, and the final plan called for two closely co-ordinated landings, the British 8th Army going in on the south-east and the US 7th Army on the south coast. Meanwhile the deception plan led the Germans to believe that the Allies were planning a descent on the mainland of Greece. This was not difficult to sell to Hitler, who had declared in December 1942 that an attack on Crete and on German and Italian bases in the Aegean Sea and the Balkan peninsula might be made 'in the foreseeable future'.[1] Even after the invasion of Sicily he thought the Allies measures in the Eastern Mediterranean indicated that they would shortly 'begin landing operations against our strong line in the Aegean, Peloponnese – Crete – Rhodes, and against the west coast of Greece with offshore Ionian Islands.'[2] At the same time Field-Marshal von Richthofen, C.-in-C. of *Luftflotte* 2, like Marshal Badoglio, felt that it would be operationally correct for the Allies to attack Sardinia rather than Sicily, and had moved the main concentration of German air defences to that island.

As a preliminary to the Sicily landings, the Allies took Pantellaria and Lampedusa, which surrendered after a severe aerial bombardment (18 May – 11 June). The rock of Pantellaria, 60 miles South of Sicily, was found to have a garrison of 11,000 Italians! They might just as well have been in a prisoner-of-war camp for all the good they were doing there. Although the Allies had dropped 6,570 tons of bombs on Pantellaria the garrison suffered very few casualties, and only two out of 54 batteries were completely knocked out. These results do not seem to have led the Allied High Command to question the efficacy of saturation bombing.

A week before the landings, the Allied air forces began (3 July) to make massive air attacks on the Sicilian airfields. The work was well done: on 9 July troops in the convoy steaming towards Sicily from Port Said could already see the summit of Etna looming over the horizon, and were gratified when not a single Axis plane put in an appearance to disturb their cruise.

The Mediterranean can make itself unpleasant if it chooses and, when it was already too late to postpone the landings, an unseasonable north wind brought foul weather and a short, heavy swell to throw the soldiers' stomachs into their mouths. Such discomforts bring their compensations: no Italian soldier expected a visit that night. But through the night the airborne troops were already winging their way towards their targets, notably the Ponte Grande, whose capture was vital to ensure the British advance on Syracuse.

This, the first Allied airborne operation of any size, was not

---

[1] Directive No. 47. 28 December 1942.
[2] Directive No. 48. 26 July, 1943.

spectacularly successful. The troops, British and American, were flown from Kairouan in Tunisia in some 400 transport aircraft and 137 gliders. Conditions were difficult because of the high wind, and many of the pilots had not had sufficient training. Many of the parachutists landed far from their objectives and a large number of gliders came down in the sea. But these were élite troops and the survivors carried out much useful work.

The seaborne landings, though opposed, were everywhere successful and rapid progress was made. On the morning of D-Day troops could be seen marching up the beach in column of threes, a spectacle one had hardly expected on the first day of the reconquest of Europe.

And far away in East Prussia Hitler informed his generals that *Citadel* – their Kursk offensive – must be called off immediately. Troops must be transferred from the Russian front to deal with the invasion of Sicily.[1]

Syracuse (10 July) and Augusta (13 July) were soon in British hands, and XIII Corps was advancing steadily towards Catania. By 13 July the leading troops were held up by an enemy rearguard at Lentini, and, to speed up the advance, landings were made that night to secure the bridges north of that town. No. 3 Commando landed from the sea at Agnone, and prevented the destruction of the Ponte dei Malati while at the same time the 1st Parachute Brigade and 151 Brigade[2] captured the Primosole Bridge over the Simeto, and gave the British an entrance to the Plain of Catania. These results were only achieved with considerable loss, owing to the presence in the area of part of the Hermann Göring division.

Firmly established on the slopes of Mount Etna, the Germans were now able to hold up the British advance, and the plain with the Gerbini airfields was to be disputed for nearly three weeks.

Meanwhile the Americans were making even more rapid progress, after beating off an armoured counter-attack by the Germans near Gela on the 11th.

On 22 July the Americans under Patton entered Palermo. The late General George S. Patton, Jr., (alias *Gorgeous Georgie*) was one of the more flamboyant characters of World War II. He was perhaps the most successful leader of armoured formations on the Allied side, combining the dash of an old-time cavalryman with the expertise of

[1] Mellenthin: *Panzer Battles*, p. 224.
[2] Three battalions of the Durham Light Infantry.

the modern panzer leader. He was careful of his turn-out, invariably wearing a highly polished helmet and a pair of pearl-handled revolvers. He had a genius for 'putting his foot in it', and distinguished himself in Sicily when, during a visit to a hospital, he slapped a soldier whom he thought to be malingering. No doubt Patton was suffering from nervous strain. Needless to say Eisenhower was acutely embarrassed, but he managed to save his temperamental subordinate from being sacrificed on the altar of democracy. The erring general was compelled to apologize not only to his victim and the hospital personnel but ordered to appear before the officers and representative groups of enlisted men of each division under his command 'to assure them that he had given way to impulse and respected their positions as fighting soldiers of a democratic nation'.[1] We are not told if that was good for discipline. A penitent Patton now grovelled before his chief. 'I am at a loss to find words with which to express my chagrin and grief at having given you, a man to whom I owe everything and for whom I would gladly lay down my life, cause to be displeased with me.'

It was General Bradley's opinion that the private whose face Patton slapped did more to win the war in Europe than any other private in the army! In Normandy Patton said: 'For God's sake, Brad, you've got to get me into this fight before the war is over, I'm in the doghouse now and I'm apt to die there unless I pull something spectacular to get me out.' His race across France (See Chapter 29) was to be a real *Blitzkrieg*.[2]

By the end of July the American advance was slowing down as it approached Mount Etna. But there was to be no long deadlock. The British 78th Division, an experienced formation, was brought over from Tunisia and used to capture the key to the German defences, Adrano (6 August). When the Americans took Randazzo also (13 August) the Etna postion was no longer tenable.

Guzzoni and his German adviser, von Senger und Etterlin, had seen from the first that their best plan was to fight a delaying action and then evacuate the main body of their fighting troops to the mainland, with as much equipment as possible. In this they differed somewhat from the ever-optimistic Kesselring (C.-in-C. South) who, 'doubtless still thinking of Dieppe,'[3] had originally hoped for a successful

[1] See Snyder: *The War – A Concise History*, p. 343.
[2] Bradley: *A Soldier's Story*, p. 357.
[3] Senger and Etterlin: *Neither Fear nor Hope*, p. 139.

counter-attack. The Axis commanders were fairly successful in getting their troops away across the narrow Straits of Messina. They are said to have concentrated 500 anti-aircraft guns astride the Straits, and by day they covered the passage by smoke. The Allied air forces sank a number of craft, but mines and coast defence batteries discouraged any attempt by naval forces to disrupt the ferry-service. When on 16 August the Americans won the race for Messina the Germans had evacuated some 60,000 men. Only 7,000 remained behind as prisoners of war.

The campaign had lasted 39 days. General Marshall estimated that it had cost the Germans 37,000 men and the Italians 130,000 – mostly prisoners. The Allied casualties in killed, wounded and missing were 31,158.

The Sicilian campaign was a mortal blow to the Axis. On 25 July Mussolini fell as the result of a palace revolution, and King Victor Emmanuel III confided the government to Marshal Badoglio. Although the Badoglio government continued to go through the motions of co-operating with the Germans, it was evident to everyone that Italy was on the verge of surrender.[1] Mussolini was imprisoned in an inaccessible hotel in the Gran Sasso, and Badoglio opened secret negotiations with the Allies, employing the captured British general, Carton de Wiart, as an intermediary. American, British and Italian representatives met in Lisbon and an armistice was signed at Syracuse on 3 September, the very day on which the Allies, after the briefest possible lull in their operations, landed at Reggio in Calabria.

The Germans had been expecting the defection of their Allies for weeks, if not months, and acted promptly. Rome was seized, and it was only with difficulty that the King and Badoglio managed to evade them. Much of the Italian fleet, including four battleships[2] and six cruisers, sailed to Malta, and surrendered early in September.

The British landing at Reggio (3 September) was not contested. It was followed by the seizure of Taranto (9 September) which, again, was not defended by the Germans.

On 9 September General Mark Clark's Fifth US Army landed in the Gulf of Salerno, South of Naples. The range of fighter cover made it practically impossible to risk a disembarkation any further north. For a time it was hoped to land an American airborne division at

---

[1] According to Ciano the idea of a separate peace had been taking root as early as the end of January 1942. (*Diary*, 28 January, p, 578).

[2] A fifth arrived later.

Rome at the same time, but the Italian grip on the airfield proved too feeble, and this bold operation was not carried out. The Allies have been severely criticised for failing to take advantage of the Italian surrender, but it must be realized that this came as no surprise to the enemy and that at least 15 German divisions were in the country. Five of these were quickly concentrated against the Salerno beach-head and at one time (11 September) it looked as if the invaders would be compelled to re-embark. The *Luftwaffe* made itself felt once more, scoring hits on the British battleship *Warspite* and the American cruisers *Philadelphia* and *Savannah* with glider bombs.[1] But the Allies had massive air support and by 15 September the worst was over. On the 16th the advance guard of the Eighth Army, which had covered some 200 miles in 13 days, made contact with the Fifth Army about 40 miles SE of Salerno, a remarkable feat and one which strained British administrative resources to the limit.

The Eighth Army now shifted the axis of its advance to the east coast, and using Brindisi and Taranto as bases, pushed up the coast to Bari, which was taken on 22 September. Foggia, with its complex of airfields, fell (27 September) and it was not until he reached the river Biferno that Montgomery encountered serious opposition. A Commando landing seized Termoli and the town was held by 78 Division against the counter-attack of 16 Panzer Division. The campaign now became a battle for the river lines. General Fuller, a hostile critic, describes the methodical way in which Montgomery overcame these successive obstacles:

'These tactics consisted in: (1) the building-up of such a superiority in every arm that defeat would become virtually impossible; (2) the amassing of enormous quantities of munitions and supplies; (3) a preliminary air and artillery bombardment of obliteration; (4) followed by a methodical infantry advance, normally begun under cover of darkness; and (5) followed by tanks, used as self-propelled artillery, to provide the infantry with fire support.'[2]

The Germans were compelled to fall back to the Trigno and then the Sangro, where they fought relentlessly, but eventually broke. On the west coast the pattern was similar. Naples had fallen on 1 October and Kesselring had then withdrawn to the Volturno, which the Americans

---

[1] These were rocket bombs which were radar-controlled, and could therefore be launched out of range of anti-aircraft artillery.

[2] Fuller: p. 270.

forced. Kesselring now fell back to the Garigliano, an obstacle whose importance is attested by its history.[1]

At this juncture (24 December) the demands of Operation *Overlord*[2] produced considerable changes in the Allied forces in the Mediterranean area. Generals Eisenhower, Montgomery and Bradley, and Air Chief Marshal Tedder, all went to England to take up new appointments. General Sir Henry Maitland-Wilson succeeded Eisenhower as Theatre Commander, and Lt.-General Sir Oliver Leese took over the Eighth Army.

Several veteran British and American formations were withdrawn to lend their experience to the cross-Channel invasion. General Alexander (15th Army Group) was left with the Eighth Army, which consisted of seven divisions, all from the British Commonwealth, and the Fifth Army (General Mark Clark) which contained five American, five British, and two French divisions, with a Polish division in reserve.

To oppose these forces Kesselring had 18 divisions. Of these five were holding down northern Italy, three were in reserve, and only 10 were actually in the line.

The Battle of the Garigliano began on the night 17/18 January and the Allies made very little progress. On the 22nd, when it was already petering out, Major-General Lucas, with 50,000 British and American troops (VIth Corps), was landed at Anzio.[3] Instead of pushing inland to cut the communications of the Germans on the Garigliano, Lucas dug-in to consolidate his beach-head. Since he made no serious attempt to advance, the Germans did not find it unduly difficult to contain him. That so unenterprising an officer should have been chosen to command an operation calling for dash and drive is scarcely credible. The lessons of Suvla Bay were forgotten.[4] Churchill called the VIth Corps an 'army of chauffeurs' and caustically compared it to 'a stranded whale'.

But in war, as in human affairs generally, the right thing often happens for the wrong reasons. The ill-success at Anzio was to make it easier for the planners to get greater strength for *Overlord*, for it brought home to the politicians the sort of situation that might arise in Normandy.

[1] Here, for example, the Spaniards defeated the French in 1504.
[2] The code name for the invasion of France.
[3] Or Nettuno.
[4] 1915.

Along the Garigliano the Germans stood fast, their hold on their great fortress of Cassino unshaken. On 29 January the Allies launched another attack on the little town, but by 4 February it had ended in failure, a failure blamed on the ancient Abbey of St Benedict, which seemed to survey the whole battlefield like a vast observation post.[1]

It was decided that until the Abbey had been obliterated the tactical problem could not be solved. The Allies dropped leaflets on the Abbey on 14 February, warning the monks and any civilians there to depart. On the 15th 254 bombers dropped 576 tons of bombs and turned the Abbey into a heap of rubble.[2] It was not as yet appreciated that the Germans were adept at constructing bunkers and strong-points in buildings. When the roof fell in and the walls collapsed the bunkers were actually strengthened. This is what happened at Cassino.

After another day's bombing the Allies attacked on the 18th, following a five hour bombardment. But mere weight of metal is a crude key to a tactical problem and it did not solve this one. The infantry were soon held up. Conditions began to bear a resemblance to the Somme and Passchendaele. General Alexander, who had had vast tactical experience on the Western Front in the First World War, very sensibly called off the attack.

Many of the details of the mounting of this brief offensive have been strongly criticized, and certainly mistakes were made. The most serious, as the defending commander, von Senger und Etterlin, has pointed out, was that:

'The plan was so similar to the first one (in January) ... that it could not hold any surprise. There was nothing new in it. I knew the terrain round Albaneta Farm, Hill 593 and Hill 444 from the day that I proceeded on foot to visit a battalion of 90 Pz. Gren. Div., when the trail of blood from the wounded that had been brought back marked for me the way up the track. These were all defensive positions in excellent condition, and they were being improved every day. According to German ideas, anyone wishing to continue the attack in the same direction from the terrain won in the earlier assault would have had to assemble a much more

---

[1] General von Senger, who commanded here, assures us that the actual building was not occupied. But how were the Allies to know that they were opposed by so punctilious a gentleman?

[2] For the faithful there was an element of wonder – the only two places to escape damage were the cell used by St. Benedict and the tomb in which his remains had rested for 1,400 years since his death. (Snyder: p. 357).

ITALY 1943–1945

powerful mass as an attacking force. To achieve this, the attacker could have ruthlessly denuded his secondary fronts, a measure that I too was constantly compelled to adopt for my defensive operations.'[1]

On 15 March another attempt was made in excellent weather. The preliminary bombing (1,400 tons) was not remarkable for its accuracy. Eighth Army commander lost his caravan headquarters three miles from Cassino, and the French Corps Headquarters at Venafro, 12 miles away, was heavily attacked.

There followed a two hour bombardment by 900 guns; then the tanks and infantry went in, only to find the Germans still strongly ensconced in their rubble-covered strongpoints. The tanks could not get through to support the infantry because of water-filled bomb-craters that resembled ponds. Experience in Sicily, not to mention the First World War, should have shown that this would be the case. After eight days this offensive, like its predecessors, was halted.

When on 11 May yet another offensive was launched, Cassino was outflanked. Despite heavy losses the Polish Corps fought its way through to the north of the town, turning it from the rear. Cassino fell on the 17th and next day the Poles took Monastery Hill.

Simultaneously the Allies broke out of the Anzio beach-head. But unfortunately General Mark Clark failed to cut the lines of communications of the Germans on the Cassino Front (Highways 6 and 7). Obsessed with the idea of getting to Rome ahead of his Allies, he permitted the main body of the enemy to escape with a loss of no more than 27,000 prisoners.

Rome fell on 4 June. President Roosevelt commented: 'The first Axis capital is in our hands. One up and two to go!'

[1] Senger and Etterlin: p. 206.

CHAPTER TWENTY-SEVEN

THE PACIFIC, 1943–44

1942
9 Dec.	Capture of Gona.

1943
2 Jan.	Buna taken.
18 Jan.	Fall of Sanananda.
9 Feb.	Guadalcanal cleared.
1/4 Mar.	Battle of the Bismarck Sea.
18 Apr.	Admiral Yamamoto killed.
30 Jun./Jul.	The Central Solomons Campaign.
5 Aug.	The Americans take New Georgia.
15 Aug.	Americans land on Vella Lavella.
3 Sep.	Capture of Salamaua.
5 Sep.	American paratroops take Nadzab airstrip.
6 Sep.	Australians seize Lae.
2 Oct.	Australians take Finschhafen.
12 Oct./	
2 Nov.	Heavy air raids on Rabaul.
1 Nov.	Americans land on Bougainville.
1/2 Nov.	Battle of Empress Augusta Bay.
6 Nov.	Second battle of the Solomons.
19/23 Nov.	Tarawa.
20/24 Nov.	Makin taken.
3 Dec.	The Cairo conference.
26 Dec.	Americans land at Cape Gloucester.

1944
29 Jan.	American task forces raid the Marshall Islands.
31 Jan./	
7 Feb.	Americans take Kwajalein Atoll.
17/21 Feb.	Eniwetok Atoll taken.

> *. . . This was the type of strategy we hated most. The Americans attacked and seized, with minimum losses, a relatively weak area, constructed air fields and then proceeded to cut the supply lines . . . Our strongpoints were gradually starved out. The Japanese Army preferred direct assault after the German fashion, but the Americans flowed into our weaker points and submerged us, just as water seeks the weakest entry to sink a ship.*

GENERAL MATSUICHI INO.

THREE campaigns, mutually supporting and more or less simultaneous, are outlined in this chapter. All were intended to bring the Allies within range of Japan. Amphibious operations would leapfrog across the Pacific, bypassing countless Japanese-held islands and leaving their garrisons to wither on the vine.

The first five months of 1943 did not take the Allies very far along the road to Tokyo. With the Germans still in Tunisia, and Operation *Husky*[1] in the offing, there was little shipping to spare. In particular the shortage of carriers was still acute. Even so two significant events took place in these months.

The loss of Gona and Buna led the Japanese to reinforce Lae and Salamaua in New Guinea. On 1 March an important convoy left Rabaul, carrying 7,000 troops in eight transports. Major General George C. Kenney, MacArthur's air commander, had 336 American and Australian planes in Papua. On 3 March they set about the convoy, sinking seven of the transports and two of the escorting destroyers. Next day they sank two more destroyers while torpedo boats accounted for the remaining transport. At least 3,500 Japanese soldiers were killed. The Allies lost five planes. Never again did the Japanese expose such a target within the range of land-based aircraft.

On 16 April Yamamoto met his end. He was flying from Rabaul to the Solomon Islands on a tour of inspection. Decoded Japanese

[1] The invasion of Sicily.

messages had given away his complete timetable. Sixteen Lightnings from Henderson Field were sent to intercept the Admiral and his escort of Zekes. Yamamoto, a martinet and a stickler for punctuality, turned up exactly on time. The Japanese considered his loss as a major defeat, but it may be questioned whether he was really the great strategist they thought him.

On 30 June MacArthur was at last ready. His objective was the airfield of Munda in New Georgia. His 34,000 raw troops, unaccustomed to jungle conditions, took six weeks to get the better of 8,000 Japanese. Munda fell on 5 August.[1]

On 15 August the Americans landed on Vella Lavella which was required as a fighter base. The final Japanese evacuation on the night 6/7 October led to the sea battle of Vella Lavella. This brisk engagement marks the end of the Central Solomons campaign in which the Americans had lost six warships and the Japanese 17.

The last three months had brought the Allies within 300 miles of Rabaul – albeit somewhat slowly. The Americans now had the initiative. Their next objective was Bougainville. On 1 November 14,000 Marines landed in Empress Augusta Bay, half way along the SW coast, opposed only by 270 Japanese infantry with an old 75.

In the early hours of 2 November Rear Admiral Omori came on the scene, hoping to get in among the transports as the Japanese had done in the Battle of Savo Island (9 August 1942). Rear Admiral Merrill handled his force notably well, and sank a cruiser and a destroyer. Omori departed well contented with the thought that he had sunk two cruisers – which was not the case. The transports were unscathed.

Halsey now retaliated with carrier strikes at Rabaul, intended to destroy aircraft and attack seven heavy cruisers which were coming down from Truk to give Merrill the *coup de grâce* for which Omori imagined he had prepared him. The Japanese cruisers were all badly damaged (5 November). On 11 November a new task group, including the *Essex*, *Bunker Hill* and *Independence*, enjoyed a highly satisfactory baptism of fire when they destroyed a large number of planes from Rabaul. Admiral Koga, discomfited, withdrew his remaining warships and planes from Rabaul to Truk.

By 14 November the build-up on Bougainville had reached 33,861 men and 23,137 tons of stores.

[1] It was on the night of 1/2 August that the Japanese destroyer *Amagiri* ran down the PT-109 commanded by Lieutenant John F. Kennedy, USNR.

Off New Ireland on 25 November Captain Arleigh A. ('31-knot') Burke's flotilla sank three new destroyers which were trying to run reinforcements into Buka. The Japanese did not score a single hit.

There were still some 60,000 Japanese on Bougainville. It took General Hyakutake a long time to concentrate them for an attack on the American perimeter, but during January and February he moved them up along the jungle tracks. By the time the attack began (9 March) General Griswold had about 27,000 fighting troops ashore. Japanese artillery destroyed or damaged over 20 planes, and their infantry made some impression on the American perimeter, but they sustained heavy losses, and by 17 March the battle had died down. Another general assault began on 23 March, but largely due to artillery counter-preparation made little progress. On the 27th the Japanese began to withdraw from the Empress Augusta Bay area.

Meanwhile MacArthur was mounting another offensive in New Guinea. His aim was to take Salamaua, Lae and Finschhafen. He prepared the way by establishing local air superiority. On 17–18 August a raid on the Japanese base at Wewak destroyed over 100 planes. General Kenney followed this up by taking the airstrip at Nadzab with 1,700 paratroops.

The Australians seized Lae (6 September) and Finschhafen (2 October) by seaborne landings. The Japanese fell back from Salamaua towards Lae on 8 September.

On 26 December MacArthur landed the 1st Marine Division on Cape Gloucester, New Britain, so as to secure control of the Dampier Strait. It was, however, no longer intended to attack Rabaul and its garrison of 100,000 men. It had been decided at Quebec in August to bypass the place by occupying Manus in the Admiralties and Kavieng in New Ireland. On 29 February the 1,000 troopers of 1st Cavalry Division landed unopposed on Los Negros Island, which an airman had reported to be unoccupied. The garrison of 4,000 failed to eject these amphibious cavaliers.

The capture of Manus Island (15 March – 25 March) was effected with remarkably little difficulty. The Seventh Fleet now controlled 'the magnificent, deep, landlocked Seeadler Harbor, fifteen miles long and four wide. Far better as a base than Rabaul, and nearer Japan,' . . .[1]

[1] Morison: *The Two-Ocean War*, p. 294.

The last of the three offensives to get under way was that against the Gilberts and Marshalls.

The first objectives were Tarawa and Makin, both of which were heavily bombed between 12–20 November, while from New Zealand, Hawaii, San Diego and even Alaska the Fifth Fleet (Vice-Admiral Raymond A. Spruance) closed in upon them. The combat troops were under the command of Major-General Holland M. ('Howling Mad') Smith, USMC, while V Amphibious Force was under Rear-Admiral R. Kelly Turner, who had already won much experience in Guadalcanal.

Tarawa, resolutely defended by Rear Admiral Shibasaki and 4,500 men, of whom only 17 were made prisoners, cost the Marines about 3,000 casualties (19–23 November). The techniques of amphibious warfare were being learned the hard way, but they *were* learned, for the Americans, with customary thoroughness, made the operation the object of intensive study, and reaped the benefit during the rest of the war. It was sheer bad luck that the leading waves had had to wade 500 yards under fire because their landing craft could not get over the coral reef offshore. But the amount of preliminary bombardment needed to soften-up the garrison was seriously underestimated by the Navy. In the event the Marines won the battle in old-fashioned style at squad level, officers in front. When the chips are down the primitive virtues still count – and they always will.

Makin was taken between 20 and 24 November. The 27th Infantry Division, stale from over-training, took their time crushing a garrison of 800 Japanese.[1] Their losses were slight but while they were making heavy weather of their task a Japanese submarine sank the escort carrier *Liscome Bay* (24 November). Kwajalein Atoll was a different story.

Nimitz now had at his disposal the powerful Fast Carrier Force Pacific Fleet, which included the *Enterprise*, the *Saratoga*, the *Essex* and three more of her class, and six light carriers. To some strategists it seemed that this force should be employed to help General MacArthur in his thrust along the New Guinea-Netherlands East Indies-Philippines axis. This would be in keeping with the principle of concentration of force. Nevertheless the Americans needed bases in the Marianas (Guam, Tinian and Saipan) in order to bomb Japan

[1] Including 500 labour troops.

with Superfortresses (B-29s). At the Cairo Conference (3 December 1943) Admiral King won approval for the dual approach.

This strategy threw the Japanese off balance. They already had plenty on their hands trying to cope with MacArthur in the Bismarck Archipelago. They decided to sacrifice their garrisons in the Marshalls and to concentrate on holding their next line of defence: the Marianas-Truk-New Guinea-Timor.

Between 29 January and 6 February four carrier task groups softened up the Marshalls, practically wiping out the Japanese air and sea forces in the process. Simultaneously Kwajalein was heavily bombarded and then taken by a series of well coordinated amphibious assaults. The Atoll, consisting of 100 coral islands grouped round a great lagoon, is the largest in the world. At least ten of the islands were defended, and Kwajalein itself, where Rear-Admiral Akiyama was well-dug in with 5,000 men, had to be taken yard by yard. Only 35 prisoners were captured. The attackers, who by this time had mastered the techniques of the amphibious assault, had only 372 soldiers and Marines killed out of the 41,000 who landed.

The Americans now proceeded to knock out the bases at Ponape and Truk. Liberators from Tarawa dealt with Ponape (15–26 February) and the fast carrier forces with Truk, sinking 200,000 tons of merchant shipping and two destroyers besides destroying about 275 planes (17–18 February).

Truk has been called the 'Gibraltar of the Pacific'. It was now so vulnerable as to be practically useless, and the Americans were able to by-pass it with impunity. For the first time a major base had been neutralized by carriers without the aid of a single land-based bomber. With Ponape and Truk out of action the capture of Eniwetok Atoll, some 330 miles WNW of the Marshalls, was effected without the interference of a single Japanese plane. The fighting followed the Kwajalein pattern. A novel feature was that the 2,000 Japanese on Parry and Eniwetok Island itself had hidden with such skill that the islands appeared to be unoccupied. Fortunately papers found elsewhere gave the game away. Once more Japanese casualties, 2,677, were far heavier than American, 339 killed and missing. But the winkling-out of a tough and fanatical enemy from bunker to bunker, with grenades and flame-throwers, was a desperate business calling for courage and training of the highest order. Robert Sherrod, a war correspondent, writing of Tarawa, gives a glimpse of one such fight.

'A Marine jumped over the seawall and began throwing blocks of fused TNT into a cocoanut-log pillbox about fifteen feet back of the seawall against which we sat. Two more Marines scaled the seawall, one of them carrying a twin-cylindered tank strapped to his shoulders, the other holding the nozzle of the flamethrower. As another charge of TNT boomed inside the pillbox, causing smoke and dust to billow out, a khaki-clad figure ran out the side entrance. The flamethrower, waiting for him caught him in its withering stream of fire . . .'[1]

The capture of the Marshall Islands meant that the Americans had broken through the outer crust of the Japanese defences. The strategy of the dual thrust had proved its worth.

[1] Robert Sherrod: *Tarawa: Portrait of a Battle*, (Duell, Sloan and Pearce, 1944).

CHAPTER TWENTY-EIGHT

THE WAR AT SEA, 1942–45

1942

19 Aug.	The Dieppe Raid.
27 Sep.	The *Stephen Hopkins* sinks the *Stier*.
8 Nov.	Operation *Torch*.
11 Nov.	Sinking of the *Hokoku Maru*.
Nov.	Admiral Sir Max Horton takes over command of the Western Approaches.
31 Dec.	The Battle of the Barents Sea.

1943

30 Jan.	Dönitz becomes Commander-in-Chief of the German Navy.
Jan./May	Unsuccessful bombing offensive against U-boat building yards and bases.
Feb.	Heavy sinking of merchantmen in the Atlantic.
8 May	Admiral Sir Bruce Fraser becomes Commander-in-Chief, Home Fleet.
May	41 U-boats sunk.
22 May	Dönitz withdraws his submarines from the North Atlantic.
10 Jul.	Allied landings in Sicily.
8 Sep.	The *Tirpitz*, and *Scharnhorst* bombard Spitzbergen.
15 Oct.	Sir Andrew Cunningham becomes First Sea Lord.
Oct.	Agreement with Portugal. Allied bases established in the Azores.
26 Dec.	The Battle of North Cape. *Scharnhorst* sunk.

1944

3 Apr.	*Tirpitz* bombed in Altenfiord.
May	German E-boats sink two LSTs during an invasion rehearsal.
6 Jun.	D Day. Operation *Overlord*.

9 Jun.	German destroyers defeated in the Channel.
14 Jun.	Admiral Sir Henry Moore assumes command of the Home Fleet.
11 Sep.	The midget submarine X24 sinks the floating dock in Bergen harbour.
15 Sep.	*Tirpitz* damaged by RAF Lancasters.
4 Oct.	The RAF destroys or damages four U-boats in Bergen.
12 Nov.	RAF Lancasters sink the *Tirpitz*.

1945

2 Jan.	Admiral Sir Bertram Ramsay killed in an aircraft accident.
8/9 Mar.	Germans from the Channel Islands surprise Granville.
11/12 Mar.	Germans from West Holland raid into the Scheldt.
7 May	The Admiralty orders all attacks to cease.

> '*The decisive point in warfare against England lies in attacking her merchant shipping in the Atlantic.*'
>
> ADMIRAL DÖNITZ. September 1939.

> '*The defeat of the U-boat ... is the prelude to all effective aggressive operations.*'
>
> WINSTON S. CHURCHILL. 11 February 1943.

BY THE end of 1942 the Allies were slowly beginning to win back their mastery at sea, for the U-boat 'wolf-packs', in their hunt for unescorted merchantmen, had been driven from the east coast of America to the Caribbean and the Gulf of Mexico. By October the American 'Interlocking Convoy System' extended as far south as Trinidad and Pernambuco. In the North Atlantic severe battles still continued. For example in August 18 U-boats sank 11 ships (53,000 tons) of convoy SC. 94 in a five-day struggle. Two submarines were sunk and four severely damaged, so this battle could perhaps be called a draw. But in September the attack on convoy ON. 127, which claimed seven victims, cost the enemy not a single U-boat. It was at this juncture, however, that Admiral Noble, Commander-in-Chief, Western Approaches, at last found that he had sufficient escorts to be able to form specially trained 'Support Groups'. New escort carriers; a short-wave (10 centimetre) radar which could detect a surfaced U-boat several miles away; and heavier depth charges, all came into service. British aircraft could now patrol 800 miles out to sea, and the area which could not be covered from Iceland, Newfoundland, North Ireland or Gibraltar was diminishing.

On 12 September U.156 sank the troopship *Laconia* with 1,800 Italian prisoners aboard. The German captain, Hartenstein, sent out messages promising not to torpedo rescue ships so long as he himself was not attacked. Several French and British ships, including the cruiser *Gloire* from Dakar, went to pick up survivors. On the afternoon of the 13th an American Army plane from Ascension Island, after flying around for about an hour, bombed the submarine. It is not known who ordered this attack, though 'the balance of probabilities suggests that it was an American authority'.[1] The upshot was that Dönitz gave an order that 'all attempts to rescue the crews of sunken ships will cease forthwith', an order for which he would have to answer to the Nuremberg Tribunal.

Between July and October 1942 the Allies lost 396 ships (over 2,000,000 tons), though many of the sinkings were far from the main Atlantic routes.

Disguised raiders were still a menace. The *Stephen Hopkins*, an American 'Liberty ship', sank the *Stier* in the South Atlantic on 27 September, a fine achievement. Two others, *Komet* and *Thor*, were accounted for soon after. The Japanese sent two 10,400 ton ships, the *Hokoku Maru* and *Aikoku Maru*, each armed with six 6-inch guns, into the Indian Ocean, where, on 17 November, an incredible fight took place. The Royal Indian Navy's minesweeper *Bengal* (733 tons), armed with a 12-pounder, and the Dutch tanker *Ondina*, with one 4-inch gun, met these formidable opponents 1,300 miles NW of Perth. They sank the *Hokoku Maru* and drove off the *Aikoku Maru*, without themselves suffering serious damage.

Dönitz continued to probe deep. In October he had five U-boats off Capetown, and in December nine off the coast of Brazil. Both groups scored heavily for a time.

Those who served in the Royal Navy in the War usually look upon the Russian convoys as the most exacting of the many duties that fell to their lot. The chances of survival if torpedoed in the Arctic were practically non-existent. Two convoys (PQ. 18 and QP. 14) fought their way through in the autumn of 1942. PQ. 18 lost 13 out of 43 ships, but shot down 41 German aircraft based on Norway, the escort carrier *Avenger* playing a decisive part. This was the turning point in the Arctic war.

Operation *Torch*[2] made very heavy claims on the Royal Navy, and for a time the number of ships arriving at Archangel and Murmansk was much diminished. *En passant* it may be remarked that the Russians were not the easiest of Allies, even refusing the British permission to land medical staff to look after sick and wounded seamen. Yet whenever a convoy was postponed for any reason Stalin protested loudly.

Malta convoys were still demanding a tremendous effort on the

---

[1] Roskill: p. 225.
[2] See Chapter 21.

part of the Royal Navy. Of 82 merchantmen that attempted to reach the island between January 1941 and August 1942 only 49 had arrived safely.

There is no evidence that at this period Hitler himself was taking much interest in the war at sea. It is true that Directive No. 23[2] was 'Directions for operations against the English war economy', but that was dated 6th February 1941. The *Führer* was preoccupied with the land fighting in Russia and in Africa. Even so the U-boat fleet had continued to expand and now numbered nearly 400 boats, of which about half were fully operational. Admiral Raeder's requests that U-boat construction be given the highest priority had – belatedly – been granted.

There were now some 450 British and Canadian escort vessels in the Atlantic, a very inadequate number if the crews were not to become utterly exhausted. 1942 had been a black year, even if prospects were beginning to look a little brighter. The Allies had lost 1,664 merchantmen (nearly 8,000,000 tons), and only a small proportion of these had been replaced. Britain's imports had dropped to one third less than the 1939 figure. Stocks of commercial oil fuel in Britain had fallen very low, and only about two months' supply remained.

Hitler, obsessed with the notion that the Allies might invade Norway, had concentrated the *Tirpitz, Lützow, Hipper, Nürnberg, Köln* and some 12 big destroyers in Norwegian waters. When on 30 December a U-boat from the strong flotilla based on Narvik reported the whereabouts of a Russian convoy, JW.51.B, Vice Admiral Kummetz came out of Altenfiord with the *Hipper, Lützow* and six destroyers.

Captain R. St. V. Sherbrooke, the commander of the escorts, had briefed his subordinates and the Convoy Commodore with great care and foresight. The cruisers *Sheffield* and *Jamaica* (Rear-Admiral R. L. Burnett) were coming down from Murmansk to meet the convoy.

Contact was made at 8.30 and for three hours Sherbrooke with five destroyers and five smaller escorts had to fight off a converging attack. The two British cruisers made a belated appearance at 11.30 – they had been pursuing a radar contact to the east instead of steering for the gun flashes – and soon made themselves felt. By 2 p.m. the battle was over and the enemy were withdrawing. The British lost

[2] Hitler: *War Directives*, pp. 56–7.

the destroyer *Achates* and the little minesweeper *Bramble*. The Germans lost the large destroyer *Friedrich Eckholdt*, while the *Hipper* herself was damaged and her speed reduced. None of the convoy was sunk, largely because in the Arctic twilight the *Lützow* had behaved with undue prudence.

Thus thanks to the skill of Sherbrooke, who was badly wounded, and the devotion of his men, five British destroyers supported by two 6-inch cruisers foiled a pocket-battleship, an 8-inch cruiser and six large destroyers.[1] The German Naval Staff described the battle as 'obviously unsatisfactory', while Hitler had one of his rages and was so rude about the German Navy that Grand Admiral Raeder resigned. Dönitz became Commander-in-Chief.

The Casablanca conference rightly decided that the defeat of the U-boats was a necessary preliminary to the invasion of Europe. For this reason the USAAF and Bomber Command, much to the disgust of the latter's Commander-in-Chief, Harris,[2] were ordered to divert a large part of their effort to the U-boat bases. Between January and May, 1943, 11,000 tons of high explosive and 8,000 tons of incendiaries were dropped on bases and building yards, but in vain: owing to the skilful construction of their pens not a single U-boat was put out of action. This fruitless offensive was one of the most serious miscalculations made by the Allied planners during the whole war.

By the beginning of February Dönitz had 100 U-boats on patrol, 37 of which were in the 'air gap' south of Greenland. Losses for February were heavy, a total of 63 ships (360,000 tons). March was even worse. Dönitz concentrated 40 U-boats against convoys SC. 121, SC. 122 and HX. 229 from New York, and 21 merchantmen were lost. 'Our escorts are everywhere too thin,' Mr Churchill told President Roosevelt, 'and the strain upon the British Navy is becoming intolerable.' Altogether in March, in all theatres, 108 ships (627,000 tons) were lost. But the worst was over. By the end of the month the support groups were operating and the pendulum began to swing the other way.

In May, thanks to Admiral Horton's skilful handling of his support groups, losses dropped still further. SC. 130 from Halifax,

---

[1] Their tonnage was 2,260–2,690. They had five 5–5·9 inch guns and 8 torpedo tubes. The British destroyers (*Onslow* class) had four guns (4–4·7 inch) and 8 torpedo tubes, 1,540 tons.

[2] See Chapter 24.

escorted by B.7 Group (Commander P. W. Gretton) and supported by No. 120 Squadron's Liberators from Iceland, got through unscathed in a battle which cost the enemy five U-boats, and Dönitz one of his sons.[1]

The month of May marks the climax of the Battle of the Atlantic. The number of merchantmen lost fell to 50 (265,000 tons), while the enemy, in all theatres, lost 41 U-boats. On 22 May Dönitz, unable to accept such losses, withdrew his submarines from the North Atlantic. Although it was some time before the Admiralty realized it, a decisive victory had been won and the Germans' grip on our lifeline had at last been loosened – and not a day too soon.

A lull followed, but Dönitz was far from abandoning the struggle. U-boats were to be produced at the rate of 40 per month. The construction of new types with a higher underwater speed was to receive the highest priority. The older boats were to be fitted with the 'schnorkel', a breathing-tube which enabled them to recharge their batteries while submerged, making them much more difficult to locate by radar. A new acoustic torpedo was to be used against escorts, and the U-boats, which had suffered much during the summer from the attentions of Coastal Command, were to be given a more powerful anti-aircraft armament.

The month of June passed without a single convoy on the North Atlantic route being attacked, though the Germans lost 17 U-boats that month.

Dönitz's strategy was always to thrust deep in search of soft spots, and his submarines scored heavily in the Indian Ocean (June) and in the West Indies and off the coasts of Brazil and West Africa. These far-flung forays depended very much on U-tankers or 'milch-cows', of which only 10 were ever completed. Four of them were sunk during the summer.

At the same period American escort carrier groups had a number of successes in the Germans' refuelling area about 400 miles NW of the Azores. Between June and August the Germans sank 58 merchantmen, but at a cost of 74 U-boats, the majority being destroyed by aircraft.

By this time only the Indian Ocean was a really profitable hunting ground for the enemy. Between June and December 1943 seven German and eight Japanese submarines succeeded in sinking 57 merchantmen (337,000 tons) in those waters. The demands of the

[1] Peter Dönitz was an officer in U.954 which was sunk by a Liberator on 19 May.

amphibious operations against Sicily and Italy had deprived the Eastern Fleet of escorts, and demonstrated once more how difficult it is for the Royal Navy – or any other – to be strong everywhere.

In mid-September Dönitz sent 28 U-boats into the North Atlantic in an effort to reassert his grip on the British lifeline. The Submarine Tracking Room in the Admiralty was alert to this development, and escort groups which had been cooperating with Coastal Command in the Bay of Biscay were re-deployed between Iceland and Northern Ireland. In a fierce battle in mid-September the enemy sank three escorts and six merchantmen at a cost of three U-boats, one of which (U. 229) was rammed by the destroyer *Keppel*.

In October two escort groups fought a double convoy through, losing only one merchantman and accounting for six U-boats.

The tactics developed by the renowned Captain E. J. Walker (2nd Escort Group) against U-boats which sought safety by diving deep are of interest.

'His method was to station a "directing ship" astern of the enemy to hold Asdic contact, while two others, not using their asdics crept up on either side, to release a barrage of depth charges by signal from the directing ship at the critical moment. The U-boat thus never knew when the depth charges were released, and could not take avoiding action while they were descending.'[1]

The escorts supported by long-range aircraft were proving more than a match for the submarine, despite its new torpedoes and other devices. Of 2,468 merchantmen which crossed the Atlantic in September and October only nine were sunk.

In October an agreement was made with Portugal by which Allied air and naval bases were established in the Azores. By the end of 1943 the Allies had definitely gained the upper hand in the Atlantic.

In mid-1943 the Home Fleet had been much reduced by the need to send ships to take part in the invasion of Sicily, though the Americans generously lent Admiral Fraser a battleship squadron and the carrier *Ranger*. The Fleet was able to reinforce Spitzbergen in June and to carry out a deception plan designed to make the Germans think that the British meant to invade southern Norway – an idea to which, as we know, Hitler was always receptive.

On 15 October Sir Andrew Cunningham became First Sea Lord in place of Sir Dudley Pound, who had become ill and who died on 21 October 1943 – Trafalgar Day.

[1] Roskill: p. 312.

In the summer of 1943 President Roosevelt was pressing for the renewal of the convoys to Russia. The Admiralty and Admiral Fraser were agreed as to the need to immobilize the *Tirpitz*, and, if possible, the *Scharnhorst* beforehand. On 22 September two midget submarines, X.6 and X.7, commanded by Lieutenant D. Cameron, RNR and Lieutenant B. G. C. Place, RN, got into Altenfiord, despite mines and defensive nets. Two-ton charges, skilfully positioned, made the giant *Tirpitz* leap out of the water and put all three of her main turbines out of action.

Russian convoys began again in November, and the first two got through unscathed. In December Rear-Admiral Bey came out of Altenfiord with the *Scharnhorst* and five destroyers to attack Convoy JW. 55.B. Admiral Fraser had foreseen this move and had taken the *Duke of York* all the way to Kola Inlet to cover the previous convoy (JW. 55.A).

In the first phase of the Battle of the North Cape Vice-Admiral Burnett handled his cruisers most intelligently and, although *Norfolk* was badly hit gave the *Duke of York* time to join in. At 4.50 *Scharnhorst*, her guns trained fore and aft, was taken by surprise when *Belfast* illuminated her with star shell. Battered by the *Duke of York* and *Jamaica* from one side and Burnett's cruisers (*Belfast*, *Norfolk* and *Sheffield*) from the other, she fought bravely for an hour. Then, with her main armament silenced and her speed reduced, she was torpedoed by destroyers. At 7.45 she sank into the icy waters of the Barents Sea, taking with her all but 36 of her crew of 2,000.

The U-boats had a bad time in the early days of 1944. Escorts were numerous, well-trained and alert. Sloops like *Wild Goose* and *Woodpecker*, to name but two, had brought submarine hunting to a fine art. It was a relentless struggle. Take the case of U.358 sunk in February; 'four frigates of the 1st Escort Group held contact for 38 hours before success came to them, and when their victim was *in extremis* she managed to sink the frigate *Gould* with an acoustic torpedo.'[1] It is hardly strange that Dönitz now gave up the unequal struggle. Between January and March 105 convoys (3,360 ships) crossed the Atlantic with a loss of only three merchantmen. Their escorts sank 29 U-boats.

With the increase in the number of escorts and escort carriers the

---

[1] Roskill: p. 354.

Russian convoys were now getting through, despite every effort on the part of the enemy.[1]

On 3 April *Tirpitz* was the victim of a surprise attack by Barracudas from carriers of the Home Fleet. She was put out of action for another three months, and her crew suffered 400 casualties. The Royal Navy lost three aircraft.

In June the German Navy and *Luftwaffe* were hard-pressed to oppose the invasion of Normandy. A number of U-boats, E-boats and destroyers lay in French ports, but the destroyers were routed by the 10th Destroyer Flotilla west of Cherbourg on 9 June and the U-boats, except for U.984 which sank four ships in a Channel convoy on 29 June, did little to impede the Allied build-up. The elusive E-boats, for all their dash, had little more than nuisance value. In fact the enemy's most dangerous weapon proved to be the pressure-operated mine.

In August the new Commander-in-Chief Home Fleet, Sir Henry Moore, began a new series of Russian convoys. As a preliminary, several abortive attempts on the *Tirpitz* were made by carrier-borne aircraft. Then on 15 September 28 RAF Lancasters operating from a primitive[2] Russian airfield near Archangel scored a hit and two near misses with 12,000 pound bombs.

Finding it impossible to repair *Tirpitz* in Norway the Germans moved her to Tromsö, to be used as a floating battery, when – as they never ceased to expect – the Allies should invade Norway. This success meant that the Home Fleet could spare the carriers *Formidable* and *Indefatigable*, which left for the Far East. *Tirpitz* met her end on 12 November, when 32 Lancasters scored three hits and several near misses with 'block-busters' – 'and the battleship turned turtle with nearly 1,000 of her crew trapped inside her'.[3] *Tirpitz* had fired her big guns once – at Spitzbergen; but if her tactical career had been undistinguished, her strategic influence, while she was intact in Altenfiord, had been of great importance.

The well-escorted Russian convoys in the second half of 1944 were extremely successful. Every one of 159 ships sent to Russia got through, and only two out of 100 merchantmen in homeward convoys were sunk. In their unavailing attacks nine U-boats were lost.

From first to last, in 40 outward convoys, 811 ships were sent to

[1] It was with a convoy in February that Captain Walker raised his personal score to 14 U-boats.
[2] Four Lancasters were damaged beyond repair on landing there!
[3] Roskill: p. 403.

Russia of which 720 arrived. They delivered 4,000,000 tons of cargo, 5,000 tanks and 7,000 planes. This was a great achievement on the part of the Royal Navy, and the Merchant Navies of Britain and the USA.

Only in the Indian Ocean were the Germans still scoring fairly heavily, due to the lack of escorts in the Eastern Fleet, but by the autumn this campaign too was on the wane, largely due to heavy casualties among the boats sent out from Germany to reinforce the enemy.

A form of stalemate had developed by the end of 1944, for although the schnorkelling U-boats were not sinking many ships, the escorts were not finding as many of them as in the days when they had ventured to operate on the surface in 'wolf-packs'. The number of German U-boats was still increasing and reached its peak of 463 boats as late as March 1945. The war was nearing its close, but still these were anxious days for the Admiralty, because, in addition, mines laid by E-boats and aircraft were taking a steady toll in coastal waters. Raids also caused some trouble. The German garrison in the Channel Islands reminded the Allies of its presence when on the night 8/9 March it surprised the little port of Granville on the neighbouring coast of the Cherbourg Peninsula, a place which had recently been the Headquarters of General Eisenhower and Admiral Ramsay. On the night 11/12 a foray by the German naval forces in West Holland into the Scheldt was sharply repulsed.

On the credit side long-range aircraft of Bomber Command had sown so many mines in the Western Baltic that the Germans had to carry out their U-boat training in Oslo Fjord, and by March their minesweeping service was beginning to break down. Beaufighters were ranging as far as the Kattegat to prey on coastal shipping.

The U-boat struggle continued bitter to the end. In April 44 boats sailed out from Norway and, using their 'schnorkels', got busy off the north-east coast of Britain. One, U.1199, actually remained submerged for 50 days! During the last five weeks of the war they sank 10 merchantmen (52,000 tons) and two small warships, though the Germans lost 23 submarines. These last did not, however, include any of the new Type XXIII which, fortunately for the Allies, came on the scene too late to be decisive. As the Russians drew near to the Baltic coast in April the Germans moved their remaining U-boats to Norway. When the surrender came 156 obeyed Dönitz's orders to surrender; 221 scuttled themselves.

Altogether the Germans had 1,162 U-boats at one time or another, of which 785 were destroyed. British ships or planes sank 500. Enemy submarines sank 2,828 Allied or neutral ships, an astronomical total of 14,687,231 tons, of which the British Merchant Navy lost nearly 11,500,000 tons.[1] Moreover, most of the 175 warships sunk by German submarines were British. During the war the Merchant Navy lost 30,248 men, and the Royal Navy, 51,578 killed and missing: of these a very large number fell victim to the U-boats.

The Germans too suffered severely. By the end of the war their mercantile traffic had ceased. Mines laid by ships and planes had sunk 604 ships (660,000 tons); and air attacks had accounted for 289 (574,000 tons). Surface ships of the Royal Navy dealt with 86 more (303,000 tons). From 1940 onwards British submarines had sunk 104 ships (318,000 tons). The Royal Navy and the RAF between them had practically destroyed the German Merchant Navy.

When the surrender came the Germans still had the cruisers *Prinz Eugen* and *Nürnberg* fit for sea. The *Scheer*, *Lützow*, *Köln* and *Emden* had been destroyed by bombing. The *Seydlitz* and *Hipper* were scuttled by their own crews The British took possession of the damaged *Leipzig*, while the wrecked *Gneisenau* and the uncompleted *Graf Zeppelin* fell into the hands of the Russians, the one at Stettin, the other at Gdynia.

These bare statistics of the war at sea give some idea of the awful struggle for sea-power, especially in the Atlantic and the Arctic; of the deadly menace of the U-boat, and the sacrifices made in the long and doubtful campaign which was only brought to its conclusion by the collapse of the German power on land.

[1] In 1939 the British Merchant Navy comprised 9,488 ships totalling 21,215, 261 tons.

CHAPTER TWENTY-NINE

OPERATION *OVERLORD*

1943

May	Washington. American and British Chiefs of Staff fix 1 May 1944 as provisional D Day.
Oct.	Eisenhower first sees the COSSAC plan.
Nov.	Rommel takes over command on the French Coast.

1944

Jan.	General Eisenhower takes command of the European invasion forces.
4 Jun.	Fall of Rome.
6 Jun.	D Day.
7/18 Jun.	The Beachhead consolidated.
13/14 Jun.	First flying bombs land in England.
17 Jun.	Hitler's conference at Margival, near Soissons.
19/22 Jun.	The Great Storm.
22 Jun.	The Battle of Belorussia begins.
27 Jun.	Americans take Cherbourg.
1 Jul.	Von Kluge takes over from von Rundstedt.
9 Jul.	British take Caen.
15 Jul.	Rommel injured.
18 Jul.	Americans take St. Lô.
20 Jul.	Hitler wounded in the Bomb Plot.
30 Jul.	Patton breaks out.
1 Aug.	Eisenhower assumes command in France.
6/7 Aug.	The Germans' Avranches offensive.
15 Aug.	Operation *Anvil*. (or *Dragoon*). The Allied landings in the South of France.
17 Aug.	Model takes over from von Kluge. Americans take St Malo.
19 Aug.	Von Kluge commits suicide.
25 Aug.	The liberation of Paris.
28 Aug.	Marseilles taken.

1 Sep.	Canadians take Dieppe.
3 Sep.	The British liberate Brussels.
	Hitler reinstates von Rundstedt as C.-in-C. West.
4 Sep.	British enter Antwerp.
7 Sep.	Americans reach the Moselle.
8 Sep.	First V-2 lands on London.
	Liège and Ostend captured.
17 Sep.	Allied airborne landings in Holland.
	Operation *Market Garden*.
18 Sep.	Fall of Boulogne and Brest.
30 Sep.	Fall of Calais.
8 Nov.	Fall of Walcheren.
28 Nov.	The first Allied convoy reaches Antwerp.

> *'He either fears his fate too much,*
> *Or his deserts are small,*
> *Who dare not put it to the touch,*
> *To win or lose it all.'*

Lines by James Graham, Marquis of Montrose, as quoted by Montgomery in his Personal Message to 21st Army Group before D Day.[1]

THE ten weeks' campaign of Normandy was one of the decisive struggles of modern times. The destruction of the German Seventh Army, half a million strong, and the liberation of France after four years of humiliating occupation, were results of the first importance, and placed the eventual outcome of the German War beyond all doubt.

The Germans, with 60 divisions, failed to repel the Allies, who could muster only 37. But the Anglo-American forces had complete command on the sea and in the air, and so it was once again a case of the victory of the better balanced force.

At the end of 1943 the Allied commanders for the invasion of Europe were appointed. General Eisenhower was to be in supreme command, with Air Chief Marshal Sir Arthur Tedder as his Deputy Commander and Lt.-General Bedell-Smith as his Chief of Staff. For *Neptune*, the cross-channel phase of the operation, all three Commanders-in-Chief were British: Admiral Sir Bertram Ramsay, General Sir Bernard Montgomery (21st Army Group), and Air Chief Marshal Sir Trafford Leigh-Mallory. For the actual invasion there were to be two armies – the American 1st Army under Lt.-General Omar Bradley and the British 2nd Army under General Miles Dempsey.

[1] In 1964 Field-Marshal Montgomery assured the author that he had not been aware that the next verse runs:

> 'Like Alexander I will reign,
> But I will reign alone,
> My thoughts did ever more more disdain,
> A rival to my throne.'

Planning had been going on in London since 1943. During the Casablanca conference Lt.-General F. E. Morgan had been appointed 'Chief of Staff to the Supreme Allied Commander (Designate)', better known as COSSAC. The number of divisions which could be landed on D Day was limited by the availability of landing craft, but Montgomery, supported by Eisenhower and Mr Churchill, succeeded in getting the force increased to five seaborne divisions and three airborne. It seemed little enough. Indeed the success of the whole operation depended upon the speed of the German concentration to meet the landings, and the success of the measures devised to distract and delay them.

Eight divisions may not sound very much, but in fact the Allies were putting forth a stupendous effort in Operation *Overlord*. The force included:

> 5,300 ships and craft,
> 150,000 men[1],
> 1,500 tanks[1],
> 12,000 planes.

The German Commander-in-Chief, West, was Field-Marshal von Rundstedt, who had 60 divisions, 11 of them armoured, with which to hold France, Belgium and Holland. He considered that the German armies were over-extended, especially in face of Allied air superiority, and suggested a withdrawal to the German frontier. This was not well-received by Hitler, who in February appointed Rommel to command the troops in France, while retaining Rundstedt in overall command. Since the two field-marshals differed as to the way in which their task was to be carried out, the arrangement was not a happy one. Von Rundstedt and Rommel were agreed that the French ports should be held to the last man, but whereas the latter wanted to fight the invaders on the beaches[2] the former thought in terms of counter-attacking before their beach-head could be consolidated. Eventually they decided upon an unsatisfactory compromise, with most of the infantry well forward and most of the armour kept back. After the arrival of Rommel a great deal of work was done on the defences.

The German layout revealed von Rundstedt's preoccupation with

---

[1] To be landed in the first 48 hours.

[2] 'The war will be won or lost on the beaches. The first 24 hours will be decisive.' Rommel.

GERMAN DISPOSITIONS ON THE INVASION COAST 6 JUNE 1944

Key
German Infantry Divisions — 352 INF. DIV
German Panzer Divisions — 21 PZ
German S.S. Panzer Divisions — 1 SS PZ
German S.S. Panzer Grenadier Div. — 17 SS PZ GR DIV

847 INF. DIV
HOLLAND
16 GAF. DIV
Amsterdam
719 INF. DIV
1 SS. PZ.
165 INF. DIV
BELGIUM
Antwerp
712 INF. DIV
48 INF. DIV
19 GAF. DIV
18 GAF. DIV
15th GERMAN ARMY
331 INF. DIV   182 INF. DIV
47 INF. DIV   326 INF. DIV   2 PZ
Calais
491 INF. DIV   85 INF. DIV
344 INF. DIV
348 INF. DIV
O London
245 INF. DIV   116 PZ   Paris
84 INF. DIV
17 GAF. DIV   R Seine
346 INF. DIV   Rouen   12 SS. PZ.
Southampton
711 INF. DIV
Le Havre
716 INF. DIV   21 PZ   PZ. LEHR
352 INF. DIV   7th
709 INF. DIV   GERMAN
Cherbourg   91 INF. DIV   ARMY   17 SS. PZ. GR. DIV
243 INF. DIV
319 INF. DIV   1st GERMAN ARMY
St. Malo   77 INF. DIV
266 INF. DIV   5 PARA DIV
Nantes
353 INF. DIV   275 INF. DIV   11 PZ
3 PARA DIV   265 INF. DIV   158 INF. DIV   708 INF. DIV
343 INF. DIV   Bordeaux
159 INF. DIV
BAY OF BISCAY   276 INF. DIV

the Pas de Calais.[1] The enemy were convinced, and Eisenhower's deception plan encouraged them in their conviction, that the Allies would strike there. Here they constructed their strongest defences, and deployed their most powerful formations. Here, at least, the defence had some depth. But for the most part the famous Atlantic Wall had no more depth than the Maginot Line, which these same Germans had bypassed so readily in 1940.

In 1944 the Germans had very much more and better armour than the French had had in 1940, but in many ways their situation bore an ironic similarity to that of Gamelin's army. Deprived of air support the Germans now sat in a long thin crust of defences and awaited their fate, unaware of the strength of their enemy, or where to expect him.

In fact, as we have seen, there were only 37 divisions under SHAEF,[2] and it was calculated that it would take seven weeks to get this force to France. Allied superiority at sea and in the air more than redressed the balance, for they enabled Eisenhower to keep the Germans dispersed before D Day and to delay their concentration in the days that followed.

Pre-D Day bombing of the French railway system did a great deal to hinder rapid troop movement. The French Resistance also played its part, by ambush and sabotage.

Still more important was the Allied Deception Plan. The 'First Army Group', a phantom formation, was concentrated in South East England. Its wireless traffic did much to prevent the Germans drawing troops from the coast between Antwerp and Le Havre. Security leaks were prevented by the prohibition of travel between England and Ireland, and by the sealing off at the end of May of a stretch of the south coast, 10 miles deep. The pre D Day bombing, though it isolated the Normandy battlefield by destroying the bridges of the Seine and the Loire, was so intense in the Pas de Calais and elsewhere that it did not betray the area selected for the invasion.

In outline, Montgomery's plan, after establishing a beachhead, was to draw the German armour into battle with the British round Caen, while the Americans, after overrunning the Cotentin Peninsula and taking Cherbourg, were to break out and then, wheeling left, drive the Germans up against the River Seine. It was a masterly

[1] In mid-July they still had 18 divisions watching the coast between Le Havre and Antwerp.
[2] Supreme Headquarters, Allied Expeditionary Force.

concept, based not only on Montgomery's knowledge of his immediate opponent, Rommel, but on the characteristics of the two great Allied armies committed to his charge – the stubbornness of the British, the dash of the Americans. As things turned out the campaign followed with fair accuracy the course Montgomery had predicted.

The chosen lodgement area was the Bay of the Seine between Cabourg and Valognes. It was selected as being the nearest stretch of beaches where the defenders were not altogether too thick on the ground. It was within range of Allied air support, and the Cotentin Peninsula gave some protection to the anchorage.

The Pas de Calais, though much nearer, was much more strongly defended; the straits were commanded by a great number of coast defence guns; and high chalk cliffs made it difficult to get away from many of the beaches.

The landings began in the early hours of 6 June when three airborne divisions were dropped to secure the flanks of the lodgement area.

On the American flank no less than 12,000 parachute troops were dropped. The US 82nd Division was to prevent a quick counter-attack from the West against the beaches, and ensure that the American seaborne divisions could break out of their beach-head so as to cut off the Cotentin Peninsula and Cherbourg. This was an essential part of Montgomery's plan.

A good deal of cloud over the coast that night hampered the navigation of pilots, many of whom were on their first operation. The anti-aircraft fire, though not very destructive, induced many of them to take evasive action, and in so doing to lose their bearings. Men of the two American airborne divisions were landed all over a twenty mile stretch of country, but many of their objectives were taken, including Ste. Mère Église and Pouppeville. A party from 82nd Division ambushed Major-General Falley, commander of the German 91st Division, while another paralysed his Battle Headquarters. 91st Division had nobody to spare to counter-attack Utah beach.

The very chaos of the American airborne landings added to the bewilderment of their enemies. What tidy-minded German intelligence officer could be expected to sort out a pattern from the far-flung reports of parachute landings that came flooding in to their headquarters?

The task of 6th Airborne Division was to seize and hold the left

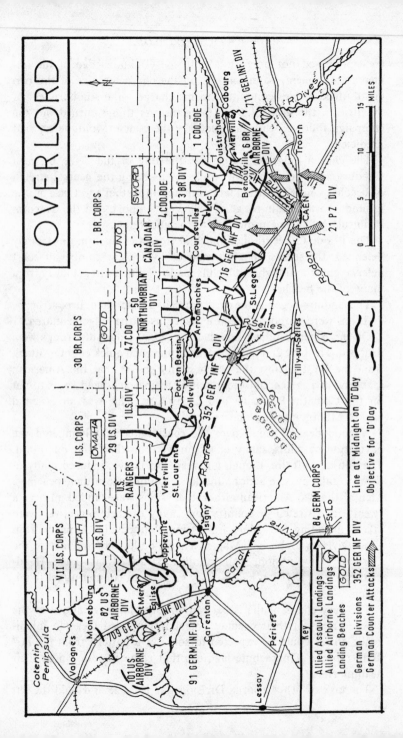

flank of the beach-head, so as to give the seaborne divisions time to get set. Here the full force of the counter-attacking panzer divisions was to be expected. Disaster here could mean that the British would be outflanked and rolled up from east to west. Were the Le Plein ridge, east of the Orne, to remain in enemy hands, the British beach-head would be displayed like a map to the German observation posts.

The bridges over the Orne and the canal at Benouville were captured by a glider-borne *coup-de-main* soon after midnight,[1] and, although 6th Airborne's drop, like those of the American divisions, was scattered, the parachutists mustered in sufficient force to secure the bridges and most of the landing-zone, where at 3.30 a.m. gliders brought in the anti-tank guns designed to receive the expected onslaught of 21st Panzer Division. At the same time five bridges over the Dives had been blown up, and Lt.-Colonel Otway's 9th Parachute Battalion, which could muster only 150 men, had stormed the Merville Battery. Reinforced early in the afternoon by the 1st Commando Brigade, and at about 9 p.m. by the 6th Air-Landing Brigade, the 6th Airborne Division had that evening a firm grip on the eastern flank of the bridgehead.

The assault on Utah Beach went pretty well according to plan; battleships, aircraft, rocket ships and destroyers neutralized the defences and cut their telephones wires. They may not have caused many casualties, but they made the Germans unhappy, confused them and kept their heads down. At 0630 the ramps went down and the leading infantry got ashore without many casualties.

Only one thing had gone wrong. The whole of the first flight had landed in the wrong place. This was partly due to the strong tide and partly to accidents to the craft responsible for navigation. The Americans proceeded to turn this accident to their advantage. Appropriately enough it fell to a Roosevelt to make one of the big decisions of D Day. Brigadier-General Theodore Roosevelt, a somewhat rheumatic veteran of 57, had persuaded his divisional commander to let him go in with the first wave 'to steady the boys'. Finding that the two leading battalions were more or less opposite the Pouppeville causeway he decided to make do with the beach he'd got rather than try to fight his way along the beach to secure the correct beach-head. It was a brave decision, for should his men fail to capture the single

---

[1] Six platoons of the 2nd Battalion of the Oxfordshire and Buckinghamshire Light Infantry, under Major R. J. Howard.

causeway ahead of them by nightfall there was going to be the world's biggest traffic jam on Utah beach – some 36,250 men and 3,500 vehicles. But an outlet from Utah was secured. It was now only a matter of time before the seaborne troops could relieve their airborne comrades beyond Ste. Mère Église.

At no point were the D Day landings nearer to failure than on Omaha beach. For this reason the landing is worth describing in some detail.

The German defensive position was naturally strong, and had been elaborately fortified. The Germans had big guns in eight concrete bunkers, 35 anti-tank guns in pill-boxes and 85 machine-guns. These were sited to cover three rows of obstacles planted below high-water mark. Inshore of these was a shingle belt, too steep for tanks and garnished with mines and barbed wire. The four beach exits were mined.

The fortified villages of Vierville, St. Laurent, and Colleville gave depth to the position, which was backed by the flooded valley of the River Aure. In sum it was a strong position, though, given reasonably expert planning, not an impregnable one. The American planning for this particular landing was not, however, of a high order.

Unduly impressed by the possibility that German shellfire would interfere with the lowering of the landing craft, the American admirals decided to perform this operation 12 miles offshore! The sea was so rough that a number of the craft were actually swamped, many were swept far to the east of their objectives, and landed their sea-sick soldiers not only in the wrong place, but late.

The frail canvas sides of the amphibious tanks were not designed for a heavy sea. One battalion was expected to swim about four miles. Of the 29 tanks launched, 27 either sank at once or were gradually swamped. The other battalion was sent in later, dryshod. Thus the first wave of infantry was left to storm the Atlantic Wall without the close support of armour.

The American planners had been offered large numbers of the 'Funnies' which their British allies had developed to deal with pillboxes, barbed wire and mines. These were Shermans converted for specialized purposes. Some were equipped to flail a way through minefields, others to lay tracks or to bridge anti-tank ditches. Some had flame-throwers or huge charges for destroying pillboxes. Such devices might be all right for the cautious and war-weary British:

the Americans preferred to see what could be done by straightforward frontal assault. Dieppe might never have been fought!

Bad luck played at least as malign a part as bad planning. Ten landing craft of the first wave sank during the run in. Wind and tide conspired to land most of the survivors in the wrong place. Most of the supporting fire, whether from the sea or the air, came down too far inland, missing the actual beach defences. The shells of the battleship *Nevada* had made such a screen of dust that observers could no longer make out their targets or perceive where the leading American troops had got to.

At close range the Germans opened a heavy fire from machine guns, artillery, and mortars, which reached a crescendo as the leading landing craft touched down on the sandbanks, and the soldiers scrambled out to make their way across the last 600 yards of flat sand, shingle, wire, and mines. Many, burdened down by their heavy equipment, fell into pools or runnels and were drowned. Some sought cover behind the beach obstacles, others could only conceal themselves by lying where the sea lapped the shore, with only their heads exposed to the merciless fire of weapons so cunningly defiladed as to be practically invulnerable.

Here an LCA[1] suffered four direct hits from mortar bombs and disintegrated; there a craft foundered 1,000 yards off-shore, and men were seen jumping overboard and being dragged down by their heavy loads.

Twenty-five minutes passed and the second wave touched down to find the first pinned at the water's edge. Already many of the leaders had fallen. No group had suffered more severely than the Army-Navy Special Engineer Task Force, who, burdened with their equipment, were invited to perform on foot the tasks carried out on the British beaches by 'the Funnies'. Only six out of 16 bulldozers got ashore and of these three were knocked out almost at once by artillery fire. Casualties among these unfortunate engineers amounted to 41 per cent of their strength, the majority being mown down in the first half hour. As often as not when they managed to prepare an obstacle for demolition they could not blow it up because their comrades were taking cover behind it!

Here and there an officer or a sergeant got his men going. One was Colonel Canham, who remarked: 'They're murdering us here. Let's move inland and get murdered.'

[1] The Landing Craft Assault, designed to carry 35 men, was bullet-proof.

Waves of men and vehicles continued to pile up along the fore-shore, only to add to the confusion. At 1.30 p.m. the German commandant told 352 Division's Headquarters that the invasion had been stopped on the beaches. Five minutes later the Chief of Staff passed the news to von Rundstedt that they had 'thrown the invaders back into the sea'. He spoke too soon.

About 10 a.m. General Huebner, the assault commander, had already taken a firm grip on the proceedings. Realizing the position on the beaches he stopped the waves of vehicles going in, and threw in more fighting troops. He called for naval gunfire support, and in response destroyers ran in to within 1,000 yards of the shore.

On the American left the 1st Division, veterans of Sicily and Salerno, though hard-hit, rallied and began to fight their way inland. One battalion made its way through a minefield to attack the village of Colleville.

On the right 29th Division, in action for the first time, was badly shaken. But small groups pushed on from the sea wall, and infiltrated as far as Vierville and St. Laurent. By midday the German artillery was beginning to run short of ammunition and in face of Allied air superiority it was impossible for columns to get through.

Nightfall found the 1st Division fairly well established round Colleville, with a bridgehead two miles deep on a front of four miles. 29th Division had a precarious hold on a strip of France two miles long and three-quarters of a mile deep. During the night the Americans were able to sort themselves out, and, with further reinforcements, the bridgehead was secured and 34,250 men were ashore.

The day's fighting had cost the Americans 3,000 casualties – about 1,000 from each of the two leading regimental combat teams. Material losses included more than 50 tanks, 26 guns and some 50 landing craft, besides 10 larger vessels. But their task had not been an easy one, and nobody could reasonably hope that a beach-head could be won without an ugly butcher's bill.

The Germans had been within an ace of repulsing the Omaha assault. But a purely static defence was not enough. A strong counter-attack was needed and this, thanks to 352 Division's misleading optimistic reports, was never laid on. General Marcks, the corps commander, launched his reserves elsewhere.

The British landings were extremely well supported by the Royal Navy. The bombardment was long and accurate, the run-in comparatively short, and the navigation accurate. There were the usual accidents inevitable in a combined operation, but most of the troops landed in the right place and at the right time. The sea was very rough, and the swimming tanks in some cases had to be landed dryshod after the infantry were already ashore. The tide was racing in and most of the under-water obstacles were already submerged when the first troops landed. This made demolition by the Sappers unexpectedly difficult, and many of the landing craft were seriously damaged.

Many of 'the Funnies' were already on the beach when the infantry landed and did splendid work in covering them across the beach.

On their right, by nightfall the British were six miles inland, with their patrols already in the outskirts of Bayeux. The veterans of 50 Division and 7th Armoured had done their work well. They had secured a beach-head big enough to allow XXX Corps to deploy properly. They had secured Arromanches so that the Mulberry harbour could be built without delay.[1] They had attracted a substantial portion of the German reserves, which spent an uncomfortable afternoon bicycling towards the coast under continuous attack from the RAF. Already that evening Major-General Richter with tears in his eyes was bewailing the fate of 716 Division: 'My troops are lost, my whole division is finished'. It was little more than the truth.

In the centre and on the left there had been substantial gains, with the 3rd Canadian and 3rd British Divisions thrusting towards Caen.

Fortunately for the Allies D Day found the Germans still at loggerheads over the employment of their armour. Certain divisions were not to be committed without Hitler's orders. Major-General Feuchtinger's 21st Panzer – the nearest to Caen – was not to move without orders from Army Group B. The strange German chain of command was greatly to Montgomery's advantage. Better still, certain of the links were actually missing – Rommel was near Ulm; Dollmann (Seventh Army) was at Rennes, running an exercise to study the

---

[1] 'The Mulberry outside the American beach-head near St. Laurent-sur-Mer was never used. It was wrecked in gale winds which blew for three days, June 19–22, 1944, the worst storm in 40 years. But the second Mulberry near the British beach-head of Arromanches was a thing of mechanical beauty, a miracle of construction, providing an outer roadstead where ocean-going vessels could anchor, and an inner roadstead, where the concrete caissons formed a fixed breakwater. Between the caissons and the shore ran ten miles of steel piers, over which the men and supplies were poured for the build-up. A million troops passed through this amazing man-made harbour or over the beaches before the end of the month. 'That Mulberry', said General Speidel, 'was of decisive significance.' (Snyder: *The War – A Concise History* p. 386).

defence of Brittany; Sepp Dietrich (1 SS Panzer Corps) was in Brussels. Even so it was as early as 6.45 a.m. that Speidel (Rommel's Chief of Staff) authorized the employment of 21st Panzer in the Caen area. Feuchtinger sent a battle-group against 6th Airborne, but this was later called off because of the deteriorating situation on the Caen-Bayeux front. During the evening some of his tanks actually reached the sea at Luc-sur-Mer (8 p.m.), but their real achievement was to hold up the British thrust at Caen from the north.

As Colonel von Oppeln-Bronowski took his battle group into action, General Marcks said to him: 'Oppeln, the future of Germany may very well rest on your shoulders. If you don't push the British back, we've lost the war.' This was exactly the situation. Everything depended on hurling the Allies back into the Channel on D Day itself, without giving them time to get dug-in. And this is precisely what the Germans failed to do.

And so in a single day the Allies had broken the Atlantic Wall – an obstacle at least as formidable as anything seen in the 1914–18 War. And yet the casualties – 9,000 out of 156,000 – did not compare with those suffered on the first day of the battle of the Somme. This is the measure of the technical and tactical advantages made in the intervening generation.

Counter-attack followed counter-attack during the first week, but all the time the Allies were building up more quickly than the Germans. The latter hoped to split the Allied front in two by a great armoured counter-offensive. This they entrusted to General Freiherr Geyr von Schweppenberg,[1] who had been a successful corps commander in Russia. Geyr was not accustomed to operating against an enemy who had complete air superiority. He set up the Battle HQ of Panzer Group West in an orchard 12 miles South of Caen, with four large wireless trucks and a conspicuous group of office caravans clearly arrayed in the open. On the evening of 10 June the RAF bombed the HQ., killed or wounded all the staff officers, knocked out the wireless trucks and most of the transport. Geyr, who was wounded, was one of the few survivors. The command now passed to Sepp Dietrich, who had no intention of carrying out the offensive Geyr had planned. Thus Rommel's hopes of putting in a counter-attack before it was too late were rudely dispelled.

By 11 June the beach-heads had been linked, as gradually the invaders won more elbow-room. By the 12th 326,547 men were

[1] Son of the Master of the Horse to the King of Württemberg.

ashore with 54,186 vehicles and 104,428 tons of stores.[1] But the great gale of 19–22 June was a fearful setback, for it completely destroyed the American 'Mulberry', besides wrecking or damaging 415 vessels.

The early capture of Cherbourg was now more vital than ever. Operations on this flank were in the capable hands of Lt.-General J. Lawton Collins, who had commanded an infantry division in the jungles of Guadalcanal. Wilmot describes his tactics:

'In the Cotentin Collins' answer to the bocage was to attack on very narrow fronts and to deliver a series of short, sharp thrusts astride two main roads. He had four regiments advancing in column of battalions, each regiment on a frontage of a thousand yards. He could afford to ignore his flanks, for the enemy had poor communications, small reserves and no tanks except obsolete French models manned by a training battalion. He drove his men hard in brief spells, relieving his leading battalions two or three times a day. In 48 hours[2] the Americans advanced five miles and fought the enemy to a standstill.'[3]

Hitler allowed his local commanders very little tactical discretion. Wilmot relates a typical instance of the kind of remote-control generalship of which the Dictator was so fond.

'When it was pointed out that there was no possibility of the existing positions being held, he shouted, 'Very well then, if they won't hold there (meaning Montebourg), they must hold here', and, taking a red pencil, he slashed a line straight across the map from one side of the peninsula to the other just south of Cherbourg.'[4]

Neither von Rundstedt nor Rommel felt strong enough to stand up to Hitler on this occasion.

Thanks to the *Führer* the Americans had already broken the four divisions that ought to have defended Cherbourg, before they actually reached that formidable fortress. Major-General von Schlieben's garrison, some 21,000 strong, included many low-category

[1] By D + 11 (17 June) 587,653 men and 89,728 vehicles were ashore.
[2] 13–15 June.
[3] Wilmot: *The Struggle for Europe*, p. 355.
[4] Wilmot: p. 357.

troops, and Todt workers as well as Russians and Poles.[1] But the very nature of the defences made the task a most difficult one and the American technique of attack is worth study.

'Dive-bombers and artillery drove the defenders in the outer entrenchments to seek the shelter of the concrete. Then the infantry, covered by a light bombardment, advanced rapidly until they were 300 to 400 yards from their objective. From there, machine-guns and anti-tank guns directed intense fire into the embrasures while demolition squads worked round to the rear of the pillbox. Then they dashed in and blew down the steel door with 'beehives'[2] or 'bazookas', thrust in pole-charges and phosphorus grenades and left the explosives and the choking smoke to do the rest. It was a slow process, but it was sure and comparatively inexpensive.'[3]

Von Schlieben surrendered on 26 June and the naval forts and arsenal capitulated next day.

The early fall of Cherbourg was a great prize for the Allies, who now possessed a first-class port even though its harbour could not be used straight away. The confidence of the German commanders in their coastal fortresses was much shaken. Hitler's inept generalship had certainly speeded up the proceedings, but the skill and certainty of General Collins's operations were most remarkable.

On the British flank no comparable progress was being made simply because the Germans had concentrated the bulk of their armour against that sector. By mid-July Dempsey's 14 divisions were pinning down 14 German divisions, including seven out of nine armoured divisions (600 tanks). Bradley's 15 divisions, with four of Patton's in reserve, were opposed by the equivalent of nine divisions with 110 tanks. It was the long slogging match round Caen which paved the way, as Montgomery had always intended, for the breakout on the American sector.

Bradley's plan for the breakout, *Cobra*, could well have foundered in the *bocage*. As he tells us:[4]

---

[1] 'You can't expect Russians and Poles to fight for Germany against Americans in France,' von Schlieben is reported to have remarked to his captors. (Wilmot: p. 360.)

[2] Explosive charges that could be stuck to the object to be demolished.

[3] Wilmot: pp. 361 and 362.

[4] Bradley: *A Soldier's Story*, p. 342.

'Previous attempts to force the Normandy hedgerows had failed when our Shermans bellied up over the tops of those mounds instead of crashing through them. There they exposed their soft undersides to the enemy while their own guns pointed helplessly toward the sky.'

At this juncture Sergeant Curtis G. Culin, Jr., devised a solution. He fitted four tusks to a light tank.

'The tank backed off and ran head-on toward a hedgerow at ten miles an hour. Its tusks bored into the wall, pinned down the belly, and the tank broke through under a canopy of dirt.'

Using Rommel's underwater obstacles for tusks every ordnance unit in Bradley's command set to and within a week three/fifths of the tanks taking part in *Cobra* had tusks – an organizational feat only possible to a nation as technically-minded as the Americans.[1]

Within the German High Command all was not well. On 17 June Hitler himself had put in a brief appearance and had held a conference at Margival near Soissons. He had demanded explanations from von Rundstedt and Rommel, and had received from the latter a forthright assessment of Allied strength which provoked an outburst from the *Führer*: 'Don't you worry about the future course of the war. Stick to your own invasion front!'

By this time Hitler was depending to some extent on his secret weapons, including the V-1 with which he had begun to bombard London on 12 June. One of these 'buzz bombs' developed a mechanical fault, changed direction and burst near the *Führer's* command post during the Margival conference. Hitler, who had talked of visiting Cherbourg next day, promptly flew back to Berchtesgaden. From this time forward he preferred to run the Western Front entirely by remote control.

Von Rundstedt continued in command until 1 July, when he had a telephone conversation with Keitel and warned him that a counter-attack on the Odon by four SS panzer divisions was being held by the British.

Keitel: 'What shall we do? What shall we do?'

Von Rundstedt: 'Make peace you fools. What else can you do?'

---

[1] Sergeant Culin was awarded the Legion of Merit. 'Four months later he went home to New York after having left a leg in Huertgen Forest'. (Bradley: p. 342).

Von Kluge, in whose loyalty Hitler had a somewhat misplaced confidence, was sent to replace von Rundstedt.

On the afternoon of the 15th July Rommel was attacked by fighters, his driver was hit, and the car crashed into a tree. Seriously injured, the Field-Marshal was carried to the nearby village of Ste Foy de Montgommery. His fighting days were done.

Five days later came the famous *Attentat* of 20 July.

Hitler was holding a conference in a wooden *Gästebaracke* at the Wolf's Lair in East Prussia. Colonel Count Claus Schenck von Stauffenberg, an officer who had been terribly wounded in Tunisia and was now chief of staff of the Replacement Army, smuggled in a bomb in his briefcase. At 12.42 the bomb went off. Stauffenberg returned to Berlin convinced that Hitler was dead, but in fact only four of more than 20 people present were killed outright. Hitler's right ear was deafened, his legs were burned and his right arm was temporarily paralysed, but that was all.

Hitler had the presence of mind to forbid the release of any information about the *Attentat*. This completely cut the ground from under the feet of the conspirators for generals who were in sympathy with them were not prepared to act unless they were absolutely certain that the tyrant was dead.

For a time the conspirators held the War Office in Berlin and their supporters in Vienna and Paris came out into the open. But that evening it was announced that the *Führer* was still alive.

Hitler's vengeance was swift and mediaeval. He denounced the conspirators as 'a small clique of criminally stupid, ambitious officers, devoid of conscience'. He saw them as blue-blooded Prussian swinehounds who could not comprehend the beauties of Nazism. In his mood of self-pity he mourned: 'The German people are unworthy of my greatness. No one appreciates what I have done for them.'

As for the plotters it was his wish that 'they be hanged like cattle.' Eight of them were, with the Reich Film Corporation's cameramen in attendance to film the scene as they hung naked and strangling. Each man took about five minutes to die. That evening in the *Reichskanzlerei* Hitler enjoyed the film not once but several times, and had it put into the syllabus of the Cadet Schools in Berlin.

The leaders of the plot had included Colonel-General Ludwig Beck, a former chief of the General Staff, and serving officers like General von Stuelpnagel the governor of Paris. Von Kluge and Rommel were both to some extent implicated.

In Normandy the Allies had by this time practically fought their way out of the *bocage*. Caen fell on 9 July and St Lô on the 18th. On 26 July General Patton's fresh US Third Army broke out from the beach-head and began to overrun Brittany. The Battle of Normandy had become the Battle of France. It was high time for the Germans to withdraw if they were to save anything from the wreck. But Hitler had not done. On 7 August a desperate German counter-thrust was launched in the direction of Avranches. Bradley's US First Army held the Mortain offensive, while Patton, swinging north, drove in towards Argentan, the British Second Army held firm and the Canadian First Army thrust south-east from Caen towards Falaise. For five awful days the German Fifth Panzer and the Seventh Armies struggled desperately to get out of the sack so formed. They left behind them 50,000 prisoners and 10,000 dead.

On 15 August the Allies landed 10 divisions[1] near Cannes (Operation *Anvil* or *Dragoon*). The Germans now evacuated the South of France and departed up the Rhône valley with all speed.

By this time Hitler had produced yet another C.-in-C. West. This was Field-Marshal Walther Model, an energetic and resourceful officer, who had the great virtue in Hitler's eyes that he did not belong to the old Prussian military families.

Von Kluge committed suicide on 19 August, after sending Hitler a final letter urging him to make up his mind to end the war. But Hitler still strove to convince his followers that the Allies would fall out among themselves, 'Whatever happens we shall carry on this struggle, until, as Frederick the Great said, "one of our damned enemies gives up in despair!" '[2]

There was little enough that Model could do to save the situation in France. All he could hope to do was to rally the remnants of his armies along the Siegfried Line.

By this time Paris itself had risen in revolt (19 August), with the gendarmerie seizing the Ile de la Cité, and the FFI,[3] 20,000 strong, fighting a pitched battle with General Choltitz's garrison, which surrendered, to the number of 10,000 on 25 August. On the 26th the great day came when at last General de Gaulle walked down the Champs Elysées in the midst of a delirious population.

The battles of Normandy and of France had cost the Germans

---

[1] Three American and seven French.
[2] Wilmot: p. 495.
[3] French Forces of the Interior.

dear. Half a million casualties, including 210,000 prisoners, and more than 2,000 tanks and assault guns had been left behind. Everywhere the Allies were surging forward. Patton was in Lorraine. Montgomery, confounding the critics who thought him slow, had sped forward to Brussels and Antwerp. And far away in Belorussia the Red Army had destroyed Army Group Centre.

When on 1 September Eisenhower himself took over control of the campaign the question was where to strike next. Montgomery felt that the Allies had not the administrative backing for two simultaneous thrusts, one at Strasbourg, another to the Ruhr. Yet Eisenhower, whose tactical ideas were often illustrated in terms of the American football field, was unwilling to hold up Patton, 'the man with the ball'.

Montgomery still hoped to bring the European war to a swift conclusion. It was to this end that Operation *Market Garden* was planned. The three airborne divisions of the First Allied Airborne Army (Lt.-General Lewis H. Brereton) were to capture the key bridges of Holland and thus open the way for the British Second Army to outflank the Siegfried Line.

The American landings at Eindhoven and Nijmegen secured the passage of the Maas and the Waal (17 September). Only at Arnhem on the Lower Rhine did this ambitious plan go awry. The 1st Airborne Division was landed too far from the bridge and this was the fundamental cause of the troubles that followed. The flak was not so heavy as it had been when Gale seized the Orne crossings on D Day. As ill luck would have it Model himself and 9th SS Panzer were in the Arnhem area when the drop took place and German reaction was swift. Bad weather and inefficient signals communications contributed to the disaster that followed. The Guards Armoured Division fought with great determination to break through to the relief of the Airborne Division.

On the night 25/26 September 2,163 survivors broke out. Of 10,000 who had landed 1,130 had been killed and 6,450 captured. The Germans estimated their losses at 3,300 killed and wounded.

It is wrong to look upon Operation *Market Garden* as a complete failure, for it had secured the passages of the Maas and the Waal. But it fell far short of the decisive results that had been hoped for, and with its end the great Allied impetus, which had carried. them triumphantly forward from the Normandy beaches, seemed – almost literally – to have 'run out of petrol'.

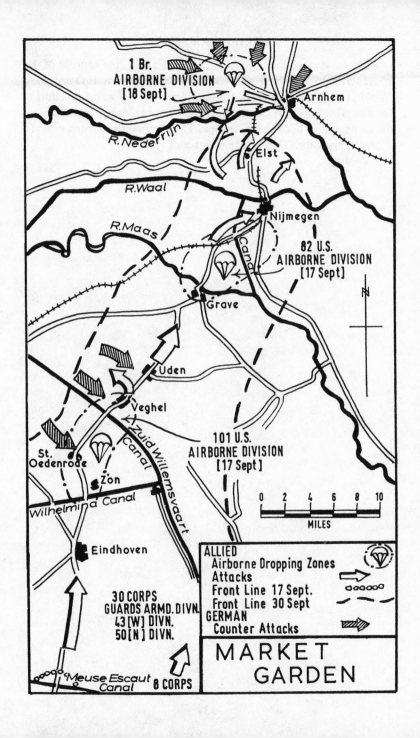

With the Russians still held up east of Warsaw, the capture of the approaches to Antwerp and its establishment as a forward base would probably have been a sounder operation of war than *Market Garden*. The fall of Walcheren on 8 November ended this phase of the campaign in north-west Europe. The Germans had been granted a breathing-space. They made full use of it.

CHAPTER THIRTY

THE EASTERN FRONT, 1944

1944

Jan.	The breaking of the Leningrad Blockade.
Mar.	Koniev's Ukraine offensive.
30 Mar.	Model replaces von Manstein.
8 Apr.	Russian offensive in the Crimea.
10 Apr.	Malinovsky liberates Odessa.
9 May	Russians retake Sevastopol.
6 Jun.	The Normandy landings.
18 Jun.	Russians break the Mannerheim Line.
22 Jun.	Soviet offensive in Belorussia.
28 Jun.	Model takes over Army Group Centre.
3 Jul.	The Russians retake Minsk.
13 Jul.	Red Army offensive in the Ukraine.
18 Jul.	Vilna captured.
20 Jul.	The Bomb Plot.
21 Jul.	Guderian becomes Chief of OKH. Staff.
23 Jul.	Fall of Lublin.
28 Jul.	Red Army takes Brest-Litovsk.
1 Aug.	Rising in Warsaw.
20 Aug.	Russian attack on Roumania.
23 Aug.	Surrender of Roumania.
25 Aug.	Finland seeks an armistice.
25 Aug.	Liberation of Paris.
30 Aug.	Malinovsky enters Bucharest and Ploesti.
4 Sep.	Cease-fire in Finland.
6 Sep.	Bulgaria sues for an armistice.
7 Sep.	Bulgaria declares war on Germany.
19 Sep.	Finland signs an armistice with Great Britain and Russia.
2 Oct.	Warsaw. General Bor-Komarewski capitulates.
7/16 Oct.	Germans evacuate the Riga area.

15 Oct.	Hungary asks for an armistice.
29 Oct.	Russians reach outskirts of Budapest.
24 Nov.	Russians cross the Danube at Mohacs.
16 Dec.	The Ardennes offensive.
26 Dec.	Russians encircle Budapest.

'The Year of the Ten Victories.'

THE SPRING of 1944 found the Germans everywhere on the defensive. In Italy the Allies were held at Anzio and Cassino; in the West Hitler conceived that a landing might take place as early as mid-February, so the withdrawal of troops or material from France, Belgium, Holland and Denmark had been forbidden (29 December 1943). In the East the *Führer* hoped to be able to hold the line of the old (1938) Russian frontier, and on 8 March, in *Führer* Order No. 11, he listed a chain of 'fortified areas' from Reval to Nikolayev, among them Vinnitsa, which had once been not one of his outposts but his Headquarters. Hitler remained surprisingly optimistic. On 2 April he outlined his current thinking in Operation Order No. 7.[1]

'The Russian offensive in the south of the Eastern front has passed its climax. The Russians have exhausted and divided their forces.

The time has now come to bring the Russian advance to a final standstill . . .

It is now imperative, while holding firm to the Crimea, to hold or win back the following line:

Dniester to north-east of Kishinev-Jassy-Targul Neamt – the Eastern exit from the Carpathians between Targul Neamt and Kolomyya-Ternopol-Brody-Kovel.'

One wonders whether Hitler expected his followers to believe that the Russians had exhausted their forces. It is impossible to be certain of the strength of the Russian services, but at the beginning of 1944 there were probably not less than 7,000,000 men in the Red Army alone.[2] In addition the Soviet air force was now vastly superior to the enemy's. Werth records a revealing conversation with an air force colonel at Uman in March 1944.

[1] Hitler: *War Directives*, p. 162.
[2] Though by that time at least 5,000,000 had been lost (Werth, p. 761).

'The German air force is much weaker now than it used to be. Very occasionally they send fifty bombers over, but usually they don't use more than twenty. There's no doubt that all this bombing of Germany has made a lot of difference to the German equipment, both in the air and on land. Our soldiers realize the importance of the Allied bombings; the British and Americans, they call them "*nashi*" – that is "*our*" people. . . A lot of German fighters now have to operate in the west and we can do a lot of strafing of German troops, sometimes without much air opposition.'

And he added:

'Those Kittyhawks and Airocobras are damned good – not like last year's Tomahawks and Hurricanes – which were pretty useless. But here we mostly use Soviet planes, especially low-flying *stormoviks* which scare the pants off the Germans . . .'[1]

To the Russians 1944 is the year of the Ten Victories. Of these the first two have already received some mention in Chapter 25.[2] The third victory came when in April the Fourth Ukrainian Front attacked Seventeenth Army in the Crimea and drove it back to Sevastopol. The Germans evacuated some 30,000 men by sea to Constanza in Roumania, but as many were left in Sevastopol, and much shipping was lost in this 'Dunkirk'. Sevastopol fell on 9 May, and Odessa had already fallen to Tolbukhin's army in April.

The fourth Russian triumph came in June when Marshal Govorov knocked Finland out of the war by breaking through the Mannerheim Line and taking Viborg (Viipuri). The Russians, with noteworthy restraint, halted at the 1940 Finnish frontier and did not push on to Helsinki.

Victory Number Five, the greatest of them all, was the liberation of Belorussia which began on 22 June. The Germans expected an offensive in the south designed to drive Army Group North Ukraine back against the Carpathians and Army Group South Ukraine into the Balkans. Hoping for a quiet summer on the central front they transferred a panzer corps to the south, depriving Army Group Centre (Field-Marshal Busch) of about 80 per cent of its tanks. On

[1] Werth: *Russia at War*, p. 787.

[2] (1) The breaking of the Leningrad Blockade (January), and the pursuit of the Germans, to the borders of Estonia. (2) Koniev's offensive across the Ukraine (February and March) when, after the Korsun encirclement, the Germans were driven right back into Roumania.

23 June the third anniversary of the German invasion of Russia, four Soviet armies began a double offensive on a 450 mile front. Zhukov, with the First and Second Belorussian Fronts, attacked towards Mogilev and Bobruisk; Vasilevski, with the First Baltic and Third Belorussian Fronts, advanced on Vitebsk and Orsha.

The Russians had made their preparations with all the thoroughness they had shown before Kursk. They had, including reserves, 166 divisions in Belorussia, with 31,000 guns and mortars, 5,200 tanks and self-propelled guns, and some 6,000 planes. A fleet of 12,000 lorries, mostly American, assured their administrative backing. For the wounded 294,000 hospital beds were in readiness.[1]

Behind the German lines 143,000 partisans were operating, and between 20 and 23 June they put practically all the Belorussian railways out of action, paralysing the German supply system.

In the first five days the Russians drove deep into the enemy lines, breaking them in six places, but Hitler, determined not to give up any more of the ground he had conquered in 1941, refused to allow his troops to fall back from parts of the front which had been by-passed. In consequence – as might have been foreseen – large numbers were cut off. The Third Panzer Army lost touch with Army Group North, the flanks of the Fourth and Ninth Armies were broken, and by the end of June the last-named had been trapped and destroyed round Bobruisk, only its Headquarters and one corps escaping. Another large body of German troops was cut off at Vitebsk and these two encirclements cost the Germans 20,000 prisoners.

Hitler now gave orders that the line of the Beresina must be held, but the Russians moved too fast and on 3 July they closed the pincers behind Minsk.

'In view of these shattering events,' writes Guderian,

'Hitler moved his headquarters in mid-July from the Obersalzberg to East Prussia. All units that could be scraped together were rushed to the disintegrating front. In place of Field-Marshal Busch, Field-Marshal Model, who already commanded Army Group A,[2] was also given command of Army Group Centre[3] – or to be more precise of the gap where that army had been. . . I knew Model well from the days when he commanded the 3rd Panzer Division in 1941 . . .; he was a bold, inexhaustible

---

[1] Werth: *Russia at War*, p. 861.
[2] Army Group North Ukraine was its actual title at this period.
[3] 28 June.

soldier, who knew the front well and who won the confidence of his men by his habitual disregard for his personal safety. He had no time for lazy or incompetent subordinates. He carried out his intentions in a most determined fashion. He was the best possible man to perform the fantastically difficult task of reconstructing a line in the centre of the Eastern Front.'[1]

The difficulty of his task will be readily appreciated from the fact that German casualties at Minsk numbered 100,000. On 17 July Werth saw 57,000 prisoners, including several generals, paraded through Moscow.

'Particularly striking was the attitude of the Russian crowds lining the streets. Youngsters booed and whistled, and even threw things at the Germans, only to be immediately restrained by the adults; men looked on grimly and in silence; but many women, especially elderly women, were full of commiseration (some even had tears in their eyes) as they looked at these bedraggled "Fritzes". I remember one old woman murmuring, "Just like our poor boys . . . also driven into the war."'[2]

Through the 250 mile gap in the German front the Russians advanced at a rate of 10 or 15 miles a day. Vilna fell into their hands on 13 July, while on the 18th Rokossovsky crossed into Poland, taking Lublin (23 July) and Brest-Litovsk (28 July). Belorussia was free and the German army had suffered a worse defeat than Stalingrad, for 25 divisions had been destroyed with casualties amounting to 350,000 men. The Russians felt that this rout avenged the terrible defeats that they had suffered in the same area in 1941. Their morale and their attitude to the Communist régime is well-illustrated by a letter which Werth received during this Battle of Belorussia. It was from Mitya Khludov, aged 19, who came from a well-known Moscow family of merchants.

'I am proud,' he wrote, 'to tell you that my battery has done wonders in knocking the hell out of the Fritzes. Also, for our last engagement, I have been proposed for the Patriotic War Order, and, better still, I have been accepted into the Party. Yes, I know, my father and my mother were *burzhuis*[3], but what the hell! I am a

[1] Guderian: p. 336.
[2] Werth: p. 862.
[3] Bourgeois.

Russian, a hundred per cent Russian, and I am proud of it, and our people have made this victory possible, after all the terror and humiliation of 1941; and I am ready to give my life for my country and for Stalin; I am proud to be in the Party, to be one of Stalin's victorious soldiers. If I'm lucky enough I'll be in Berlin yet. We'll get there – and we deserve to get there – before our Western Allies do. If you see Ehrenburg[1], give him my regards. Tell him we all have been reading his stuff . . . Tell him we really hate the Germans after seeing so many horrors they have committed here in Belorussia. Not to mention all the destruction they've caused. They've pretty well turned this country into a desert.'[2]

When Hitler moved to Rastenberg in July, the invasion of the Reich seemed imminent; indeed as early as 31 May Martin Bormann, the Nazy Party Chancellor, had sent a circular letter to all Gauleiters explaining the task of the Party in such an eventuality. It was at Rastenberg, while the Battle of Belorussia was drawing to its bloody close, that the *Führer* so narrowly escaped Colonel von Stauffenberg's time-bomb. His survival clinched the struggle for power between the Party and the Army, 'at once the most suspect and the most dangerous body in the State'.[3] The plot has already been discussed in this work[4], but certain appointments that followed may be mentioned here. One was that of Colonel General Schörner, an officer whose loyalty to the Nazi party was only equalled by his self-esteem, to command Army Group North. Hitler empowered him to employ

'all available forces and materials of the Armed Forces and the Waffen SS, of non-military organisations and formations, of Party and civilian authorities, in order to repel enemy attacks and preserve our Baltic territories (Ostland).'[5]

Another was the selection of the Reichsführer S.S. Herr Himmler to replace General Fromm, the commander of the Replacement Army, who had been hanged for his part in the plot.

[1] Ilya Ehrenburg, a leading Russian journalist and personality, who denounced the Germans often and eloquently in *Pravda* and *Red Star*.

[2] Mitya did not live to see Berlin. He was wounded a few days later and after writing that he was feeling better and would soon be back with his battery, died, like thousands more, in some overcrowded field hospital. Werth: p. 763.

[3] Hitler: *War Directives*, p. 174.

[4] Chapter 29.

[5] Hitler: *War Directives*. p. 175.

A third was the appointment of Guderian, who had played no part in the attempt on Hitler's life, as Chief of Staff of the OKH in place of Zeitzler, who had been sick for some time, and whose relations with his master had not been improved by the series of disasters on the front for which OKH had to answer.

Guderian reached the *Wolfschanze* on 21 July and reported to Hitler, who

'seemed to be in rather poor shape; one ear was bleeding; his right arm, which had been badly bruised and was almost unusable, hung in a sling. But his manner was one of astonishing calm as he received me.'

According to Guderian the *Führer* soon got over the physical effects of the bomb.

'His already existing malady, plain for all to see in the trembling of his left hand and left leg, had no connection with the attempt on his life. But more important than the physical were the moral effects. In accordance with his character, the deep distrust he already felt for mankind in general, and for General Staff Corps officers and generals in particular, now became profound hatred. A by-product of the sickness from which he suffered is that it imperceptibly destroys the powers of moral judgment; in his case what had been hardness became cruelty, while a tendency to bluff became plain dishonesty. He often lied without hesitation, and assumed that others lied to him. He believed no one any more. It had already been difficult enough to deal with him; it now became a torture that grew steadily worse from month to month. He frequently lost all self-control and his language grew increasingly violent. In his intimate circle he now found no restraining influence, since the polite and gentlemanly Schmundt had been replaced by the oafish Burgdorf.'[1]

The failure of the attempt to assassinate Hitler (20 July) was hardly less of a relief to Stalin than to the intended victim. The last thing the former wanted was to see the Nazi regime replaced by a pro-Western Government, now that the Anglo-American armies were established on the Continent. Having battered the Germans unmercifully, he meant to give them the *coup de grâce* in their home country.

[1] Guderian: p. 342. Hitler's Senior Military Aide, General Rudolf Schmundt had been mortally wounded by the bomb on 20 July. He was succeeded by General Wilhelm Burgdorf.

With the Germans in flagrant disarray the Russians scored Victory Number Six. In July they overran the Western Ukraine, including Lwow, and won a bridgehead beyond the Vistula at Sandomierz, south of Warsaw. The victory was marred in Western eyes by the failure to take that city, or to relieve its heroic inhabitants who rose on 1 August, under the leadership of General Bór-Komarowski, in a desperate endeavour to throw off the German yoke.

There has been no lack of Polish, British and American writers to put a sinister interpretation upon this episode. Captain Cyril Falls, whose work is distinguished by his balanced judgment, concludes that it is 'most improbable' that the Red Army 'stood by and watched with satisfaction the slaughter and capture of elements which might have proved troublesome to it when it set about organizing as Soviet territory the belt of Poland which it had recovered'.[1] Werth, who goes into the whole question[2] most thoroughly, comes to much the same conclusion, while admitting that the Russians would have eliminated Bór-Komarowski himself one way or another. Werth had the advantage of discussing the whole question with General Rokossovsky[3], the commander responsible, at Lublin on 26 August, 1944, while the struggle was still in progress. Rokossovsky, who was himself of Polish blood, told Werth that on about 1 August a German counter-attack by three or four armoured divisions had driven his troops back about 65 miles. The insurgents, he said, had started their uprising on their own without co-ordinating it with the Russians. Even in the best circumstances the Red Army could not have got to Warsaw before mid-August. At the time of the interview the Germans were doing their damnedest to reduce the Russian bridgeheads across the Vistula. 'Mind you,' Rokossovsky continued, not without reason, 'we have fought non-stop for over two months now. We've liberated the whole of Belorussia and nearly one fourth of Poland; but, even the Red Army gets tired after a while. Our casualties have been very heavy.'

The Russians were bitterly criticised at the time for not allowing British and American planes to land behind their lines, after dropping supplies to the insurgents. Rokossovsky explained that the military situation east of the Vistula was very complicated – presumably due to his recent reverse. 'And we just don't want any British and

[1] Falls: *The Second World War*, p. 230.
[2] Werth: part 7, Cap. VIII.
[3] 1st Belorussian Front.

American planes mucking around here at the moment.' He was of the opinion that, since General Bór's men were only holding out in isolated spots, most of the supplies would fall into German hands anyway. Allied experience at Arnhem and elsewhere seems rather to support this view.

Guderian's comments are also of interest:
'It may be assumed that the Soviet Union had no interest in seeing these (pro-London) elements strengthened by a successful uprising and by the capture of their capital . . . But be that as it may, an attempt by the Russians . . . to cross the Vistula at Deblin on July 25 failed, with the loss of thirty tanks . . . We Germans had the impression that it was our defence which halted the enemy rather than a Russian desire to sabotage the Warsaw uprising.'

It is hardly surprising that the Germans should have massed strong forces around Warsaw, since they blocked the direct Russian route to the Fatherland.

Ill-armed though they were, the Poles were remarkably successful at first. By 6 August much of the city was in their hands. On the 8th the sadistic Gruppenführer S.S. von dem Bach-Zelewski, an expert in anti-partisan warfare, came on the scene. He had at his command the Kaminski Brigade, composed largely of Russian turncoats and the Dirlewanger S.S. Brigade, recruited from paroled German convicts. These formations were not squeamish. According to Clark 'Prisoners were burned alive with petrol; babies were impaled on bayonets . . .; women were hung upside down from balconies in rows.'[1] Still the Poles held out with the utmost tenacity. Rumours of the atrocities reached Guderian, who taxed von dem Bach with them, and was told that because of the desperate nature of the street-fighting his men had abandoned all moral standards. He had lost control of them. This was too much for Guderian, who complained to Hitler. The latter had been privy to Himmler's plan to extinguish the revolt by sheer violence and terror, but even so Guderian had his way. Von dem Bach, finding the wind had changed, sent the Kaminski Brigade to the rear and had its commander shot! In another age the Borgias might have found employment for such an officer.

The Poles held out with desperate courage, prolonging the unequal struggle in the sewers of their city. But at length they were compelled to surrender (2 October); 300,000 had lost their lives. The Ghetto

[1] Clark: *Barbarossa*, p. 337.

had been destroyed in 1943. Now Hitler ordered that the whole city be razed to the ground (9 October). When the Russians entered in January 1945 they found that about nine-tenths of it had been demolished.

While the struggle for Warsaw was in progress, the Red Army was winning Victory Number Seven. On 20 August the Russians thrust southwards into Moldavia and Roumania with an army consisting of about 90 infantry divisions, besides 41 tank and three cavalry formations. Army Group South Ukraine (General Friessner) was partly German and partly Roumanian. The Russian onslaught was deliberately directed against the latter, with the aim of knocking Roumania out of the war. They offered little resistance and some even turned against their allies. The Germans, though they resisted fiercely, were cut off by 23 August and 16 divisions were destroyed. Losses were estimated at 60,000 killed and 106,000 prisoners. The bag is said to have included 338 planes, 830 tanks and self-propelled guns, 5,500 pieces of artillery and 33,000 trucks. On 30 August Malinovsky entered Bucharest and Ploesti, while Tolbukin pushed on into Bulgaria.

The Roumanian troops had shown themselves rather less than enthusiastic for Hitler's cause and on 23 August King Michael showed himself to be of their mind when he had Marshal Antonescu imprisoned in the Palace. General Hansen and his German Military Mission were interned and an armistice with Russia was signed on 12 September.

Victory Number Eight was the freeing of Estonia and most of Latvia. This had the effect of alarming the Finns, who now sued for peace. The armistice was signed on 19 September. The Russians refrained from occupying Finland, a gesture calculated to reassure the Scandinavian peoples.

In October the Russians invaded Hungary and Czechoslovakia, and joined hands with the Yugoslavs in liberating Belgrade: Victory Number Nine. In Hungary fierce fighting continued well into 1945.

The last Russian success of this their year of victories took place in the far north when the Germans were expelled from Petsamo and driven back into Northern Norway.

No objective account of the war on the Eastern Front can avoid the question of German war crimes and atrocities. It is thought that the

Germans took well over 3,000,000 prisoners in 1941 alone, and in all perhaps 5,000,000. Of these, it seems that only about 1,000,000 survived, It is, of course, impossible to produce accurate statistics, but it is certain that very many died while prisoners. Nor did they succumb to starvation alone. There is ample evidence that great numbers were shot, gassed, or tortured to death. It is easy to say that these crimes were committed by the S.D. or the S.S., but the German Army cannot escape a share of the responsibility. General Reinecke, Chief of the General Army Office of the OKW, known as 'der kleine Keitel', excused the killing of Commissars and Bolsheviks on the grounds 'that the war between Germany and Russia was unlike any other war. The Red Army soldier . . . was not a soldier in the ordinary sense, but an ideological enemy. An enemy to the death of National-Socialism, and he had to be treated accordingly.'[1] The Russians were *Untermensch* – sub-human – that was the underlying concept of the arrogant conquerors.

Nearly 3,000,000 Russians were deported to Germany for slave labour. They were not well treated. Early in 1942 Rosenberg complained to Keitel that only a few hundred thousand were still fit for work, and Göring told Ciano that some of the prisoners of war had resorted to cannibalism. Wittily he added that some had gone rather too far and had eaten a German sentry. The Reichsmarschall had a sense of humour all his own.

The extermination of the Jewish population was systematic. Alexander Werth cites the example of Klooga in Estonia where he

'saw the charred remains of some 2,000 Jews, brought from Vilno and other places, who had been shot and then burned on great bonfires they themselves had been ordered to build and light.'

A few had escaped. One told Werth of a kindly S.D. man who comforted a weeping child with the words 'My little one, don't cry like this, death will soon come.'[2]

The Germans have only themselves to thank if their critics see among their less lovable characteristics a pleasure in inflicting pain, which accords oddly with their well-known vein of self-pity. Forgetfulness one would not expect in people so efficient. Yet such an ornament of the German Army as Field-Marshal von Manstein could allege at Nuremberg that an order he had signed had 'escaped his memory entirely'. It stated that:

[1] Werth: p. 705.
[2] 'Aber Kleiner, weine doch nicht; bald kommt der Tod.' Werth: p. 702.

'The Jewish-Bolshevist system must be exterminated . . . The German soldier comes as the bearer of a racial concept. (He) must appreciate the necessity for the harsh punishment of Jewry . . . The food situation at home makes it essential that the troops should be fed off the land, and the largest possible stocks should be placed at the disposal of the homeland. In enemy cities, a large part of the population will have to go hungry. Nothing, out of a misguided sense of humanity, may be given to prisoners-of-war or to the population, unless they are in the service of the German Wehrmacht.'[1]

Himmler put things rather more bluntly when, speaking at Poznan in 1941, he said:

'I am not interested in the slightest if 10,000 Russian females die of exhaustion digging an anti-tank ditch for us, provided the ditch is dug.'

Even so Manstein's order was in the best Nazi manner, and he belonged neither to the S.S. nor the S.D. but to the German Army which, we are invited to believe, knew nothing of the barbarities committed by their fellow-countrymen – nothing of Belsen, nothing of Auschwitz, nothing of the systematic devastation as they fell back from Belorussia.

By comparison the atrocities committed at random by the Russians were child's play. Arson, murder, robbery and rape marked their conquering progress, but at least these crimes were not organized or even condoned by higher authority. A Russian major told Werth that 'many German women somehow assumed that "it was now the Russians' turn", and that it was no good resisting.' The most ignorant Kazakh knew enough German to say 'Frau, komm'. It was sufficient. The wheel had come full circle.

[1] Werth: p. 706.

CHAPTER THIRTY-ONE

FROM THE MARIANAS TO THE PHILIPPINES

1944

19 May	Wakde taken.
27 May/ *22 Jun.*	Fighting for Biak.
6 Jun.	The Normandy Landings.
15 Jun./ *9 Jul.*	Americans take Saipan.
11 Jun.	Bombing attacks on the Marianas.
19/20 Jun.	The Battle of the Philippine Sea.
18 Jul.	The Tojo cabinet resigns.
21 Jul./ *8 Aug.*	Americans take Guam.
24 Jul./ *1 Aug.*	Americans take Tinian.
25 Aug.	The Liberation of Paris.
12/16 Sep.	The Quebec Conference opens.
12/15 Sep.	Admiral Halsey's carriers raid the Philippines.
15 Sep./ *24 Nov.*	Fighting on Peleliu.
15 Sep.	Capture of Moratai.
3 Oct.	Joint Chiefs of Staff decide to liberate Manila and Luzon.
4 Oct.	First airfield ready on Moratai.
12/14 Oct.	Air battle over Formosa.
23 Oct.	Angaur captured.
20 Oct.	The Americans land on Leyte.
23/25 Oct.	The Battle of Leyte Gulf.
15 Dec.	Americans land on Mindoro.
25 Dec.	Capture of Palompon.

1945

9 Jan.	Americans land at Lingayen Gulf, Luzon.

26 Feb.	Corregidor in American hands.
4 Mar.	Manila cleared.
30 Jun.	Eighth Army takes over from Sixth Army on Luzon.
15 Aug.	End of offensive action against Japan.
25 Aug.	Yamashita surrenders.

> *'Dawn came none too soon for the Marines – but it found them still there.'*[1]   SAMUEL ELIOT MORISON.

IN THE Pacific the two-pronged thrust drove deeper. In the south-west General MacArthur's operations were designed to pave the way for a landing on Mindanao in the Philippines on 15 November. In the Central Pacific the objective was the Marianas – a thousand-mile leap on the way to Japan.

With Manus in his hands and Rabaul sealed off, MacArthur lost no time in completing the conquest of New Guinea. Early in April General Kenney knocked out the Japanese air base at Hollandia with massive bombing attacks. MacArthur followed up with a well-planned combined operation (22 April) and by 3 May the place was in his hands. During the next three months he pushed westwards and in a series of four seaborne landings secured the rest of New Guinea as well as the island of Biak, which was needed for its airfields. The garrison, 10,000 men under Colonel Kuzume, was almost as numerous as the American landing force, and it was well dug-in.

The aggresive Admiral Toyoda[2] was planning a big naval battle and realized that American heavy bombers from Biak might intervene. He decided to reinforce the island from Mindanao but was foiled twice. He then concentrated a really strong force, including the big battleships *Yamato* and *Mushashi*, which might well have done the trick. But before he could strike he became aware of the threat to the Marianas from Spruance's Fifth Fleet and felt compelled to concentrate in the Philippine Sea. Colonel Kuzume was left to his fate, though he contrived to hold out until 22 June, and exacted a toll of 6,238 casualties.[3]

With Hollandia, Wakde and Biak in his hands, MacArthur could prepare to fulfil the vow he had made when he left Corregidor.

---

[1] Saipan. 16 June, 1944.

[2] Koga, Yamamoto's successor, had been killed in an airplane accident about 1 April.

[3] They included 438 killed, 2,300 wounded and 3,500 died from typhus.

In the Central Pacific the Americans now faced the vast leap from the Marshalls to the Marianas. Vice-Admiral Kelly Turner, who with Guadalcanal, Tarawa and the Marshalls behind him, qualified as *the* expert on amphibious warfare, had 535 ships and 127,571 troops[1] at his disposal.

In Saipan, which the Japanese regarded as part of the homeland, General Saito had 22,700 men, while the unfortunate Admiral Nagumo – the man who had lost the carriers, and indeed the Pacific War, at Midway – had a flotilla of small craft and 6,700 sailors. After April, thanks to the successes of American submarines, the garrison received no reinforcements.

On 11 June Admiral Mitscher's four fast carrier groups began bombing the Japanese airfields. On 13 and 14 June the battleships carried on the softening-up process. D-day was the 15th. By nightfall 20,000 troops were ashore, though 2,000 of them were casualties. The Japanese fought skilfully, making excellent use of artillery and mortars to compel the American amphtracs to disgorge their troops at the water's edge instead of carrying them well inland.

The Marines spent a bad night.

'The Japanese saw to it that nobody slept for more than a few minutes. After a series of probes, their big effort was announced at 0300 June 16 by a bugler; and with much screaming, brandishing of swords and flapping of flags the enemy launched an attack that was supposed to drive the Marines into the sea. As the Japanese fell others replaced them, and the fighting on this flank did not reach its climax until sunrise, at 0545. Five Marine Corps tanks then stopped the last attack, and the Japanese withdrew under a blanket of gunfire from the cruiser *Louisville* and destroyers *Phelps* and *Monssen*, leaving about 700 dead on the battlefield. Dawn came none too soon for the Marines – but it found them still there.'[2]

The Japanese had no intention of leaving the Marianas to their fate as they had the Marshalls. Already a powerful fleet was on its way. The American commanders, Spruance, Turner and Holland Smith, knew this as well as Saito. Cancelling the landing on Guam due to take place on 18 June, they put their reserve infantry division ashore

[1] Five divisions, of which three belonged to the U.S. Marine Corps.
[2] Morison: *The Two-Ocean War*, p. 329.

and sent the transports off to the eastward until such time as the crisis should blow over.

Admiral Toyoda, with new air groups at his command, was determined to try the old Yamamoto strategy of annihilating the US Pacific Fleet at one fell swoop. First Mobile Fleet (Vice-Admiral Ozawa) had concentrated at Tawi Tawi, west of Mindanao, on 16 May. The Japanese had hoped to lure the Americans south, but the news from Saipan told Toyoda that he must seek his decisive battle in the Marianas.

The Japanese fleet was thoroughly outclassed by the Americans:

	United States	Japanese
Fleet carriers	7	5
Light carriers	8	4
Battleships	7	5
Heavy cruisers	8	11
Light cruisers	13	2
Destroyers	69	28
AIRCRAFT		
Fighters	475	222
Dive-bombers	232	113
Torpedo-bombers	184	95
Float planes	65	43
	956	473[1]

Spruance's main handicap was that he was more or less anchored to Saipan, since he had to cover the troops ashore.

June 19 was fair and cloudless. Still unaware of Ozawa's position the Americans began operations by attacking Guam, and a series of dogfights ensued, in which the Hellcats shot down more than their own number of Japanese aircraft.

Meanwhile the first wave was coming over from Ozawa's carriers and 'The Great Marianas Turkey Shoot' was on. The Japanese got one hit on South Dakota in Admiral Lee's battle line, but not one reached the carriers. The Hellcats got 45 out of 69 enemy planes.

During this phase American submarines had sunk two Japanese carriers, first the Shokaku, a veteran of Pearl Harbor; then the big new flagship Taiho, which, struck by a single torpedo, plunged swiftly

[1] In addition Ozawa could hope for some help from about 100 planes based on Guam.

to the cold depths of the Pacific, taking three-quarters of the crew with her.

Six of Ozawa's second raid got through to the carriers, only to be shot down by combat air patrols or anti-aircraft fire. About 20 attacked the battle line, and there were near-misses on several battleships. This time the Japanese lost 98 out of 130 planes. Most of the third wave of 47 aircraft got safe back to the *Junyo* and the *Ryubo* for the simple reason that they failed to find their target. Of about a dozen which did get through seven were shot down. The fourth raid, 82 planes, was launched at 1100. Nine survived.

While this was going on, Mitscher's bombers had been making heavy attacks on Guam.

The Philippine Sea was by far the biggest carrier battle of the war. In the unequal struggle the Japanese lost two carriers and 346 planes. The United States lost 30 planes, besides taking one single hit on a battleship. The Japanese pilots, outnumbered and seriously short of training, were simply shot out of the skies by vastly more experienced aviators.

On the 20th three American carrier groups pursued Ozawa eastwards. They did not find him until 1540. Then Mitscher launched 216 planes in an all-out strike, which sank the carrier *Hiyo* besides damaging the *Zuikaku* and other vessels. The Americans shot down 65 of Ozawa's 100 surviving carrier planes, for a loss of 20. It was pitch dark by the time they got back to their carriers, and, although in defiance of Japanese submarines Mitscher ordered his ships to light up, 80 planes crashed or were ditched, having run out of fuel. Even so the Americans lost no more than 130 aircraft and 76 airmen in the two days of battle. The Japanese got back to Okinawa (22 June) with 35 out of 430 planes. Once more their carrier air groups had been practically wiped out, and Spruance had hit the Japanese Navy in the way that hurt most.

It was now only a matter of time before the Marianas must fall. Resistance on Saipan ended on 9 July. The Americans had 14,000 casualties, the Japanese at least 24,000 killed. Although 1,780 prisoners were taken, half of them Koreans, hundreds of Japanese civilians committed suicide by jumping off the cliffs. Saito and Nagumo themselves committed *hara-kiri*.

On Guam[1], the most important of the Marianas, resistance was

[1] The Americans had bought Guam from Spain in 1899.

less determined than on Saipan. Even so its capture cost 7,081 casualties. By mid-August the Americans were in effective control of the Marianas. And on 18 July the cabinet of General Tojo had resigned.

The Americans were now thinking ahead to the final assault on Japan. One school of thought, which included Admirals King and Nimitz, wished to take Formosa and either make their base there or on the China coast. MacArthur headed the other school which wished to retake Luzon and make that the jumping-off place. He felt that not to liberate the Filipinos at the earliest possible moment would be a betrayal, and that thereafter no Asiatic would ever trust an American again. But it was not only for political reasons that the General had his way. Formosa was very strongly defended and, since most of the coast of China was in Japanese hands, there was little real prospect of establishing a base in the area.

In September Admiral Halsey with his *Essex* class carriers boldly sailed up within sight of land and bombarded the Japanese air bases in the Philippines. The few enemy planes that appeared were shot down. So much for the theory that carriers could never operate within range of shore-based planes. Meanwhile the Quebec Conference was thrashing out the course of future operations. The news of Halsey's success came in time for President Roosevelt and Winston Churchill to agree to the invasion of Leyte on 20 October. The projected operation to take Mindanao was cancelled, and the whole programme was speeded up by two months. This was a remarkable demonstration of strategic flexibility, but the administrative backing was there, and the amphibious assault that followed was a model.

Peleliu in the Palau Group was one of those islands which Nimitz might well have bypassed. But he felt that the Palaus would be needed as staging points and, as the veteran 1st Marine Division was already at sea, he ordered that the operation go forward, despite the recent change of plan.

By this time the Japanese were trying new tactics. Instead of meeting the Americans on the beach, as they had done in the past with such notable lack of success, their idea now was to site their main position well in rear, and to keep a strong reserve for counter-attack.

On Peleliu Colonel Nakagawa adopted a cross between the old and the new tactics, for his men fought hard for the beaches and inflicted 1,110 casualties on D Day. By the 18th the Marines had fought their way to the airfields, but north of it they were faced by

Umurbrogal Ridge, which was honey-combed with strongpoints hewn out of the soft coral rock and immune from bombardment from ship or plane. The Americans

'. . . would reach a cave mouth after a bloody battle, only to find that it was deserted, or capture a peak and smell cooking being done by cave-dwelling Japanese resting comfortably beneath. The biggest cave, encountered on 17 September, contained more than a thousand Japanese. The only weapon to cope with them was a new long-range flame-thrower, first mounted on LVTs[1] and later on Sherman tanks, which threw a wicked tongue of fire that could penetrate 40 or 50 feet and even lick around a corner.'[2]

Nakagawa held out until the night of 24/25 November, when he committed suicide. His 5,300 men were no more. They had taken 1,950 Americans with them.

As a preliminary to the invasion of Leyte four carrier groups attacked Formosa and neighbouring airfields in China (12/14 October). The Americans destroyed over 500 planes for the loss of 76, besides inflicting immense bomb damage on military installations. Three American ships were damaged, but none of them fatally.

For the assault on Leyte the Americans assembled 738 ships, including 17 carriers. The landings went with great precision, and were comparatively uneventful (20 October). By midnight on the 21st the Americans had landed 132,000 men and 200,000 tons of stores, besides taking the harbour of Tacloban and the airfields there and at Dulag.

The Japanese Navy was too scattered to concentrate in time to interfere with the vulnerable ship-to-shore movement phase of the Leyte landings. But, undeterred by the debacle in the Marianas, Admiral Toyoda was still seeking the opportunity for a knock-out blow. Japanese strategists believed quite rightly in keeping the enemy guessing. They liked to achieve this not only by deception, which was very reasonable, but by dividing their forces in the hope of putting in an appearance suddenly where they were least expected. This called for good timing, which in turn demanded a higher standard of communications than the Japanese had achieved.

One would think that by October 1944 the most obtuse and re-

[1] Landing Vehicle, Tracked (Amphtrac).
[2] Morison: p. 427.

actionary admiral would have noticed the value of air power. In this respect the Combined Fleet, though it still had four carriers,[1] was completely outclassed. Ozawa came out of the Inland Sea with no more than 116 planes. There simply had not been time to train new pilots since their air groups had had the stuffing knocked out of them over the Philippine Sea. The wonder is that the Japanese gave their opponents such a run for their money in the battle of Leyte Gulf, one of the most intricate of the whole war.

The Japanese approached from two directions: the main force under Vice-Admiral Kurita coming from North Borneo and Ozawa from Japan. Kurita was to destroy the fleet under Kincaid which was supporting the landing. Ozawa was to lure Halsey away to the north.

Kurita had 5 battleships, including the giants *Yamato* and *Mushashi*, 12 heavy cruisers and 19 destroyers. A smaller force under Vice-Admiral Nishimura and including two battleships was to co-operate with Kurita. Since all four carriers were with Ozawa, the striking force depended for its air support on such land-based planes as were in range.

Ozawa was an officer of great ability, second only to Yamamoto, and he played his part with skill. As in the Philippine Sea battle American submarines scored heavily. They shadowed Kurita and sank his flagship, the heavy cruiser *Atago*, in the early stages of the operation (23 October). Then a carrier borne attack smote the *Mushashi* which turned turtle and plunged to the depths with most of the crew.

Convinced that Kurita had been hard hit and was probably retiring, Halsey turned north to oppose Ozawa and his carriers. Kincaid was left to his own devices. But Kurita, so far from withdrawing, pushed on at 20 knots, making for the San Bernardino Straits. Nishimura was also bearing down on Kincaid who, to meet this two-pronged thrust, had battleships, intended for ship-to-shore bombardment (and already seriously short of ammunition), and small escort carriers, devoid of armour and intended only for troop and convoy support. Halsey spent the night 24/25 October speeding away from Leyte in search of Ozawa. Kurita spent that same night dashing in towards the invasion fleet. Kincaid was ready to repel an attack from the southward, where Rear-Admiral Oldendorf lay in wait for Nishimura in the Surigao Straits with six battleships[2] and

---

[1] *Zuikaku, Zuiho, Chitose* and *Chiyoda.*
[2] Five being survivors of Pearl Harbor.

eight cruisers arrayed to cross the T as the Japanese approached. It was the school-solution to a sort of naval problem which hardly ever actually occurs. Nishimura, who forged ahead with determined gallantry, was practically blasted out of the water. This Battle of Surigao Straits was Tsushima over again.[1] Admiral Shima, who was supporting Nishimura, withdrew with a discretion unusual in a Japanese commander. The cruiser *Mogami*, a survivor of Midway, was sunk, as well as the battleship *Yamashiro*. The dawn of 25 October found Halsey 300 miles north of Leyte, still looking for Ozawa; Kincaid's covering force preening itself on one of the most satisfactory night actions ever fought; and the main Japanese striking force, all unsuspected, steaming down the east side of Samar towards Leyte, having traversed the San Bernardino Strait during the night without the least opposition.

The Battle of Samar began when at 6.45 a.m. Kurita sighted the northern group of Kincaid's escort carriers under Rear-Admiral C. A. F. Sprague. They were operating about 40 miles offshore, providing support for the troops already ashore.

Both sides were equally surprised. In theory Sprague's force hadn't a chance. With his speed and firepower Kurita should have been able to make short work of these carriers. But Sprague kept his head, and he and his command improvised tactics suitable to an occasion for which no manual caters. Airmen and light surface craft alike attacked with reckless courage, as the carriers made off eastwards at $17\frac{1}{2}$ knots. The Americans lost three escort vessels but they managed to hit two cruisers and to check Kurita's onslaught.

Even before Sprague ordered the three destroyers *Hoel*, *Heermann* and *Johnston* to counter-attack, the commander of the last-named, Commander Ernest E. Evans, a Cherokee, 'called all hands to General Quarters, and passed the word "Prepare to attack major portion of Japanese Fleet".' *Johnston* went down fighting, but not before she had torpedoed *Kumano* and engaged the battleship *Kongo* with 5-inch gunfire.

While the fumbling Japanese admiral paused to ascertain damage, Avengers and Hellcats from all three American carrier groups set about him with sufficient fury to cripple two cruisers and to convince Kurita that he had the main American carrier force on his back. He sank the carrier *Gambier Bay*, but at 0911 he decided to withdraw. His staff had mistaken destroyers for cruisers and escort for fleet

[1] In 1905 Togo defeated Rozhdestvenski at the Battle of Tsushima Strait.

carriers. When he should have formed battle line he was worrying about cruising in anti-aircraft formation. He estimated that Sprague's force, whose maximum speed was $17\frac{1}{2}$ knots, was making 30.[1]

As if the escort carriers had not had enough to put up with for one day, the 25 October saw the first of the celebrated *Kamikaze*[2] raids. They hit two carriers among other vessels and sank the carrier *St. Lo*.

On 25 October Halsey's aircraft discovered Ozawa and sank all four of his aircraft carriers and a destroyer in the Battle of Cape Engano.

Brooding over a supposed affront[3] the American admiral then wasted a vital hour and failed to block Kurita's escape route through the San Bernardino Strait, thus robbing Admiral Lee of his chance of a good old-fashioned battlewagon shooting match.

The complicated Japanese plan had failed; Ozawa, playing the part of the tethered goat, had sacrificed his carriers in vain. Kurita, cast in the role of the hunter, had missed a sitting target.

Halsey made two grave errors in the battle of Leyte Gulf, but by sinking all four carriers he more than compensated for these lapses. Oldendorf showed how to carry out one of the classic manoeuvres of naval warfare. Sprague showed how to play a completely unpredictable battle 'off the cuff'. But no amount of cleverness will win a battle. Without the cool courage of men like his Cherokee captain, Sprague's battle would have been lost.[4]

The fighting for Leyte soon began to resemble the struggle for Guadalcanal two years earlier.

The Japanese had 365,000 troops in the Philippines and by 'Tokyo Express' tactics built up their forces on Leyte to about 45,000. But by 1 November 101,635 Americans were ashore under General Krueger (Sixth Army).

The *Kamikaze* campaign got into its stride and the carriers *Belleau*

[1] 'I knew you were scared, but I didn't know you were that scared,' said another Admiral to Sprague, when, after the war, he read Kurita's report.

[2] *Kamikaze* – Divine Wind. This was the name of the typhoon which smote the fleets sent against Japan by Kublai Khan in 1281.

[3] He misinterpreted a signal from Nimitz as a criticism. See Morison: *The Two-Ocean War*, pp. 466–7 for this illuminating episode.

[4] The airmen too had distinguished themselves. The Air Group Commander in *Gambier Bay*, Lt.-Commander Edward J. Huxtable, had 'guided his Avenger for two hours through the flak to make dry runs, once flying down a line of heavy cruisers to divert them from their course and throw off their gunfire for a few precious minutes.' (Morison: p. 460).

Wood, Intrepid and *Franklin* were badly damaged, and at least 45 planes destroyed. *Lexington* was hit a little later.

Severe American air strikes against Japanese reinforcement shipping (13/14 and 25 November) provoked a fierce reaction. The *Kamikazes* hit *Intrepid, Cabot* and *Essex* (25 November).

General Yamashita, the conqueror of Singapore, was sent to take command of the defence. As General Eichelberger (Eighth US Army) put it . . . 'Yamashita, the rainy season, and evil terrain made Leyte hard going for the military calendar-keepers.'[1] By the end of November most of the island was in American hands and 35,000 Japanese who could no longer look for any reinforcement faced 183,242 Americans. Already 24,000 Japanese had died. American casualties included 2,260 killed, and considerable numbers died of dysentery and tropical diseases.

Their desperate resort to *Kamikaze* tactics brought the Japanese a real revival of air power. The *Kamikaze* Corps had been organized in 1944 by Rear-Admiral Arima. What with the American introduction of proximity fuses for anti-aircraft shells, and the ever-growing skill of their fighter pilots, it had become virtually impossible for a conventional bomber to hit an American ship.

The Japanese tactics were now to crash onto an enemy ship and obsolescent aircraft could be used – at twice the normal range. The spread of petrol and the explosion of the bombs were bound to inflict heavy casualties and damage for the loss of one semi-trained pilot. Nor did the Japanese temperament reject such desperate measures.

The *Kamikazes* had considerable successes against convoys between Leyte Gulf and Mindoro, where the Americans had landed on 15 December. But this was nothing to the attack on the Luzon Attack Force. During the three days bombardment (6/9 January) which preceded the landing in Lingayen Gulf, the *Kamikazes* struck time and again. The vessels hit during this nightmare period included the battleship *New Mexico*,[2] the light cruiser *California*, HMAS *Australia* – four times – and several destroyers. But by 12 January the Japanese had practically used up every plane they had in the Philippines.

The US Sixth Army's fight for Manila itself was bitter, for, although Yamashita had ordered the evacuation of the capital, Rear-Admiral Iwabachi held out with the 20,000 men of his naval

[1] Lt.-General Robert L. Eichelberger: *Jungle Road to Tokyo*, (Odhams, 1951).
[2] Lt.-General Herbert Lumsden, Winston Churchill's liaison officer at MacArthur's Headquarters, was among the killed.

base. In his fanatical defence, the beautiful city with the ancient Spanish walled town of Intramuros was razed to the ground – the price of liberation.

The Sixth Army's campaign for Luzon lasted 173 days and cost it 37,854 casualties.[1]

On 30 June Eighth Army, which had finished off the Japanese on Leyte, took over on Luzon. Its commander, Lt.-General Eichelberger, claims that his Army 'set up an all-time record for swift amphibious movements' and had fifty-two D-days between Christmas 1944 and the Japanese surrender. 'In one forty-four day period alone these troops conducted fourteen major landings and twenty-four minor ones. . . . 8 Army fought on Leyte, on Luzon, on Palwan and the Zamboanga Peninsula, on Panay and Bohol and Negros, on Mindanao, Mindoro, and Marinduque, on Cebu and Capul and Samar. And on a score of smaller islands which . . . are remembered by most G.Is only as "faraway places with strange-sounding names".'

The Philippines were recovered island by island, and it was not until after the end of the war that Yamashita surrendered with the 50,000 men that remained to him.

When soldiers of 11 Airborne Division fighting their way to Manila found the Japanese position protected by salvaged 5-inch naval guns, they sent word to their HQ saying: 'Tell Bill Halsey to stop looking for the Jap fleet. It's dug in on Nichols Field.' By the time the Americans had done with it in the Marianas and at Leyte Gulf it might just as well have been.

---

[1] In addition the U.S. and Australian Navies lost 2,000, mostly from *Kamikaze* attacks.

CHAPTER THIRTY-TWO

BURMA VICTORY

1942
Dec.   British offensive in the Arakan.

1943
Feb./May The first Chindit expedition.
Apr.   In the Arakan the British withdraw to Buthidaung.
Aug.   South-East Asia Command (SEAC) set up.

1944
11 Jan.   XV Corps takes Maungdaw.
3 Feb./
May   Japanese offensive in the Arakan.
5 Mar.   Second Chindit expedition begins.
15 Mar.   Japanese offensive in Assam.
22 Mar.   Japanese take Tamu.
24 Mar.   Death of Wingate.
7 Apr.   Siege of Kohima.
17 May   Merrill's Marauders take the southern airfield at Myitkyina.
7 Jun.   Japanese retreat from Imphal and Kohima.
3 Aug.   Fall of Myitkyina.
19 Aug.   Japanese quit Assam.
Oct.   General Stilwell recalled to America.
3 Dec.   Fourteenth Army takes Kalewa.

1945
3 Jan.   Reoccupation of Akyab.
7 Jan.   The Ledo Road completed.
28 Feb./
4 Mar.   Fourteenth Army takes Meiktila.
20 Mar.   Capture of Mandalay.
3 May   Rangoon recaptured.

> '*On the other side of the room, seated by the situation map, lit by a shaded light, were the officer on duty and a younger colleague who had recently joined the Headquarters. The older officer was speaking in the voice of assured authority. He placed his finger firmly on the map. "Uncle Bill", he announced, "will fight a battle here", "Why?" not unreasonably asked the youngster. "Because", came the answer, "he always fights a battle going in where he took a licking coming out"!*'

> FIELD-MARSHAL SLIM.

THE British reconquered Burma, only to give the country its independence almost immediately afterwards. In consequence there are those among the veterans of the Fourteenth Army who wonder what they were fighting for in that far-away corner of an Empire which was on the eve of voluntary dissolution. But their contribution to the strategy of the Far East War was very real. The 'Forgotten Army' did not fight in vain. Its efforts not only saved India from invasion, but, still more important, helped to keep China in the fight, and thereby enabled the Chinese to tie down at least one-third of the Japanese army throughout the war. Although the Burma Road had been cut, the Allies still managed to supply the Chinese by the air-ferry service over the 'Hump Route' which cleared the Himalayas at an altitude of 23,000 feet.

General Marshall had no illusions as to the importance of keeping Chiang-Kai-Shek in the war.

> 'If the armies and government of Generalissimo Chiang-Kai-Shek had been finally defeated, Japan would have been left free to exploit the tremendous resources of China without harassment. It might have made it possible when the United States and Britain had finished the job in Europe, and assaulted the Japanese home islands, for the government to flee to China, and continue the war on a great and rich land mass.'

The Americans put enormous resources into the campaign in Burma.

By the end of 1942 the British were beginning to think once more in terms of the offensive.

A new and strange British commander had appeared on the scene. This was Brigadier Orde Wingate an officer who had already acquired something of a reputation in Abyssinia. He had managed to 'sell' to Churchill the idea of long-range penetration and between February and May 1943 waged a private war beyond the Chindwin, where his men cut the railway from Mandalay to Myitkyina in 75 places (March). The survivors of the Chindits returned after suffering immense hardships, and abandoning considerable numbers of sick and wounded to the Japanese, who, for their part, reacted very little to these pinpricks. The Press made much of the exploits of these men, which was justifiable at a time when morale in Burma was still being built-up after the retreat of 1942. Wingate himself became a sort of reincarnation of 'Lawrence of Arabia'. It must, however, be conceded that the first Wingate expedition showed that in the jungle the Japanese were not invincible. More important it demonstrated the value of the new technique of air supply. It also offset the grim failure of attempts, early in 1943, to recapture Akyab and its important airfield, by means of an advance down the Arakan coast.

In August 1943 South-East-Asia Command (SEAC) came into being. The Supreme Commander was Lord Louis Mountbatten, who as Chief of Combined Operations had already gained an intimate knowledge of inter-service cooperation, besides being an inspiring leader, at a time when leadership and training were the key to the situation. The men of the Fourteenth Army – British, Indian, Gurkha, African – had to be made to believe that they were as good as the Japanese 'supermen'. They had to learn to live and move in the jungle, to patrol with boldness and cunning, to get used to having Japanese parties behind them trying to draw their fire and make them give their positions away.

In a war where no man was a non-combatant, and a country of rivers and jungle-clad mountains, physical fitness was of paramount importance. It was a tremendous problem in an army where in 1942 120 men were evacuated sick for every one wounded. Malaria, dysentery, mite typhus and skin troubles were the chief diseases. At the end of 1942 one division of 17,000 had 5,000 sick. In some units hardly enough men were left to look after the mules and drive the vehicles.

It was partly a question of discipline. The strictest health precautions were imposed, especially against malaria. Research into tropical diseases; the introduction of mepacrine and other drugs; the treatment of the sick in forward areas instead of evacuating them to India – this meant an absence from duty of weeks instead of months. The arrival forward of surgical teams; evacuation by light aircraft from airstrips cut out of jungle or ricefield, the innovation of jeep ambulances; and the gallant, devoted work of doctors, nurses, the American Field Service volunteers and others – all served to diminish the ravages of disease and to increase the chances of recovery for the wounded.

The immediate aim of Mountbatten's command was straightforward. It was to re-establish land communications with China. The methods of achieving this aim were necessarily complex. There was to be an offensive in northern Burma in the winter of 1943–4; the Ledo Road from Assam, which was then being built[1], was to be extended so as to join the old Burma Road at Mongyu near Lashio. A pipeline was to be built from Calcutta to Assam, and another parallel to the Ledo Road. Supplies flown over 'the Hump' were to be doubled – 20,000 tons a month was the new target. Advanced bases were to be set up in China, from which Allied aircraft could bomb Japan and Manchukuo.

The main objective was Myitkyina with its three airfields. Once they were in Allied hands it would be possible to shorten the journey to China and cut out the climb over 'the Hump'.

Three Allied offensives were to take place simultaneously. Stilwell's Chinese-American Army[2] was to thrust down the Chindwin to Myitkyina. The Chindits[3] were to be flown into Burma to cut the communications of the Japanese facing Stilwell and to disrupt an expected offensive into Manipur. In the Arakan XV Corps (Lt.-General A. P. F. Christison) was to retake Akyab.

The British offensive in the Arakan was violently counter-attacked. The Japanese in their usual fashion went round the flanks and got behind their opponents. There was no lack of confusion and afright, hospitals and headquarters were overrun, general officers vanished into the jungle in their pyjamas, but instead of pulling out as they had so often been compelled to do in the past, the British stuck tight,

[1] The Ledo road was built between December 1942 and 7 January 1945. It was built by coolie labour, working under the supervision of American engineers, and zigzagged for miles over precipitous mountains.

[2] Two Chinese divisions trained in India and 'Merrill's Marauders'.

[3] 3rd Indian Division was their official designation.

formed brigade and divisional boxes and hung on. That this was possible was due entirely to command of the air. At last the British had a secure line of communications. The boxes were able to hold out simply because they were supplied from the air. This was to be the great feature of the war in Burma. The Chindits were supplied from the air, and so, when the Japanese invaded Assam, were Imphal and Kohima. Reinforcements – a complete division[1] – were flown in from the Arakan.

Admiral Mountbatten has emphasized the extent to which the reconquest of Burma depended upon air supply:

> 'It was not just a question of auxiliary air supply, because 96 per cent of our supplies to the Fourteenth Army went by air. In the course of this campaign we lifted 615,000 tons of supplies to the armies, three quarters of it by the US Air Force and one quarter by the Royal Air Force; 315,000 reinforcements were flown in, ...; 110,000 casualties were flown out, ... In our best month – March, 1945 – we actually lifted 94,300 tons. During that time the American Air Transport Command were building up their 'Hump' traffic, so that by July they had reached their peak of 77,500 tons per month.'[2]

And this in spite of the fact that they had only about half the aircraft they needed for their exacting task. The American pilots aimed to get the war over as quickly as possible. If that meant flying all day, seven days a week, for 18 months on end, they were prepared to give it a try.

On 15 March 1944 the Japanese took the offensive. They meant to get into the Brahmaputra valley and overrun the airfields which were supplying China. Had they been successful they might well have pushed on to invade eastern India.

Slim, with singular foresight, had flown out many administrative troops – *bouches inutiles* – before the storm came. The battle lasted three months. By the beginning of June the two armies were strangely interlocked: in the north two British divisions round Kohima; between them and Imphal two Japanese divisions; around Imphal and Palel four more British divisions; and south of them a Japanese division and a brigade. Outnumbered by two to one, the Japanese eventually cracked and recrossed the Chindwin in disorder. They

[1] The 5th Indian Division.
[2] 'The Strategy of the South-East Asia Campaign,' Admiral the Viscount Mountbatten. *Journal of the Royal United Services Institution*, November 1946.

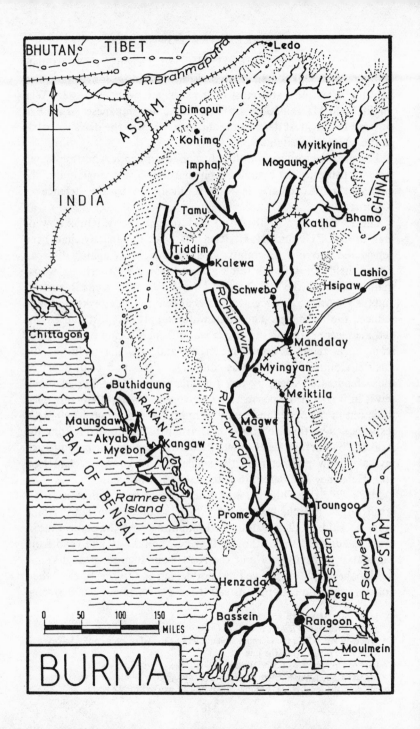

BURMA

had lost most of their tanks and lorries, and at a conservative estimate 250 guns and 53,000 men. Five divisions[1] could no longer be called fighting formations, and most of the survivors were exhausted. Well might Field-Marshal Slim comment that 'the Japanese Army had suffered the greatest defeat in its history'.[2] It was the decisive battle of the whole campaign.

This great victory was not lightly won. Fourteenth Army alone had suffered some 16,700 casualties, but had not lost a single gun. The desperate nature of the fighting is illustrated by the defence of Kohima.

The 13 day siege (5–18 April) was an epic to rival Lucknow or Hazebrouck[3]. Colonel H. U. Richards who, fortunately, had been considered too old to command a brigade in Wingate's 'Special Force', held out with a scratch garrison, some 2,500 strong, whose main units were the 4th Queen's Own Royal West Kent Regiment[4] and the 1st Assam Regiment. A series of determined attacks gradually reduced the perimeter. The main water supply was lost and by the end men were crawling out to get water from a spring only 30 yards from a Japanese position. No-man's-land was the width of the District Commissioner's tennis court.[5] At night jitter raids deprived the defenders of sleep, by day the Japanese infantry hurled themselves in waves at the perimeter. The wounded were often compelled to lie out in the open, and many were hit a second time. Their stout resistance gave time for the 5th Division to be flown in from the Arakan, but before relief came Richards' men had been squeezed into a narrow perimeter on the single feature known as Garrison Hill. Here they had determined to make their last stand.

Meanwhile the Chindits, whose leader had been killed in an air crash on 24 March, were waging their second campaign. Tribute must be paid to their valour and endurance. At the same time it must be admitted that although they cut the railway and road from Mandalay to Myitkyina and the road from Bhamo to Myitkyina, the Japanese fighting Stilwell did not detach any troops to clear their lines of communications. Instead Take Force, about 6,000 strong,

---

[1] 15th, 18th, 31st, 33rd and 54th.

[2] Slim: *Defeat into Victory*, p. 359.

[3] Where in April 1918 the German advance was halted when even cooks, bakers and butchers were thrown into the line.

[4] Part of 161 Brigade of 5th Division.

[5] Mr (later Sir) Charles Pawsey, who went through the whole siege, had great influence with the local Nagas among whom he had worked for 22 years.

was formed from 53 Japanese Division, which was then arriving in Burma. This improvised formation attempted to capture 'White City' and destroy 77 Brigade, but was bloodily repulsed after heavy fighting. The chief effect of the second Chindit expedition 'was to delay for a couple of months two infantry and one artillery battalions of the Japanese 15 Division on their way to take part in the offensive against Imphal.'[1] All in all it seems that these excellent troops would have been far better employed in the vital battle for Imphal.

Stilwell himself advanced but slowly and it was not until 4 August that he took Myitkyina. In October Chiang-Kai-Shek, who disliked his rugged mentor, contrived to get him recalled to America.[2]

In December the British crossed the Chindwin and the Japanese retired to the Irrawaddy. Slim now confused them by bringing his left-hand corps across to his right flank and effecting a crossing of the Irrawaddy south of Mandalay.

The motto of the Fourteenth Army was 'God helps those who help themselves' and not the least remarkable feature of this campaign was the way in which a flotilla was improvised to cross the river.

By the end of February 1945 the Fourteenth Army had reached the vital communications centre of Meiktila. Bitter fighting followed. The Army Commander himself witnessed the last stage of a minor attack typical of thousands made in the three long years of the Burma campaign.

'The fire of Brens and rifles swelled in volume; the tank's gun thudded away. Suddenly three Gurkhas sprang up simultaneously and dashed forward. One fell, but the other two covered the few yards to the bunkers and thrust tommy-guns through the loopholes. Behind them surged an uneven line of their comrades; another broke from the spinney, bayonets glinting. They swarmed around the bunkers and for a moment all firing ceased. Then from behind one of the hummocks appeared a ragged group of half a dozen khaki-clad figures, running for safety. They were led . . . by a man exceptionally tall for a Japanese . . . Twenty Gurkha rifles came up and crashed a volley. Alas for Gurkha marksmanship! Not a Japanese fell; zigzagging they ran on. But in a few seconds, as the Gurkhas fired again, they were all down, the last

[1] Slim: p. 267.

[2] This is hardly strange, for Stilwell, who despised Chiang-Kai-Shek, always referred to him both in public and in private as 'The Peanut'. Still, if he lacked the social graces, 'Vinegar Joe' could at least get a Chinese army to advance.

to fall being the tall man. The tank lumbered up, dipped its gun and, with perhaps unnecessary emphasis, finished him off. Within ten minutes, having made sure no Japanese remained alive in the bunkers, the two platoons of Gurkhas and their Indian-manned tank moved on to their next assignment ... A rear party appeared, attended to their own casualties, and dragged out the enemy bodies to search them for papers and identifications. It was all very business-like.'[1]

Meanwhile in the Arakan XV Corps suddenly came to life again and in a fast moving amphibious campaign retook Akyab (3 January 1945), and inflicted a sharp reverse on the Japanese at Myebon (12 -13 January). This was followed up by the landing of 3 Commando Brigade (22 January) at Kangaw which cut the Japanese communications in the Arakan, and proved the decisive battle of that campaign.

The fighting for Meiktila and Mandalay, the great battle for Central Burma, had exhausted General Kimura's reserves. Too late he decided to withdraw, and Fourteenth Army beat him in the race for Toungoo, largely because a secret force of Karen Guerrillas, organized well in advance, delayed the retreating Japanese with ambush after ambush.

It was now a question whether the British could reach Rangoon before the monsoon should break. On 3 May that race too was won.

By that time the survivors of Kimura's broken army were scattered all over the country, and, although there was still a great deal of mopping-up to be done before the final Japanese surrender, the campaign in Burma was won.

The Fourteenth Army had the defeats of 1942 behind it; the jungle, malaria, and the monsoon to contend with; it was always low in priority for equipment of every kind, from landing-craft and parachutes to more mundane comforts such as a bottle of beer or a loaf of bread instead of the eternal 'compo' rations. Its triumph against every adversity has a dramatic quality all its own. Many contributed nobly to the good work, but one will be remembered when all the rest are forgotten – Field-Marshal Slim.

[1] Slim: p. 438.

CHAPTER THIRTY-THREE

THE ARDENNES

1944

20 Oct.	Americans take Aachen.
3 Nov.	Jodl briefs the three army commanders of Army Group B.
28 Nov.	First Allied convoy reaches Antwerp.
2 Dec.	Hitler's Berlin Conference.
11/12 Dec.	Hitler's final briefing at the 'Eagle's Nest' near Siegenberg, Hesse.
16 Dec.	German offensive begins.
18 Dec.	101st Airborne Division reaches Bastogne. Dense fog over battlefield.
19 Dec.	Sixth Panzer Army held up.
21 Dec.	Germans take St. Vith. The weather improves.
22 Dec.	Bastogne summoned to surrender.
23 Dec.	The weather clears.
24 Dec.	High water-mark of the German advance.
25 Dec.	German spearhead crushed near Dinant.
30 Dec.	Patton and Manteuffel clash round Bastogne.

1945

3 Jan.	Hodges attacks.
8 Jan.	Hitler agrees to limited withdrawals.
9 Jan.	Patton breaks out of Bastogne.
12 Jan.	Russian winter offensive begins.
13 Jan.	Hitler orders a retreat on the Western front.
16 Jan.	Patton and Hodges meet at Houffalize.
28 Jan.	The battle ends.

> '*Soldiers of the West Front, your great hour has struck. Every-thing is at stake!*' - VON RUNDSTEDT. 15 December 1944.

NOT since Pearl Harbor had the Americans received so rude a shock as when the dawn of 16 December 1944 was broken by the thunder of a thousand guns: German guns, heralding a most deter-minded onslaught.

Ever since July, Hitler, with a strategic sense which one is com-pelled to admire, had been building up a reserve, a *masse de manoeuvre*, of 250,000 men. It was little enough for a two-front war, nor were they the soldiers of 1940, but it was still a force capable of delivering a heavy blow. And it was commanded by von Rundstedt, a man of whom miracles could still be expected. He had already performed one when he stabilized the German line on the Western Front after the débâcle in Normandy. Now he performed another by concentrating Hitler's last army (Model's Army Group B) in the Eifel area without attracting the attention of the American High Command. How did the Allied intelligence fail to see a quarter of a million men, their vehicles and 1,100 tanks? They saw what they wanted to see. The Germans, they thought, were licked – and anyway who would think of mounting an offensive in the Ardennes in the middle of winter? A certain number of suspicious troop movements were reported by prisoners, civilians and by airmen, but their signi-ficance was discounted. As the Germans hoped, these were thought to be reinforcements for the fighting round Aachen.

Although von Rundstedt was to command the offensive, he did not favour it. It was Hitler's own brain-child. Physically the *Führer* was not the man he had been before the bomb attempt of 20 July. Lt.-General Hasso von Manteuffel saw him as 'a stooped figure with a pale and puffy face, hunched in his chair, his hands trembling, his left arm subject to a violent twitching which he did his best to conceal, a sick man apparently borne down by the burden of his responsibility. When he walked he dragged one leg behind him.' But this miserable, shambling creature could still make himself obeyed. Whatever his physical condition his will-power was unimpaired. Temperamentally unstable, he was incapable of playing a waiting game. He deliberately sought a decision. Moreover that acute if unbalanced mind could detect certain factors in favour of his plan.

In 1940 the Ardennes had been the weak link in the French chain. Now the Monschau-Echternach sector was the weakest part of Eisenhower's front. Lt.-General Courtney H. Hodges (First Army) was holding 85 miles with only five divisions and three of them (2, 4 and 28) had suffered heavily in the recent fighting round Aachen. Only about 100 miles to the NW. was Antwerp, the great Allied supply base, which had recently been opened to seaborne traffic. The German commanders knew the narrow roads of the Ardennes with their hairpin bends and steep hillsides very well. They had come that way in 1940. Bad weather could be expected to nullify the Allied air superiority. Otto Skorzeny's Panzer Brigade 150, disguised in American uniforms, would cause confusion behind the lines.[1]

Von Manteuffel had a conversation with Hitler on 2 December, when the latter admitted that there was

> 'a certain disparity between the distant objective of Antwerp and the forces which were to capture it. However, he said, this was the time to put everything on one throw of the dice, "for Germany needs a pause to draw breath". Even a partial success, he believed, would retard the plans of the Allies by eight to ten weeks, . . . Temporary stabilization on the Western Front would enable the Supreme Command to move forces from there to the threatened central sector of the Eastern Front.'[2]

The German generals were not unnaturally concerned about the question of air cover. After the Berlin conference Manteuffel told Hitler that 'in our sector of the front we never saw or heard a German aeroplane these days'. He received this curious reply:

> 'The *Luftwaffe* is being deliberately held back. Göring has reported that he has three thousand fighters available for the operation. You know Göring's reports. Discount one thousand, and that still leaves a thousand to work with you and a thousand for Sepp Dietrich.'[3]

[1] 'The importance of Operation *Greif* has been grossly exaggerated since the war.' (Von Manteuffel).

[2] Freidin: *The Fatal Decisions*, p. 219.

[3] Freidin: p. 225.

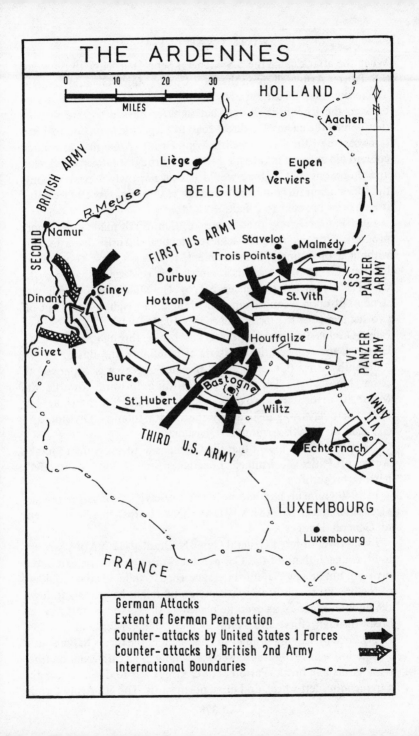

THE ARDENNES

0 10 20 30
MILES

HOLLAND

Aachen

Liège

Eupen
Verviers

BELGIUM

BRITISH ARMY

R. Meuse

SECOND

Namur

FIRST US ARMY

Stavelot
Trois Points
Malmédy

Durbuy

Ciney

Hotton

St. Vith

S.S. PANZER ARMY

Dinant

Houffalize

VI PANZER ARMY

Givet

Bure

Bastogne

St. Hubert

Wiltz

VII ARMY

THIRD U.S. ARMY

Echternach

LUXEMBOURG

Luxembourg

FRANCE

German Attacks
Extent of German Penetration
Counter-attacks by United States 1 Forces
Counter-attacks by British 2nd Army
International Boundaries

When the attack came the S.S. General Sepp Dietrich with the Sixth S.S. Panzer Army fell upon the US V Corps (Major-General Leonard T. Gerow) and thrust towards Liège. The Americans were driven back to the Eisenborn Ridge, but in three days desperate fighting they denied the enemy the direct road to Liège, the main communications centre of Bradley's Twelfth Army Group. A German armoured column did succeed in thrusting forward through Malmédy, Stavelot, and Stonmont, but as luck would have it narrowly missed not only the Allies' main fuel dump but Hodges' H.Q. at Spa. By 19 December it had been brought to a halt.

Fifth Panzer Army, though weaker than Sixth made much more progress. Von Manteuffel achieved tactical surprise by attacking without a preliminary bombardment, relying on close cooperation between his armour and his infantry. His onslaught shattered the US VIII Corps (Major-General Troy H. Middleton), which was strung out upon a long front. On Manteuffel's right a corps cut off two regiments of the inexperienced US 106th Division in the Schnee Eifel. On his left two panzer corps broke through the US 28th Division, and reached the outskirts of Houffalize and Bastogne.

Seventh Army (General Erich Brandenberger) was supposed to cover Manteuffel's left flank by thrusting forward towards the Meuse. It made some progress at first especially on the right, but after a few days was held up by the US 4th Infantry Division and elements of the 9th Armoured Division.

Dietrich's failure meant that the Germans were not going to retake Antwerp. Hitler determined nonetheless to exploit Manteuffel's narrow breakthrough.

In 1940 Gamelin had had no theatre reserve, no *masse de manoeuvre*. Eisenhower had the XVIII Airborne Corps; this he now sent to General Hodges.

Eisenhower ordered General Omar N. Bradley (12th Army Group) to attack each flank of the German breakthrough with an armoured division. But he saw that if Model succeeded in widening the shoulders of the breakthrough Bradley's army group might be split right down the middle. Practical as ever, he placed all the US forces north of the break-through (First and Ninth Armies) under Montgomery (21st Army Group), leaving Bradley in command of the forces to the south.

Like Joffre in 1914 Eisenhower was willing to give up ground rather than let his line break. Patton (Third Army) was to disengage, make a tremendous left wheel, and drive northwards. The 6th Army Group in Alsace would have to take over Patton's sector in the Saar even if this meant giving ground in Alsace and perhaps abandoning Strasbourg. General de Gaulle was *not* pleased. But in fact the Germans were in no position to mount another offensive, and although the northern corner of Alsace was evacuated, Strasbourg itself was saved.

While Eisenhower was taking a grip on the situation, his front line troops, though hard-pressed, were putting up a fight which compared more than favourably with the resistance of the French IXth Army in 1940. The unfortunate Corap had had few if any tanks. It was the American armour that won time for Eisenhower's measures to take effect. The 7th Armoured Division denied St Vith to the enemy until 21 December. Part of the 10th Armoured Division delayed von Manteuffel just long enough to allow 101st Airborne Division to establish itself in Bastogne.

Bastogne stood like a rock. Fifth Panzer Army unable to drive through had to go round, shedding considerable forces to contain the improvised fortress. Summoned to surrender (22 December) Brigadier-General Anthony McAuliffe, a modern Cambronne, curtly answered 'Nuts'.[1]

The Germans had not quite shot their bolt. Sixth Panzer Army got going again and Manteuffel's two panzer corps drove on westward and on Christmas Eve his 2nd Panzer Division was in sight of the Meuse, near Celles, three miles east of Dinant. But the attack had lost its momentum.

Meanwhile the Allied counter-attack was getting under way. The weather had cleared and 5,000 Allied planes were strafing the transport strung out nose to tail all the way to the German frontier. In the words of General Arnold 'We prepared to isolate the battlefield.' Moreover it was air supply that saved Bastogne, while Patton pushed up from the south to its relief.

In the line north of the gap Montgomery had three American corps under Hodges (V, XVIII Airborne and VII) with the British XXX Corps in reserve on the Meuse. Hodges' centre was still vulnerable and to shorten it Montgomery evacuated a salient round Vielsalm – *reculer pour mieux sauter* is no bad tactical axiom.

The US 2nd Armoured Division (VII Corps) cut off and destroyed Manteuffel's spearhead at Celles on Christmas Day. Next day the

[1] At the battle of Waterloo the French general Baron Pierre-Jacques-Etienne Cambronne, when summoned to surrender, replied with the single word 'Merde', though polite historians usually render his reply as '*La Garde meurt mais ne se rend pas!*'

US 4th Armoured Division broke through to Bastogne. Thus ended the first phase of the battle.

By Christmas Day von Rundstedt realized that the battle had been lost, but Hitler was not the man to admit defeat or to cut his losses. Instead he thought up a new double offensive. He would begin by taking Bastogne and then, wheeling north, would take the First Army in flank while a secondary attack engaged it from the direction of Roermond. In the New Year he would mount yet another offensive in Alsace.

At the same time Eisenhower was planning a counter-offensive which had rather more substance. Bradley and Montgomery were to strike simultaneously.

Bastogne was still the storm centre. The corridor to the town was only a mile wide in places. Patton was determined to drive off the two German corps that were squeezing its lifeline. At the same time Manteuffel was concentrating for the attack which would rid him once and for all of this thorn in his flesh. On 30 December they met head on, and locked in a deadly winter battle which ranged blindly and fiercely through the snow-clad woods and ravines of the Ardennes.

By the time the battle died down the Germans were spent. On 8 January 1945 Hitler reluctantly agreed to limited withdrawals, and next day Patton broke out of Bastogne. Model, helped by a break in the weather, began to disengage his forces. On the 13th, owing to the Russian winter offensive, the German Supreme Command withdrew Sixth S.S. Panzer Army from the Ardennes battle, and permitted a general retreat. Patton and Hodges joined hands at Houffalize on the 16th and Bradley was able to resume command of his army and restore his original line. By 28 January it was all over.

The battle cost the Allies 76,980 casualties, but it ruined Hitler's last reserve army both morally and physically. The Germans lost 70,000 casualties and 50,000 prisoners, besides 5-600 tanks and 1,600 planes. The Russians had launched their great winter offensive on 12 January, and Hitler no longer had his *masse de manoeuvre* to meet it: a terrible price to pay for the six weeks delay it imposed on the Western Allies.

It was a great victory. Even so the Germans, though less well trained than three years earlier, had hacked a wound 50 miles deep in the American line. They had fought with all their old devotion. The more credit to the Americans who beat such men.

The part of the air forces must not be underrated. The *Luftwaffe* was still able to send over 700 aircraft on New Year's Day, 1945 to attack Allied airfields and to destroy nearly 200 planes on the ground. On 22 January the Anglo-American air forces claimed to have destroyed 4,200 pieces of heavy equipment; railway engines and trucks, tanks, motor and horse-drawn vehicles.[1]

There are those who regard General Eisenhower as a very indifferent general, little more than a sort of Grand Liaison Officer. It is true that in the battle of the Ardennes his original lay-out was faulty. Major-General Fuller even goes so far as to say:

'The enormity of Eisenhower's distribution can be measured by supposing that it had been made in May, 1940. Had it been, then there can be little doubt that his armies would have suffered a similar fate to Gamelin's.'[2]

But this is going altogether too far, and ignores the fact that up to mid-December 1944 Eisenhower had had the initiative on the Western front, and was not simply sitting waiting to be attacked. Once the battle began he made the right decisions and he made them in time. In the event his 33 divisions mauled 26 German divisions. One can only judge a general by his works, good or ill, and it seems to the present writer that Eisenhower's stature is greatly enhanced by this macabre winter battle.

> '*Few, few shall part where many meet*
> *The snow shall be their winding sheet*
> *And every turf beneath their feet*
> *Shall be a soldier's sepulchre.*'[3]

[1] Fuller: *The Second World War*, p. 548.
[2] Fuller: p. 349.
[3] Thomas Campbell: *Hohenlinden*.

CHAPTER THIRTY-FOUR

ITALY, 1944–45

1944

4 Jun.	The fall of Rome.
6 Jun.	D Day: Normandy.
10 Jun.	Americans reach Civitavecchia.
22 Jun.	The 8th Army breaks the Trasimene Line.
15 Jul.	Fifth Army attacks the Arno Line. French take Poggibonsi.
18 Jul.	The Poles take Ancona.
19 Jul.	Leghorn taken.
23 Jul.	Fall of Pisa.
4 Aug.	The British enter Florence.
15 Aug.	*Anvil.* Allied landings in the South of France.
26 Aug.	Offensive on the Adriatic coast.
Aug./Nov.	Operations delayed by rain.
13/17 Sep.	Battle of the Gothic Line.
21 Sep.	The Canadians take Rimini.
5 Oct.	The British land in Greece.
14 Oct.	The British occupy Athens.
21 Nov.	Allied offensive begins.
5 Dec.	Canadians occupy Ravenna.
6 Dec./ 5 Jan.	Civil War in Athens.
15 Dec.	German counter-attack on Lucca.

1945

9 Apr.	The Poles break the Comacchio Line.
11 Apr.	1st New Zealand Division crosses the River Santerno.
19 Apr.	The Americans break through the Argento Gap and occupy Bologna. The pursuit begins.
26 Apr.	The Brenner Pass sealed.

26 Apr.	The fall of Verona and Genoa.
	Collapse of German resistance.
29 Apr.	Murder of Mussolini.
29 Apr./	
2 May	Surrender of German units and commanders in Italy.
2 May	New Zealanders occupy Trieste.

'The Italian campaign – more, probably than any other – abounds with drama and romance. The background as it unfolded evoked continual memories of Italy's great past; in the foreground in sharp strident contrast there was the momentous advance of modern armies . . . The scene called to mind Italian masters of every age and school: if the ruins of Cassino resembled the cold desolation of Dante's Nine Circles of Hell, the countryside very often recalled the canvases of Bellini.'   FIELD-MARSHAL ALEXANDER.[1]

WITH THE invasion of Normandy, Italy took second priority among the campaigns of the Anglo-American Allies in Europe. Even so their presence in the peninsula was a standing threat not only to Germany's southern frontier, but also to her position in the Balkans – a third front.

The Allies were to milk their Italian armies to find divisions for *Dragoon* – the invasion of the South of France – and other fronts. The Germans did not venture to thin out the troops opposing them, continuing to maintain 25 divisions in Italy. The value of the great Allied victory in the Battle for Rome may be measured by the number of divisions which the Germans were compelled to subtract from their armies elsewhere to reinforce Italy. The Hermann Göring Division from France, the 20th *Luftwaffe* Field Division[2] from Denmark, the 42nd Jäger and the 162nd Turkoman[2] Divisions from the Balkans, and the 19th *Luftwaffe* Field Division[2] from Belgium.

His defeat compelled Kesselring to fall back 150 miles to the Gothic Line, a strong defensive position running from Pisa to Rimini. General Alexander, for his part, saw his opportunity of breaching the northern Apennines before the Germans could get set there. On 7 June he ordered Eighth Army to advance 'with all possible speed direct on the general area Florence-Bibbiena-Arezzo and

[1] Quoted by Linklater: *The Campaign in Italy*, p. 9.
[2] See Senger und Etterlin: *Neither Fear nor Hope*, for an appraisal of these divisions, which were not entirely battle-worthy.

Fifth Army direct on the general area Pisa-Lucca-Pistoia'. The two Army Commanders were authorized to take extreme risks in order to secure these vital strategic areas. They were not to concern themselves unduly with the security of their flanks. The aim was to get into the valley of the Arno and break the Apennine line from Florence to Bologna. In order to save transport and bridging material for this dual offensive, the advance on the Adriatic flank was temporarily halted.

The Allies crossed the Tiber without delay and thrust forward in pursuit of the defeated enemy, advancing 75 miles in 12 days. The arrival of XIV Panzer Corps slowed down the American advance up the coast of the Tyrrhenian Sea, but they had advanced another 35 miles by 23 June.

In the centre the British Eighth Army fought its way forward against resolute opposition, taking Perugia on 20 June. There followed the fierce eight day battle for the Lake Trasimene line, which was broken by the 28th.

Meanwhile on the Adriatic coast, after a lull, with both sides thin on the ground, the Polish Corps, rested after Cassino, had come into the line. Pressing forward with characteristic impetuosity it took Ancona on 18 July.

Next day the US Fifth Army reached Leghorn. Working with their usual skill and efficiency the American engineers soon had the port in working order. By 23 July Fifth Army had occupied Pisa. There followed a lull, with the Americans still south of the River Arno.

The Eighth Army entered Florence,[1] wounded but still beautiful, on 4 August.

As early as the autumn of 1943 the Todt Organization, with plenty of forced Italian labour at its command, had been constructing the Gothic Line. This position in the Etruscan Apennines was designed to deny the Po Valley to the Allies, and so protect 'the under-belly of Europe'. The fall of Cassino and Rome had galvanized the German engineers who, while their compatriots were winning them time by their dogged rearguard actions at Lake Trasimene and elsewhere, were working hard to complete their defences. But, formidable though these were, they were never completely finished.

The departure of the French Expeditionary Corps to take part in the landing in the south of France had deprived General Alexander of his best mountain-troops. Beyond question they would have been

[1] Although they did much damage, the Germans spared the Ponte Vecchio.

invaluable, and as Linklater has pointed out, might have found and exploited the weak point in the German position at Firenzuola.

General Leese now put forward a plan to surprise the Germans by an attack on the Adriatic flank, and roll up their line from the east, instead of continuing to thrust northwards from Florence. General Truscott's successes in the south of France, where he had rapidly taken Marseilles and Toulon, seemed to augur well for the prospects of the assault on the Gothic Line. And indeed at first all went well, for it was breached at the first assault. But unfortunately, the Line backed by range after range of forbidding mountains, and the excellent road system in the Po Valley permitted Kesselring to make the best possible use of his mobile reserves. The breaching of the Gothic Line was not followed by any rapid progress. Although 3,000 prisoners were taken in the first fortnight's fighting, British casualties numbered 8,000. About 100 tanks had been lost and the Germans' Panzer, which outgunned any Allied tank except the Churchill, besides being very well-armoured, was causing a good deal of concern.

Meanwhile the Fifth Army, gravely weakened by the demands of *Dragoon*, had regrouped with the British XIII Corps under its command, and was also pushing forward towards the Gothic Line. The Germans, who had had to send troops to face the British on the Adriatic Coast, now fell back to the main defences of the Line.

The Germans laboured under the disadvantage that they could not tell where General Clark would strike. When it did come, his blow fell on Il Giogo Pass. Tremendous artillery fire demoralized the defenders: one corps' artillery fired nearly 13,000 rounds on 17 September, which 'was quite a normal day'.[1] After a fortnight's fighting the Fifth Army also had broken the Gothic Line in several places.

The Eighth Army was now at the southern edge of the Po delta, a complex of canalized rivers and streams, where the Germans had systematically demolished bridges and culverts. The area was thickly populated, and the strongly-built farms and villages lent themselves to defence. The weather, too, favoured the defenders. It was a terrible autumn. Rain and floods turned streams to torrents and brought mud to rival the Flanders variety of the First World War. Not only was the tactical situation affected: the administrative machinery of the army became seriously clogged. To the tired troops the lack of warm clothing, and of reasonable accommodation, were very real hardships.

[1] Linklater: *The Campaign in Italy*, p. 378.

At this juncture General Leese was appointed Commander-in-Chief of the Allied Land Forces in South-East Asia, and was succeeded in command of the Eighth Army by General McCreery (8 August).

Despite the weather and the flooding the Eighth Army made considerable progress in mid-October by a series of attacks astride Highway 9. As each river obstacle was reached the British crossed the upper waters and turned it by moving through the foothills. This offensive had, however, the effect of shortening the German line in the hills south of Bologna, which city was now seriously threatened by the US Fifth Army.

It had become evident to the Allied Commanders that it was not going to be possible to give the Germans in Italy the *coup de grâce* until the spring of 1945. The aim of the Allied operations was now to keep the Germans fully occupied so as to prevent them withdrawing troops to their Eastern or Western Fronts. Starved of replacements the Allies did not find this easy, particularly as they had at the same time to find a garrison for Greece. The more tired the troops became the more they needed gunfire support, and by October the shortage of ammunition had become a serious problem, and the allotment of shells was down to 25 rounds per gun per day for field guns, and 15 for medium and heavy.

At the same time General von Vietinghoff's Tenth Army, though it had been able to meet the first phase of the Eighth Army's winter offensive without drawing on his general reserve, had also been severely mauled. The Allies kept up the pressure as best they could and by Christmas were established on their winter line, the River Senio. The Canadians had taken Ravenna on 5 December, but the Fifth Army's offensive had still not wrested Bologna from the enemy.

There was some local fighting during the winter, as when at Christmas the Germans launched a sudden counter-attack, routed the US 92nd Negro Division and threatened the Fifth Army's communications with Leghorn. This particular situation was restored by 8th Indian Division, borrowed from Eighth Army. But on the whole the winter was quiet and the Allies rested and built-up their armies for the final onset. Replacements of men and materials were now plentiful. By the time the spring weather came morale was high.

Both sides now withdrew troops from Italy. The Combined Chiefs of Staff moved the 1st Canadian Corps to North-Western Europe, while the Germans' 16th S.S. and 356 Divisions were taken from von Vietinghoff, who had succeeded Kesselring in command of Army

Group C. The Germans still had rather more than 23 divisions besides six of Italian Fascists. The US Fifth Army (now under General Truscott) was faced by the Fourteenth Army; the Eighth by the German Tenth. And behind the lines some 50,000 Italian Partisans were amusing themselves with sabotage and guerrilla warfare.

By this time the Allied air offensive had wrecked the German lines of communications. All the Po bridges had been destroyed in the autumn of 1944. Fine weather in February and March left railway-yards, roads, bridges, and supply-dumps at the mercy of the XXIInd Tactical Air Command and the Desert Air Force. The railway through the Brenner Pass was almost continuously interrupted. According to von Senger[1] the Allied 'air superiority had become so preponderant that nobody dared show himself on the roads in daylight'.

On 24 March General Mark Clark, the commander of the Fifteenth Army Group, issued orders for the final offensive. His aim was to destroy the German armies south of the Po, to force the passage of that river, and to take Verona.

The Eighth Army attacked on 9 April after a tremendous artillery bombardment, and with strong support from fighter-bombers. The Germans were holding the banks of the Senio in force, and five of their forward battalions were practically obliterated by the preliminary bombardment. The flame-throwing Crocodile tanks played a decisive part, and everywhere good progress was made.

On the 14th the US Fifth Army began its attack, and achieved a considerable degree of surprise. At first the Germans regarded it as a diversionary operation. A breakthrough was made between LI Mountain Corps and XIV Panzer Corps. This the Germans had insufficient reserves to meet. Since all his communications with Germany ran through Verona, von Vietinghoff was particularly sensitive to the pressure from Eighth Army near Comacchio. For this reason he had concentrated two of his three reserve divisions there. Thus the American attack, the second phase of the Allied offensive against the so-called Genghiz Khan Line, was very successful and on 21 April Bologna was at last occupied by Polish and American troops.

The German army was beginning to disintegrate. General von Senger describes[2] the hazards of re-crossing the Po.

[1] Senger und Etterlin: *Neither Fear nor Hope*, p. 229.
[2] Senger und Etterlin: pp. 300–301.

'My H.Q. staff was dissolved into separate groups. At dawn on the 23rd we found a ferry at Bergantino. Of the thirty-six Po ferries in the zone of 14th Army, four only were still serviceable. Because of the incessant fighter-bomber attacks it was useless to cross in daylight. As the level of water in the Po was low, many officers and men were able to swim across. The access road at Revere was blocked by many columns of burning vehicles. I had to leave my cars behind. In the twilight we crossed the river, and together with my operations staff I marched the twenty-five kilometres to Legnano. We were unable to establish any communications. Major-General von Schellwitz, who after General Pfeiffer's death[1] had assumed command of the remnants of 65 and 305 Inf. Divs., was captured south of the river.'

Later he was able to organize some sort of front between Lake Garda and the Pasubio Pass, with a few fresh troops – including a Parachute officers' School and an S.S. Mountain School – but there were no guns, and the roads to the North were 'filled with an unending stream of stragglers'.

With the fall of Verona on the 26th the German forces in Italy had been cut in two. The same day Genoa surrendered to the Partisans.

On the Eighth Army front only the German Parachute Divisions were still in good order. All the rest had been well battered. On 19 April General Keightley sent his Vth Corps through the Argenta Gap, making for Ferrara and Bondeno to cut off the Germans retreating from Bologna. There were a few formations, notably the 29th Panzer Grenadier Division, still prepared to put up a desperate resistance in the face of grievous losses. But by the 25th April it was all over. On that day

'Lieut.-General the Graf von Schwerin, commanding the LXXVIth Corps, surrendered with some formality – and the remnants of his champagne – to the 27th Lancers, and declared his inability to continue fighting with a few Divisional Headquarters which had no troops under command. His opinion was substantiated by the wreckage on the river bank, where among hundreds of loose horses and draught oxen a thousand pieces of artillery and eighty tanks lay in the discard, and a vast concourse of carts and wagons – pressed into service and crowded with the accoutrements of flight – stood smouldering or lamed on broken wheels. Fourteen

[1] Lt.-General Pfeiffer, commander of 65 Infantry Division, was killed at the bridge at Finale.

thousand prisoners were in the Vth Corps's cages to increase the evidence of an Army's mortality.'[1]

The end came when on 2 May General von Vietinghoff's plenipotentiaries presented themselves at the palace of Caserta to surrender.

Benito Mussolini had not survived the collapse of his Allies. Rescued by the daring of Otto Skorzeny, the German partisan leader, from his inaccessible prison in the Gran Sasso, he had become once more the figurehead of Fascism – or what remained of it – in Northern Italy. As the Allies closed in on Milan, Mussolini, his mistress, Carla Petacci, and a few diehard adherents, taking with them a fortune in gold, made for Switzerland. On the night of 28 April, by the merest chance, a Communist, Lt.-Colonel Valerio, discovered them in a farmhouse near Lake Como. Soon afterwards he shot them. When Carla Petacci pleaded for their lives he said: 'I execute the will of the Italian people.' It is charitable to doubt whether his countrymen would have wished her death as well as that of the fallen dictator, but in the temper of the hour she may have been spared worse things. In Milan an hysterical mob subjected the lifeless corpses and those of a dozen other dead Fascists to revolting indignities. They were in merciless mood.

The long campaign, which had lasted 600 days, was over. Even before the final surrender the defence of Italy had cost the Germans 556,000 casualties. The Allies had lost 312,000 killed and wounded, of which 59,000 was the 8th Army's share.

Once the concentration for Normandy had got under way the Allied commanders had been handicapped because they never received strategic priority. Indeed, at one time or another 21 divisions were withdrawn to fight in other theatres. Even so, in 1944 the presence of the Allied armies in Italy had contained no less than 55 enemy divisions in the Mediterranean area.

General Fuller is pleased to describe the Italian campaign as one 'which for lack of strategic sense and tactical imagination is unique in military history.'[1] No doubt the tactics of the campaign could have been more enterprising had it been possible to have provided more landing craft, or more formations specially trained in mountain warfare.

[1] Linklater: p. 465.
[2] Fuller: p. 261.

Perhaps, at times, the campaign lacked subtlety both in its strategy and its tactics. Nevertheless by the crude yet warlike standards of divisions employed and casualties inflicted, the Allies had very much the better of the bargain in Italy.

CHAPTER THIRTY-FIVE

THE END IN GERMANY

1945

12 Jan.	Red Army offensive begins.
17 Jan.	Russians enter Warsaw.
18 Jan.	Rokossovsky takes Modlin.
19 Jan.	Koniev captures Cracow.
20 Jan.	Cherniakhovsky takes Tilsit.
21 Jan.	Cherniakhovsky captures Gumbinnen.
	Rokossovsky takes Tannenberg.
23 Jan.	Koniev enters Silesia and reaches the Oder.
28 Jan.	End of the Battle of the Ardennes.
10 Feb.	Rokossovsky takes Elbing.
13 Feb.	Fall of Budapest.
23 Feb.	Zhukov takes Poznan.
6 Mar.	Allies take Cologne.
7 Mar.	Capture of Remagen bridge.
22 Mar.	Patton crosses the Rhine.
23 Mar.	Montgomery crosses the Rhine.
28 Mar.	Gdynia taken.
29 Mar.	Capture of Mannheim.
30 Mar.	Fall of Danzig.
1 Apr.	Paderborn. Meeting of US First and Ninth Armies.
	Russians denounce the Soviet-Japanese neutrality pact.
8 Apr.	Fall of Bremen.
9 Apr.	The French take Karlsruhe.
	Vassilevsky takes Königsberg.
10 Apr.	Capture of Hannover.
12 Apr.	Death of President Roosevelt.
13 Apr.	Russians take Vienna.
20 Apr.	Nuremberg taken.
21 Apr.	Model commits suicide.
	The French take Stuttgart.
23 Apr.	Patton reaches the Czech frontier.

25 *Apr.*	Americans and Russians meet at Torgau.
26 *Apr.*	Malinovsky enters Brno.
27 *Apr.*	Russians and Americans meet in Germany.
1 *May*	Hitler commits suicide.
2 *May*	Fall of Berlin and Lübeck.
8 *May*	Unconditional surrender of Germany.

> '*Even if we could not conquer, we should drag half the world into destruction with us, and leave no one to triumph over Germany . . . We shall never capitulate, no never! We may be destroyed, but if we are we shall drag a world with us – a world in flames.*'   HITLER, 1934.

His morale bolstered by the flattery of such courtiers as Göring and Ribbentrop, Hitler remained singularly unmoved by the disasters of 1944. When on 24 December Guderian outlined the Russian dispositions, the Dictator ridiculed his forecasts. Himmler echoed his leader:

> 'You know, my dear Colonel-General, I don't really believe the Russians will attack at all. It's all an enormous bluff. The figures given by your department "Foreign Armies East" are grossly exaggerated. They're far too worried, I'm convinced there's nothing going on in the East.'

The demands of the Ardennes offensive and the refusal to withdraw the 30 divisions from the Courland peninsula left the Eastern front of 750 miles relatively thinly held. Guderian worked hard to build up a reserve but was far from satisfied with the result. When Hitler, in one of his more gracious moments, thanked him for his efforts, Guderian gloomily replied:

> 'The Eastern Front is like a house of cards. If the front is broken through at one point all the rest will collapse, for twelve and a half divisions are far too small a reserve for so extended a front.'[1]

It was fair comment.

When the Ardennes offensive was still raging, Churchill sent a message to Stalin (6 January) in which he described the battle as 'very heavy' and asked whether the Western Allies could 'count on a major Russian offensive on the Vistula front, or elsewhere, during January' . . .

[1] Guderian: p. 387.

It was with profound relief that Churchill received Stalin's reply which said that:

'in view of the position of our allies on the Western Front, Headquarters of the Supreme Command has decided to complete the preparations at a forced pace and, disregarding the weather, to launch wide-scale offensive operations against the Germans all along the Central Front not later than the second half of January.'

He was better than his word. The Red Army began its offensive on 12 January and was rewarded with a swift breakthrough. By the 17th they were in Warsaw. Koniev overran southern Poland, making for Silesia. Zhukov pushed on through central Poland, thrusting for the very heart of Germany; Rokossovsky advanced northwards on Danzig. In the north Cherniakhovsky was overrunning East Prussia and in the south Petrov was crossing the Carpathians.

By the end of the month the Red Army was on the Oder, and had penetrated the provinces of Silesia and Brandenberg. In Berlin there was panic, and thousands of Germans, slave labourers, and prisoners of war, trekked westwards through the freezing winter.

On 30 January the doomed Dictator broadcast to his followers for the last time, assuring them that by sparing his life on 20 July the Almighty had shown that He wished him to continue as their *Führer*, a conclusion which the events of his career scarcely seem to have warranted. He adjured the people to fight on and defeat 'the hordes that England had called up from the steppes of central Asia'.

On 3 February the Russian advance reached the Oder, only 36 miles east of Berlin, and by early March had cleared Silesia. Hitler used up most of his remaining reserves in a vain attempt to relieve Budapest, which fell on 13 February.

The conclusion of the Ardennes battle (28 January) left the Germans facing seven great armies west of the Rhine. Despite unfavourable weather in February the Allies fought their way forward, and by 13 March the whole of the west bank of the river was in their hands. It was bitter fighting all the way, for now the Germans were fighting for the Fatherland. If there was despair in their hearts, there was fanaticism as well. The British and Canadian soldiers who battled their way through the forests of the Reichswald and the Hochwald have grim memories of those days. But it was fighting that cost the enemy dear. The Germans lost 60,000 casualties and 293,000 prisoners between the start of the Reichswald offensive and the day (23 March) when the Allies stood poised and ready to cross the Rhine.

Meanwhile an all-out air offensive struck at German communications. Sometimes as many as 16,000 sorties were made in a day. On both 22 and 23 February 20,000 tons of bombs were dropped. The *Luftwaffe* could do nothing to protect the Reich from this devastating onslaught.

At one vital point the watch on the Rhine proved less than vigilant. On 7 March Sergeant Alexander A. Drabik of Holland, Ohio, led a platoon of the us 9th Armoured Division across the Ludendorff bridge at Remagen between Bonn and Cologne.

> 'We ran down the middle of the bridge, shouting as we went. I didn't stop because I knew that if we kept moving they couldn't hit me. My men were in squad column and not one of them was hit. We took cover in some bomb craters. Then we just sat and waited for the others to come. That's the way it was.'[1]

This was a windfall indeed – well might Eisenhower call it 'One of my happy moments of the war.'

Hitler reacted in his usual heavy-handed way. Four officers whom he considered to blame were court-martialled and shot.[2] Von Rundstedt was dismissed for the last time, and to take his place Field-Marshal Kesselring was summoned from Italy. He introduced himself to his new staff with the words 'Well, gentlemen, I am the new V-3'.

The Germans fought hard to seal off the Remagen bridge-head. Jet dive bombers, V-2 rockets and long-range artillery shells were hurled at the bridge, but when on 17 March it eventually collapsed the Americans had already pushed several divisions across.

Still Germany struggled on, and despite the decision to give Herr Himmler command of Army Group Vistula – a truly astonishing appointment – even managed to stage a brief counter-offensive in mid-February.

Every day now brought Hitler some evil tidings, but with the portrait of Frederick the Great hanging over his desk he could still take heart: 'When bad news threatens to crush my spirit I derive fresh courage from the contemplation of this picture. Look at those

---

[1] Snyder: *The War – A Concise History*, p. 426, quoting Sergeant Drabik.

[2] Ironically enough Captain Bratke, whose duty it was to demolish the bridge was taken prisoner and so outlived the *Führer's* wrath.

strong blue eyes, that wide brow. What a head!'[1] Certainly the *Führer* did not lack tenacity – and like his hero he couldn't be sacked!

Meanwhile in the south Patton's US Third Army had been reducing the Saar-Moselle area, a task he had completed by 23 February, and clearing the west bank of the Rhine. On the night of 22 March he suddenly crossed south of Mainz, losing only 28 casualties in the process. Far away in Berlin Hitler and his staff discussed this disaster on a sector that they knew only too well was practically unguarded – 'Is there no panzer brigade or something like that which could be sent there?' the *Führer* demanded, to be told that except for five tank-destroyers (*Jagdtiger*) in a repair shop at Sennelager everything had been committed.[2]

With his world collapsing about him, Hitler, showing a determination worthy of a better cause, maintained the unequal struggle. He now decided to proclaim a 'Scorched Earth' policy, telling Speer, when he protested:

> 'If the war is lost, the German nation will also perish. This fate is inevitable. There is no need to take into consideration the basic requirements of the people for continuing even a most primitive existence . . . Those who will remain after the battle are those who are inferior; for the good will have fallen.'[3]

Such was the man in whom the Germans had, with so few exceptions, put their trust.

North of the Ruhr the crossing of the Rhine was effected in more formal style than on Patton's front. The nature of the obstacle, which is lucidly described by Fuller, made this imperative:

> 'The width of the Rhine on Montgomery's front was between four hundred and five hundred yards, liable to increase from seven hundred to one thousand two hundred yards at high water, and the mean velocity of the current was about three and a half knots. With this breadth of water to cross, the whole operation was organized on amphibious lines – it was an inland waterborne invasion.'[4]

Montgomery, in his precise, calculating way, laid on a set-piece

[1] Guderian: p. 416.
[2] Wilmot: p. 756.
[3] Wilmot: p. 757.
[4] Fuller: p. 359.

attack. A shattering bombardment, of an hour's duration, opened the proceedings, then the 1st Commando Brigade crossed and seized Wesel. Meanwhile the 2nd British Army and the US Ninth Army were crossing north and south of that town respectively.

These strokes were followed up next day by a massive demonstration of airborne power. The British 6th Airborne from East Anglia and the US 17th Airborne from near Paris, escorted by 2,153 planes of the Tactical Air Forces, and carried in 1,572 planes and 1,326 gliders, landed beyond the Rhine. They were within range of artillery support from the west bank, and happily their casualties were not heavy.

Once across the Rhine the Allies could at last strike into the Ruhr, the industrial heart of Germany, the home of Krupp of Essen, Thyssen of Mülheim and a hundred lesser firms sprawled from Dortmund and Duisburg to Solingen and Hamm. In vain the *Führer* declared that the Ruhr was a fortress. There was no longer any magic in that formula. As March drew to its close the US First and Ninth Armies swung round the Ruhr in a double envelopment; the classic pincers movement in which the Nazis had so often crushed their foes. The two armies met near Paderborn on 1 April, trapping Model in a vast net 80 miles in diameter. By 18 April 400,000 Germans had been taken, and on the 21st Model, who had been declared a war criminal by the Russians, shot himself in a wood near Duisberg.

While Army Group B was being crushed in the vice, the German front was everywhere disintegrating. To the southward the American and French armies drove forward with unrelenting vigour. Patton reached Frankfurt on 29 March. Mannheim, Magdeburg, Leipzig, Bayreuth, all fell with bewildering speed. On 12 April the US Ninth Army reached the Elbe near Magdeburg. They were now only 60 miles from Berlin.

By the end of March the Red Army had entered Austria and on 13 April Vienna itself was taken. In the north Danzig had fallen on 30 March.

By this time the German soldiers scarcely knew what was going on. The support of tanks or planes was a thing of the past. Supply was uncertain, communications broke down. Units and formations, left for days on end without orders, had to sort things out for themselves as best they could. The number of 'missing' began to increase, as at long last defeatism began to spread through the *Wehrmacht*. The long-deferred Allied victory was in sight.

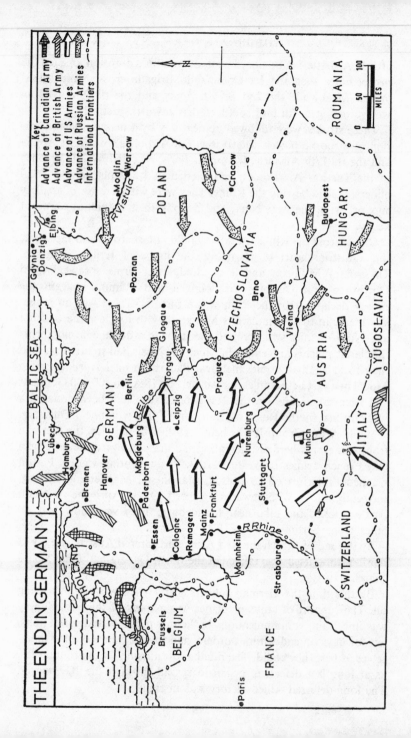

President Roosevelt did not live to see it. On 12 April he died suddenly of a cerebral haemorrhage, and was succeeded by the Vice-President, a former county judge from Missouri, Harry S. Truman. Hitler had long hoped for an event such as 'the miracle of the House of Brandenburg', which had saved Frederick the Great in the Seven Years War.[1] This miracle he saw in the death of the great American who had dealt him so many mortal blows. Yet, though Hitler himself did not live long enough to discover it, he had as relentless an enemy in Truman as in Roosevelt, and one who was to prove in every way equal to the great office to which he was so suddenly and tragically called.

It was not until 16 April that Zhukov and Koniev launched their final offensive. Within two days the T.34s were racing through Saxony. In Berlin Hitler prepared to make his last stand. On the 16th April the *Führer*, living to the last in his fantasy world, issued an Order of the Day to his soldiers on the Eastern Front.

'The hordes of our Judeo-Bolshevist foe have rallied for the last assault. They want to destroy Germany and to extinguish our people ... Colossal artillery forces are welcoming the enemy. Countless new units are replacing our losses ...

'This moment, which has removed from the face of the earth the greatest war criminal of all ages, will decide the turn in the fortunes of war.'

But his course was run. This was to be his last Order of the Day; he had little more than a week to live. His last days were bitter. On 23 April a telegram came from Göring, suggesting that as Hitler had decided to remain at his post in the fortress of Berlin, he, Göring, should 'take over, immediately, the total leadership of the Reich'. This provoked an explosion! Göring was a *Schweinhund*, and a drug addict! It was a stab-in-the-back! Göring, guilty of high treason, would be spared the death penalty, but must resign his high offices forthwith.

Next came the news that Himmler, his *treuer Heinrich*, through the mediation of the Swedish Count Folke Bernadotte, had endeavoured to open surrender negotiations. When the news filtered through to his Berlin bunker, Hitler went into another paroxysm of frustrated fury. 'Nothing is spared me! No loyalty is kept, no honour observed!

[1] The Czarina Elizabeth had died in 1762, and had been succeeded by the Czar, Peter III, who admired Frederick and withdrew Russia from the War.

There is no bitterness, no betrayal that has not been heaped upon me!'

On the night of 28/29 April, with the Russians only a few hundred yards away in the Potsdamer Platz, he married the faithful Eva Braun in the bunker in the garden of the Chancellery. Next, day after naming Admiral Dönitz as his successor, and poisoning his dog, he shot himself and went to join the 30 million who had fallen victim to his ambitions. His body was burnt. On 2 May the survivors of the Berlin garrison surrendered.

The British had crossed the Elbe on 29 April and on 2 May British, American and Russian troops met on the shores of the Baltic. On 4 May Field-Marshal Montgomery accepted the unconditional surrender of Dönitz's plenipotentiaries, Admiral von Friedeburg and General Kinzel, on Lüneberg Heath. Hostilities were over, but the document which formally concluded the Second German War was that signed at Rheims on 7 May, by Air Chief Marshal Tedder, representing Eisenhower, and by Marshal Zhukov and Field-Marshal Keitel. The document signed, a telegram was sent to the Combined Chiefs of Staff. It read:

'The mission of this Allied Force was fulfilled at 3 a.m., local time, 7 May 1945. Eisenhower.'

CHAPTER THIRTY SIX

IWO JIMA AND OKINAWA

1944

3 Oct.	Joint Chiefs of Staff Directive for the capture of Iwo Jima.
24 Nov.	B-29s from the Marianas begin bombing Tokyo.

1945

19 Feb./	
16 Mar.	Iwo Jima secured.
9/10 Mar.	Air raids on Japan. 83,793 killed.
26 Mar.	British Pacific Fleet joins the Americans.
6 Apr.	Landings on Okinawa.
7 Apr.	*Yamato* sunk.
12 Apr.	Death of President Roosevelt.
13 Apr.	American push on Okinawa.
28 May	450 Super-Fortresses attack Yokohama.
2 Jun.	660 Super-Fortresses attack Kure and other towns.
18 Jun.	Lt.-General Buckner killed.
20 Jun.	Okinawa: Japanese civilians surrendering *en masse*.
21 Jun.	End of organized resistance.
22 Jun.	Lt.-General Ushijima commits suicide.

O Lord! Thou knowest how busy I must be this day:
If I forget Thee, do not Thou forget me.
            SIR JACOB ASTLEY[1] at Edgehill, 23 October 1642.

AT LAST the time for the assault on Japan itself drew near.

Iwo Jima, $4\frac{1}{2}$ miles by $2\frac{1}{2}$, is the central island of the Volcano group and lies half way between Saipan, in the Marianas, and Tokyo. It was uninhabited except for its garrison. The Americans wanted it as an emergency landing place for their B-29s from the Marianas, which had begun bombing Japan on 24 November 1944. The Americans had given the Japanese plenty of time to make a fortress of an island which, had the Joint Chiefs of Staff decided to capture it immediately after the Marianas, could have been taken practically unopposed. Iwo Jima took 6,800 tons of bombs and 22,000 shells, from 5-inch to 16-inch in calibre, before the invasion began. But the defences skilfully tunnelled into the sides of the extinct volcano, Mount Suribachi, were proof against these attentions.

D-Day was 19 February 1945. The run-in went like clockwork, but once ashore things were different. The amphtracs found volcanic ash and cinders poor going and the terraces of Mount Suribachi practically insurmountable. The Japanese brought down a tremendous volume of mortar fire from the mouths of cleverly constructed tunnels. Of the 30,000 Marines landed that day 2,400 were hit. The beach-head was far short of that planned, but there was no counterattack. General Kuribayashi was conserving his strength.

Iwo Jima was one more island which the US Marines had to take yard by yard, fighting up bare slopes against a strongly entrenched enemy. The Japanese fought to the last and of a garrison of over 20,000 only 216 were taken prisoner. Thirty per cent of the American landing force became casualties.

The *Kamikazes* could play little part, for their bases were too far

---

[1] Sergeant-Major General of the Royalist Foot at Edgehill. A chaplain had the words of Astley's prayer printed on cards, and distributed to the Marines before the landing on Iwo Jima. (Morison: *The Two-Ocean War*, p. 517).

away. 21 February was a bad day, however, for one crashed the *Saratoga*[1] and destroyed 42 planes. Another wrecked the *Bismarck Sea*.

Okinawa,[2] 67 miles long by from three to 20 miles wide, was defended by Lt.-General Mitsuru Ushijima and some 90,000 men. Tenth Army (Lt.-General Simon Bolivar Buckner), not far short of 300,000 strong,[3] was given the task of taking it.

By this time very heavy raids by B-29s were going in against Japanese cities. These 'rocked the nation to its very foundations'.[4] Fast carrier raids (18–21 March) were not so successful, *Wasp*, *Yorktown* and *Franklin* all suffering serious damage from *Kamikazes*. Even so 161 Japanese aircraft were shot down.

The landings on Okinawa began on 1 April 1945 after five days of preliminary bombardment. All went well that Easter Sunday and by the evening Yontan and Kadena airfields were in American hands. The Japanese had retired from the beach area and 50,000 troops were ashore. General Ushijima did not intend to try conclusions with the invaders until they were beyond the effective range of naval gunfire support. Thus a week elapsed before the real fighting began.

Before that time a serious attempt was made to relieve the garrison. A sortie by the beautiful giant *Yamato* (72,908 tons),[5] the light cruiser *Yahagi* and eight destroyers was to follow up a mass attack by *Kamikazes*.

On 7 April Mitscher's task groups found the 'Special Surface Attack Force' (Vice-Admiral Ito) as it passed through Van Diemen Strait. From 1232–1417 plane after plane bombed and torpedoed the force, reducing the decks of the *Yamato* to a shambles. At 1423 she went down with 2,488 men. *Yahagi* and four destroyers were sunk. The Americans lost 15 planes. Japan now had only one battleship left, *Haruna*.

Her fleet crippled, Japan now depended on the *Kamikazes*, although conventional bombing continued. The period 6 April to 22 June was made hideous by the massed attacks bearing the charming title of *Kikusui*, which, being translated, means 'floating chrysanthemum'.

---

[1] She survived to meet her end from an American atomic bomb at Bikini!

[2] The island had belonged to Japan since 1879.

[3] 172,000 combatant and 115,000 non-combatant troops.

[4] Morison: p. 528, quoting Japanese sources.

[5] She was 863 feet long and had nine 18-inch guns. Range: 22½ miles. Crew: 2,767. Speed 27·5 knots.

It has been estimated that more than 3,000 *Kamikazes* were flown in these weeks. They sank 21 ships, and damaged 66.[1] When one adds to this hundreds of attacks by conventional aircraft one begins to comprehend the ordeal of the fleet supporting the Okinawa invasion. It was the most costly naval campaign of the war. But statistics do not really tell us what it was like. One example must suffice.

There were 355 *Kamikazes* in the first *Kikusui* attack which concentrated against the destroyers *Leutze* and *Newcomb*. The latter was attacked five times in swift succession. The first *Kamikaze* hit her after-stack, the second was splashed, and the third crashed right down through the ship and blew up, destroying the engine rooms. ' "With intentions of polishing us off," wrote her skipper, Commander I. E. McMillan, "a fourth plane raced toward *Newcomb* from the port beam and although under fire by her forward batteries came through to crash into the forward stack, spraying the entire amidships section of *Newcomb*, which was a raging conflagration, with a fresh supply of gasoline." Flames shot up hundreds of feet, followed by a thick pall of smoke and spray which so completely covered the destroyer that sailors in nearby battleships thought that she had gone down.'[2]

The British carriers[3] of the Pacific Fleet (Vice-Admiral Sir Bernard Rawlings), which had been operating with the Americans since 26 March, though their fuel capacity did not compare with that of the American carriers, were better able to cope with the *Kamikazes*, which did only local damage to their steel decks.

As early as 8 April 82 Marine Corsairs were operating from the captured airfields of Yontan and Kadena, though both were still under shellfire. Land-based planes were soon able to thicken up the carrier-based Combat Air Patrols and bring some relief to the destroyers on radar picket duty.

By 19 April the Americans, with four-fifths of the island in their hands, had 160,000 men ashore. They were up against the fortified Japanese position across the three-mile waist of the island. The defences were as tough as anything the Americans had met on the long road from Guadalcanal. But by mid-June the Japanese were

[1] 43 had to be scrapped: the other 23 were out of action for more than 30 days. See Morison: p. 544, for an interesting table of the effects of *Kikusui* attacks.

[2] Morison: p. 545. Both the destroyers had to be scrapped, but thanks to almost incredibly efficient rescue work lost only 47 killed and missing.

[3] *Indomitable, Victorious, Illustrious* and *Indefatigable.*

almost worn down. When on 18 June Lt.-General Buckner was killed by shellfire, while observing one of the last attacks of the campaign, his work was nearly complete.

On 20 June civilians were surrendering *en masse* and next day Major-General Geiger was able to report that organized resistance was at an end. At dawn on 22 June, when American grenades were already exploding nearby, Lt.-General Ushijima, in full uniform, accompanied by his Chief of Staff, Lt.-General Cho, in a white *kimono*, emerged from their Headquarters cave, seated themselves on a quilt covered by a white cloth, bowed to the eastern sky, and, with the assistance of an Adjutant, committed *hari-kiri*. In the words of a Japanese eye-witness 'both generals had nobly accomplished their last duty to the Emperor.'[1]

They had certainly exacted a heavy toll of American life. The war might be long lost but there was no falling-off in the resolute resistance of the obedient, fanatical, fatalistic Japanese soldier. In taking Okinawa, Tenth Army lost 7,613 killed and 31,800 wounded. The United States Navy had 4,900 sailors killed and 4,800 wounded; 34 ships and craft sunk, 368 damaged.

As it turned out, General Carl Spaatz's US Army Strategic Air Force was to strike the mortal blow against Japan. He had the Eighth Air Force (Lt.-General J. H. Doolittle) in Okinawa and the Twentieth (Lt.-General N. F. Twining) in the Marianas. With amazing speed the Americans constructed 23 airstrips on Okinawa, and by the end of the war 18 groups of heavy and medium bombers and fighters were operating from that hard-won base.

Okinawa was, however, much more than an air base. Admiral Nimitz summarized its strategic value thus:

'Establishment of our forces on Okinawa has practically cut off all Japanese positions to the southward as far as sea communications are concerned. It has made the Japanese situation in China, Burma, and the Dutch East Indies untenable and has forced withdrawals which are now being exploited by our forces in China.'

That Japan was beaten was clear enough. But would she surrender without an invasion that could cost another 50,000 American lives? President Roosevelt had not lived to see victory. While the fight for Okinawa was at its height he had died suddenly. His successor, the unknown Harry S. Truman, was to have an early opportunity to show the world the calibre of his decisions.

[1] Only about 7,000 of their men were taken prisoner.

CHAPTER THIRTY-SEVEN

THE BOMB

1945

Feb.	Americans recapture Manila.
7 Apr.	The *Yamato* sunk.
21 Jun.	Resistance ends on Okinawa.
22 Jun.	Imperial Presence Conference.
16 Jul.	Atomic bomb tested in New Mexico.
6 Aug.	An atomic bomb is dropped on Hiroshima.
8 Aug.	Russia declares war on Japan.
9 Aug.	An atomic bomb is dropped on Nagasaki.
14 Aug.	Unconditional surrender of the Japanese Government.
2 Sep.	The Japanese surrender signed in Tokyo Bay.
5 Sep.	British reoccupy Singapore.
7 Dec.	Yamashita executed.
22 Dec.	Tojo hanged.

> '*A fission bomb of superlatively destructive power will result from bringing quickly together a sufficient mass of element U-235. This seems as sure as any untried prediction based upon theory and experiment can be.*'
> Report of the secret committee of the National Academy of Science. Washington, 6 November 1941.

BY MAY 1945 the Japanese knew they were beaten, but President Truman did not know they knew. The Japanese wanted to find a way out of their predicament, but always in the background was the stumbling block of Unconditional Surrender. After the loss of Manila in February the Emperor consulted certain elder statesmen, including Prince Konoye. All were agreed that peace was desirable, but they did not know how to bring it about.

When in April the *Yamato*, newest and biggest of Japanese battleships, was sunk, all hope of victory at sea vanished. Nothing could be done to help the armies in Burma and Yunan. The Emperor resolved to seek peace. On 22 June he summoned the Imperial Presence Conference, and gave orders that the question of ending the war as quickly as possible should be considered. This, commented a Court official, 'in those days of frenzied chauvinism was an act which required an extraordinary resolution, involving a grave risk even to the august person of an emperor'.[1]

Hiroshima ('the broad island'), the seventh largest town in Japan, stood where the seven arms of the river Ota pour into the inland sea. Arsenal, harbour, factories, oil refineries and warehouses formed a triangle, inhabited by 343,000 civilians and a garrison of perhaps 150,000 soldiers. For all the horror of its fate it was certainly 'a military target' by the standards already established in World War II. Estimates vary as to how much it had already suffered from bombing during raids in March and April.

At nine minutes past seven on the morning of 6 August four B-29s

---

[1] Flower and Reeves: *The War*, p. 1027.

appeared in the cloudless sky and the sirens sounded. By 7.31 they had disappeared and the all-clear went.

Meanwhile a single Superfortress, named the *Enola Gay*, and piloted by Colonel Paul W. Tibbets, had released one bomb, which had descended five miles by parachute and burst over the target. It left no crater.

The casualties were approximately 78,000 killed, 10,000 missing, and 37,000 injured, not counting those who were to suffer later from exposure to gamma rays.

So bald a statement hardly conveys the horror of what happened. A Japanese journalist describes the scene:

'Suddenly a glaring whitish pinkish light appeared in the sky accompanied by an unnatural tremor which was followed almost immediately by a wave of suffocating heat and a wind which swept away everything in its path.

Within a few seconds the thousands of people in the streets and the gardens in the centre of the town were scorched by a wave of searing heat.

Many were killed instantly, others lay writhing on the ground screaming in agony from the intolerable pain of their burns. Everything standing upright in the way of the blast – walls, houses, factories, and other buildings – was annihilated and the debris spun round in a whirlwind and was carried up into the air. Trams were picked up and tossed aside as though they had neither weight nor solidity. Trains were flung off the rails as though they were toys. Horses, dogs and cattle suffered the same fate as human beings. Every living thing was petrified in an attitude of indescribable suffering. Even the vegetation did not escape. Trees went up in flames, the rice plants lost their greenness, the grass burned on the ground like dry straw.

Beyond the zone of utter death in which nothing remained alive houses collapsed in a whirl of beams, bricks and girders. Up to about three miles from the centre of the explosion lightly-built houses were flattened as though they had been built of cardboard. Those who were inside were either killed or wounded. Those who managed to extricate themselves by some miracle found themselves surrounded by a ring of fire. And the few who succeeded in making their way to safety generally died twenty or thirty days later from the delayed effects of the deadly gamma-rays. Some of the reinforced concrete or stone buildings remained standing, but their interiors were completely gutted by the blast.

About half an hour after the explosion, whilst the sky all around Hiroshima was still cloudless, a fine rain began to fall on the town and went on for about five minutes. It was caused by the sudden rise of over-heated air to a great height, where it condensed and fell back as rain. Then a violent wind rose and the fires extended with terrible rapidity, because most Japanese houses are built only of timber and straw.

By the evening the fire began to die down and then it went out. There was nothing left to burn. Hiroshima had ceased to exist.'[1]

Stunned by the blast, the Jesuit priest Father Wilhelm Kleinsorge found himself wandering round the garden of his mission, dressed only in his underclothes. Nearby he could hear his housekeeper crying in Japanese: 'Our Lord Jesus Christ, have pity on us!' And on the other side of the world Winston Churchill attributed to 'God's mercy' the fact that American and British, not German, scientists had discovered the secret of atomic power.

On 25 August Minoru Suzuki dictated a letter to his parents thanking them because despite their meagre resources they had allowed him to study first at college, then at Tokyo University. He was going to die. 'Autumn will come, the chirping of the crickets, the forest despoiled of its foliage will remind you of my death, but do not weep.' It was in exquisite taste. His hands had been burnt away.

The dropping of the Hiroshima bomb was followed by an ultimatum, which was ignored.

On 9 August a second bomb was dropped on the port of Nagasaki, a city of 250,000 inhabitants. Unconditional surrender followed on 14 August.

The Imperial Rescript

We, the Emperor, have ordered the Imperial Government to notify the four countries, the United States, Great Britain, China and the Soviet Union, that We accept their Joint Declaration. To ensure the tranquillity of the subjects of the Empire and share with all the

[1] Quoted by Flower and Reeves: pp. 1031 and 1032, from Marcel Junod., *Warrior without Weapons*, (Cape, 1951).

countries of the world the joys of co-prosperity, such is the rule that was left to Us by the Founder of the Empire of Our Illustrious Imperial Ancestors, which We have endeavoured to follow. To-day, however, the military situation can no longer take a favourable turn, and the general tendencies of the world are not to our advantage either.

What is worse, the enemy, who has recently made use of an inhuman bomb, is incessantly subjecting innocent people to grievous wounds and massacre. The devastation is taking on incalculable proportions. To continue the war under these conditions would not only lead to the annihilation of Our Nation, but the destruction of human civilization as well. How could We then protect Our innumerable subjects, who are like new-borne babes for Us? How could We ask the forgiveness of the divine spirits of Our Imperial Ancestors? When Our thoughts dwell on those of Our subjects who died in battle, those who fell as victims of their duty, those who perished by a premature death, and on the families they have left behind them, We feel profoundly upset.

. . . It is Our desire to initiate an era of peace for future generations by tolerating the intolerable and enduring the unendurable. Capable of maintaining the national policy and placing Our trust in the perfect sincerity of Our good and faithful subjects, We will always be with you. Let all the countries, like one single family where tradition is handed down from son to grandson, have firm faith in the indestructible character of the Land of the Gods. Remembering Our heavy responsibilities and the length of road yet to be covered, concentrating all Our strength on the construction of the future, animated by deep morality and firm honesty, We swear to hold the flower of Our National policy very high, resolved not to remain backward in the general progress of the world. We ask you, Our subjects, to be the incarnation of Our will.

HIROHITO.[1]

All over Japan his people listened to the Emperor addressing them for the first time. Some stretched out at full length, foreheads touching the floor, to receive his commands. When it was over many wept, then, bowing to each other politely, they went their way. 'The Emperor knows better than we do what should be done.'

[1] 15 August, 1945. Flower and Reeves: pp. 1034 and 5.

A few, like Vice-Admiral Onishi, the commander of the *Kamikaze*, and General Sugiyama, the Chief of Staff, committed *hara-kiri*, but there was no wave of suicides.

The surrender was signed aboard the US battleship *Missouri* anchored in Tokyo Bay on Sunday 2 September 1945. For the Americans the war had lasted three years, eight months, and 25 days. At the ceremony the Americans flew not only the flag that had been flying over the Capitol in Washington on the day of Pearl Harbor, but oddly enough, the historic flag – with only 31 stars – which Commodore Perry had flown when he first landed on Japanese soil in 1853. Perhaps some who were present reflected that it might have been better had he never set foot there!

General MacArthur made a short speech and announced that he meant to discharge his responsibilities with justice and tolerance. Next the instrument was signed by two delegations.[1] General Mac-Arthur then led a short prayer for peace – which was followed closely by the flight of 436 Superfortresses over Tokyo.

Japan too saw its version of the Nuremberg tribunal. On 19 November MacArthur ordered the arrest of 11 Japanese war leaders. With an accurate historical sense he sought to punish war crimes that had taken place as long ago as the 'thirties when the Japanese had seized Nanking. Prince Konoye, who had thrice been premier of Japan, and who, had justice been done, would probably have been acquitted, committed suicide before he could be taken. Tojo, the brains of the war party and virtual dictator, had not been so lucky. He wished to commit *hara-kiri*, but had nobody to assist by decapitating him after the ceremonial disembowelment. When he was about to be arrested on 11 September he shot himself in the chest. The Americans found him wearing full uniform and six rows of medal ribbons. He was not mortally wounded – his pistol was only a ·32.

While a prisoner he said to a Japanese reporter: 'I am sorry for the peoples of Greater East Asia. I will shoulder the whole responsibility. I hope they will not go amiss in dealing with the situation. The war of Greater East Asia was a just war. With all our strength gone we finally fell. I do not wish to stand before the victor and be tried as the vanquished' ... To some Americans he said: 'You are the victors and you are now able to name who was responsible for the war.

[1] The defenders of Corregidor and Singapore, Lt.-Generals Wainwright and Percival, recently released from Japanese prisoner-of-war camps, were among the signatories.

But historians 500 or 1,000 years from now may judge differently.'
It is a thought that no victor can afford to ignore.

He went to the gallows on 22 December leaving this valedictory
verse:

> *It is good-bye,*
> *Over the mountains I go today*
> *To the bosom of Buddha*
> *So, happy am I.*[1]

Who are we to condemn those who play the game by an altogether
different set of rules?

The case of General Yamashita, the Tiger of the Philippines,
excites less pity. The sadism of his troops was well attested. There
were those who alleged that, among other atrocities, his soldiers had
poured petrol on women's heads and then set fire to them. Yamashita's denial that he had any knowledge of such doings was unconvincing. He was executed on 7 December 1945, the fourth
anniversary of Pearl Harbor.

Wisely the Americans kept Emperor Hirohito on the throne of
his ancestors, and refrained from trying him as a war criminal. He
had, of course, attended meetings of those who planned the war,
but his spiritual control over his subjects was such that it was clearly
simpler for the occupation forces to support him. At a time when the
Japanese nation had been shaken to its very soul by an unbelievable
and unparalleled defeat at the hands of a despised enemy, they needed
something to cling to. Loyalty to their Emperor must at least be left
them. Doubtless this decision prevented terrible disorders and
accelerated the process of rebuilding the democratic and industrious
Japan we know today.

[1] Snyder: *The War – A Concise History*, pp. 542 and 543.

CHAPTER THIRTY-EIGHT

PARTING SHOTS

'*We are now about to enter upon a new chapter in the history of mankind. We should thank God for Hitler. He has done a great service to the world. He has brought us back to a realization of brute facts. He has got us away from ideals and rhetoric. Facts are the only things that matter. Hitler has shown that Hell is still here on Earth. He has, in fact, taken the lid off Hell, and we have all looked into it. That is his service to the human race.*'

FIELD-MARSHAL SMUTS, 1944.

AN INTERNATIONAL tribunal sat at Nuremberg from 20 November 1945 to 1 October 1946 and tried 24 of Hitler's chief associates, some of whom have figured in these pages. Göring, von Ribbentrop, Keitel, Jodl and Bormann were among those condemned to hang.[1] Admiral Raeder was sent to prison for life; Dönitz and Speer for 20 years. In 1965 the time limit for Nazi trials was extended until 31 December 1969.[2]

A generation that has only seen him ranting on some ancient newsreel might be inclined to underrate Hitler, but though unbalanced he was a formidable opponent. General von Mellinthin, a keen observer and no friendly critic, gives an interesting thumbnail sketch:

'... Hitler was an incredibly clever man, with a memory far beyond the average. He had terrific willpower and was utterly ruthless; he was an orator of outstanding quality, able to exercise an hypnotic influence on those in his immediate surroundings. In politics and diplomacy he had an extraordinary flair for sensing the weakness of his adversaries, and for exploiting their failings to the full. He used to be a healthy man, a vegetarian who neither smoked nor drank, but he undermined his constitution by taking sleeping powders and pep pills, chiefly during the later years of

[1] Göring poisoned himself. Bormann was tried *in absentia*.
[2] For a detailed discussion of the trial see Snyder: *The War – A Concise History.*

417

the war. Although his health deteriorated, his mind remained amazingly alert and active until the very end.'[1]

Why, despite these powers and his undoubted tenacity, did he lose?

It may be that he underrated his opponents. Despising democracy and the quest for peace, he evidently came to regard Great Britain and the United States as utterly effete. In this he fell victim to his own rhetoric and the wishful thinking of the incompetent von Ribbentrop. His own service as a front-line soldier in the First World War should have warned him against this line of thought.

It is easy to criticise the Allies for going into the war ill-prepared. But while Hitler's preparations for a land campaign were excellent it is usually forgotten that the *Wehrmacht* was only ready for campaigns on the continent. When in 1940 Great Britain failed to surrender after the fall of France the *Luftwaffe*, largely for lack of long-range bombers, was not quite up to the task of subduing the RAF. The German navy was inadequate to clear the Channel, and the U-boat fleet, which at the outbreak of war was rather weaker than the British submarine force, was not able to cut Britain's Atlantic life-line, though later it came near to doing so.

Hitler certainly had a high opinion of himself as a soldier. He had been decorated twice in the First World War and his experiences then had probably given him confidence. He had a certain tactical flair, demonstrated by his supporting Manstein's plans for the 1940 campaign. He alleged that he had studied Clausewitz and Schlieffen. The German victories in Poland and France appeared to him in the light of personal triumphs. Then when his will-power enabled his army to ride the storm, when his generals wanted to retreat in that awful Russian winter, he became convinced that he was another Frederick.

But in fact his personal command on the Eastern Front was disastrous for Germany. His habit of playing off OKW and OKH against each other – divide and rule – made for inefficiency and confusion. His continual interference in detail – so contrary to Roosevelt's methods – was the root of countless calamities. His main fault was his inability to concentrate on one aim at a time.

After the Axis defeats of November 1942, when Faith took the place of Reason in German planning, his already unscrupulous character rapidly deteriorated. It says much for the tactical power of the defensive and the tenacity of the German soldier that the Reich

[1] Mellenthin: *Panzer Battles*, p. 354.

kept going for another three years after such blows as Stalingrad and Tunis. Thanks to the *Schnorkel* and the V.2 Hitler remained dangerous to the last – particularly to Britain.

The inordinate length of the war is easily explained by Allied unpreparedness and the devastating series of early defeats.

The war had certain general features which are worthy of comment, and some may be the pattern of things still to come. Most of the campaigns began without the formality of a declaration of war. The use of the 'fifth column', of guerrillas and partisans was widespread, and though often effective frequently led to brutal atrocities by either side.

The value of a balanced force was forcibly demonstrated by the early German campaigns, when aircraft and tanks were such successful ingredients of the *Blitzkrieg*.

The interrelation of land, sea and air was well-illustrated. It was, for example, the capture of their bases by land forces that put an end to the V.2 and U-boat campaigns. The bomber offensive, by drawing the *Luftwaffe* home to defend the Fatherland, paved the way for the amphibious operations against Sicily, Italy and Normandy. A fresh idea, still of great military use, was air-supply.

The verdict of history will probably be that the admirals, generals and air-marshals of the Second World War, Allied and Axis alike, were a far more competent lot than their predecessors of the First. Even so, one detects at times a certain conservatism – reluctance to admit that the carrier is mightier than the battleship; a tendency to combat the *Blitzkrieg* with methods already inappropriate in 1918. But this criticism could be taken too far.

The power of broadcasting to enable the war leaders to indoctrinate their followers was amply demonstrated by such masters as Churchill, Roosevelt, and, it must be said, Goebbels.

It may be that minor tactics have changed very little in the last twenty years. One captures a pillbox or destroys a tank much as one did in those distant days. But the grand tactics of war were changed at a blow when the bomb fell on Hiroshima.

It is easy to condemn President Truman for ordering that the bombs be dropped, and indeed, Mr Churchill for his concurrence. Living as we do in an age when not one but several nations have far more destructive weapons, we may well regret the opening of the nuclear period of Military History. But to be fair we must look at the situation as President Truman saw it in August 1945. He did not know that the Emperor had already (8 June) ordered his ministers to seek to end the war as quickly as possible. He *did* know the desperate devotion of the Japanese forces, the *Kamikaze* spirit, their 'no surrender' attitude. However much he may have exaggerated probable Allied losses in the invasion of Japan, his statement that he saved every one of them cannot be parried. Few modern generals would hesitate to slay the enemy, military and civilian, guilty or innocent, if by so doing they could save their own men. How long would they enjoy their confidence if they did?

From a moral point of view the bombing of cities from the air, a form of war in which the Axis rather than the Allies led the way, is hard to justify. At the same time one can make a case for saying that the bombing of Hamburg (July 1943) was just as atrocious as that of Hiroshima. A bomb is still a bomb, however big its destructive potential. If the equivalent of 20,000 tons of TNT is coming does it matter whether is comes from one or 1,000?

From the strictly military point of view it is worth pointing out that one atomic bomb was a more effective weapon than a number of bombs dropped in a conventional raid by Superfortresses, even supposing that the capacity of the latter exactly equalled one atomic bomb. The principles of war, which guide commanders in their conduct of operations, call attention to the need to plan for Surprise and Concentration of Force. Nor is this view entirely cynical. The Germans had stood up to terrible bombing. Let none think that the Japanese did not equal, or indeed excel, in courage their allies: chauvinistic, patriotic, fatalistic, obedient, they were ready to go on as long as the Emperor required them to. Only the grim reaping scythe of Hiroshima and Nagasaki could prepare them for his change of mind.

But if, reluctantly, one must conclude that Mr Truman's decision was justified, this is not to say that the whole sorry tale of bombing from Warsaw and Rotterdam to Dresden and Nagasaki does anything but dishonour to the human race. World War II was total, military and economic. Almost everywhere military targets were surrounded by the dwellings of ordinary people. Seldom did the attacker, like the British at Dieppe (19 August 1942), spare the civilians at the risk of adding to their own military casualties. The history of war is a tale of violence in which civilian and soldier alike suffer.

Even the limited wars of the eighteenth century show this. Frederick the Great was not notably squeamish, to take only one example. Faced with a life and death struggle, there are no holds barred and atrocities find justification whenever their perpetrators 'get away' with them. Any weapon is permissible so long as it is effective. If poison gas was not employed in World War II it was not because it had been found too horrible in World War I but because it had proved insufficiently destructive. Such is the morality of war.

If there is any hope for the future it is that the powers will dread the use of weapons so world-ravaging as those they now possess. But history does not support the view that people are either so prudent or so benevolent. Who can tell whether we may not see the day when the United States will use the bomb against China, rather than see her equally well armed?

Military History is about people, about how they react to the stresses and strains of war. If the techniques of war change, the human spirit remains immutable. In war primitive virtues still count. It follows that, however much weapons development may alter tactics, the study of past wars is still worth while, and especially so if one is capable of recognizing one's own bias, and setting aside such things as inter-service rivalry and jealousy of one's allies.

It is as yet too early to expect the final verdict of History on the rights and wrongs of World War II, and the way it was conducted. The full story has not yet been told. We are too near the events, which this book attempts to outline.

But it is not too early to say something of the nature of war itself, its strange fascination. It is easy to denounce it for its horrors and its hardships; to condemn it for its cruelty and the suffering it brings. Dr. Johnson once said: 'Every man thinks meanly of himself for not having been a soldier, or not having been at sea.' To which Boswell replied: 'Lord Mansfield does not.' Johnson: 'Sir if Lord Mansfield were in a company of admirals and generals who'd seen service he'd wish to creep under the table!'

The veteran has compassion for the civilians hurt, the soldiers slain – even the enemy soldiers – but, having survived a hundred perils, he would not have things other than they were, for he thinks the better of himself for his campaigning days. He remembers the good times, the careless – almost carefree – life of disinterested comradeship amidst brave and generous friends. His senses reject the memory of the butcher's shop that was an observation post until the Japanese scored a direct hit, and the sickly sweet smell of corpses rotting in a Sicilian farmyard. He is glad that when the challenge came he achieved rather more than he thought he would. However regrettable it may be, there are still a great many men in this world who feel quite different from the common run of mortals because they have been under fire. It is as though it were some sort of hall-mark. And, though they may not admit it, there are thousands who would like to have proved themselves in the ancient ordeal of combat. The marvels of the industrial revolution and of modern science must not conceal from us the primitive being that lurks within us all. The peaceful British, driven into a corner in 1940, fought back with a determination that almost amounted to savagery. In some this atavistic reaction may have left a sense of guilt. The majority, though they had not previously regarded themselves as warriors, look back on the part they played in overthrowing the Axis, with nothing but satisfaction.

We live in a technological age. But it is an age in which people whose interests are opposed still strive to solve their problems by force, though their methods may be those of the economist, the politician and the diplomat. Perhaps two World Wars have bred a brand of statesman capable of keeping the lid on Hell. It does not seem likely, for we are not specially skilful in selecting our masters. Let us therefore remember the words of Santayana: 'He who forgets his History is condemned to relive it.'

SELECT BIBLIOGRAPHY

ANON: *Effects of Strategic Bombing on the German War Economy.* The United States Strategic Bombing Survey.

BELFIELD, E., and ESSAME, H.: *The Battle for Normandy.* Batsford, 1965.

BOWEN, Elizabeth: *Heat of the Day.* Jonathan Cape, 1946.

BRADLEY, General Omar N.: *A Soldier's Story of the Allied Campaigns from Tunis to the Elbe 1939-1945.* Eyre & Spottiswoode, 1951.

BRODIE, Bernard: *Strategy in the Missile Age.* Oxford University Press, 1959.

BROWN, Cecil: *Suez to Singapore.* Random House, 1942.

BRYANT, Arthur: *The Turn of the Tide* (The memoirs of Field-Marshal Lord Alanbrooke). Collins, 1957.

BUCKLEY, C. H. R.: *Greece and Crete, 1941.* H.M.S.O., 1952.

BULLOCK, Alan: *Hitler. A Study in Tyranny.* Odhams, 1953.

CARVER, Major-General Michael: *El Alamein.* Batsford, 1962.

CHUIKOV, Marshal Vasili I.: *The Beginning of the Road.* MacGibbon & Kee, 1963.

CHURCHILL, Sir Winston S.: *The Second World War.* Vols. I-VI. Cassell, 1948–1954.

CIANO, Count Galeazzo: *Ciano's Diary* (Ed. Malcolm Muggeridge). Heinemann, 1946.

CLARK, Alan: *Barbarossa.* The Russian-German Conflict 1941–5. Hutchinson, 1965.

COOPER, R. W.: *The Nuremberg Trial.* Penguin 1947.

CUNNINGHAM, Admiral of the Fleet Viscount: *A Sailor's Odyssey.* Hutchinson, 1951.

DE GUINGAND, Major-General Sir Francis: *Operation Victory.* Hodder & Stoughton, 1947.

DERRY, T. K.: *The Campaign in Norway.* H.M.S.O., 1952.

ELLIS, Major L. F.: *The War in France and Flanders.* H.M.S.O., 1953.

ELLIS, Major L. F.: *Victory in the West.* Vol. I. *The Battle of Normandy.* H.M.S.O., 1962.

FALLS, Captain Cyril: *The Second World War*. Methuen, 1948.

FERGUSON, S. and FITZGERALD, H.: *Studies in the Social Services*. H.M.S.O., 1954.

FLOWER, D., and REEVES, J.: *The War (1939–1945)* Cassell, 1960.

FRANKLAND, Noble: *The Bombing Offensive Against Germany*. Faber, 1965.

FREIDIN, Seymour and RICHARDSON, William (Ed.): *The Fatal Decisions*. Michael Joseph, 1956.

FULLER, Major-General J. F. C.: *The Second World War*. Eyre & Spottiswoode, 1948.

GOUTARD, Colonel A.: *The Battle of France, 1940*. Frederick Muller, 1958.

GUDERIAN, General Heinz: *Panzer Leader*. Michael Joseph, 1952.

HANCOCK, W. K., and GOWING, M. M.; *British War Economy*. H.M.S.O., 1949.

HARRIS, Marshal of the RAF Sir Arthur: *Bomber Offensive*. Collins, 1947.

HART, Captain B. H. Liddell: *The Other Side of the Hill*. Cassell, 1948.

HEYDECKER, J. and LEEB, J.: *The Nuremberg Trials*. Heinemann, 1962.

HITLER, Adolf: *Mein Kampf*. Hurst and Blackett, 1938.

HITLER, Adolf; *War Directives*. (Ed. H. R. Trevor-Roper). Sidgwick & Jackson, 1954.

LINKLATER, Eric: *The Campaign in Italy*. H.M.S.O., 1951.

MEDLICOTT, W. N.: *The Coming of War in 1939*. Routledge & Kegan Paul, 1963.

MELLENTHIN, F. W. VON: *Panzer Battles (1939–1945)*. Cassell, 1955.

MONTGOMERY, Field-Marshal Viscount: *El Alamein to the River Sangro*. Hutchinson, 1948.

MONTGOMERY, Field-Marshal Viscount: *Memoirs of Field-Marshal Montgomery*. Collins, 1958.

MONTGOMERY, Field-Marshal Viscount: *Normandy to the Baltic* Hutchinson, 1958.

MOOREHEAD, Alan: *African Trilogy*. Hamish Hamilton, 1944.

MORISON, Prof. Samuel Eliot: *The History of the US Naval Operations in World War II* (in 10 Vols.). Oxford University Press, 1963.

MORISON, Prof. Samuel Eliot: *The Two-Ocean War 1939–1945*. Little, Brown & Co./Oxford University Press, 1963.

O'BRIEN, Terence H.: *Civil Defence*. H.M.S.O., 1955.

ROMMEL, Field Marshal: *The Rommel Papers*. (Ed. B. H. Liddell Hart). Collins, 1953.

ROSKILL, Captain S. W. (R.N.): *The Navy at War*. Collins, 1960.

RUMPF, Hans: *The Bombing of Germany*. Muller, 1963.

SENGER UND ETTERLIN, General Frido von: *Neither Fear nor Hope*. Macdonald, 1963.

SLIM, Field-Marshal Viscount: *Defeat into Victory*. Cassell, 1956.

SNYDER, Louis L.: *The War – A Concise History 1939–1945*. Robert Hale, 1962.

SPEIDEL, Lt.-General H.: *We Defended Normandy*. Jenkins, 1951.

WARLIMONT, Walter: *Inside Hitler's Headquarters*. Weidenfeld & Nicolson, 1964.

WERTH, Alexander: *Russia at War, 1941–45*. Barrie & Rockliffe, 1964.

WILMOT, Chester: *The Struggle for Europe*. Collins, 1952.

INDEX

NOTE: References to the tables and quotations at the beginning of each chapter and to maps, are given in italics; illustrations are referred to, *illus.*, all found together between pages 176 and 177. N refers to footnote.